Homegrown Handmade

Art Roads and Farm Trails

North Carolina Department of Cultural Resources and North Carolina Cooperative Extension

Published by John F. Blair, Publisher

The paper in this book meets the guidelines for permanence and durability of the Committee on Production Guidelines for Book Longevity of the Council on Library Resources.

First Printing 2008

Design by The Roberts Group and Angela Harwood

Library of Congress Cataloging-in-Publication Data

Homegrown handmade : art roads and farm trails / North Carolina Department of Cultural Resources and North Carolina Cooperative Extension.

p. cm.

Includes index.

ISBN 978-0-89587-355-2 (pbk. : alk. paper) 1. North Carolina--Tours. 2. Automobile travel--North Carolina--Guidebooks. 3. Country life--North Carolina--Guidebooks. 4. Arts, American--North Carolina--Guidebooks. 5. Farms--North Carolina--Guidebooks. 6. Agriculture--North Carolina--Guidebooks. I. North Carolina. Dept. of Cultural Resources. II. North Carolina Cooperative Extension Service.

F267.3.H66 2008

917.5604'44--dc22

2008001769

Contents

Acknowledgments

This project came about only because of the help of thousands of people in communities all across the eastern, Piedmont, and foothills regions of North Carolina. Special thanks to Cultural Resources Secretary Lisbeth C. Evans, Mary B. Regan, Dr. Edwin Jones, Dr. Wanda Sykes, Ed Emory, Lin Nichols, Southeast Agri-Cultural Tourism Task Force, North Carolina Cooperative Extension, Carol Kline, Pat Cabe, Joe Newberry, Rebecca Moore, Wayne Martin, Becky Anderson, Richard Clark, Greta Lindt, Suzanne Wood, Feather Phillips, Sue Clark, Ginny Culpepper, Deane and Bailey Phelps, and Maryanne Friend for sharing vision, advice, and encouragement.

Thanks also go to past and present Cultural Resources employees Lindy J. Allen, Judy F. Easley, Nancy Hawley, and LeRae Umfleet for providing many of the photographs in this guidebook. Additional photos are from Communications Services, College of Agriculture and Life Sciences, North Carolina State University.

Homegrown Handmade: Art Roads and Farm Trails builds upon and complements two guidebooks produced by *HandMade in America—Farms, Gardens, and Countryside Trails of Western North Carolina* and *The Craft Heritage Trails of Western North Carolina*.

This book was made possible by the following organizations:

Introduction

If you delight in discovery and want travel that comes alive through encounters with music, storytelling, farm stewards of the good earth, and kitchens that prepare local favorites, then this book—and the project it represents—is for you.

Homegrown Handmade blends two of North Carolina's proudest legacies: the arts and agriculture. We call it "Agri-Culture." A fun example is an artfully designed corn maze.

With this guide, you can explore "Art Roads and Farm Trails" that wind through some of the prettiest spots North Carolina has to offer, in 76 mostly rural counties. The self-directed trails take you off the beaten path to find artisans and attractions of all sorts—talented jewelers and folks who make fresh goat cheese, organic farms and riding stables, sassy blues and fine art—all with a healthy dash of fresh food, friendly hoteliers, and tips from insiders.

The trails were designed by the people who live there in a unique alliance among the North Carolina Arts Council, North Carolina Cooperative Extension, and HandMade in America, with support from the North Carolina Department of Cultural Resources and project funding from the Golden LEAF Foundation.

Agri-Cultural tourism generates income for artisans, farmers, and small-town entrepreneurs. It also boosts employment and diversifies local economies. Thanks to people like you, this kind of tourism is the fastest growing in the industry.

To help you sample the rural life and learn about unique communities, we scouted out a wealth of events, activities, and adventures, from harvest festivals to potteries to museums to corner cafés. Each of the 16 trails tells a different story. Putter around "Hushpuppies, Pimento Cheese, and Sweet Tea" for some authentic North Carolina food experiences. Journey the "Front Porch to Back Forty" to recapture days gone by with a touch of au courant arts. Or rumble "Rock Stew Ramble," a savory stew of traditional coastal life.

It has been said that when you shake a tree in North Carolina, a musician will fall out . . . and usually land on an artist! Whether you are day-tripping or enjoying a leisurely vacation, you will find art galleries, festivals, state historic sites, horse farms, produce stands and you-pick farming operations, parks and preserves, and locally owned restaurants and picturesque bed-and-breakfast inns. Kids and grandkids will find plenty of fun things to do, from animal rides to corn mazes to contests to music to stage performances and even hands-on demonstrations.

Local folks wrote the criteria for inclusion in the project. So come find the tradition of talent in North Carolina with a visit to the places featured on these trails. You'll help sustain the rural economy and meet some wonderful people.

Criteria

Our team—made up of farmers, artists, tourism and cultural leaders, merchants, and educators—developed guiding principles for the sites in these trails to ensure their quality.

Hours and Days of Operation

Our goal is to ensure that sites are open to the traveling public for a minimum of 20 hours per week. Exceptions are for things like festivals, annual events, tours, and artists' home studios and galleries that are accessible by appointment only.

Site Interpretation

Our goal is that sites on the trails feature appropriate interpretive materials to enhance the visitor's experience. Sites may be staffed or not.

Authentic and Unique Site Content

Our goal is that the sites be authentic and unique, or that they reflect the region.

a. **Restaurants.** Our goal is to cover those that meet five of these criteria:

- Show local art on the walls or display cases and/or use handcrafted items as tableware
- Have interpretive materials about art or history
- Regularly have live music
- Feature locally grown produce
- Offer indigenous food
- Serve indigenous recipes
- Have offerings authentic to the establishment
- Be architecturally significant
- Be popular with locals
- Have a unique, authentic regional claim to fame
- Have a health inspection of A or better

b. **Farms.** Our goal is to highlight those that combine agriculture and the arts, such as farms with crafts for sale, photography classes, hayrides, learn-how-to-grow programs, or on-site B&Bs.

c. **Art galleries.** Our goal is to feature those that regularly display original works by North Carolina artists or produce exciting exhibits or events.

d. **Retail stores.** We want to ensure that stores offer a significant proportion of North Carolina products.

e. **B&Bs/Inns.** We want to ensure there is a connection to authentic North Carolina culture.

High-Appeal Sites

Our goal is to promote what makes living in North Carolina a unique experience. Our sites reflect a flavor of homegrown, handmade, and absolutely wild products and events unique and authentic to our state.

Cleanliness, Safety, Accessibility, and Signage

All sites must be clean and free of threats to human health and safety.

For physically challenged visitors, indoor sites must be ADA compliant. Sites providing outdoor experiences should show that attention has been given to handicapped individuals, even if it involves providing notice that a particular activity is not conducive to their safety.

How to Use This Book

The Art Roads and Farm Trails cover three geographic regions: the coast, the Piedmont, and the foothills. (North Carolina's mountain region is the subject of two other books: *The Craft Heritage Trails of Western North Carolina* and *Farms* and *Gardens and Countryside Trails of Western North Carolina*. See www.handmadeinamerica.org for more information.)

The table of contents lists all the trails. Attractions are organized by town or city; the counties that make up the trails are listed in the table of contents and the trail descriptions as well.

For each attraction, you'll see a legend noting whether it accommodates groups, has signage, has restrooms, has parking, and is handicapped accessible. Another legend signifies whether the attraction is an art site, an agricultural site, or an "other" site. Homegrown Handmade also has its own Web site (www.homegrownhandmade.com), which you can visit for more information and helpful links.

More about Homegrown Handmade and Its Partners

Homegrown Handmade was formed with a grant from the Golden LEAF Foundation, a nonprofit that supports projects to boost economic development in rural communities. The Golden LEAF (Long-term Economic Advancement Foundation) was created to receive one-half of North Carolina's funds from the tobacco Master Settlement Agreement. The Golden LEAF Foundation is helping North Carolinians make the transition from a tobacco-dependent economy through grants and investments that will positively affect the long-term economic advancement of the state.

The founding partners—the North Carolina Arts Council, the North Carolina Cooperative Extension, and HandMade in America—share a common mission to promote and sustain North Carolina's rich agricultural and cultural heritage and its rural economies.

Homegrown Handmade's goal is to stimulate statewide sustainable cultural tourism and to showcase the state's rural riches in as many communities as possible. The Art Roads and Farm Trails developed by the alliance's staff help link tourists with the farmers, artisans, and entrepreneurs who live in these communities. Until recently, www.homegrown-handmade.com was the only way for tourists and interested residents to learn about the Agri-Cultural trails created by this alliance. This guidebook was produced with the help of additional grant funds from the Golden LEAF Foundation.

The **North Carolina Arts Council** provides links to the state's 2,300 arts organizations, draws on the resources of the North Carolina Department of Cultural Resources, and oversees trail criteria and marketing. **North Carolina Cooperative Extension** works with farmers, families, and communities to develop and enhance agritourism ventures in order to provide viable alternatives to traditional agricultural enterprises. Cooperative Extension gathers research on local economies, environmental concerns, and quality-of-life enterprises and shares its findings with leaders in agritourism. **HandMade in America** develops, promotes, and markets rural tourism sites in the western part of the state and has helped Homegrown Handmade develop and expand rural tourism systems statewide.

For more information on the partners that make up the Homegrown Handmade alliance, visit www.ncculture.com, www.ncarts.org, and www.ces.ncsu.edu. More information on the project's funding source, the Golden LEAF Foundation, can be found at www.goldenleaf.org.

Tips for Your Trip

To make the most of your travels along the Art Roads and Farm Trails described in this book, you might want to bring along the following:

- A sketchbook and a camera. It goes without saying that you'll be seeing some pretty spectacular sights—ones you'll want to recall again and again. Make your trip one for the memory book.
- A measuring tape. If you find the perfect headboard or armoire at a country antiques store, you'll need to make sure it'll fit when you get it home.

• A cooler with ice. If you're a day-tripper planning on stopping at roadside produce stands or farmers' markets, you'll want to make sure any perishables—meats, cheeses, salads, and delicate produce—stay fresh.

• Cash. Many small farm stands and other independent businesses don't accept credit cards or checks.

• A map. Even if you've gotten directions for the destinations along the trail, you'll want to have a recent North Carolina map within easy reach. You can get one by calling the North Carolina Department of Transportation at 877-DOT-4YOU or by going to www.ncdot.org. For more travel information, you can call the North Carolina Division of Travel and Tourism at 800-847-4862.

Legend

- Arts & Crafts Location
- Agricultural Location
- Other Location

- Accomodates Groups
- Parking Available
- Signage
- Handicap Accessible
- Restrooms

Homegrown Handmade

Rock Stew Ramble

Beaufort, Hyde, Martin, Tyrrell, and Washington Counties

What rock is not hard, hides its stripes in water, and often ends up in a muddle? A rockfish, of course. And a muddle is just another name for a stew. "Rock Stew Ramble" is like a riddle. Follow it and find things that are more than they seem.

What waving bands of purple, pink, red, and gold look like a shimmering sunset reflected in Pamlico Sound?

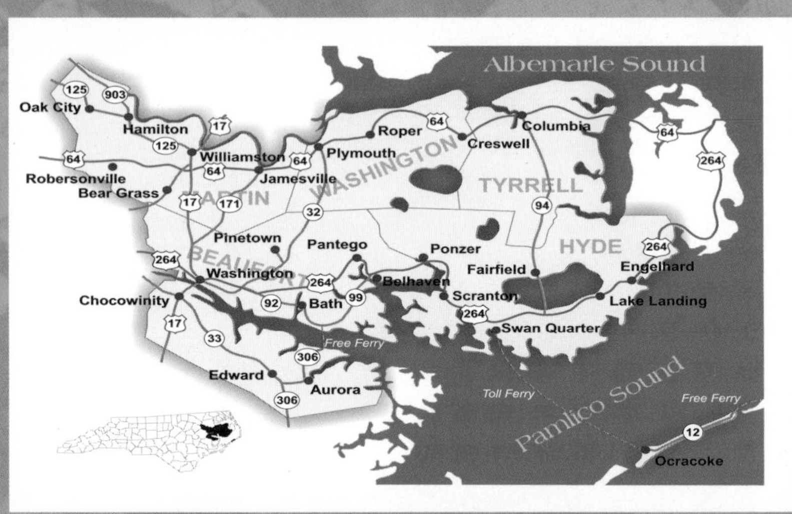

Sunflowers wave over Terra Ceia Farms (p. 22).

Which piercing light leads ships safely ashore and pays homage to days gone by?

Will those crab pots bring in a fisherman's livelihood or be garden art next to the marigolds?

This is the kind of journey where you can find sharks' teeth in a field. Visit a lake that grew giant corn. Tap your toes to a different kind of island music on Ocracoke. Discover a church where quilts occupy the pews.

Like the stone soup of the old story, "Rock Stew Ramble" begins with a watery blend of unlikely elements that become a rich, satisfying stew.

Read on for town-by-town descriptions of the unique attractions that make up the "Rock Stew Ramble" trail.

Aurora/Beaufort County

Aurora Fossil Museum

Dig in one of North America's largest phosphate mines and you'll find fossilized bones, teeth, shells, and coral. These and more are on display at the Aurora Fossil Museum. Take a self-guided tour, watch a video, and browse the gift store. Across the street is fossil-rich material waiting for young and old collectors alike. 400 Main St., Aurora, NC 27806. Mon.–Sat., 9 A.M.–4:30 P.M.; Sun., 1–4:30 P.M. Free. (252) 322-4238; www.aurorafossilmuseum.com

Bath/Beaufort County

Palmer-Marsh House at Historic Bath State Historic Site

Bath Creek Stables

Spend the weekend experiencing life on the farm at Bath Creek Stables. There's plenty to do, including wagon rides, tending livestock, horseback riding, camping, and bedding down in a real bunkhouse. 241 Stell Rd., Bath, NC 27808. Open Fri.–Sun. Fees are charged. (252) 923-5645; bathcreekstables@yahoo.com

Historic Bath State Historic Site

Stroll the tree-lined streets of North Carolina's oldest town (established in 1705) and follow in the steps of Blackbeard the Pirate. Edward Teach, better known as Blackbeard, is said to have married a local girl and settled in Bath around 1716. 207 Carteret St., Bath, NC 27808. Nov.–March, Tues.–Sat., 10 A.M.–4 P.M.; Apr.–Oct., Mon.–Sat., 9 A.M.–5 P.M.; Sun., 1–5 P.M. Admission fee. (252) 923-3971; www.bath.nchistoricsites.org

Inn on Bath Creek B&B

Inn on Bath Creek B&B

This lovely, three-story B&B offers five cozy guest rooms just an easy stroll from Bath's historic district. 116 S. Main St., Bath, NC 27080. (252) 923-9571; www.innonbathcreek.com

Jean's Shoppe

This shop sells a complete line of basket-making and chair-caning supplies, as well as baskets of all descriptions. The shop's owner, Jean Bowen, makes them all, as well as the lovely porcelain dolls you'll find on display. 99 Croatan Ave., Bath, NC 27080. Sat., 10 A.M.–5 P.M.; Sun., 1–5 P.M.; and by appointment. (252) 923-4131; JEBowen@gotricounty.com

Jean's Shoppe

Old Town Country Kitchen

Be sure to stop between the bridges at the Old Town Country Kitchen. Popular among locals and tourists alike, the restaurant offers a full breakfast, lunch, and dinner menu. You'll feel right at home. 436 Carteret St., Bath, NC 27080. Sun.–Tues., 7 A.M.–2 P.M.; Wed.–Thurs., 7 A.M.–8 P.M.; Fri.–Sat., 7 A.M.–8:30 P.M.; closed Tues. during winter. (252) 923-1840; deboyd@redscable.com

Old Town Country Kitchen

Bear Grass/Martin County

Deadwood

This unique park promises fun for the whole family with miniature golf, a picnic area, a snack bar, a gift shop, and a train ride. See the Western-style opera house with exciting shows and performers. Thursday evenings feature a dinner theater. Visitors also enjoy live music at the Smokehouse Grill. 2254 Ed's Grocery Rd., Bear Grass, NC 27892. Fri., 5:30–10 P.M.; Sat., 5 P.M.–2 A.M.; Sun., noon–9 P.M. (252) 792-8938 or (252) 792-8516; www.deadwoodnc.com

Green Acres

Green Acres welcomes campers with 175 tent, camper, and RV campsites with full hookups. Children's playgrounds, a game pavilion, a snack bar, miniature golf, and nine-hole, par-three "pasture golf" courses provide entertainment. Enjoy nature trails, swimming pools, and a lake for fishing and paddling. 1679 Green Acres Rd., Bear Grass, NC 27892. (888) 792-3939; www.greenacresnc.com

Belhaven/Beaufort County

Belhaven Inn

Located just a block from the water and the Intercoastal Waterway, the inn features three beautifully appointed rooms and a hearty breakfast. 402 E. Main St., Belhaven, NC 27810. (252) 943-6400; www.belhaveninnnc.com

Belhaven Memorial Museum

Belhaven Memorial Museum

The museum—listed in "Scary Museums" by RoadsideAmerica.com—features an eclectic collection including 30,000 buttons, a flea "bride and groom," and a dress worn by a 700-pound woman. 211 E. Main St., Belhaven, NC 27810. Thurs.–Tues., 1–5 P.M. Free. (252) 943-6817 or (252) 943-3055; www.washingtonnctourism.com

Farm Boys Restaurant

This local favorite—especially popular with the after-school crowd—is known for its biscuits, hamburgers, hoagies, French fries, and onion rings. Diners can eat at the picnic tables with a view of beautiful Pungo Creek. 216 Pamlico St., Belhaven, NC 27810. Mon.–Fri., 8 A.M.–6 P.M. (252) 943-3295

Fish Hooks Café

This brightly lit, family-friendly, fish-themed restaurant has appetizers, soups, salads, sandwiches, pastas, and fresh local seafood. The "Little Guppies" menu for children makes eating out more pleasant for parents, too! 231 E. Main St., Belhaven, NC 27810. Tues.–Thurs., 11:30 A.M.–2:30 P.M. and 5–8 P.M.; Fri.–Sat., 11 A.M.–2 P.M. and 5–8:30 P.M.; Sun., 11 A.M.–2 P.M. (252) 943-9948

The Helmsman Restaurant

The Helmsman offers a full menu of soups, salads, and entrées and a buffet of both hot and cold items. 238 Pamlico St., Belhaven, NC 27810. Mon.–Fri., 11 A.M.–2 P.M. and 5–8 P.M.; Sat., 11 A.M.–2 P.M. and 5–8:30 P.M.; Sun., 11 A.M.–2 P.M. (252) 943-3810

River Forest Manor Marina & Shipyard B&B

This handsome Victorian home has been converted into an inn, marina, and restaurant complex. Take a stroll down by the water and see yachts docked for a stay at the marina. The Sunday buffet alone is worth the trip. 738 E. Main St., Belhaven, NC 27810. (252) 943-2151 or (800) 346-2151; www.riverforestmarina.com

The Thistle Dew Bed and Breakfast

This Queen Anne Victorian–style B&B is more than 100 years old. Its three double bedrooms face the water and have private baths. Each room is decorated with art and antiques. Guests at The Thistle Dew enjoy a full breakfast each morning. 443 Water St., Belhaven, NC 27810. (888) 822-4409

Wine & Words

This unique shop features North Carolina wines from the Yadkin Valley and specialty foods from such home-state producers as Forge Mountain, Salem Bakery, and B&B Pecan Processors. The bookstore specializes in local history, nature, and culture. The Back Bay Café emphasizes fresh ingredients from area farmers and local waters. 413 Pamlico St., Belhaven, NC 27810. Wed.–Fri., noon–6 P.M.; Sat., noon–5 P.M.; Sun., noon–3 P.M. (252) 944-2870 or (252) 964-4196; www.wineandwords.biz

Wine & Words

Chocowinity/Beaufort County

Cliff's Seafood

This eatery features a family-dining atmosphere with an emphasis on fresh seafood and steaks. 2871 US Hwy 17 S., Chocowinity, NC 27817. Tues.–Fri., 11 A.M.–2 P.M. and 4–8 P.M.; Sat., 11 A.M.–9 P.M.; Sun., 11 A.M.–8 P.M. (252) 946-5203; cliffsseafood@earthlink.net

Southside Farms

This working farm features prepicked and pick-your-own berries and vegetables. Strawberries, cabbage, broccoli, potatoes, onions, and greenhouse tomatoes take center stage. 320 Harding Ln., Chocowinity, NC 27817. Mon.–Fri., 7 A.M.–6 P.M.; Sat., 7 A.M.–2 P.M. (252) 946-2487; www.southsidefarms.com

Twin Lakes Camping Resort

Twin Lakes features 424 campsites for RVs, trailers, and tents, as well as cabin and cottage rentals. Guests can moor their boats along the waterfront bulkhead. Summer programs include a "Mighty Mysterious Weekend," featuring treasure hunts and magicians, and "Water Wars," in which water-pistol fights erupt between campers and staff. 1618 Memory Ln., Chocowinity, NC 27817. Sun.–Thurs., 8 A.M.–9 P.M.; Fri.–Sat., 8 A.M.–11 P.M. Rental fees. (252) 946-5700; www.twinlakesnc.com

Waters Produce

Fresh peaches at Waters Produce

This family-owned and -operated business specializes in fresh seasonal fruits, including strawberries, which you can pick or buy prepicked. You can also purchase peaches, fresh vegetables, garden plants, and flowers. 1890 Gray Rd., Chocowinity, NC 27817. March–July, Mon.–Fri., 8 A.M.–6 P.M.; Sat., 8 A.M.–1 P.M.; Aug.–Oct. 1, Mon., Wed., and Fri.–Sat., 10 A.M.–6 P.M. (252) 946-5915 or (252) 402-5717; watersproduce@vol.com

Columbia/Tyrrell County

Ashbee Dora Vineyards

In the fall, you can pick your own grapes from among six muscadine varieties. The vineyard is located in the Gum Neck community. Grapevine Landing Rd., Columbia, NC 27926. (252) 796-1957 or (757) 204-4130

B&B on the Sound at Lasseters Landing

Discover this waterfront B&B, popular among nature enthusiasts. Birders are elated by the abundance of rare and endangered species. 42 Lasseters Landing, Columbia, NC 27925. (252) 796-3379; www.lassetersrlanding.com

Ben Franklin Store

Remember old-fashioned tin ceilings? This store—the oldest Ben Franklin location in the state—has them, along with buttered popcorn, yard goods, penny bubblegum, and more. Main St., Columbia, NC 27925. Mon.–Sat., 9:30 A.M.–5:30 P.M. (252) 796-2231; wjwhite@beachlink.com

B&B on the Sound at Lasseters Landing

The Brickhouse Inn B&B

The Brickhouse Inn, formerly known as the Combs-Hussey House (1890), is a beautiful example of the Victorian style, with scalloped millwork, a wraparound porch, and a gazebo. 415 Main St., Columbia, NC 27925. (252) 766-3333; www.thebrickhouseinn.com

Cabin Fever Reliever Creative Arts Retreat

Defeat the winter blues and nurture your interests in the arts by attending a Cabin Fever Reliever getaway. Instruction in fine crafts, traditional music, and fine arts is available. The retreat is held at the Eastern 4-H Environmental Education and Conference Center. 201 Main St., Columbia, NC 27925. Held in mid-Feb., Thurs.–Sun. Tuition covers fees, meals, and lodging. (252) 796-2787; www.pocosinarts.org

Pocosin Arts, Inc. (p. 12)

Columbia Theater Cultural Resources Center

This old theater has been newly renovated to present exhibits about the history of farming, fishing, and forestry in the greater Pocosin region. You can also visit The Box Office Antiques and Gifts for a unique shopping experience. 304 Main St., Columbia, NC 27925. Tues.–Fri., 10 A.M.–4:30 P.M.; Sat., 10 A.M.–2 P.M. Admission fee. (252) 766-0200; www.partnershipforthesounds.org

Original theater seats at Columbia Theater Cultural Resources Center *Partnership for the Sounds*

Doris' Store

Stop in for hoop cheese, hand-woven baskets, a quick snack, and the latest on what's happening in the community. 1310 N. Gum Neck Rd.,

Columbia Theater Cultural Resources Center *Partnership for the Sounds* (p. 9)

Columbia, NC 27925. Mon.–Sat., 6:15 A.M.–5:30 P.M. (252) 796-1417

Duard Brickhouse Produce

Here, you can pick your own produce and pay by the honor system. Choose from collards, corn, broccoli, cabbage, tomatoes, squash, zucchini, okra, beets, and beans. Rte. 1209 (Soundside Rd.), Columbia, NC 27925. (252) 796-0579

Flemz Market & Deli

The name is short for Fleming, the family that owns this down-home deli. You'll find local newspaper clippings, photos, posters, and other artifacts along with the sub sandwiches, hoop cheese, and soft drinks. 401 N. Road St., Columbia, NC 27925. Mon.–Thurs., 6 A.M.–8 P.M.; Fri.–Sat., 6 A.M.–9 P.M. (252) 796-3536; jimmyfleming2@earthlink.net

4-H Livestock Show

4-H Livestock Show *Tyrrell Hall*

If you've never been to a 4-H livestock show and sale, you're in for a treat. Kids ages five to 18 proudly show off their animal husbandry skills. The broad smiles on the blue-ribbon winners' faces are contagious. Tyrrell Hall, US Hwy 64 E., Columbia, NC 27926. Held the third Wed. in Apr. dee_furlough@ncsu.edu

Full Circle Crab Company

1366 US Hwy 64 E., Columbia, NC 27925. Summer, daily, 5 A.M.–8 P.M.; winter, daily, 6 A.M.–6 P.M. (252) 796-9696; www.ncagr.com/NCproducts/showsite.asp?ID=100130

Harry Lee Davis Roadside Potato Stand

This quaint roadside produce stand is known for its potatoes—red and sweet. Payment is by the honor system. US Hwy 64 E., Columbia, NC 27925. Open seasonally; call for available produce. (252) 796-8742

Historic Columbia Walking Tour

Stop by the Tyrrell County Visitors Center and pick up a tour brochure. 203 S. Ludington Dr., Columbia, NC 27925. Year-round. Free. (252) 796-2781 or (252) 796-0723; www.visittyrrellcounty.com

McClees Restaurant

Harry Lee Davis Roadside Potato Stand

McClees serves fresh and savory dishes, including seafood, homemade soups, and desserts. The handmade pottery soup bowls were made by a local potter. Beautiful local juniper paneling and the original tinwork ceiling recall early Main Street commercial interiors. 203 Main St., Columbia, NC 27925. Tues.–Sat., 6 A.M.–2:30 P.M.; Sun., 8 A.M.–2:30 P.M. (252) 796-1567

Mitchell's Barbershop

Once upon a time, there were places where men swapped yarns and little boys had to sit on a board laid across the arms of a barber's chair to get their hair cut. Remember the powder dusting after the ordeal? It's still there at Mitchell's Barbershop. 202 Main St., Columbia, NC 27925. Mon.–Tues. and Thurs.–Sat., 8 A.M.–5 P.M. (252) 796-6871

Owen's Taxidermy

Make your trophy-sized fish or game a permanent fixture. 308 N. Road St., Columbia, NC 27925. Mon.–Fri., 9 A.M.–5 P.M. (252) 796-5931; taxidermy@mchsi.com

Pledger Hardware

You'll find everything you need for farm, shop, home, and garden, from washers to washboards to washing machines. At Christmas, the owners roll out the bicycles and polish the pocketknives. 308 Main St., Columbia, NC 27925. Mon.–Fri., 7:30 A.M.–5:30 P.M.; Sat., 7:30 A.M.–noon. (252) 796-3361

Pocosin Arts Folk School & Steamed Blue to Red Hot Crab Dinner and Auction

Enjoy the exhibits of fine crafts and folk art. Visit the teaching studio. Enjoy demonstrations in pottery, spinning, quilting, and weaving. And on the third Saturday in September, check out the organization's Steamed Blue to Red Hot Crab Dinner and Auction. It's a complete crab fest followed by a fun-filled auction of the region's best original arts and crafts. 201 Main St., Columbia, NC 27925. March 21–Dec. 24, Tues.–Fri., 10 A.M.–5 P.M.; Sat., 10 A.M.–2 P.M.; and by appointment. Admission is free; tuition is charged for classes. (252) 796-2787; www.pocosinarts.org

Pocosin Arts, Inc.

Scuppernong River Festival

On the second Saturday in October, you can enjoy activities ranging from an early-morning 5K run to canoe races, a horseshoe-pitching competition, antique car displays, a big parade, a street dance, and a fireworks display. Main St., Columbia, NC 27925. (252) 796-2781 or (252) 976-1371; www.visittyrrellcounty.com

Tyrrell County Courthouse

The courthouse, built in 1903, features turn-of-the century architecture. Included at this site are the county's veterans' memorial and a Civil War monument. 403 Main St., Columbia, NC 27925. Mon.–Fri., 8:30 A.M.–5 P.M. (252) 796-6281; www.visittyrrellcounty.com

Tyrrell County Library

The Tyrrell County Library contains literature about the county's history and genealogy and features works by local artists and photographers. Travelers can plug into the free cyber café and catch up with their e-mail. 414 Main St., Columbia, NC 27925. Mon.–Thurs., 10 A.M.–8 P.M.; Fri., 10 A.M.–6 P.M.; Sat., 10 A.M.–1 P.M. (252) 796-3771; www.pettigrewlibraries.org/photoCatalogList.asp

Pocosin Arts, Inc.

Tyrrell County Visitors Center/ Walter B. Jones, Sr., Center for the Sounds

Tyrrell County Visitors Center
Partnership for the Sounds

203 S. Ludington Dr., Columbia, NC 27925. May–Oct., Mon.–Sat., 9 A.M.–5 P.M.; Sun., 1–5 P.M.; Nov.–Apr., Mon.–Sat., 9 A.M.–5 P.M. (252) 796-0723; www.partnershipforthesounds.org or www.visittyrrellcounty.gov

Creswell/Washington County

Conman's Hunting Guide Service & Vacation Cottages

Mike and Connie Noles run a guide service specializing in black bear, whitetail deer, and tundra swan. Rabbit, turkey, and quail hunts are also available. The couple's fully furnished cottages provide family fun on the lake and great fishing opportunities. 6693 Shore Dr., Creswell, NC 27928. (800) 668-7124; www.homestead.com/conmans

Davenport Homestead

The homestead has been preserved as a faithful representation of rural North Carolina life in the 1700s. Take the self-guided tour and see rooms filled with authentic household goods, or visit during the annual celebration, held the first Saturday of June. Mt. Tabor Rd., Creswell, NC 27928. Open year-round by appointment. Free. (252) 797-4336 or (252) 793-1377; www.visitwashingtoncountync.com

Somerset Place State Historic Site

Somerset Place, one of 27 state historic sites, demonstrates North Carolina plantation life. 2572 Lake Shore Rd., Creswell, NC 27928. Apr.–Oct., Mon.–Sat., 9 A.M.–5 P.M.; Sun., 1–5 P.M.; Nov.–March, Tues.–Sat., 10 A.M.–4 P.M.; Sun., 1–4 P.M. Free. (252) 797-4171; www.somersetplace.nchistoricsites.org

Edward/Beaufort County

Bennett Vineyards

The sandy soil of the old Wiley T. Bennett Plantation produces Mount Vernon White, Scuppernong White, Charlestowne Red, Muscadine Red, Roanoke Red, and a Blush. Bennett offers trail rides that include a hot dog lunch, a pig-picking dinner, and musical entertainment. 6832 Old Sandhill Rd., Edward, NC 27821. Mon.–Fri., 10 A.M.–3 P.M.; call for tours. Admission is free; fees are charged for trail rides. (252) 322-7154 or (877) 762-9463

Somerset Place State Historic Site *N.C. Historic Sites* (p. 13)

Engelhard/Hyde County

Alligator River Growers

If you haven't tasted a Mattamuskeet sweet onion from North Carolina's far eastern Hyde County, you're missing out. The short growing season is from early June through late July. 3278 Airport Rd., Engelhard, NC 27824. Mon.–Fri., 7:30 A.M.–5 P.M. (252) 925-9731 or (877) 430-6768; www.alligatorrivergrowers.com

Big Trout Marina & Campground/Restaurant

Big Trout caters to boaters, campers, and seafood lovers on the waterfront, where you can watch the fishing boats and pleasure boats coming and going. The café serves fresh seafood daily, including oysters, shrimp, flounder, and trout, as well as plenty of fresh vegetables. 72 Summerlin Rd., Engelhard, NC 27824. (252) 925-6651

Engelhard Seafood Festival

This annual festival features rides, live animals, beauty pageants, music, and fresh local seafood! Engelhard, NC 27824. Held the weekend of the third Sat. in May; events run Fri. evening and all day Sat. Free. (252) 926-9171 or (888) 493-3826; www.hydecounty.org

Gibbs Store, LLC

Visit this old-timey hardware store and you can almost smell the oiled sawdust on the floor. Just ask Greg Gibbs for anything from iron pans to hunting supplies. 35095 US Hwy 264, Engelhard, NC 27824. Open Mon.–Sat. (252) 925-4511

Gull Rock Seafood

975 Gull Rock Rd., Engelhard, NC 27885. Open seasonally during daylight hours. (252) 925-1951

Historic Lake Landing Landmarks

Take this driving tour and see 25 homes, churches, commercial structures, and other buildings listed on the National Register of Historic Places. The tour showcases superior examples of surviving rural architecture. US Hwy 264 and Rte. 1108/1114, Engelhard, NC 27824. Year-round. Interior tours are limited to churches. Free. (252) 926-9171 or (888) 493-3826; www.hydecounty.org

Hotel Engelhard

This hotel is in a prime location for bird watchers, hunters, and fishermen. It features an on-site restaurant and one RV hookup. 34901 US Hwy 264, Engelhard, NC 34901. (252) 925-2001 or (800) 290-5311; www.Hotelengelhard.de.vu

Marco Gibbs Seafood

36676 US Hwy 264, Engelhard, NC 27885. Open seasonally during daylight hours. (252) 925-6301

Martelle's "Feed House" Restaurant

Martelle's features regional home-cooked cuisine for lunch and dinner. From seafood to chops, you'll find it at Martelle's. There's also a gift shop and an oyster bar. 33301 US Hwy 264, Engelhard, NC 27824. Open Tues.–Sun. (252) 925-1799; www.martellesfeedhouse.com

Octagon House

The eight-sided structure was constructed with no posts except for the windows and doors. It's one of the few

The Octagon House
NC Echo
(p. 15)

octagonal homes in the state, and one of only two in North Carolina built in the 19th century. 30868 US Hwy 264, Engelhard, NC 27824. Open Thurs.–Fri. Free. (252) 925-4150

Fairfield/Hyde County

Cox Crab Pots

The crab-pot builder is still in demand in eastern North Carolina, where crabs remain plentiful. Stop by Cox Crab Pots and see how this ancient craft is carried out. 2374 Newlands Rd., Fairfield, NC 27826. Open year-round during daylight hours. Free. (252) 926-1966

A Glimpse of Historic Fairfield

The tour begins with a stop at the Hyde County Chamber of Commerce for a brochure. Fairfield, NC 27885. Year-round during daylight hours. Free. (252) 926-9171 or (888) 493-3826; www.hydecounty.org

Hyde Away Motel

A favorite of fishermen and hunters, the motel provides a central location on mainland Hyde County for sportsmen to pursue their interests. It offers guest rooms as well as mobile homes for larger groups. 6491 NC Hwy 94, Fairfield, NC 27826. (252) 926-8101

Hyde Trail Ride

Equestrians will love the views afforded by trails along the banks of Lake Mattamuskeet. The annual event begins at Wysocking Bay and eventually winds through a cypress swamp and along waterfowl impoundments filled with thousands of migrating waterfowl. 2089 Piney Woods Rd., Fairfield, NC 27826. Held the second Sat. in Apr. (252) 926-9171 or (888) 493-3826; www.hydecounty.org

Mattamuskeet Fresh Produce

During the growing season, this facility is used to process, pack, and ship corn, green beans, squash, cucumbers, and other truck crops grown by Hyde County farmers. But the farmers are always willing to give visitors a tour and sell some produce. 2089 Piney Woods Rd., Fairfield, NC 27826. (252) 926-1040

Osprey Nest Campground, RV Park & Boat Ramp

At this campground on Hyde County's mainland, you'll find easy access to Lake Mattamuskeet, along with showers and other amenities. 6234 Piney Woods Rd., Fairfield, NC 27826. Open daily year-round. (252) 926-4491; www.ospreynestcampground.com

Simmons Lakeside Lodge

A shoreline dotted with graceful cypress trees gives the lodge a postcard view of Lake Mattamuskeet. Hunting and fishing opportunities abound, and guide service is available. 5811 Piney Woods Rd., Fairfield, NC 27826. (252) 926-1441

Hamilton/Martin County

Fort Branch Confederate Earthen Fort

2883 Fort Branch Rd., Hamilton, NC 27840. Apr.–first week of Nov., Sat.–Sun., 10 A.M.–5 P.M., and by appointment. (252) 792-6605, (252) 776-8566, or (800) 776-8566; www.fortbranchcivilwarsite.com

Fort Branch Confederate Earthen Fort

Walking Tour of Historic Hamilton

Tour brochures are available at the Martin County Travel & Tourism office. 100 E. Church St., Hamilton, NC 27892. (252) 792-6605 or (800) 776-8566; www.visitmartincounty.com

Jamesville/Martin County

Berry Tyme Farms

Here, you can pick your own delicious strawberries from easy-to-access rows. The plants are healthy, with plump, ripe berries kept clean on plastic. Ready-picked berries are available, too! 1504 Wendell Modlin Rd., Jamesville, NC 27857. May 1–June 1, Mon.–Sat., 7 A.M.–7 P.M. (252) 792-6916

Cypress Grill

Originally, this charming grill was one of the many riverside fishing shacks where local men cooked, played cards, and socialized. Today, the Cypress Grill is widely known for its fried fish and roe. 300 N. Stewart St., Jamesville, NC 27846. Open Jan.–Apr., coinciding with the annual herring run. (252) 792-4175; www.roanokeriver.com/news_features/cypressgrill.htm

Mackey's Ferry Peanuts and Gifts

Locally grown peanuts are prepared daily here. Stop by the gift shop, where you'll find local flavor even among the gift packages. 30871 US Hwy 64 E., Jamesville, NC 27846. Open daily, 9 A.M.–6 P.M.; closed Christmas and Thanksgiving. (252) 793-2993; www.mfpnuts.com

Roanoke River Paddle Trail and Canoe Camping Platforms

Paddlers from all over love this unique trail. Ten unusual camping platforms in the swamps and lowlands of the basin provide spectacular opportunities. Roberson's Marina, US Hwy 64 and Gardner's Creek, Jamesville, NC 27857. Reservations are required. (252) 792-3583 or (252) 798-3920; www.roanokeriverpartners.org

Roanoke River Paddle Trail

Oak City/Martin County

Jackson's Greenhouses

Jackson's offers a wide variety of healthy bedding plants, hanging baskets, and other fresh greenery for the home or office. Oak City, NC 27857. (252) 798-2435

Southern Comfort B&B

Though located on a working farm, the inn features

the convenience and style implied by its name. It has two bedrooms in a farmhouse and a separate bunkhouse popular with hunters and paddlers. 15909 NC Hwy 125 N., Oak City, NC 27857. (252) 798-7081

Ocracoke/Hyde County

Bella Fiore Pottery

Visit with Sarah Fiore, who produces pottery with rich, vivid hues of yellow, green, blue, and other colors. The gallery also features watercolors, carvings, handmade jewelry, and photography produced by island artists. 109 Lighthouse Rd., Ocracoke, NC 27960. Open year-round. (252) 928-1421; www.ocracokeisland.com/bella_fiore_pottery.htm

British Cemetery

The HMS *Bedfordshire*, one of 24 ships sent by Britain to help protect America's coastal shipping, was sunk by a German sub in 1942. When the bodies of seamen washed ashore, the people of Ocracoke buried them in this small cemetery. 202 British Cemetery Rd., Ocracoke, NC 27960. Open year-round during daylight hours. (252) 926-9171 or (252) 926-9041; www.hydecounty.org

Deepwater Theater

Catch local talent, including The OcraFolk Opry, a troupe that spins yarns and performs a variety of music from acoustic rock to bluegrass. 82 School Rd., Ocracoke, NC 27960. Evening performances, June–Oct. The cost is $12 for adults and $6 for children. (252) 928-4280; www.molassescreek.com

Downpoint Decoy Shop

Here, you can find a wide variety of handmade duck decoys, an enduring symbol of North Carolina's low country. Check out the collection of old fishing lures, wooden and paper gun-shell boxes, paddles, and almost anything nautical. 340 Irvin Garrish Hwy, Ocracoke, NC 27960. Open daily, noon–4 P.M. (252) 928-3269

Howard's Pub & Raw Oyster Bar

Fresh-caught seafood dishes delight locals and visitors alike. Visitors enjoy the island memorabilia on the walls and the only water-view restaurant deck in Ocracoke. 1175 Irvin Garrish Hwy, Ocracoke, NC 27960. Open daily, 11 A.M.–2 A.M. (252) 928-4441; www.howardspub.com

Ocracoke Historical Interpretative Trail

Ocracoke's historical, natural, and cultural attractions are featured on this island tour. Pick up a brochure at the Hyde County Chamber of Commerce. Ocracoke, NC 27960. Year-round during daylight hours. Free. (252) 926-9171 or (888) 493-3826; www.hydecounty.org

Ocrafolk Festival

Ocracoke Island

Ocrafolk Festival Poster

Ocracoke Lighthouse

The beacon of this famous light—the oldest lighthouse in operation in North Carolina—shines for 14 miles. Though visitors can no longer enter the lighthouse, a trip to the grounds is worth the visit. Ocracoke, NC 27960. Open year-round. Free. (252) 926-9171 or (888) 493-3826; www.hydecounty.org

Ocracoke Lodging

For lodging information about Ocracoke, go to www.ocracokevillage.com or www.ocracokeisland.com.

Ocracoke Preservation Society/David Williams House

David Williams was the first captain of the Coast Guard lifesaving station on Ocracoke. Here, you can view artifacts from the Civil War and Fort Ocracoke and learn the history of the early Coast Guard. 49 Water Plant Rd., Ocracoke, NC 27960. Apr.–Nov., Mon.–Sat. Free. (252) 928-7375; www.ocracokepreservation.org

Hyde County's Talking Historical Places *Hyde County*

Ocracoke Visitor Center/Cape Hatteras National Seashore

38 Irvin Garrish Hwy, Ocracoke, NC 27960. (252) 928-4531

Ocracoke Lighthouse's beam shines 14 miles.

The Ocrafolk Festival

The three-day event features performances from local and regional musicians, tales by Ocracoke storytellers, and food. Howard St. and School Rd., Ocracoke, NC 27960. Held in early June, Fri.–Sun. (252) 928-3411; www.ocrafolkfestival.org

Over the Moon

This little shop features jewelry, pottery, woodwork, garden art, and other creations by more than 100 local and regional artists and artisans. 64 British Cemetery Rd., Ocracoke, NC 27960. Open year-round. (252) 928-3555

Owen's Veggies

Stop by this family-owned market for produce and locally made fig preserves, jams, jellies, and hot pepper and herb vinegars. Call ahead to find out what's fresh! 439 Lighthouse Rd., Ocracoke, NC 27960. Easter–Oct., Sun.–Fri., 10 A.M.–6 P.M.; Sat., noon–6 P.M. (252) 928-3811

Secret Garden Gallery

Watercolors, oils, handmade gold and silver jewelry, and handmade contemporary furniture are among the wonderful things on display. Special exhibitions are held every two weeks from March through November. 72 Back Rd., Ocracoke, NC 27960. Feb.–Nov., 10 A.M.–6 P.M. (252) 928-2598; www.art-on-ocracoke.com

The Sunflower Center for the Arts

The Sunflower Gallery features handmade jewelry, art glass, and other gifts, plus paintings by local and regional artists. 172 Back Rd., Ocracoke, NC 27960. Easter–Oct., Mon.–Fri., 10 A.M.–5 P.M.; Sat., 10 A.M.–noon. (252) 921-0188; www.ocracokeisland.com/sunflower_center1.htm

Pantego/Beaufort County

Gathering a bouquet at Terra Ceia Farms

Terra Ceia Farms

Stop by this farm—one of the largest bulb producers on the East Coast—for cut flowers, bulbs, and perennials. 3810 Terra Ceia Rd., Pantego, NC 27810. (252) 943-2865 or (800) 858-2852; www.TerraCeiaFarms.com

Pinetown/Beaufort County

Oden's Store & Antiques

You'll find an array of antiques alongside the general merchandise in this turn-of-the-century country store. There's an especially good selection of glassware and crystal. 15191 US Hwy 264 E., Pinetown, NC 27865. Mon.–Sat., 11 A.M.–5 P.M. (252) 943-2956; odenstore@yahoo.com

Petals & Produce

Looking for seasonal fruits and vegetables? You'll find them at Petals & Produce. There are lots of greenhouse bedding plants, shrubs, container plants, and small trees, too. 19821 US Hwy 264 E., Pinetown, NC 27865. Mon.–Fri., 8 A.M.–5:30 P.M.; Sat., 8 A.M.–3 P.M. (252) 943-3116

Plymouth/Washington County

Academy Antiques

This shop sells treasures of long ago, including furniture, glassware, and lamps. 108 E. Water St., Plymouth, NC 27962. Open daily, 11 A.M.–9 P.M. (252) 793-6100 or (252) 217-8696

Askew's Farm & Nursery

Askew's is an old family farm that offers plants, shrubs, and other greenery for sale. Visit the Chicken Koop with its hand-painted items and a variety of crafts. 3542 NC Hwy 32 S., Plymouth, NC 27962. Mon.–Sat., 8 A.M.–5 P.M. (252) 793-2797

Barber Shop Antiques

The Barber Shop sells antiques, collectibles, and junk. You'll find deals for real! 1224 US Hwy 64 W., Plymouth, NC 27962. Mon.–Sat., 8 A.M.–5 P.M., and by appointment. (252) 809-2466

The Battle of Plymouth Living History Weekend

This event features a reenactment of the Battle of Plymouth. This last major Confederate victory of the Civil War was the largest battle fought in North Carolina. 302 E. Water St., Plymouth, NC 27962. Held the third weekend in Apr. (252) 793-1377; www.livinghistoryweekend.com

The Book and the Cup

Enjoy freshly ground gourmet coffees, lattes, smoothies, and decadent homemade desserts while gazing at the Roanoke River. Books and creative gift items are available, too! 111 W. Water St. #1, Plymouth, NC 27962. Mon.–Sat., 8 A.M.–6 P.M. (252) 791-0295; bookandcuphsd@embarq.net

Brush Creek Yachts

Marvin Spencer is a master boatbuilder known for his art as well as his craft. You'll find an assortment of handmade canoes and wooden boats of all sizes and types in various states of construction or repair. 208 W. Water St., Plymouth, NC 27962. (252) 482-3753; www.brushcreekyachts.com

Farm City Festival

There's lots of fun at this festive event in historic downtown Plymouth the weekend before Thanksgiving. 128 E. Water St., Plymouth, NC 27962. Begins Fri. at 5:30 P.M. at the Mini Park; Sat. events start at 10 A.M. Free. (252) 793-2163; www.visitwashingtoncountync.com/attractions/farm_city_festival.htm

Garden Spot Café

Garden elements are painted on the walls of this café. A wrought-iron garden table provides a delightful view of Main Street and a perfect place to nod and smile at passersby. Fresh salads, wraps, and decadent desserts hit the spot. 124 W. Water St., Plymouth, NC 27962. Mon.–Tues.,

11 A.M.–2 P.M.; Wed.–Fri., 11 A.M.–2 P.M. and 5–8 P.M. (252) 793-3600; jenjimmy@earthlink.net

Gingerbread Bakery

This bakery features pastries and biscuits to die for and a buffet lunch on weekdays. US Hwy 64 W., Plymouth, NC 27962. Mon.–Fri., 5 A.M.–5 P.M.; Sat., 5 A.M.–noon. (252) 793-9334

Historic Plymouth Walking Tour

Historic Plymouth Walking Tour, Ausbon House *Doward Jones, Jr.*

Plymouth ranks among the top 10 Civil War sites in the Carolinas and is the site of the state's largest battle. Visitors can learn about naval vessels of the period and see a prewar building that survived a Union raid. A free tour guide is available at the Port O' Plymouth Museum. Plymouth, NC 27962. (252) 793-1377

The Little Man

This half-century-old burger joint is known for its special sauce and delicious, generously portioned fries. 170 US Hwy 64 E., Plymouth, NC 27962. Open daily, 5 A.M.–11 P.M. (252) 793-2484

Norm's Ice Cream Shop

Take a break from shopping and treat yourself to a sundae. 108 E. Water St., Plymouth, NC 27962. Open daily, 11 A.M.–9 P.M. (252) 793-6100 or (252) 217-8696

Port O' Plymouth Museum/CSS *Albemarle*

Exhibits tell about the Battle of Plymouth and Washington County. A 3/8-scale replica of the 63-foot CSS *Albemarle* is moored behind the museum. Groups can arrange to see the gunboat cruise up the Roanoke and fire its guns. 302 E. Water St., Plymouth, NC 27962. Tues.–Sat., 8 A.M.–5 P.M. The cost is $1 for adults and $.50 for children. (252) 793-1377

Ram *Albemarle* Restaurant

If you miss breakfast, you can get it here until 11:30 A.M., Tuesday through Saturday. Then the restaurant switches over to a luncheon buffet. Friday night features a special seafood buffet. 303 US Hwy 64 W., Plymouth, NC 27962. Tues.–Sun., 5 A.M.–10 P.M. (252) 793-3388

CSS *Albemarle* *NC Echo*

Roanoke Basin Gallery

Doward Jones, Jr.'s, skillful eye for textures, lights and darks, and composition is reflected in his award-winning photography. You'll find pottery by local potters, books about the region, and antiques collected by local collectors. 210 W. Water St., Plymouth, NC 27962. Mon.–Fri., 8 A.M.–5 P.M. (252) 793-4777; d.jonesjr@mchsi.com

Roanoke Oyster Bar

Fresh oysters (in season, of course), delicious steamed shrimp, and outstanding crab legs are featured here. Live entertainment can be found most Saturday nights. 107 E. Water St., Plymouth, NC 27962. Apr.–Sept., Mon.–Sat., 5–10 P.M. (252) 793-1039

Roanoke River Lighthouse

This replica of the Roanoke River Light reveals some of the fascinating details of a lightkeeper's lonely, often harsh existence. Plymouth, NC 27962. Tues.–Sat., 11 A.M.–3 P.M.; Sun., 1–4 P.M. Admission fee. (252) 217-2204 or (252) 793-1377

Roanoke River Paddle Trail and Canoe Camping Platforms

Paddle by day and spend the night camping on unique platforms in the swamps and lowlands of the river. Windsor, NC 27983. Open year-round. (252) 792-3583 (reservations) or (252) 798-3920 (office); www.roanokeriverpartners.org

Virginia Dare Antiques, Baskets, and Cane Seats

This shop offers country and primitive antiques and beautiful handmade baskets. 18945 NC Hwy 32 N. (Acre Station), Plymouth, NC 27962. Spring–New Year's, Fri.–Sat., 10 A.M.–5 P.M., and by appointment; Jan.–March, Fri.–Sat. (252) 927-3172; vdrh@gotricounty.com

Washington County Arts Council

The council, created in 1978, supports excellence in the arts through events and shows. 206 W. Water St., Plymouth, NC 27962. (252) 793-8248; brookds@earthlink.net

Roanoke River Lighthouse (p. 25)

Washington County Farmers' Market

You'll find fresh fruits and vegetables and friendly farmers here. There are homemade items, too! Plymouth, NC 27962. May–Dec., Tues., 8 A.M.–1 P.M.; Fri., 3–7 P.M.; Sat., 8 A.M.–5 P.M. (252) 793-2163

Washington County Library

If you have small children, visit during the special storytelling time. 201 E. Third St., Plymouth, NC 27962. Wed., 10–11:15 A.M. (252) 793-2113

Wildlife Museum & Gallery

Get a closeup look at mounted wildlife from North America and Africa. There's a sensory section where visitors can feel differences in textures among animal hides, horns, and antlers. 111 W. Water St., Plymouth, NC 27962. Mon.–Fri., 9 A.M.–4 P.M. Admission is $3. (252) 793-3248; www.visitwashingtoncountync.com

Ponzer/Hyde County

A-Bell Gallery

Ann Bell's watercolor "painted memories" reflects her childhood in the Depression era. The artist has been called "the Grandma Moses of North Carolina." The gallery also features a unique collection of antique household goods. 39308 US Hwy 264, Ponzer, NC 27810. Open by appointment. (252) 943-2059

American Peat Company

This peat operation is the world's largest. Chances are your garden has peat from this mine! 2786 Hyde Park Canal, Ponzer, NC 27810. Call ahead. (252) 935-5287

Riverside Campground & Cottages

This campground on the banks of the Pungo offers campsites, cabins, and cottages. A convenient boat ramp lets you glide into the black water. 272 Riverside Campground Rd., Ponzer, NC 27810. (252) 943-2926

Wildlife Museum & Gallery

Thomasina's B&B

Thomasina's features three guest rooms near the river and four national wildlife refuges. Homemade breakfast rounds out this pleasant experience. 28 Riverside Campground Rd., Ponzer, NC 27810. (252) 943-2097; www.thomasinasbandb.com

Robersonville/Martin County

Carolina Country Fresh (formerly Scattered Acres)

This pick-your-own strawberry farm and produce stand carries local arts and crafts, produce, soy candles, and more. US Hwy 64, Robersonville, NC 27871. Produce stand, Apr.–Christmas; berry patch, mid-Apr.–early June. (252) 795-2926 or (252) 795-4903; www.carolinacountryfresh.com

East Carolina Motor Speedway

Fans come here for the late-model stock cars and the sportsman-class race on a hard-surface racetrack. 2918 US Hwy 64 Alt., Robersonville, NC 27871. Apr.–Oct., Sat., 6 P.M. Admission fee. (252) 792-1116; www.ecmsracing.com

Filling Station

Part of this unusual restaurant was actually built as a pack house in 1901. It serves eastern-style barbecue and seasonal favorites like fresh herring. 7309 US Hwy 64 Alt., Robersonville, NC 27871. (252) 795-3496

St. James Place

This restored Gothic Revival Primitive Baptist church now houses a remarkable collection of Southern folk art and pottery. More than 100 North Carolina quilts—including 42 African-American examples—are draped over pews. US Hwy 64 and Outerbridge St., Robersonville, NC 27871. Open year-round by appointment. (252) 795-3936, (252) 795-4719, or (252) 795-4576; www.visitmartincounty.com/SiteDetail.asp?ID=5

Restored Gothic Revival church houses St. James Place. *NC Echo*

Roper/Washington County

Roper Peanut Festival

This event is a celebration of local culture and agriculture. A highlight is the crowning of the Peanut Festival Queen, who must be at least 75 to qualify. Downtown Roper, NC 27962. Held the second Sat. in Sept. (252) 793-5156

Scranton/Hyde County

Quilts and pottery at St. James Place

Mayo's Commercial Fishing Supply

See how crab pots are made. 854 Puddin Hill Rd., Scranton, NC 27875. Open year-round during daylight hours. Free. (252) 926-8601

VanHorn's Campground and Marina

Also known as Bayside, this campground offers cabins, RV hookups, and easy access to Pamlico Sound. 480 Germantown Rd., Scranton, NC 27875. (252) 926-6621; wallyvanhorn2003@yahoo.com

Swan Quarter/Hyde County

Equils Seafood

275 Creekside Dr., Swan Quarter, NC 27885. Open seasonally during daylight hours. (252) 926-9802

Mattamuskeet Campground

360 NC Hwy 94, Swan Quarter, NC 27885. (252) 926-0911

Mattamuskeet Lodge

Lake Mattamuskeet is a remarkable waterfowl sanctuary and wildlife refuge. The lodge is listed on the National Register of Historic Places. Visitors can tour by car or bicycle. 38 Refuge Rd., Swan Quarter, NC 27885. Access to the building is restricted, but the grounds are open year-round during daylight hours. Free. (252) 926-9171 or (888) 493-3826; www.hydecounty.org

Mattamuskeet Lodge

Mattamuskeet Seafood

Whether you'd just like to see how blue crabs caught in the nearby waters of Pamlico Sound are processed or whether you'd like to purchase fresh crabmeat or handmade crab cakes in season, this is the place to visit! 24694 US Hwy 264, Swan Quarter, NC 27885. Open seasonally by appointment. (252) 926-2431

Newman Seafood

Newman Seafood is the place to go if you want fresh local seafood right off the boat. Be sure to take the time to visit the crab shedding facility. If you've never witnessed a crab shed its shell, this is the place to do it. Soft crabs are a real find here! 644 Landing Rd., Swan Quarter, NC 27885. Open seasonally during daylight hours. (252) 926-1288

Rose Bay Oyster House

Rose Bay shucks oysters for packing and for sale to the public. Take a tour or just take home some oysters. 7794 US Hwy 264, Swan Quarter, NC 27885. Open seasonally during daylight hours. (252) 926-9151

Washington/Beaufort County

Beaufort County Arts Council

The gallery and gift shop feature the works of local artists. 108 Gladden St., Washington, NC 27889. Tues.–Fri., 9 A.M.–4 P.M.; Sat., 10 A.M.–2 P.M. Free. (252) 946-2504; www.beaufortcountyartscouncil.org

Black Brothers Farm

Visit this working farm for ultrafresh strawberries and greenhouse tomatoes. 681 Black Rd., Washington, NC 27889. Dec.–May, Mon.–Sat. Call for tours. (252) 946-7092

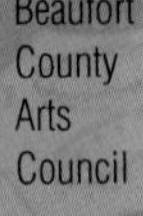

Beaufort County Arts Council

The Blind Center

This not-for-profit center teaches independent-living skills to the visually challenged. To support these activities, the center offers hand-woven textile pieces; bead, clay, and ceramic works; cane stools and chairs; and more. 221 N. Harvey St., Washington, NC 27889. Mon.–Fri., 10 A.M.–4 P.M. (252) 946-6208 or (252) 946-2436; www.theblindcenter.org

Carolina House B&B

Built in 1880, the Carolina House is listed on the National Register of Historic Homes. It features four guest rooms furnished with beautiful antiques. 227 E. Second St., Washington, NC 27889. (252) 975-1382; www.carolinahousebnb.com

East Carolina Wildlife Arts Festival & NC Decoy Carving Championship

This event features wildlife exhibits, local arts and crafts, and food. Highlights include goose and swan calling, an auction, and a competition for the best carved decoys and wildlife pieces in the state. PO Box 1713, Washington, NC 27889. Held at the end of Jan. Admission is $8 for one day or $10 for two days. (252) 946-2897; www.eastcarolinawildfowlguild.com

Historic Washington-Beaufort Visitor Center & Walking Tour

The tour begins at the visitor center. 138 S. Market St., Washington, NC 27889. Mon.–Fri., 9 A.M.–5 P.M.; Sat.–Sun., 10 A.M.–4 P.M. Free. (252) 948-9415 or (800) 999-3857; www.washingtonnctourism.com

King Chicken Drive-In

This Beaufort County institution features biscuits, burgers, barbecue, and chicken. 601 Carolina Ave., Washington, NC 27889. Mon.–Wed., 5:30 A.M.–11 P.M.; Thurs.–Sat., 5:30 A.M.–12:30 A.M.; Sun., 6–11 A.M. (252) 946-4594

The Meeting Place Café

This café offers homemade soups, quiches, sandwiches, and baked goods, including the chef's famous homemade poppy seed muffins, which are served free with lunch. 225 W. Main St., Washington, NC 27889. Mon.–Sat., 11 A.M.–3:30 P.M. (252) 975-6370; tmcp@excite.com

The Moss House

This beautiful 1902 Victorian home provides gracious accommodations in the heart of historic downtown Washington. A full Southern gourmet breakfast is served each morning. 129 Van Norden St., Washington, NC 27889. (252) 975-3967 or (888) 975-3393; www.themosshouse.com

North Carolina Estuarium

North Carolina's first aquarium focusing exclusively on sounds and coastal rivers boasts more than 200 displays. Stop in the gift shop for unique items, or take a water tour. 223 E. Water St., Washington, NC 27889. Tues.–Sat., 10 A.M.–4 P.M. Admission is $3 for adults and $2 for students; children under five are free. (252) 948-0000; www.partnershipforthesounds.org

Overhead view of Mattamuskeet Lodge (p. 29)

Raindrop Ridge Farm

This farm specializes in herbs and older plant varieties. 1356 Camp Leach Rd., Washington, NC 27889. The greenhouses are open daily, mid-March–June. (252) 923-9251; raindropherbs@beaufortco.com

Riverwalk Gallery

This cooperative gallery owned by area artists offers a wide array of artwork, including paintings, pottery, photography, fabric art, and jewelry. 139 W. Main St., Washington, NC 27889. Mon.–Sat., 10:30 A.M.–5 P.M. (252) 974-0400

A Slice of Heaven Dessert, Tea & Coffee Bar

Customers can select fresh strawberry napoleons, fresh cobblers, an array of Belgian chocolate desserts, and pies from the owner's own recipes. 210 W. Main St., Washington, NC 27889. Wed.–Thurs. and Sun., 10 A.M.–5 P.M.; Fri.–Sat., 10 A.M.–5 P.M. and 7–11 P.M. (252) 948-2300

Smoke on the Water Festival

This lively festival in late October features a pork and chili cookoff and is home to the North Carolina State Barbecue Championship. Enjoy the music provided by local and regional musicians. Children's activities keep tots and teens busy. Washington, NC 27889. (252) 974-2632

Tranter's Creek Resort & Campground

Whether you stay in your tent, in your camper, or in a creek-side cabin, Tranter's activities and ideal location guarantee a relaxing stay. Guests enjoy the large pool, the game room, the boat ramp, the camp store, and much more. 6573 Clark's Neck Rd., Washington, NC 27889. Office hours, Mon.–Thurs., 9 A.M.–6 P.M.; Fri.–Sat., 9 A.M.–9 P.M.; Sun., 10 A.M.–6 P.M. (252) 948-0850; www.tranterscreekresort.com

Whitaker's Barn

Located in a quaint little barn, Whitaker's sells beautiful outdoor plants and local produce. You'll also find homemade jams and jellies, honey, and other regional products, as well as fresh North Carolina Christmas trees and wreaths during the holiday season. 1101 John Small Ave., Washington, NC 27889. Mon.–Sat., 8:30 A.M.–5:30 P.M. (252) 946-4883

Woolard Produce

There's nothing like seasonal fresh berries and produce! At Woolard Produce, you'll find fresh strawberries, blackberries, greenhouse tomatoes, sweet corn, collards, watermelons, and more. 101 Belgian Ln., Washington, NC 27889. (252) 975-1756

Williamston/Martin County

Big Mill B&B

This charming inn is located on 200 acres of farmland and forest. In winter, you can sit by a fire in the large stone fireplace in your suite and see Canada geese as they land on the lake. On a balmy summer day, stroll under the trees or in the grapevine orchard and smell the Cape jasmine. 1607 Big Mill Rd., Williamston, NC 27892. (252) 792-8787; www.bigmill.com

Clark's Pharmacy

This working pharmacy and soda fountain features hand-stirred vanilla and cherry Cokes, fresh orangeades and lemonades, packaged sandwiches, snacks, and coffee. It's a downtown gathering spot for young and old! 142 W. Main St., Williamston, NC 27892. (252) 792-2151; www.visitmartincounty.com

Cobb's Corner Restaurant

Try the famous "Banana Fritters" for dessert. Local hand-stitched and embroidered pillowcases, handkerchiefs, and other handmade items are on display for sale. Cobb's is located at the Holiday Inn. 101 East Blvd., Williamston, NC 27892. (252) 792-6493

Farm Life Disc Golf

Test your skills on this unique 18-hole disc golf course with a pond, fruit trees, and a stream. All holes are par-three. Disc sales and rentals are available. Your whole family will enjoy the fun! 1233 Kent Roberson Rd., Williamston, NC 27892. Apr. 1–Dec. 15, open daily during daylight hours. (252) 792-3196

Haughton Hall B&B

203 Haughton St., Williamston, NC 27892. (252) 792-0070; www.haughtonhallnc.com

Jenkins Antiques

This sprawling display of antiques, collectibles, and reproductions is spread throughout an 1857 farmhouse. 2427 US Hwy 17 S., Williamston, NC 27892. (252) 792-1766

Martin County Arts Center & Council

The council maintains changing displays of arts and crafts by regional artisans, including unique furniture and other wood items, paintings, glass and metal objects, textiles, and more. The "Alive After Five" celebration is held each third Thursday. 160 E. Main St., Williamston, NC 27892. Thurs.–Sat., 10 A.M.–4 P.M. (252) 792-5142; www.martincountync.com/mc/arts/

Martin County Farmers' Market

Locally grown fresh produce, homemade goodies, and crafts are available. Take home a basketful! 4001 W. Main St. Ext., Williamston, NC 27892. May–Dec., Fri.–Sat., 7 A.M.–1 P.M. (252) 792-1621 or (252) 792-1900

Martin County Travel & Tourism

100 E. Church St., Williamston, NC 27892. Mon.–Fri., 9 A.M.–5 P.M. (252) 792-6605 or (800) 776-8566; www.visitmartincounty.com

Martin Supply

From hoop cheese to locally made jams, jellies, honey, and molasses, you'll enjoy a glimpse of times past. Besides farm supplies, you'll find a full line of hunting and sporting goods, as well as men's and women's apparel. 217 Washington St., Williamston, NC 27892. (252) 792-2123; www.visitmartincounty.com

The Message of Easter

The moving story of Easter is told with full pageantry, great production values, and period costumes each year by members of the Farm Life community. 2925 Piney Grove Church Rd., Williamston, NC 27892. Offered the Fri. before Palm Sunday through the Mon. after Easter, 8:15 P.M. Free. (252) 792-1342;www.messageofeaster.com

Morningstar Nature Refuge

Morningstar is a beautiful private wildlife refuge that offers guided and self-guided tours. The Wind Walker Observatory alone is worth the trip. You'll also find a research lab, a library, a wildlife museum, a wetland boardwalk, private gardens, and fabulous exhibits. 1967 Meadow Branch Rd., Crane Meadow Ridge, Williamston, NC 27892. Open by appointment. Free. (252) 792-7788; www.morningstarrefuge.org

Morningstar Nature Refuge *Gail L. Roberson*

R&C Restaurant

If you want collards and backbone, go on Monday. For rutabagas, visit on Tuesday. Specials are offered each day, accompanied by unique thin, crispy cornbread. 211 Washington St., Williamston, NC 27892. (252) 793-3161; www.visitmartincounty.com

Roanoke Inn B&B

This charming Queen Anne features more than comfortable sleeping quarters. Lovely architectural details include pressed-tin ceilings, three fireplaces, and inlaid heart-wood floors. There's a convenient high-speed Internet connection, too. 201 S. Biggs St., Williamston, NC 27892. Open March–Dec. Dining is by reservation only. (252) 792-7288; www.roanokeinn.org

Shamrock Restaurant

Steaks, seafood, and good, old-fashioned home cooking are always on the menu. The old-style lunch buffet is one of a few left in eastern North Carolina. 101 West Blvd., Williamston, NC 27892. Mon.–Sat., 6 A.M.–9 P.M.; Sun., 7 A.M.–9 P.M. (252) 792-5007

Shaw's Barbeque

Shaw's is known across the state for some of the best eastern North Carolina barbecue around. It also features melt-in-your-mouth cheese (or ham, egg, or sausage) biscuits at breakfast and other country specialties. US Hwy 64 Alt., Williamston, NC 27892. Open Mon.–Sat. (252) 792-5339; www.visitmartincounty.com

Sunnyside Oyster Bar

This seasonal restaurant has been a local treasure since the early 1930s. It's been featured on ABC's *Good Morning America* and is listed on the National Register of Historic Places. Enjoy oysters, shrimp, or scallops while you sit in the cozy original wooden booths. 1102 Washington St., Williamston, NC 27892. (252) 792-5339; www.visitmartincounty.com

The Trading Post

This eclectic collection of used furniture, household items, and other interesting estate finds is a favorite spot for antique hounds. You never know what you'll discover here! 404 Martin Luther King, Jr., Dr., Williamston, NC 27892. (252) 792-6346

Terra Ceia Farms (p. 22)

Walking Williamston: A Tour of Historic Williamston

Start this walking tour at the Martin County Travel and Tourism office. 100 E. Church St., Williamston, NC 27892. Free. (252) 792-6605 or (800) 776-8566; www.visitmartincounty.com

Wright Brothers Mural

This delightful mural greets everyone who enters the Williamston post office. Painted in 1940 by Philip von Saltza, it is one of 43 murals and other works of art installed in North Carolina public buildings between 1938 and 1943. 121 E. Main St., Williamston, NC 27892. Year-round during business hours. Free.

Roanoke River Paddle Trails (p. 18)

Front Porch to Back Forty

Bertie, Chowan, and Perquimans Counties

To get a real sense of this place, drive with your windows down . . . at least for a while. Let the summer perfume of honeysuckle and wisteria stir your sensuous side.

During harvest season, the unmistakable aroma of freshly dug peanuts will send you searching for a big bucket of the tasty treats. You won't look long. Plenty of them are available at roadside stands and sidewalk shops that are loaded with personality, great food, and handmade treasures.

Enjoy exploring the outdoors at Bennet's Mill Pond. *Sue Clark* (p. 40)

Stop in at a local gallery and discover a new artist. Be inspired by the motion of a woven metal sculpture or the music of a glass wind chime. Let the eyes in a portrait speak to you.

This is open farm country. It spreads out between small towns and communities, each with a unique personality. Sample them all and then, at the end of the day, think back on your experiences while relaxing in a friendly B&B. Pick a rocker on the front porch and listen to the music of the katydids or the crowd cheering for a home run at a baseball game just down the street. No matter where you start on this trail, you'll find interesting characters, delightful talent, and a genuine welcome waiting for you.

Read on for town-by-town descriptions of the unique attractions that make up the "Front Porch to Back Forty" trail.

Colerain/Bertie County

Seagull Café

This charming little fish house on the Chowan River offers fresh herring, herring roe, and fresh perch during the spring season. The café is open during the annual herring run each year, as well as in the fall. The fall menu includes trout, corn herring, oysters, and shrimp. And don't forget the dessert choices, which include homemade lemon and chocolate meringue pies and banana pudding. 147 River Rd., Colerain, NC 27924. Open Wed.–Fri. from the first Wed. in Oct. through the Fri. before Thanksgiving; also open March–Apr. (252) 356-4387

Edenton/Chowan County

Acoustic Coffee

Great coffee, a friendly atmosphere, and live music—what else could you ask for? Muffins, scones, brownies, and cookies are baked on-site daily. Hats, T-shirts, coffee mugs, and CDs by local musicians are for sale, too. 302 S. Broad St., Edenton, NC 27932. Mon.–Thurs., 7 A.M.–4 P.M.; Fri., 7 A.M.–4 P.M. and 6:30–9:30 P.M. for music; Sat., 8 A.M.–5:30 P.M. or until 9 P.M. when there's a performance. (252) 482-7465; www.acoustic-coffee.com

By Hand Gallery & Studio

Belvidere Bed & Breakfast

This waterfront inn features two guest rooms with queen beds. A full breakfast greets lodgers each morning. The innkeepers also offer river tours. 306 Colony Dr., Edenton, NC 27932. (252) 482-1622; www.belviderebandb.com

Bennet's Mill Pond

Bennet's Mill Pond teems with wildlife and waterfowl. There are fishing platforms, boat docks, and over 200 acres of quiet, navigable water. Rocky Hock Rd., Edenton, NC 27932. Open sunrise–sunset. (252) 482-8595; ecrd@ncmail.net

By Hand Gallery & Studio

This eclectic gallery offers a variety of handmade items. You'll see the works of the artist-in-residence, one-of-a-kind wheel- and hand-created clay pottery, sculpture, glass works, pine-needle baskets, and fiber art. Ask about classes, too. 301 N. Broad St., Edenton, NC 27932. Apr.–Dec., Thurs.–Sat., 10 A.M.–5 P.M. (252) 619-2300; bfreeman203@earthlink.net

Cannon's Ferry Heritage River Walk

Cannon's Ferry Heritage River Walk

Follow the signs and learn about the Cannon's Ferry fishing industry and its impact on the region. The walk is located at one of the most beautiful points along the Chowan River. As you saunter, you'll find a picnic area and a canoe and kayak launch area. Off Hwy 32, Edenton, NC 27932. Open daily. (252) 482-8595; ecrd@ncmail.net

Captain's Quarters Inn

It's a short walk to Albemarle Sound from this quaint eight-room inn located in the historic district of Edenton. It was refurbished in 1994. Dinner, served by reservation, is cooked by an award-winning chef. 202 W. Queen St., Edenton, NC 27932. (252) 482-8945 or (800) 482-8945; www.captainsquartersinn.com

Chicken Kitchen

This eatery opened its doors in 1971 and has been a fixture in the community ever since. For those who want country cooking on the go, the Chicken Kitchen has drive-through service. 809 N. Broad St., Edenton, NC 27932. Mon.–Sat., 6 A.M.–8:30 P.M.; Sun., 6:30 A.M.–9:30 P.M. (252) 482-4721; http://home.earthlink.net/~chickenkitchenedenton

Chowan Arts Council and Gallery Shop

The gallery features works by 150 area and regional artists, from handmade jewelry and pottery to stunning photography, vivid oils, and watercolors. Guest musicians, poets, and other artists perform throughout the year. 200 E.

Church St., Edenton, NC 27932. Mon.–Sat., 10 A.M.–4 P.M.; Sun., 1–4 P.M. (252) 482-8005; www.chowanarts.org

Chowan County Courthouse

This 1767 structure is considered by some to be the finest Georgian courthouse in the South. The courthouse is a national historic landmark. E. King St., Edenton, NC 27932

Chowan County Tourism Development Authority

116 E. King St., Edenton, NC 27932. Mon.–Fri., 9 A.M.–5 P.M. (252) 482-3400 or (800) 775-0111; www.visitedenton.com

The Cupola House *Historic Edenton State Historic Site*

The Cupola House

Built in 1758 for Francis Corbin, an agent of Lord Granville, one of the eight Lords Proprietors, this structure is considered the finest wooden example of the Jacobean style of architecture in the South. The house is included on tours originating from Historic Edenton State Historic Site. 408 S. Broad St., Edenton, NC 27932

Dunlow Farm

You can pick your own strawberries or buy them prepicked at the Dunlow Farm. Vegetables are available in season, too. 1426 Paradise Rd., Edenton, NC 27932. Apr.–June, Mon.–Sat., 7 A.M.–dusk. (252) 482-7367

Edenton Boat Slips

If you're cruising by boat, you can tie up at the newly constructed breakwater on Edenton Bay. Transient boat slips with electric and water hookups are available. Clean restrooms and shower facilities are on the premises, too. Located at the foot of Broad St., Edenton, NC 27932. Apr.–Oct., 9 A.M.–9 P.M. (252) 482-7352 or (252) 482-2832; www.townofedenton.com

Chowan Arts Council & Gallery *Sue Clark*

Edenton Harbor Kayak Rentals

Here, you can rent kayaks and tour the shores of beautiful Edenton Bay or discover the twists and turns of Pembroke Creek. Located at Colonial Park at the foot of Broad St., Edenton, NC 27932. Mon.–Fri., 8 A.M.–5 P.M.; from May to July, it is also open Sun., 9 A.M.–9 P.M. A one-person kayak costs $10 per hour or $35 per day; a two-person kayak costs $15 per hour or $45 per day. (252) 482-2832 or (252) 337-4488; www.townofedenton.com

Dunlow Farm

Edenton Historic Commission/Barker House

Edenton Harbor Kayak Rentals

The historic Barker House is the home of the Edenton Historic Commission. It's also a popular site for outdoor meetings, weddings, or just sitting in the rocking chairs overlooking Edenton Bay. 505 S. Broad St., Edenton, NC 27932. Mon.–Sat., 10 A.M.–4 P.M.; Sun., 1–4 P.M.; closed Dec. 23–25 and New Year's. Free. (252) 482-7800; barkerhouse@inteliport.com

Edenton Music & Water Festival

This free festival featuring jazz, blues, gospel, and country music is held on the third Saturday in June. Canoe and kayak rental facilities are nearby. Guided paddle tours and competitive kayak and Sunfish races are also part of the fun. On the waterfront, Broad St., Edenton, NC 27932. (252) 482-8005; www.chowanarts.org

Edenton Historic Commission/ Barker House
NC Echo

Emmerich Theatre Production Company

The company offers full-length Broadway-style musicals and original Christian plays in the heart of rural North Carolina. The Rocky Hock Playhouse, home of the company, hosts comedies and full-length plays. 126 Evans-Bass Rd., Edenton, NC 27932. The cost is $14 for adults, $13 for

Edenton Music & Water Festival (p. 43)

seniors, and $8 for children under 12; special rates are available for groups. (252) 482-4621; www.rockyhockplayhouse.com

The Garden Shack

This little store features locally grown produce, homemade jams and jellies, handcrafted picnic tables, classic Adirondack chairs, and lots more. 930 Virginia Rd. (Hwy 32), Edenton, NC 27932. Mon.–Fri., 7:30 A.M.–5 P.M.; Sat., 8 A.M.–2 P.M. (252) 482-1100

The Garden Shack

Granville Queen Inn

This lovely inn (circa 1907) features nine guest rooms with antique furnishings and private baths. The innkeepers serve a full breakfast. 108 S. Granville St., Edenton, NC 27932. (252) 482-5296 or (866) 482-8534; www.granvillequeen.com

Historic Edenton State Historic Site

Granville Queen Inn

Edenton, North Carolina's second-oldest town, was settled around 1685 and incorporated in 1715 as the "Towne on Queen Anne's Creek." In 1722, it was named to honor Governor Charles Eden. The site offers a 14-minute audiovisual program, exhibits, a gift shop, and information. 108 N. Broad St., Edenton, NC 27932. Apr.–Oct., Mon.–Sat., 9 A.M.–5 P.M.; Sun., 1–5 P.M.; Nov.–March, Tues.–Sat., 10 A.M.–4 P.M.; Sun.; 1–4 P.M. Tours are at set times; guided walking and trolley tours are $7 for adults and $3.50 for children and students. (252) 482-2637; www.edenton.nchistoricsites.org

Historic Hicks Field/Edenton Steamers

Hicks Field is the home of the Edenton Steamers, a Coastal Plain League baseball team. In 1995, Hicks Field was added to the National Register of Historic Places. 111 E. Freemason St., Edenton, NC 27932. (252) 482-4080; www.edentonsteamers.com

Lords Proprietors' Inn

Historic Edenton State Historic Site *N.C. Division of State Historic Sites*

Located in the heart of Edenton's historic district and within walking distance of Albemarle Sound, the Lords Proprietors' Inn offers guests elegant accommodations, some of the finest cuisine in eastern North Carolina, and genuine hospitality. 300 N. Broad St., Edenton, NC 27932. (252) 482-3641 or (888) 394-6622; www.edentoninn.com

May Play Day

For excellent rural entertainment, food, and kids' games, don't miss May Play Day, held on the grounds of the Rocky Hock Community Building. 101 Court St., Edenton, NC 27932. Held the first Sat. in May. (252) 482-3400; www.edenton.com

Robin Sams Gallery

Robin Sams is highly regarded for her oils and watercolors. Working in a realistic style, she concentrates on the effect of light on form, as well as on color relationships. She paints portraits, landscapes, and figures; her portraits of pets are especially endearing. 315 Broad St., Edenton, NC 27932. Thurs.–Sat., 11 A.M.–4 P.M. (252) 482-1075; www.robinsams.com

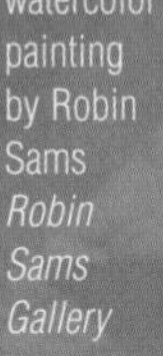

St. Paul's Episcopal Church

This second-oldest church building in North Carolina was begun in 1736. The parish, organized under the first Vestry Act of 1701, holds the oldest charter in the state. The site is included on tours originating from Historic Edenton State Historic Site. Broad St. and Church St., Edenton, NC 27932

A watercolor painting by Robin Sams *Robin Sams Gallery*

Trestle House Inn

This inn sits on five acres and overlooks water on three sides, with a lake refuge above and behind the viewing deck. Its five guest rooms—all named after local waterfowl—offer views of a canal popular with the area's winged residents. 632 Soundside

Rd., Edenton, NC 27932. (252) 482-2282 or (800) 645-8466; www.trestlehouseinn.com

Westover General Store

Look carefully—strangers may find it difficult to believe that this culinary treasure is housed in what appears to be an old service station. Most of the folks who live in Edenton and Chowan County know Westover for some of the best deli sandwiches south of New York. 801 W. Queen St., Edenton, NC 27932

Wilbur Ray Bunch Farms

Wilbur Ray Bunch Farms

Those who stop here enjoy fresh food together with friendly folks. Bunch's farm stand offers fresh local produce in season, as well as local honey and other treats. Come in July or early August to enjoy the famous Rocky Hock melons from "out the county." Since they're sugary-sweet and very juicy, the recommended method of eating them is over the sink or near a hose! 2833 Rocky Hock Rd., Edenton, NC 27932. (252) 221-4594

Hertford/Perquimans County

Beechtree Inn

The Beechtree Inn property is studded with 17 houses constructed from the mid-18th to the early 19th century. Three are open as guest houses, each with all the modern amenities and furnished with period pieces and reproductions. Emilio's Bistro adds to the experience. 948 Pender Rd., Hertford, NC 27944. Emilio's is open Mon.–Thurs. and Sat. nights. (252) 426-1593 (inn) or (252) 426-7815 (restaurant); www.beechtreeinn.net

Covent Garden Inn

The Covent Garden Inn (circa 1916) is in the Colonial Revival style. Rooms are available with private or semiprivate baths. Each is climate-controlled for comfort. The handsome parlor offers a cozy fireplace, a grand piano, cable TV and a VCR, books, and games. 107

Covent Garden, Hertford, NC 27944. (252) 426-5945; www.visitperquimans.com

Beechtree Inn
NC Echo

1812 On the Perquimans—A Coastal Plantation Inn

This circa 1812 home has been converted into a charming bed-and-breakfast inn. It features a country setting, boating, croquet on the lawn, and, for a small additional cost, a sumptuous breakfast with fish, spoon bread, fried green tomatoes, and more. 385 Old Neck Rd., Hertford, NC 27944. (252) 426-1812

Hertford Hardware Store

One trip to this old-fashioned, turn-of-the-century hardware store will have you strolling down memory lane. Nails are still sold by the scoop and seeds by the handful. Cold bottled Cokes are available from an antique machine. 146 N. Church St., Hertford, NC 27944. (252) 426-5211; shaste@intelliport.com

Hertford Hardware Store

Hertford Supply

If you're after great peanuts, pick up "the Pride of Perquimans" at this favorite gathering spot for area farmers. It's just the place to see what it takes to farm these days. 809 Edenton Rd., Hertford, NC 27944. Mon.–Fri., 7:30 A.M.–5 P.M.; Sat., 7:30 A.M.–noon. (252) 426-5591

Hertford Supply

Hobbs Furniture Classes

Early American furniture-building classes focus on everything from Chippendale chairs to nightstands. Classes are offered for students of all skill levels and ages. 948 Pender Rd., Hertford, NC 27944. (252) 426-7815; www.hobbsfurniture.com

Indian Summer Festival

This old-time street festival brings energy and good times to Hertford and Winfall. The celebration includes local music, foods, and crafts. Boat rides are given between Hertford and

Hobbs Furniture Classes (p. 47)

Winfall. The event is held in conjunction with the Hearth and Harvest Festival at the Newbold-White House. 118 W. Market St., Hertford, NC 27944. Held the second Sat. in Sept. (252) 426-1425

Jesse Byrum Farm Stand

Jesse Byrum has become a Hertford fixture, and his locally grown produce is well known for its value. In fact, Jesse guarantees it! If your melon is not sweet enough, you can exchange it for another. Jesse's truck is usually parked at the corner of Church St. and Grubb St., Hertford, NC 27944. Mon.–Sat., 10 A.M.–5:30 P.M.

Newbold-White House

Built in the early 1700s, the Newbold-White House is the oldest known brick house in North Carolina that is open to the public. It contains period furnishings and household goods that were typical of Quaker families in early America. The museum shop has pottery, local crafts, jewelry, handmade toys, stained glass, and more. 151 Newbold-White Rd., Hertford, NC 27944. (252) 426-7567; www.newboldwhitehouse.com

Northeast Dragway

You can take in the excitement of auto racing at the dragway, which features a one-eighth-mile track. Both local and regional race teams compete. 1099 Lake Rd., Hertford, NC 27944. March 16–Nov., Fri.–Sat. evenings. (252) 254-2066 or (252) 264-3430

Indian Summer Festival (p. 47)

Perquimans Antique Trail

Interested in old treasures? Stop by the Perquimans County and Town of Hertford Visitor Center and get a copy of the *Guide to Antiques*. 118 W. Market St., Hertford, NC 27944. (252) 426-5657; www.visitperquimans.com

Perquimans Arts Center/Perquimans Arts League

Located in historic Hall of Fame Square in downtown Hertford, the center features original artwork, jewelry, painted furniture, photography, pottery, baskets, greeting and note cards, and many more craft items from local artists. 109 N. Church St., Hertford, NC 27944. Tues.–Sat., 11 A.M.–3:30 P.M. (252) 426-2020

Perquimans County Farm Tour

The tour is offered only during even-numbered years. Included are farms, plantations, a cotton gin, produce outlets, 4-H exhibits, and demonstrations. 608 S. Edenton Rd., Hertford, NC 27944. Admission fee. (252) 426-5428; www.visitperquimans.com

Newbold-White House A Colonial Quaker Homestead & Museum Shop

Springfield Bed & Breakfast Inn

This beautiful inn is located in a historic farmhouse constructed in 1896. 962 S. Edenton Rd., Hertford, NC 27944. (252) 426-8471; www.springfieldbb.com

Strick's Family Campground

This RV campground overlooking the Perquimans River has 45 sites with full hookups. Its guests can access the river via the campground's boat dock and pier. Harvey Point Rd., Hertford, NC 27944. Reservations are required. (252) 426-7920

Timmy's Bait & Tackle

You'll find a full line of tackle and marine supplies at Timmy's. You can even rent a small fishing boat or a pontoon boat. 160 Creek Dr., Hertford, NC 27944. (252) 426-5837

Woodard's Pharmacy

When was the last time you had an old-fashioned hand-dipped ice-cream cone? When was the last time you paid 50 cents for one? Bring back the memories and visit Woodard's Pharmacy. Sandwiches and freshly squeezed orangeades, limeades, and lemonades are also available. 101 N. Church St., Hertford, NC 27944. (252) 426-5527

Windsor/Bertie County

Annual Junior Fishing Tournament

This event is especially for those ages one to 16. United States Fish and Wildlife representatives are on hand. Food and prizes are offered. The Windsor Area Chamber of Commerce, Trade Mart, and the Windsor Rotary Club sponsor the event. 102 N. York St., Windsor, NC 27983. Held in June. Advance registration is free. (252) 794-4277; www.windsor-bertie.com

Bertie County Peanuts

Growing peanuts for over 100 years, processing peanuts since 1915, and cooking peanuts for the past decade, Bertie County Peanuts is one of the oldest family-owned and -operated firms of its kind in the county. 217 US Hwy 13 N., Windsor, NC 27983. Mon.–Fri., 7 A.M.–5 P.M.; Sat. during busy season, 7 A.M.–noon. (252) 794-2909 or (800) 457-0005; www.pnuts.net

Bunn's Barbeque

Established in 1938, Bunn's is the county's oldest restaurant. The building predates the Civil War. You'll find great barbecue and Brunswick stew, locally grown vegetables, and homemade pies. Be sure to notice the local artwork and ceramics displayed throughout. 127 N. King St., Windsor, NC 27983. (252) 794-2274

Hammerhead Oyster Bar

This restaurant serves up a variety of steamed seafood. Hammerhead is located in the old post office building in the historic district of Windsor. Along with your seafood, you'll enjoy music by local bands. Artwork and local memorabilia are available, too. 117 N. King St., Windsor, NC 27983. Open Sept.–Apr. (252) 794-5960

Historic Windsor Walking Tour

Windsor has 17 historic homes and buildings listed in its National Register Historic District. Tour pamphlets are available at the Windsor–Bertie County Chamber of Commerce, 102 N. York St., Windsor, NC 27983. Mon.–Fri., 9 A.M.–5 P.M. (252) 794-4277; www.windsor-bertie.com

Hope Plantation

This lovely plantation features the 1803 Palladian-style Hope Mansion, the home of former North Carolina governor David Stone (1770–1818), the King Bazemore House (circa 1763), and the Roanoke-Chowan Heritage Center. 132 Hope House Rd., Windsor, NC 27983. Apr.–Oct., Mon.–Sat., 10 A.M.–5 P.M.; Sun., 2–5 P.M.; Nov.–March, Mon.–Sat., 10 A.M.–4 P.M.; Sun., 2–5 P.M.; closed Thanksgiving and Dec. 21–Jan. 2. The cost is $8 for adults, $7 for seniors and college students, and $3 for guests 18 and under. (252) 794-3140; www.hopeplantation.org

The Inn at Gray's Landing

This antique-filled bed-and-breakfast inn offers spacious bedrooms with private baths. It's located in a 1790 home furnished with period antiques and reproductions. A full English breakfast is served. 401 S. King St., Windsor, NC 27983. (252) 794-2255 or (877) 794-3501;www.grayslanding.com

Hope Plantation

Livermon Recreational Park & Mini Zoo

This site features over 30 different species of foreign and domestic animals. 104 York St., Windsor, NC 27983. Summer, Mon.–Fri., 8 A.M.–8 P.M.; Sat.–Sun., 9 A.M.–8 P.M.; winter, daily, 8 A.M.–5 P.M. Free. (252) 794-5553; www.windsor-bertie.com

Winfall/Perquimans County

Old Hickory Antiques

This little shop specializes in antiques and collectibles. 1164 Ocean Hwy N., Winfall, NC 27985. Mon.–Sat., 9 A.M.–5 P.M. (252) 264-2533

Edenton Walking Tour: A Step into Revolutionary Days

Lace up your walking shoes and take in the sights and sounds of historic Edenton, the second-oldest town in North Carolina. The Edenton Walking Tour is designed to delight both history buffs and architecture aficionados as it takes you past some of the oldest and most unique buildings in the state. Highlights of the tour include the Chowan County Courthouse (circa 1767), which is thought to be the oldest in continuous use in North Carolina. The Cupola House (circa 1758) is believed to be the oldest building in town, and its interior is noted for period furnishings. There's a tiny mark on a windowpane in one of the children's rooms that records the rhyme, "When this you see, Remember me." It's dated April 15, 1835. Down the street, St. Paul's Episcopal Church (begun in 1736) is a fine example of an early colonial church. The grounds feature monuments dating from the early 1700s. Inside are a 15th-century solid brass chandelier and communion silver that dates from 1725. Then there's the Barker House (circa 1782), perhaps the most photographed historic structure in Edenton. Its early residents led a rebellion against English tea taxes. Rounding out the tour is the James Iredell House (circa 1773), named for North Carolina's first attorney general and George Washington's appointee to the United States Supreme Court. Free tour brochures and maps are available at the Chowan County Tourism Development Authority on East King Street.

High Tide on the Sound Side

Camden, Currituck, Dare, and Pasquotank Counties

There's no place quite like the northern leg of North Carolina's Outer Banks, where ferries and a modern bridge join the mainland to the narrow strip of sand with the sound lapping on one side and the Atlantic Ocean pounding on the other. There's a silence here, broken only by the cry of sea gulls and crashing waves along the road to new and breezy experiences.

You can spend time in an entire village that's been restored by locals who care deeply about legends and history, and visit the area's own Currituck Lighthouse. Hunters will find the remote, untouched areas beyond the paved road especially beckoning, and you'll gasp in delight when one of numerous species of ducks, herons, and egrets lifts majestically on fragile wings from the green protection of the marsh grasses both here and on the mainland's numerous fingers of land.

Deeper inland, you'll want to visit Elizabeth City, known worldwide as "the Harbor of Hospitality." Here, in this well-known Intracoastal Waterway location, the Rose Buddies present the ladies on any docking vessel with a rose of welcome. Step into the area and indulge in visual arts, drama, and musical culture. Breathe in the hush of an ancient cemetery or join the clamor of a festival. You won't have to look far to find collections of carved waterfowl decoys in shops everywhere.

Back on the Outer Banks, you'll spot the gleaming monument to the beginnings of flight at Kitty Hawk, where echoes of flying machines still hang in the air. Cross over to Roanoke Island to attend a production of *The Lost Colony*, the longest-running outdoor drama in North Carolina, where you'll delve into the mysteries surrounding the disappearance of North Carolina's earliest settlers. Enjoy the fragrant beauty of the Elizabethan Gardens. View the *Elizabeth II* docked in Manteo's harbor while picnicking on the grounds of Festival Park. Spend the night at a quaint bed-and-breakfast down the road and watch the moon rise over the water after sundown. Hear the fishing boats leave the dock at sunrise. Contract to fish with them beyond the ocean's spray in deep waters that sparkle in the sun.

Visit prolific vineyards and serene little wineries nestled into the sound-side landscape next to rows of sunflowers, and select your favorite vintage in the tasting room.

Indulge in succulent handpicked fresh fruits and crunchy vegetables from open-air roadside markets. Buy today's catch to cook, or feast on just-out-of-the-water seafood cooked to savory perfection at a remote little restaurant around the bend.

Thrill to the view from the top of the famous Cape Hatteras Lighthouse, and discover the Bodie Island Lighthouse near Oregon Inlet. Visit an old store museum full of artifacts collected by a hermit beachcomber. Stroll through numerous art galleries full of nature-inspired oil paintings, watercolors, sculptures, and stained-glass creations.

Enjoy choosing, from all over this four-county watery wonderland, wind chimes, mobiles, and jewelry handcrafted from shells, driftwood, precious and semiprecious stones, and metals to depict the area's lighthouses, birds, turtles, and fish. Or purchase a colorful handbag, rug, or tote woven from rags of abandoned clothing and discarded men's ties.

Read on for town-by-town descriptions of the unique attractions that make up the "High Tide on the Sound Side" trail.

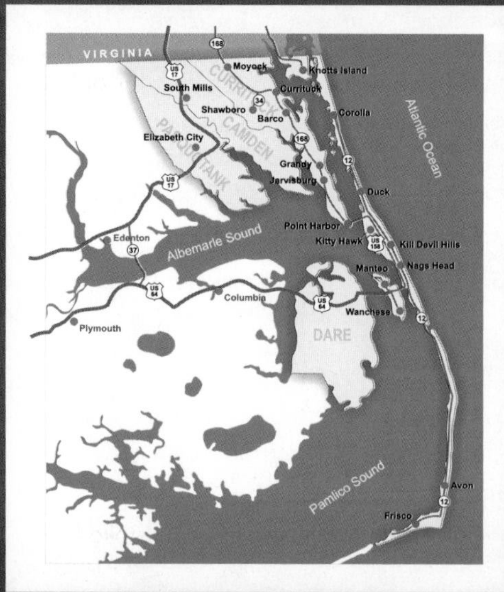

Avon/Dare County

Studio 12

Studio 12 has an exceptional collection of ready-to-paint pottery for both young and old. You can paint a true treasure to remember your Outer Banks vacation or purchase a beautiful ready-to-take-home treasure. 40534 NC Hwy 12, Avon, NC 27915. Apr.–mid-June and August 8–Dec., Mon.–Sat., 9:30 A.M.–6 P.M.; mid-June–Aug. 7, daily, 9:30 A.M.–6 P.M. The cost is $15 to $35 per person. (252) 995-7899; www.studio12hatteras.com

Barco/Currituck County

Currituck Wildlife Festival *N.C. Arts Council*

Currituck County Public Library

The library features an ongoing exhibit of art. 4261 Caratoke Hwy, Barco, NC 27917. Mon.–Fri., 9 A.M.–6 P.M.; Sat., 8:30 A.M.–5 P.M. (252) 453-8345; www.youseemore.com/EARL

Currituck Wildlife Festival

Held the first weekend after Labor Day, the festival features the nation's best wildlife carvers, wildlife artists, and decoy collectors, as well as excellent food, all under one roof. Come listen to the latest hunting stories along with Currituck historical folklore. Currituck High School, 4203 Caratoke Hwy, Barco, NC 27917. Sat.–Sun., 10 A.M.–5 P.M. Admission is $5. (252) 453-2479

Morris Farm Market

Morris Farm Market

Morris Farm Market provides a fun, down-home atmosphere and some of the best produce in town. Families love to sample the fresh melons and ciders and view the market's many tractors. 3784 Caratoke Hwy, Barco, NC 27917. May–mid-Sept., daily, 8 A.M.–8 P.M. (252) 453-2837; morrisfarms@lycos.com

Palmer Inn B&B

The inn is a restored homestead with lovely Victorian décor. Guests enjoy elegantly appointed rooms with private baths and awaken to the tantalizing aroma of homemade bread, muffins, pancakes, and fresh fruit. 3861 Caratoke Hwy, Barco, NC 27917. (252) 453-3896 or (252) 453-6286; www.palmerinn.com

Corolla/Currituck County

Corolla Schoolhouse in Historic Corolla Village

The 1890 schoolhouse, restored in 1999, has exhibits about the village and its inhabitants. Schoolhouse Ln. and Corolla Village Rd., Corolla, NC 27927. (252) 453-0171

Corolla Schoolhouse *Currituck County Travel & Tourism Department*

Currituck Outer Banks Visitors Center

Stop here for brochures, maps, and other tourist information. 500 Hunt Club Dr., Corolla, NC 27927. Open seasonally, daily, 9 A.M.–5 P.M. (252) 453-9612; www.visitcurrituck.com

Historic Corolla Village

Unpaved paths invite you to stroll in the ocean breeze and discover quaint historic homes and unique shops and restaurants. You can also admire the village garden with its indigenous and heirloom plants. Schoolhouse Ln. and Corolla Village Rd., Corolla, NC 27927. (252) 453-9612; www.visitcurrituck.com

The Inn at Corolla Light

Guests enjoy full access to unlimited Outer Banks amenities, including the acclaimed Oceanfront Corolla Light Resort with its Olympic-sized pools, children's facilities, and play areas, the acclaimed Clubhouse Café, and of course the wide, wonderful Corolla beaches! (252) 453-0335 or (800) 215-0772; www.corolla-inn.com

Outer Banks Center for Wildlife Education

This center is dedicated to coastal ecology and the culture of coastal North Carolina. Exhibits, daily classes, and outdoor programs are offered. 1160 Village Ln., Corolla, NC 27927. Daily, 9 A.M.–6 P.M. Free. (252) 453-0221; www.ncwildlife.org

The Whalehead Club at Currituck Heritage Park

Completed in 1925, the 21,000-square-foot structure on 39 acres was originally a private residence. The Art Nouveau architecture, Tiffany lighting fixtures, copper-shingled roof, and five stately chimneys stand majestically on the shores of Currituck Sound. Currituck Heritage Park, 1100 Club Way, Corolla, NC 27927. Apr.–Oct., 10 A.M.–6 P.M.; Nov.–March, 9 A.M.–5 P.M. Fees are charged for house tours. (252) 453-9040; www.whaleheadclub.org

The Whalehead Club *NC Echo*

Currituck/Currituck County

Currituck County Arts Council Art Extravaganza Art Show and Sale

This annual show features paintings, photography, woodwork, pottery, jewelry, and decoy carvings. Currituck County High School, 4203 Caratoke Hwy, Currituck, NC 27929. Held the third Sat. in March, 10 A.M.–3 P.M. Free. (252) 232-2634

Currituck County Arts Council

Historic Currituck Courthouse

The historic Currituck Courthouse was constructed in 1842 on the site of the 1700s courthouse. 153 Courthouse Rd., Currituck, NC 27929. Mon.–Fri., 8 A.M.–5 P.M. (252) 232-0719; www.co.currituck.nc.us

Old Currituck County Jail

Built in 1857, this is one of the oldest county prisons in North Carolina. It features 1:3 brick bonding, gable parapets, a dentiled brick cornice, and tooled stone lintels and sills characteristic of mid-19th-century construction. 153 Courthouse Rd., Currituck, NC 27929. Mon.–Fri., 8 A.M.–5 p.m., or by appointment. Free. (252) 232-0719; www.visitcurrituck.com

Duck/Dare County

Greenleaf Gallery

This is a showcase for artists from North Carolina and Virginia. The gallery offers an exciting and diverse selection of American art glass, fine functional and decorative ceramics, woodwork, and designer jewelry. 1169 Duck Rd., Duck, NC 27949. Mon.–Sat., 10 A.M.–5 P.M.; Sun., 10 A.M.–3 P.M.; closed Jan.–Feb.; exhibits held May–Sept. (252) 261-2009; www.outer-banks.com/greenleaf

Elizabeth City/Pasquotank County

Albemarle Craftsman's Fair

At this fair, you can watch master craftsmen and enjoy works in wood; quilts; decoys; birds and other figurines; silver, wire, and glass jewelry; stained, slumped, and carved glass; wrought iron; and clay. 200 E. Ward St., Elizabeth City, NC 27909. Held the last weekend in Oct. Admission fee. (252) 335-4680; www.albemarlecraftsmansfair.com

The Albemarle Potato Festival

Celebrate everything "potato" with potato-bag races, potato-peeling contests, and the best potato pies and French fries. Main St., Elizabeth City, NC 27909. Held on a Sat. in mid-May. (252) 331-2199; www.ncagr.com/markets/commodit/horticul/potatoes/festival

Clay Gardens Pottery Studio

Create your own work in this "make it and take it" pottery class. You can mold the clay, paint your masterpiece, and take it home to show off. 301 N. Hughes Blvd., Elizabeth

City, NC 27909. Tues., 3–5 P.M.; Wed., 7–9:30 P.M.; Thurs., 3–7 P.M. (252) 335-2324, (252) 333-5503, or (252) 335-1733; www.claygardens.com

Elizabeth City Area Convention & Visitors Bureau

Tourist information on the Elizabeth City area is available here. 400 S. Water St., Elizabeth City, NC 27909. Open daily, 9 A.M.–5 P.M.; closed on major holidays. (252) 335-5330; www.discoverec.org

Elizabeth City State University Performing Arts

The university offers plays, musical productions, choir performances, dramas, and other performing arts, as well as art galleries and art shows. 1704 Weeksville Rd., Elizabeth City, NC 27909. (252) 335-3400; www.ecsu.edu

Take in a show by Elizabeth City State University Performing Arts. *ECSU/University Relations & Marketing*

Elizabeth City State University Planetarium

From August to June, the planetarium presents programs covering space exploration, science fiction, and current astronomy. Laser shows are offered year-round. The planetarium is on the campus of ECSU. 1704 Weeksville Rd., Elizabeth City, NC 27909. Year-round, Mon.–Fri., 8 A.M.–5 P.M. Reservations are required. Free. (252) 335-3759; www.ecsuplanetarium.org

Episcopal Cemetery

This cemetery is on the National Register of Historic Places. Pay special attention to the cast-iron fences from the 19th and early 20th centuries. The gravestones are equally remarkable—one, dating from 1724, is among the oldest in North Carolina. 507 E. Ehringhaus St., Elizabeth City, NC 27909. Free self-guided tour. (252) 338-1686; www.christchurch-ecity.org

Harbor Nights Music Series

The series features music, street entertainers, and locally grown produce from farm vendors. Mariners Wharf Park, Water St., Elizabeth City, NC 27909. Held July–Aug., the first Fri. of the month, 5:30 P.M. (252) 338-6997

Tour Hide-N-Wood Gardens *Elizabeth City Area Convention & Visitors Bureau*

Hide-N-Wood Gardens

Here, you can see demonstrations of intensified gardening techniques on small fruits and vegetables. Portions of the garden have been designed as a native plant habitat by the National Park Service. A self-guided tour is available. 923 Wellfield Rd., Elizabeth City, NC 27909. March 1–Oct. 30, daily, 8 A.M.–5 P.M. (252) 312-4970; duanemcs@inteliport.com

Historic Districts Walking Tours

The tours of the National Register Historic Districts include the largest number of brick antebellum commercial buildings in the state. Beautiful early-19th- and 20th-century buildings house specialty shops, antique shops, restaurants, and art galleries. Free brochures are available at the Elizabeth City Area Convention & Visitors Bureau. 400 S. Water St., Elizabeth City, NC 27909. Mon.–Sat., 9 A.M.–5 P.M.; closed holidays. (252) 335-1733; www.discoverec.org

Kenyon-Bailey

For years, Kenyon-Bailey has sold handmade birdhouses and other garden items. There's also a full array of garden tools, supplies, and plants to choose from. Be sure to enjoy lunch in its small restaurant. 407 McArthur Dr., Elizabeth City, NC 27909. (252) 335-5882

P

Mariners' Wharf

"Rose Buddies" greet visiting yachts with a rose for the lady on board and an invitation to the entire crew to experience this port of call. Visitors can dock for 48 hours without charge. The waterfront is just steps away from restaurants, delis, bakeries, and sources for provisions. 400 S. Water St., Elizabeth City, NC 27909. Mon.–Sat., 9 A.M.–5 P.M. (252) 335-5330 or (866) ECI-TY4U; www.discoverec.org

Moth Boat Regatta

Interest in the moth—a small, single-handed racing sailboat—has been revived in Elizabeth City. The regatta, held the third Saturday in September, includes boat tours of the harbor, art shows, craft booths, music, and the traditional Museum of the Albemarle Barbecue Chicken Dinner. Moth Boat Park, Elizabeth City, NC 27909. Free. (252) 335-1453; www.northeast-nc.com/moa/mothboat.cfm

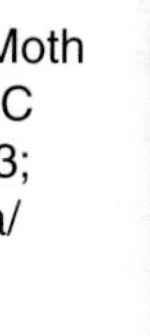

Watch the Moth Boat Regatta. *Elizabeth City Area Convention & Vistiors Bureau*

Muddy Waters Coffee Shop

This shop offers a fine selection of coffees, along with exotic munchies to enjoy inside or alfresco. 100 W. Main St., Elizabeth City, NC 27909. Mon.–Fri., 6 A.M.–10 P.M.; Sat., 7 A.M.–9 P.M.; Sun., 8 A.M.–6 P.M. (252) 338-2739

Museum of the Albemarle

Artifacts from American Indians, English colonists, African-Americans, and the people of today are exhibited in galleries that include architectural, agricultural, industrial, military, and maritime venues. 501 S. Water St., Elizabeth City, NC 27909. Tues.–Sat., 9 A.M.–5 P.M.; Sun., 2–5 P.M.; closed on major state holidays. (252) 335-1453; www.museumofthealbemarle.com

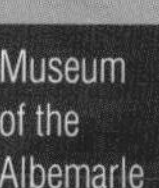

Museum of the Albemarle

Pasquotank Arts Council

The council and its gallery showcase the work of over 1,050 local and regional artists. Exhibitions feature painting, pottery, jewelry, decoy carving, photography, basketry, stained glass, and handmade dolls. 609 E. Main St., Elizabeth City, NC 27909. Mon.–Wed. and Fri.–Sat., 10 A.M.–5 P.M.; Thurs., 10 A.M.–7 P.M. (252) 338-6997; www.pasquotankarts.org

Pasquotank County Farmers' Market

This market, one of the largest in the region, offers a wide variety of fruits, vegetables, and homemade products. Located next to the Cooperative Extension Center, Elizabeth City, NC 27909. May–Dec., Tues. and Fri.–Sat., 8 A.M.–4 P.M. (252) 338-3954

Performing Arts Series, College of the Albemarle Auditorium

Student, local, and professional productions include concerts, touring productions, and a full musical presentation in the spring. 1208 N. Road St., Elizabeth City, NC 27909. Admission fee. (252) 335-0821 or (800) 335-9050; www.albemarle.cc.nc.us/acadaff/finearts/schedule.htm

Port Discover

Port Discover

This hands-on science center allows kids and their families to explore and interact with science. Programs are offered in environmental and marine sciences, aviation science, biology, physical sciences, health and wellness, agricultural sciences, and planetary sciences. 613 E. Main St., Elizabeth City, NC 27909. Tues.–Sat., 1–5 P.M. Free. (252) 338-6117; www.portdiscover.org

Tundevisual Art Studio

Artist Tunde Afolayan creates original paintings, prints, and experimental media. His thematic compositions are captured in vibrant colors, allowing figurative images to adopt expressive, abstract qualities, as well as representational styles. 312 S. Griffin St., Elizabeth City, NC 27909. Open by appointment. (252) 267-5981; www.tundevisualart.com

Tundevisual Art Studio

Frisco/Dare County

Frisco Native American Museum & Natural History Center

Exhibits include the universally recognized artifact collection of the Chirichiua Apache, the tribe of Geronimo. Visitors can enjoy self-guided nature trails and live exhibits. The annual powwow is held each April. 53536 NC Hwy 12, Frisco, NC 27936. Tues.–Sun., 11 A.M.–5 P.M., or by appointment. Admission fee. (252) 995-4440; www.nativeamericanmuseum.org

Frisco Native American Museum & Natural History Center

Grandy/Currituck County

Glass Sensations

These designer glass applications add beauty to any home, using hundreds of colors and textures to create any scene or design you desire. Every handcrafted application is unique. Stained glass overlay can be applied to any glass surface in your home. 6328 Caratoke Hwy, Grandy, NC 27939. Open by appointment. (252) 453-0980; www.glasssensations.com

Glass Sensations

Soundside Orchard

This is one of the very few produce markets that grows and sells its own peaches. Fresh honey and homemade peach jams and jellies are available, as are asparagus, muscadine grapes, collards, and salad greens. 6378 Caratoke Hwy, Grandy, NC 27939. Apr.–Nov., daily, 8 A.M.–6 P.M. (252) 453-0181; www.localharvest.org/farms/m11462

Jarvisburg/Currituck County

B. J.'s Carolina Café

This family-owned and -operated eatery specializes in eastern North Carolina barbecue, plus ribs and chicken, locally grown fresh produce in season, seafood, steaks, and hamburger steaks smothered in gravy and onions. 7069 Caratoke Hwy, Jarvisburg, NC 27947. Tues.–Sun., 8 A.M.–8 P.M. (252) 491-5222; bjncbbq@yahoo.com

Sanctuary Vineyards

Native American and vinifera grapes are planted among scenic coastal farmlands. The vineyards are caressed by sparkling sunrises and kissed by ocean breezes. 6957 Caratoke Hwy, Jarvisburg, NC 27947. Open daily, 10 A.M.–6 P.M. Free. (252) 207-9377 or (800) 637-2446; www.sanctuaryvineyards.com

Kill Devil Hills/Dare County

Billy's Seafood, Inc.

Each morning, family members catch what is sold that afternoon. Other local fisherman dock at the back door with their catch of the day. You'll even get tips on how to prepare your finds. Billy's also sells cooked crab legs, steamed crabs, and shrimp. Located on Colington Island behind Wright Brothers National Memorial, Kill Devil Hills, NC 27948. March–Thanksgiving, daily, 9 A.M.–6 P.M. (252) 441-5978

KDH Cooperative Gallery & Studios

KDH Cooperative Gallery & Studios

Artist Julie Moye showcases the work of fellow local artists, whose media include oils, acrylics, watercolors, pastels, pen-and-ink, ceramics, jewelry, fibers, furniture, candles, pottery, glass, and metals. 502 S. Croatan Hwy, Kill Devil Hills, NC 27948. Mon.–Sat., 10 A.M.–6 P.M. (252) 441-9888; www.kdhcooperative.com

Kitty Hawk/Dare County

Monument to a Century of Flight

This monument recognizes significant accomplishments in aviation history. It is located on the grounds of the Aycock

Brown Welcome Center in Kitty Hawk at Milepost 1.5. (252) 441-6584 or (252) 473-5558; www.icarusinternational.com/

Monument to a Century of Flight

Pat's Watercolors

The artist's Outer Banks–inspired subjects include lighthouses, wildlife, and colorful flowers, with an emphasis on the bearded iris. She also takes commissions and teaches watercolor classes. 32 Ginguite Trail, Kitty Hawk, NC 27949. Open by appointment. (252) 261-4659; lewtroiani@cs.com

Knotts Island/Currituck County

Martin Orchard & Vineyards

Seasonal pick-your-own peaches, apples, bunch grapes, and muscadine grapes are available here, plus yummy asparagus in the spring. The owners also produce vinifera grapes for wine. Rt. 1256 (Martin Farm Ln.), Knotts Island, NC 27950. Produce stand, daily, 8 A.M.–6 P.M.; winery, daily, noon–6 P.M. (252) 429-3542 or (252) 429-3564; www.martinvineyards.com

Moonrise Bay Vineyard

Moonrise Bay Vineyard

This vineyard features 14 acres planted with Merlot, Cabernet Sauvignon, Nebbiolo, Syrah, Chambourcin, Chardonnay, and Sauvignon Blanc. You can experience the grapes through a tour or tasting. 134 Moonrise Bay Landing, Knotts Island, NC 27950. Open daily, noon–5 P.M. Tasting fees. (252) 429-9056 or (866) 888-9463; www.moonrisebaywine.com

The Peach Basket

The Peach Basket

Peaches, plums, nectarines, pears, and apples are handpicked each morning. You can also shop for jams and other treats, including diabetic jams and diabetic peach pies and cobblers. 208 South End Rd., Knotts Island, NC 27950. June–early Sept., Mon.–Sat., 9 A.M.–7 P.M. (252) 429-3317 or (252) 429-3358; dsaustin@cox.net or KIPeachfarmer@verizon.net

Manteo/Dare County

Dare County Arts Council & Gallery

Approximately 80 local artists display their special creative skills and talents in this Manteo gallery. Among the featured items are original paintings, reproductions, pottery, glass, photography, jewelry, and works in fiber, metal, and mixed media. Exhibits are changed the second Wednesday of each month, and shows are held throughout the year. The gallery features an artist each first Friday from April through December. 104 Sir Walter Raleigh St., Manteo, NC 27954. Mon.–Fri., 10 A.M.–6 P.M.; Sat., noon–4 P.M. Free. (252) 473-5558; www.darearts.org

Endless Possibilities

Endless Possibilities

Using clothing and linens from six fundraising thrift shops, studio volunteers weave beautiful cloth from rags and in the process help women and children in need. All products are sold in the in-house gallery, with proceeds going to a local women's crisis hotline. 105 Budleigh St., Manteo, NC 27954. Mon.–Sat., 10 A.M.–5 P.M. (252) 475-1575; www.ragweavers.com

The Gaskins Gallery

This family gallery specializes in original paintings, prints, hand-thrown pottery, ornaments, and tiles. The owners also do custom framing and display Fenton glass and other glasswork. 40462 North End Rd., Manteo, NC 27915. Mon.–Fri., 10 A.M.–4 P.M.; Sat., 10 A.M.–noon. (252) 995-6617

The Lost Colony Outdoor Drama

In 1587, some 120 men, women, and children established the first English colony in the New World, then vanished without a trace, leaving historians and archaeologists with one of America's most perplexing mysteries. Written by Pulitzer Prize–winning playwright Paul Green, *The Lost Colony* tells their story in the dramatic setting of historic Waterside Theatre on Roanoke Island. 1409 National

Park Rd., Manteo, NC 27954. June–Aug., nightly, 8:30 P.M. Admission fee. (252) 473-2127; www.thelostcolony.org

The Lost Colony Production *Guy Albertelli*

Outer Banks Arboretum & Teaching Garden

The winding brick walkways take you past plant hybrids suitable for a coastal climate. You can also meander through a gathering area and butterfly, aquatic, and dune gardens. 517 Budleigh St., Manteo, NC 27954. Mon.–Fri., 8 A.M.–5 P.M. (252) 473-4290; www.ces.ncsu.edu/dare

Roanoke Island Festival Park

Step aboard the *Elizabeth II*, a 69-foot, square-rigged sailing ship like the one used by Sir Walter Raleigh's colonists. History is told by interpreters who wear clothing of the period. Visit the Settlement Site, complete with soldiers. Explore 400 years of Outer Banks history by touring the Roanoke Island Adventure Museum. One Festival Park, Manteo, NC 27954. Mid-Feb.–March and Nov.–Dec., 9 A.M.–5 P.M.; Apr.–Oct., 9 A.M.–6 P.M. Fees are charged. (252) 475-1500; www.roanokeisland.com

Roanoke Island Festival Park

Roanoke Island Inn

This waterfront inn was the home of the innkeeper's great-great-grandmother in the 1860s. It offers guests the privacy of outside entrances, a comfortable lobby, and a well-stocked innkeeper's pantry. A second-floor porch overlooks the Roanoke Island Marshes Lighthouse and the Manteo waterfront. 305 Fernando St., Manteo, NC 27954. (252) 473-5511 or (877) 473-5511; www.roanokeislandinn.com

Silver Bonsai Gallery

Kathryn and Ben Stewart exhibit and sell their unique handcrafted jewelry, as well as a wide variety of local and regional arts and crafts and an impressive collection of bonsai trees and supplies. 905 US Hwy 64, Manteo, NC 27954. Mon.–Sat., 10 A.M.–6 P.M.; closed in Jan. (252) 475-1413; www.silverbonsai.com

Moyock/Currituck County

Peck Basket General Store

This gift shop and folk-art studio features yard décor and local Currituck decoys. The shop's original counters, cash registers, daybooks, and scales lend authenticity, as do old-time snacks, candy, peanuts, jellies, jams, pork rinds, and gifts. 2132 Caratoke Hwy, Moyock, NC 27958. Open daily, 10 A.M.–5 P.M. (252) 232-3518; www.peckbasket.com

Nags Head/Dare County

Beachcomber Museum/Mattie Migdette's Store

This collection of large fossils, driftwood, messages in bottles, rare shells, beach glass, and artifacts was amassed by legendary Nags Head beachcomber Nellie Myrtle Pridgen. Her mother used to run a grocery store out of the building in which the collection is housed. 4008 S. Virginia Dare Trail, Nags Head, NC 27954. Open only on Thurs. in Aug., 10 A.M.–5 P.M. Free. (252) 473-5558

Melvin's Studio

James Melvin paints seascapes, lighthouses, ethnic art, landscapes, coastal art, and more. Although his media vary, his theme is consistent: peace. 124 Woodhill Dr., Nags Head, NC 27959. Mon.–Sat., 10 A.M.–5 P.M. (252) 441-5319 or (866) 635-8463; www.melvinsstudio.com

Seaside Art Gallery

This gallery features works by local and contemporary artists, as well as a wonderful selection of art by masters such as Picasso, Chagall, Renoir, and others. It also sells estate jewelry, sculptures, porcelain, art glass, and original animation art by Disney, Warner Brothers, Hanna-Barbera, and United Features. 2716 S. Virginia Dare Trail, Nags Head, NC 27959. Memorial Day–Labor Day, Mon.–Sat., 10 A.M.–6 P.M.; Labor Day–

"Certain Stars" by E M Corsa from the Seaside Art Gallery

And certain stars shot madly from their spheres, to hear the sea-maid's music

Memorial Day, Mon.–Sat., 10 A.M.–5 P.M. (252) 441-5418 or (800) 828-2444; www.seasideart.com

Point Harbor/Currituck County

Native Vine Tasting Room

Visitors learn about the state's 400-year-old wine history, see vintage winemaking equipment and memorabilia, and taste North Carolina–made wines. The shop sells wines from more than 15 state wineries, including its own. 9138 Caratoke Hwy, Point Harbor, NC 27964. Mon.–Sat., 10 A.M.–6 P.M.; Sun., noon–5 P.M. Tasting fees. (252) 491-5311; www.nativevine.com

"Love Boat" by Eric Waugh from the Seaside Art Gallery

Shawboro/Currituck County

Powells Roadside Market

This old-fashioned roadside stand sells strawberries, asparagus, peaches, watermelons, cantaloupes, pumpkins, and Christmas trees. 2138 Caratoke Hwy, Shawboro, NC 27973. Apr.–Dec. 15, daily, 8 A.M.–8 P.M. (252) 232-2547

Roberts Ridge Farm

Fresh vegetables are available here. 501 N. Indiantown Rd., Shawboro, NC 27973. June 28–Aug. 12, daily, 7 A.M.–7 P.M. (252) 336-4793 or (252) 202-9665; robertsridge1@hotmail.com

South Mills/Camden County

Dismal Swamp Canal Welcome Center

The welcome center is a destination in itself, with picnic tables, grills, and local crops like cotton and tobacco planted in small, decorative plots. The waterside walkway often has yachts and sailboats docked there, since the Dismal Swamp Canal is part of the Intracoastal Waterway. 2356 US Hwy 17 N., South Mills, NC 27976. Tues.–Sat., 9 A.M.–5 P.M. Free. (252) 771-8333 or (877) 771-8333; www.dismalswamp.com

Wanchese/Dare County

Broad Creek Fishing Center & Marina

Only minutes away from Oregon Inlet, Nags Head, and downtown Manteo, the center offers 15 different types of fishing charters and specialty trips. The full-service ship's store is fully stocked with everything you'll need or want for your day of angling. 708 Harbor Dr., Wanchese, NC 27981. Open daily, 5 A.M.–6 P.M. (252) 473-9991; www.broadcreekfishingcenter.com

The "C" Shed

The name comes from the *C* that begins each of the owner family's names. The unrelated items available here are considered collectibles by some, vintage goods by others; the shop also carries unusual items created by local artists. 24 Hickman Ln., Wanchese, NC 27981. (252) 473-6261

The "C" Shed

Carolina Decoys

Former engineer Nick Sapone is well known for his canvas decoys, especially his canvas Canada geese and white swans. He has been a featured carver at numerous waterfowl arts-and-crafts shows. 292 The Lane, Wanchese, NC 27981. Open by appointment. (252) 473-3136

Island House of Wanchese B&B

This quaint B&B features four rooms, one suite, and a hearty buffet breakfast. Guests can cool off and relax with complimentary iced tea in the evening. 104 Old Wharf Rd., Wanchese, NC 27981. (252) 473-5619; www.islandhouse-bb.com

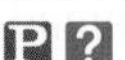

NICK-E

This stained-glass studio offers lamps, panels, three-dimensional work, sun catchers, specialty items, and custom work. The owners also teach classes. 813 Old Wharf Rd., Wanchese, NC 27981. Mon. and Thurs.–Sat., 10 A.M.–4 P.M., or by appointment. (252) 473-5036; nicke@pinn.net

"Once Upon a Time" at Tunde-visual Art Studio (p. 62)

O'Neal's Sea Harvest, Inc.

Fishermen and crabbers unload their locally caught products directly from their boats to O'Neal's docks. The business also sells frozen seafood, a locally published cookbook to aid in preparations, and T-shirts and sweatshirts. 622 Harbor Rd., Wanchese, NC 27981. May–Sept., Mon.–Sat., 9 A.M.–5 P.M. (252) 473-4535; www.onealsseaharvest.com

Queen Elizabeth from *The Lost Colony* Production (p. 66)

Music, Millponds, and Mousetraps

Gates, Halifax, Hertford, and Northampton Counties

Travel this trail and be prepared for surprises. Contrasts are everywhere—you'll find examples of delicate beauty and utilitarian strength.

You'll wonder, Whose strong hands created these intriguing porcelain pots? What level of aggravation brought about these effective—and very creative—mousetraps?

You'll see something as refined as neoclassical wall coverings and as sturdy as a locally hand-wrought butcher's

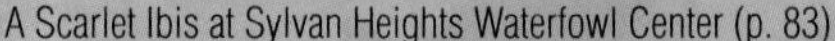

A Scarlet Ibis at Sylvan Heights Waterfowl Center (p. 83)

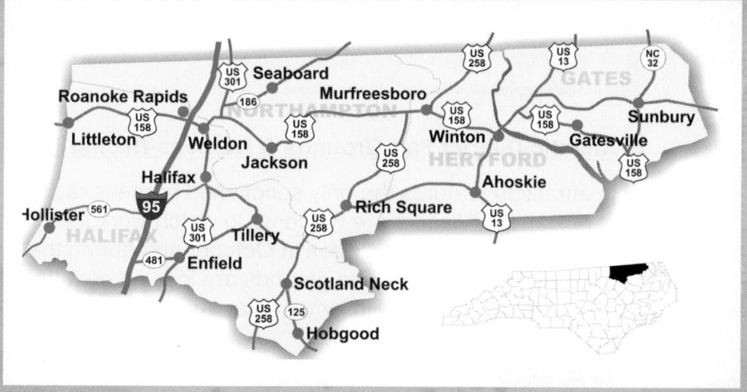

hook. You'll delight to the voices of a musical ringing out near a lush rural landscape.

Within the same day, you can look down from a mountain cliff and paddle around moss-covered cypress trees in an old millpond. You can even run whitewater rapids, though you're not in the mountains.

In a single 19th-century landmark—the Roanoke Canal's stone archway—you'll find both graceful curves and enduring strength. A colorful Native American basket illustrates the marriage of beauty and function.

Here in these communities, something as small as a peanut can cause a whole town to celebrate, and a watermelon seed can inspire an Olympic-worthy spitting competition!

For help planning your trip, read on for town-by-town descriptions of attractions along the "Music, Millponds, and Mousetraps" trail.

Ahoskie/Hertford County

Atlantic District Fair Grounds & Harness-Racing Track

This attraction features the only sanctioned harness racing east of Raleigh. Visitors are welcome to watch workouts. Races are held during fair week in October and during the second weekend in May. The grounds are located next to the R. L. Vann School. 1 Holloman Ave., Ahoskie, NC 27910. (252) 332-4533

The Gallery Theatre

The cast is local but the performances have Broadway quality. Productions run throughout the year. 115 W. Main St., Ahoskie, NC 27910. Admission is $7–$8 for adults and $5–$6 for children; group rates are available. (252) 332-2976

Jernigan House Bed & Breakfast Inn

Jernigan House Bed & Breakfast Inn

Listed on the National Register of Historic Places, this inn offers three bedrooms with many amenities. Each room features a queen-sized bed, a telephone, cable TV, a VCR, and a computer data port. 209 S. Catherine Creek Rd., Ahoskie, NC 27910. (252) 209-5455 or (866) 294-8212; www.jerniganhouse.com

Meherrin Indian Tribal Headquarters/Meherrin Indian Village

The Meherrin Indian tribal grounds are located between Ahoskie and Murfreesboro within five miles of the original 1700s reservation. Today, special tribal gatherings take place in the spring and fall. A traditional Thanksgiving feast is held annually. 852 Hwy 11, Ahoskie, NC 27910. (252) 398-3321

Enfield/Halifax County

A&B Milling/Aunt Ruby's Peanuts

People go nuts for Aunt Ruby's peanuts! And yes, there's a real Aunt Ruby. This thriving mail-order business has been around for 60 years. You can buy raw shelled peanuts, roasted redskins, and even chocolate clusters. Gift packages and catalogs are available, too. 200 Halifax St., Enfield, NC 27823. Mon.–Fri., 8 A.M.–5 P.M.; Sat., 8 A.M.–noon. (252) 445-3161 or (800) PEA-NUTS; www.auntrubyspeanuts.com

Enfield Peanut Festival

This family-fun event features good food, arts and crafts, farm equipment displays, amusements, music, dancing, and, of course, the famous peanut! The festival runs for two days in the fall. Call for dates. (252) 445-5122, ext. 2; www.enfieldnc.org

Garysburg/Northampton County

First Railroad

The first railroad in the state was completed in 1833 from Petersburg, Virginia, to Blakely, North Carolina, on the Roanoke River a short distance southeast of this marker. The marker is located at the junction of US Hwy 158 and Hwy 301 at the Roanoke River bridge southwest of Garysburg. Garysburg, NC 27831. (252) 534-1383

Gatesville/Gates County

Merchants Millpond State Park

Quiet waters, abundant greenery, fish, and wildlife make this a wonderful Southern swamp and a rare ecological community. You can camp, canoe, fish, picnic, hike, and watch regional birds and birds on the national flyway. 71 US Hwy 159 E., Gatesville, NC 27938. Nov.–Feb., 8 A.M.–6 P.M.; March and Oct., 8 A.M.–7 P.M.; Apr.–May and Sept., 8 A.M.–8 P.M.; June–Aug., 8 A.M.–9 P.M.; closed Christmas. Fees are charged for camping and canoes. (252) 357-1191; www.ncsparks.net/memi

Enfield Peanut Festival

Merchants Millpond State Park *N.C. Division of Parks and Recreation* (p. 75)

Old Gates County Courthouse

The old Gates County Courthouse is a rare example of a Federal-style seat of local government. Today, it serves as a county library with exhibits about the Gates County area. 115 Court St., Gatesville, NC 27938. Mon.–Tues. and Thurs.–Fri., 10:30 A.M.–6 P.M.; Sat., 9:30 A.M.–12:30 P.M. (252) 357-0110; ralimaf@hotmail.com

Swamp Fest

Plan for a fun family day at this gathering, which focuses on arts and crafts, games, lots of good food, live music, and even a little education. Gates County Community Center, 130 US Hwy 158 W., Gatesville, NC 27938. Held the first Sat. in Oct., 11 A.M.–7 p.m. (252) 357-0677

Halifax/Halifax County

Allen Grove Rosenwald School

This well-preserved school building is where many African-Americans were educated from the 1920s until the late 1950s. Rural Life Center, Halifax, NC 27839. Open by appointment. (252) 583-1821

First for Freedom Outdoor Drama

First for Freedom is the story of the first act by a colony leading toward the Declaration of Independence. The Halifax Resolves were signed here on April 12, 1776—a date so important that it's included on North Carolina's state flag. Halifax County Courthouse, Hwy 301, Halifax, NC 27839. Call for a schedule. (800) 522-4282

Halifax County Corn Maze

For confusion, laughter, and just plain fun, you can't beat the Halifax County Corn Maze. It can be as challenging as you like—with maps, clues, and helpers there to make sure it's fun for everyone. Dog Pound Rd., Halifax, NC 27839.

July 31–Oct. 30, Fri.–Sat., 5 P.M.–dusk. Call for details and directions. (252) 583-5161

Halifax County 4-H Rural Life Center

The center offers visitors a view of farm life in the early 1900s. On the first weekend in October, the "farmscape" comes to life during the Harvest Days Festival. 13763 Hwy 903, Halifax, NC 27839. Open by appointment except during the Harvest Days Festival. Free. (252) 583-1821 or (252) 583-5161; www.halifaxnc.com/4hrurallife

Historic Halifax State Historic Site

Created in 1758, Halifax County was named for George Montagu, second earl of Halifax. Halifax the town, like the county, is laden with history from the Revolutionary War period, when North Carolina became the first colony to declare its independence from England. 25 St. David St., Halifax, NC 27839. Tues.–Sat., 10 A.M.–4 P.M.; Sun., 1–5 P.M. Free. (252) 583-7191; www.halifax.nchistoricsites.org

Tavern at Halifax State Historic Site *N.C. Division of Parks and Recreation*

Peoples General Store

You'll find the real thing here—locally hand-forged hooks, hinges, pot racks, snakes, key rings, towel bars, toilet-tissue holders, plant hangers, and made-to-order items, all fashioned by an experienced blacksmith. 16 S. King St., Halifax, NC 27839. Sat., 10 A.M.–4 P.M., and by appointment. (252) 583-1338; peoplesn@schoolink.net

The Pines

Get your Christmas tree right off the farm. There are many sizes and species to select from. The Pines also sells accessories, wreaths, and garlands. The staff will machine-shake and net-bag your tree. US Hwy 301 N., Halifax, NC 27839. Nov. 29–Dec. 22, noon–dusk. (252) 537-3636; twgregory@coastalnet.com

Hobgood/Halifax County

Hobgood Cotton Festival

Visit the arts-and-crafts vendors. Eat lunch at the fire department or at one of the tempting food wagons. Hop a ride on a cotton trailer or a monster truck. Enjoy gospel, bluegrass, country, and rock-and-roll music. Downtown Hobgood, NC 27843. Held the second Sat. in Oct. (252) 826-4573; www.townofhobgood.com

Hollister/Halifax County

Haliwa-Saponi Tribe Pow Wow

The Haliwa-Saponi Tribe Pow Wow is a 2½-day celebration featuring American Indian dancing and singing and displays and sales of native crafts and food. Cash prizes are awarded in the dance and drum competitions. Haliwa Indian School, Hwy 56, Hollister, NC 27844. Held the third weekend in Apr. Admission is $5 for ages seven–61 and $4 for ages 62 and up; children up to six are free. (252) 586-4017; www.haliwa-saponi.com

Jackson/Northampton County

Northampton County Museum

This museum features hands-on activities that help children understand the natural resources and history of Northampton County. It includes native animals, reptiles, and birds; American Indian artifacts, including projectile points and pottery; and a chronological walk-through of Northampton County's history. US Hwy 158, Jackson, NC 27845. Wed.–Fri., 11 A.M.–5 P.M.; Sat., 9 A.M.–2 P.M. Free. (252) 534-2911; www.museum.com/jb/museum?id=29707

Haliwa-Saponi Tribe

Sir Archie

Here, you'll find the North Carolina historic marker for this foundation sire of American thoroughbred racehorses. His progeny included Timoleon, Boston, Lexington, and Man O' War. The horse died in 1833 at Mowfield, North Carolina. US Hwy 158 W., Jackson, NC 27845. (252) 534-1383

Sir Archie Highway Historical Marker *N.C. Highway Historical Marker Program*

Thornbury Plantation Hunting Lodge

Visitors come to this lodge for some of the finest hunting in eastern North Carolina. It features four bedrooms that sleep 12. It also provides linens, housekeeping, and a walk-in cooler to store your game until departure. The lodge offers delicious meals, stands, and guides. Jackson, NC 27845. Call for reservations. (252) 583-2842; www.huntthornbury.com

Littleton/Warren County

Bear Swamp Hunting Preserve

Bear Swamp Hunting Preserve's activities include deer, quail, chukar, pheasant, and duck hunting and European tower hunts for pheasant. Guests enjoy comfortable on-site lodging with all the amenities, as well as guides and stands. 14300 Hwy 48, Littleton, NC 27850. (252) 586-6065; www.bearswamp2hunt.com

Lakeland Cultural Arts Center/Dinner Theater

This site showcases musicals, comedies, revues, and classic productions. Performances are offered year-round on Friday and Saturday evenings, with some Sunday matinees. Reservations are recommended but not required. 411 Mosby Ave., Littleton, NC 27850. Admission is $5–$15. (252) 586-3124 or (877) 330-0574; www.lakelandartscenter.org

Lakeland Cultural Arts Center

Murfreesboro/Hertford County

Brady C. Jefcoat Museum of Americana/Historic Murfreesboro

You'll see a dog-powered washing machine, a delightful collection of mousetraps, rows and rows of music boxes and phonographs, air rifles—the list of objects collected here is almost endless. 201 W. High St., Murfreesboro, NC 27855. Sat., 11 A.M.–4 P.M.; Sun., 2–5 P.M.; tours may be arranged. Admission is $3–$7. (252) 398-8054 or (252) 398-5922; www.murfreesboronc.org/historic/tour/jefcoat

A dog-powered washing machine at Brady C. Jefcoat Museum

Chowan College/Green Hall Gallery

The Green Hall Gallery in the Department of Visual Arts offers a changing exhibit of works by student and faculty artists. 200 Jones Dr., Murfreesboro, NC 27855. (252) 398-6306

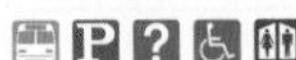

Colonial Riverport Village Tour/Murfreesboro Historical Association

This popular walking tour organized by the Murfreesboro Historical Association includes the Deale-Vincent Blacksmith Shop, which re-creates a full-scale forge typical of those used in the 19th century; the John Wheeler House, built in 1812 and representative of an upper-class family home; the McDowell Columns Building on the campus of Chowan College, a fine example of pre–Civil War architecture; the 1790 William Rea Museum, the state's oldest brick structure, featuring a Gatling gun and salvage from the Gatling Plantation; and the Winborne Building (circa 1870), currently the site of the Parker Country Store Collection. 116 E. Main St., Murfreesboro, NC 27855. Mon.–Fri., 9 A.M.–5 P.M. Free. (252) 398-5922; www.murfreesboronc.org

Murfreesboro Historical Association

Hertford/Northampton Farmers' Market

The market offers a wonderful array of locally grown produce. Homemade jellies, jams, and

other goods are also for sale. US Hwy 158, Murfreesboro, NC 27855. Sat., 7:30 A.M.–sellout. (252) 358-7822

Hertford/ Northampton Farmers' Market

The Historic Murfreesboro Gift Shop

This beautiful little store features more than 100 original paintings by regional artists, including Barbara Sant, Polly Forbes, Peggy Brinkley, Lib Nelson, Nancy Spruill, Nancy Breed-Marchant, and the late Geri Parker. 318 Williams St., Murfreesboro, NC 27855. Thurs., 3–6 P.M.; Fri., noon–6 P.M.; Sat., 11 A.M.–5 P.M.; and by appointment. (252) 398-5610; www.murfreesboronc.org/giftshop

Murfreesboro Watermelon Festival

This lively summer fair highlights the joys of the watermelon—seeds and all! Activities include food, rides, street dances, pony rides, watermelon games, and a large antique, collectibles, and crafts fair. Feeling competitive? Try your skills at seed spitting. Downtown Murfreesboro, NC 27855. Late July–early Aug. (252) 398-5922; www.murfreesboronc. org /watermelon.html

Lovely handmade baskets at the Historic Murfreesboro Gift Shop

Parker's Ferry

The many ferries operated by the North Carolina Department of Transportation in the state's eastern and coastal regions are often called "the Tar Heel Navy." Parker's Ferry is the smallest. It's a two-car, inland ferry that provides a scenic five-minute trip across the Meherrin River. The ferry operates year-round. It is located about six miles north of Murfreesboro. Hwy 258 N., Murfreesboro, NC 27855. March 16–Sept. 15, 6:30 A.M.–6 P.M.; Sept. 16–March 15, 7 A.M.–5 P.M.

Murfreesboro Watermelon Festival *Brenda Watson*

Roanoke Rapids/Halifax County

Fridays in the Park

Celebrate Friday with this free monthly music series. Bring your own lawn chair or blanket and relax to bluegrass, country, barbershop, jazz, and beach music. Centennial Park, Roanoke Ave., Roanoke Rapids, NC 27870. May–Sept., Fri., 6:30 P.M.–sunset. Free. (252) 537-3513 or (252) 535-1687; www.roanokerapidsnc.com

Halifax County Visitors Center

1640 Julian Allsbrook Hwy, Roanoke Rapids, NC 27870. Mon.–Fri., 8:30 A.M.–5 P.M. (252) 535-1687 or 800-522-4282; www.visithalifax.com

Roanoke Canal Museum and Trail

This historic 7.5-mile trail parallels the Roanoke River from Roanoke Rapids to Weldon. The Roanoke Canal Museum, which opened in September 2005, is housed in the old powerhouse, situated on the canal locks. It features interactive, child-friendly exhibits. 15 Jackson St. Ext., Roanoke Rapids, NC 27870. The trail is open daily, sunrise–sunset; the museum is open Tues.–Sat., 10 A.M.–4 P.M. Free. (252) 537-2769 or (800) 522-4282; www.roanokecanal.com

Roanoke Valley Farmers' Market

There's nothing quite like the sights, sounds, and aromas of a farmers' market. You can select from a wide variety of vegetables, fruits, and homemade goods like fresh-baked bakery products. US Hwy 158 W., Roanoke Rapids, NC 27870. June–Nov., Tues., Thurs., and Sat., 7 A.M.–sellout. (252) 537-3513 or (252) 537-8187

Beautiful teaset at the Historic Murfreesboro Gift Shop (p. 81)

Twin Magnolias Bed & Breakfast

This spacious inn is operated by a creative mother-daughter team specializing in business travelers, especially women traveling alone. The grounds include a large garden with a fishpond. 300 Jackson St., Roanoke Rapids, NC 27870. (252) 308-0019; www.angelfire.com/biz/twinmagnolias

Puna Teal at Sylvan Heights *Harrold Stiver*

Windy Farms

Stop by this quaint little produce stand for delicious veggies, fruits, and melons, all fresh from the farm. US Hwy 158 and Zoo Rd., Roanoke Rapids, NC 27870. May–Oct., Tues.–Sat. (252) 537-9089

Scotland Neck/Halifax County

Crepe Myrtle Festival

Held on the second Saturday in August, the festival showcases the beauty of the crepe myrtle in Scotland Neck. Visitors enjoy food, entertainment, crafts, and festivities. It's a great time for the entire family. 1310 Main St., Scotland Neck, NC 27874. (252) 826-3152; www.townofscotlandneck.com/festival.htm

Sylvan Heights Waterfowl Center

This unique waterfowl center, associated with the North Carolina Zoological Society, is known internationally for its research, training, breeding, and reintroduction programs. A special "First in Flight" bird show promises to entertain audiences of all ages. 4963 Hwy 258, Scotland Neck, NC 27874. Oct.–March, Tues.–Sun., 9 A.M.–4 P.M.; Apr.–Sept., Tues.–Sun., 9 A.M.–5 P.M.; closed Christmas. Call for fees. (252) 826-3186; www.shwpark.com

King Eider at Sylvan Heights *Ollie Treadway*

Seaboard/Northampton County

Christie's

Christie's

Christie's sells fresh farm produce, plants, and gifts, including fresh-cut flowers. 7761 US Hwy 158, Seaboard, NC 27876. Mon.–Sat., 10 A.M.–6 P.M. Call for available seasonal items. (252) 534-1604

P ?

Severn/Northampton County

Hampton Farms

Family-owned and operated since 1917, Hampton Farms has been called "the premier roaster and marketer of in-shell peanuts in the United States." It handled more than 24 billion—that's billion with a *b*—pounds last year. Severn, NC 27877. (757) 654-1400;www.hamptonfarms.com

Tillery/Halifax County

The Remembering Tillery Project

The Remembering Tillery Project honors an experimental New Deal program that resettled small farmers in the 1930s and 1940s. The 18,000-acre site was one of 113 resettlement experiments conducted nationwide and was the largest African-American project in the nation. The majority of the participating farmers were descendants of plantation slaves who lived in the Roanoke River region. 321 Community Center Rd., Tillery, NC 27887. Call to arrange a tour. (252) 826-3244 or (252) 826-3017

Weldon/Halifax County

The Center at Halifax Community College

This popular facility brings theater, dance, music, and Broadway tours to Halifax County. The Coffee Series focuses on speakers, musicians, and theatrical performances. Special children's programming is offered during school hours, and families can enjoy evening shows. US Hwy 158 and College Dr., Weldon, NC 27890. Call or see the Web site for schedule. (252) 536-4221 or (252) 538-4331; www.halifaxcc.edu

Ducky Derby

This is a fun festival for the whole family. You'll find food, crafts, rides for the kids, music, and, of course, racing duckies! River Falls Park, Hwy 301, Weldon, NC 27890. Held the third Sat. in Aug., 10 A.M.–3 P.M. (252) 537-3513 or (252) 535-5767; www.rvchamber.com

Farmers Exchange

A must-see for treasure seekers, the exchange offers garden supplies, antiques, housewares, collectibles, and snacks, too. 110 Washington Ave., Weldon, NC 27890. Open on Sat.

Winton/Hertford County

C. S. Brown Cultural Arts Center

The center preserves the multiethnic heritage and honors the cultural contributions of African-Americans to North Carolina and the nation. It offers programs of performing and visual arts. The center is housed in historic Brown Hall (circa 1886) on the campus of Chowan Academy, a school for black youth. A collection of West African and African-American artifacts is also on display. 511 Main St., Winton, NC 27986. Mon.–Fri., 9 A.M.–1 P.M. Program fees. (252) 358-1127; www.ncculturetour.org/csbrown

A large collection of music boxes and phonographs await you at Brady C. Jefcoat Museum (p. 80)

Coastal Treasure Chest

Carteret, Craven, and Pamlico Counties

You won't need a treasure map for this sparkling gem of a trail. There's a prize at every turn.

Discover crystal, enamel, gold, and silver in the form of unique jewelry. Watch one craftsman shape the back of an heirloom chair and another carve the wings of a decoy. Listen to the lyrical brogue of an old-time Outer Banker or the rhythmic lines sung by chanteymen working their nets long ago.

At a popular farmers' market or roadside stand, enjoy luscious fruits and vegetables still warm from the sun. Dine where the locals do on seafood so fresh you'll feel guilty about eating it.

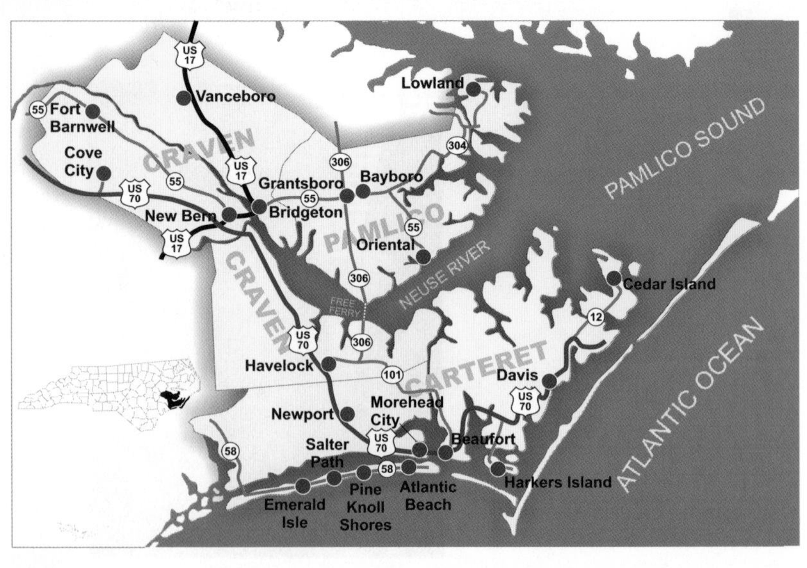

Unique Pottery at Handscapes Gallery (p. 90)

Quaint seaside villages, ancient live oaks, wild ponies, dazzling sunsets, sails in the wind, and nets cast out to sea from handcrafted wooden boats—this trail is made for inspiration. Remote, wild, and beautiful, it will take you from lush farm country to seaside wilderness with just a touch of city in between.

Create your own adventure today and see why this part of North Carolina is called "the Crystal Coast." Read on for town-by-town descriptions of the attractions that make up the "Coastal Treasure Chest" trail.

Tour the gardens and the palace at Tryon Palace (p. 100).

Atlantic Beach/Carteret County

Fort Macon State Park

Fort Macon State Park

Built between 1826 and 1834, this is one of the finest coastal forts on the Eastern Seaboard. It hosts frequent reenactments. E. Fort Macon Rd., Atlantic Beach, NC 28512. Nov.–Feb., 8 A.M.–6 P.M.; March and Oct., 8 A.M.–7 P.M.; Apr.–May and Sept., 8 A.M.–8 P.M.; June–Aug., 8 A.M.–9 P.M.; closed Christmas. Free. (252) 726-3775; www.ncsparks.net/foma

Morris Marina Kabin Kamps

This marina offers ferry service to Cape Lookout. The rustic but comfortable cabins on Cape Lookout are popular among hard-core fishermen and outdoor-loving families. 1000 Morris Marina Rd., Atlantic Beach, NC 28511. Open daily, 8 A.M.–5 P.M.; during fishing season, 6 A.M.–5 P.M. (252) 225-4261; www.portsmouthisland.com

P ?

Bayboro/Pamlico County

Bay River Pottery

The potter specializes in lovely "smoke-painted" raku, carved and pierced stoneware, unique flower-arranging vessels, and copper and clay sculptures. 107 S. Water St., Bayboro, NC 28515. Gallery, daily, 8 A.M.–6 P.M.; pottery demonstrations are by appointment. (252) 745-4749; www.bayriverpottery.com

Rivers Edge Family Campground

Located on the lovely Bay River, the campground has a 200-foot pier, a boat ramp, bathhouses, full amenities for RVs, and a play area for kids. 149 Tempe Grit Rd., Bayboro, NC 28515. Open year-round. (252) 559-3603; www.riversedgefamilycampground.com

Beaufort/Carteret County

Beaufort Grocery Company

Beaufort Grocery Company

You'll find no milk or eggs here, just fabulous seafood, fine wine, and scrumptious goodies like the chef's Cobb salad, gumbo, and crab cakes. Check out the artwork, too. 117 Queen St., Beaufort, NC 28516. Wed.–Mon., lunch and dinner; open Sun. for brunch. (252) 728-3899; www.beaufortgrocery.com

Beaufort Historic Sites Tours

See Beaufort on a double-decker bus with Beaufort Historic Sites Tours.

Meet in the 100 block of Turner Street for a walking tour of this delightful and historic town. Turner St., Beaufort, NC 28516. Mon.–Sat., 9:30 A.M.–5 P.M.; Sun., noon–4 P.M. Guided tours cost $6 for adults and $4 for children. (252) 457-5003; www.beauforthistoricsite.org

Clawson's 1905 Restaurant & Pub

Clawson's offers casual dining in a former grocery store. It features seafood, steaks, salads, and sandwiches, as well as live music and works by local artists. Fishtowne Java & Ice Cream is located at the entrance. 425 Front St., Beaufort, NC 28516. Mon.–Sat., 11:30 A.M.–9:30 P.M.; dinner is also served on Sun. at 4:30 P.M. from Memorial Day to Labor Day. (252) 728-2133; www.clawsonsrestaurant.com

Coastal Community Market

Clawson's 1905 Restaurant & Pub

Pack a picnic with dried fruits, nuts, earth-friendly gourmet foods, cheeses, olives, Oriental products, and diet products. You'll also find local bread, produce, and pickles. 606 Broad St., Beaufort, NC 28516. Mon.–Tues. and Thurs.–Sat., 11 A.M.–5 P.M.; Wed., 11 A.M.–7 P.M. (252) 728-2844; www.coastalcommunitymarket.com

Down East Gallery

Down East Gallery

Alan Cheek's paintings illustrate a bone-deep understanding of the Outer Banks. Lighthouses and surging seas glow in stunning acrylics. 519 Front St., Beaufort, NC 28516. Mon.–Sat., 10 A.M.–5 P.M. (252) 728-4410; www.alancheek.com

Handscapes Gallery

Visit Handscapes and you'll know why it was chosen by *NICHE* magazine as one of the top 100 retailers of American crafts. You'll find pottery, jewelry, glasswork, and more by 150-plus artisans. 410 Front St., Somerset Square, Beaufort, NC 28516. Summer, Mon.–Sat., 10 A.M.–9 P.M.; Sun., noon–5 P.M.; winter, 10 A.M.–6 P.M. (252) 728-6805 or (888) 346-8334; www.handscapesgallery.com

Mattie King Davis Art Gallery

Mattie King Davis Art Gallery

Carteret County's oldest art gallery is on the grounds of the historic Rustell House (circa 1732). It features original works by over 100 local and regional artists. 150 Turner St., Beaufort, NC 28516. Mon.–Sat., 10 A.M.–4 P.M. (252) 728-5225 or (800) 575-7483; www.beauforthistoricsite.org/mkdartgallery.htm

Miss Marie's Gallery

North Carolina pottery, photography, jewelry, paintings, quilts, and hand-painted furniture are sold here. 114 Queen St., Beaufort, NC 28616. Tues.–Sat., 11 A.M.–5 P.M.; Sun., noon–5 P.M. (252) 728-0908 or (888) 724-1177; www.missmariesgallery.com

N.C. Maritime Museum

North Carolina Maritime Museum

No visit to Beaufort is complete without a stop at the North Carolina Maritime Museum. It's filled with fascinating displays that bring the maritime history of this area to life. The gift shop features an extensive array of publications, prints, and unique maritime memorabilia. 315 Front St., Beaufort, NC 28516. Mon.–Fri., 9 A.M.–5:30 P.M.; Sat., 10 A.M.–5 P.M.; Sun., 1–5 P.M. Free. (252) 728-7317; www.ncmaritime.org

Cove City/Craven County

A Day at the Farm

This working farm featured on UNC-TV's *North Carolina Weekend* is for kids and adults. You can take a hayride, visit the animals, and try your luck in the corn maze. Say hello to Abraham, the trick goat seen on *World's Funniest Animals*. Guided tours of the dairy barns, an old-fashioned smokehouse, a vintage kitchen, a washhouse, and a corncrib help make your visit even more authentic. Overnight accommodations are available in the pack house. 183 Woodrow McCoy Rd., Cove City, NC 28523. Admission fee. (252) 514-9494 or (877) 514-1251

Kirkman Farm

Discover what it takes to grow corn, soybeans, wheat, rye, oats, hay, and pumpkins. The kids will get a kick out of feeding and petting the barnyard animals, including goats, potbelly pigs, rabbits, ponies, cows, and a miniature donkey. You can wander through a corn maze, roam the pumpkin patch, and enjoy a hayride tour of Christmas lights and a nativity scene—all in season, of course. 5255 Hwy 55 W., Cove City, NC 28523. Open by appointment; closed Jan.–Feb. Admission fee. (252) 638-1847

A Day at the Farm

Emerald Isle/Carteret County

Cap'n Willis Seafood Market

Cap'n Willis's own boats bring in a daily catch of tuna, grouper, snapper, crabs, and other fresh seafood. You can buy great crab cakes ready to cook! 7803 Emerald Dr., Emerald Isle, NC 28575. Open March–Dec. (252) 354-2500

Miss Marie's Gallery

Cap'n Willis Seafood Market (p. 91)

Emerald Isle Inn and B&B by the Sea

Guests relax and unwind in an oceanfront inn featuring amenities-loaded suites, not to mention patios with swings. 502 Ocean Dr., Emerald Isle, NC 28594. (252) 354-3222

Village Creek Farm

Want it fresh? At Village Creek Farm, you can sample delicious strawberries, peaches, melons, tomatoes, and veggies of all sorts—organic, too! 690 Biddle Rd., Fort Barnwell, NC 28526. Mid-March–Sept., Mon.–Sat., 7 A.M.–7 P.M.; Sun., 1–6 P.M. (252) 523-9518

Grantsboro/Pamlico County

Michael Brown, Chair Maker

Michael Brown is an artist in wood who takes timeless and classic designs to new dimensions. You'll find beautiful tables, cabinets, and chairs to suit traditional and contemporary tastes. 670 Howell Rd., Grantsboro, NC 28529. (252) 249-1348; www.michaelbrownchairmaker.com

Ol' Country Festival

This annual fair is worth the trip for the rides, vendors, food, and fun. Pamlico Community College, Grantsboro, NC 28529-0185. Held the first Sat. in May, 10 A.M.–3 P.M. (252) 249-1851

Salt Water Fly Fishing Academy

Learn to fly-cast at this academy featured on the Fox Sports network. You can take a four-hour hands-on class or a weekend fishing safari with everything from equipment and rigging to on-the-water instruction. 1313 Old Bay River Rd., Grantsboro, NC 28529. (252) 745-3500; www.flyfishcarolina.com

Cape Lookout National Seashore

Harkers Island/Carteret County

Core Sound Waterfowl Museum

Don't miss the Core Sound Waterfowl Museum. More than a collection of artifacts, it tells the story of hunters, fishermen, guides, carvers, boatbuilders, quilters, and storekeepers who have lived along Core Sound for centuries. It is located adjacent to Cape Lookout. 1785 Island Rd., Harkers Island, NC 28531. Mon.–Sat., 10 A.M.–5 P.M.; Sun., 2–5 P.M. (252) 728-1500; www.coresound.com

Lowland/Pamlico County

Lyle & Shirley's

The owners grow their own crabs for soft-shell recipes. How fresh is that? They make divine hush puppies, too. 580 Oyster Creek Rd., Lowland, NC 28552. Thurs., 11 A.M.–7 P.M.; Fri.–Sat., 11 A.M.–8 P.M.; Sun., 11 A.M.–2 P.M. (252) 745-4902

Morehead City/Carteret County

Arts & Things

You'll discover paintings, prints, stone and wood sculpture, stained glass, pottery, and art glass at this waterfront shop. You can even take a class. 704 Evans St., Morehead City, NC 28557. Mon.–Sat., 10 A.M.–6 P.M. (252) 240-1979 or (252) 808-3168; www.arts-things.com

Bistro-by-the-Sea

Fine food, wine, spirits, and live music create a special dining experience. Since the bistro is a member of Carteret Catch, all seafood served here is fresh and local! 4031 Arendell St., Morehead City, NC 28557. (252) 247-2777; www.bistro-by-the-sea.com

Bistro-by-the-Sea guarantees fresh, local seafood.

Café Zito

The eclectic menu features the owner-chef's Mediterranean

favorites, organic chicken, lamb, local produce, and seafood, all of it served in a National Register of Historic Places home with changing artwork. 105 S. 11th St., Morehead City, NC 28557. Tues.–Sat., 5:30–10:30 P.M.; Sun., 11 A.M.–2 P.M. (252) 726-6676; www.cafezito.com

Carolina Artist Studio Gallery

This sun-filled gallery run by more than two dozen artists offers original photography, paintings, hand-painted stoneware, jewelry, drawings, etchings, textiles, glazed pottery pieces, and amazing handmade furniture. 800 Evans St., Morehead City, NC 28557. Tues.–Sat., 10 A.M.–5 P.M. (252) 726-7550; www.carolinaartiststudio.com

Carteret Contemporary Art

Fresh, arresting contemporary art by regional artists is presented in a lively gallery. A dash of art consulting is offered, too. 1106 Arendell St., Morehead City, NC 28557. Mon.–Fri., 10 A.M.–5 P.M.; Sat., 10 A.M.–4 P.M. (252) 726-4071; www.twogalleries.net

Enjoy country music at the Crystal Coast Jamboree.

Crystal Coast Jamboree

Expect two hours of high-energy entertainment that blends comedy and dancing with everything from country and gospel oldies to patriotic salutes. It's one of the hottest tickets at the beach. 1311 Arendell St., Morehead City, NC 28557. Admission fee. (252) 726-1501;www.crystalcoastjamboree.com

Down East FolkArts Society

The society sponsors music, dance, and storytelling by traditional, multicultural, and contemporary folk artists. Most concerts are held at Trent River Coffee Company in New Bern or Clawson's 1905 Restaurant in Beaufort. PO Box 3489, Morehead City, NC 28557-3489. (252) 504-2787; www.downeastfolkarts.org

El's Drive-In

At this local institution, carhops will bring you some of the best shrimp burgers (and cheeseburgers, too, for landlubbers) and milk shakes around. 3706 Arendell St., Morehead City, NC 28557. Sun.–Thurs., 10:30 A.M.–midnight; Fri.–Sat., 10:30 A.M.–1 A.M. (252) 726-3002

Fill your head with maritime knowledge at The History Place.

The History Place

Come lunch with a storyteller, see a play, hear music, and soak up local history at this lively spot. The gift shop and the tearoom are delightful! 1008 Arendell St., Morehead City, NC 28557. Tues.–Sat., 10 A.M.–4 P.M. Free. (252) 247-7533; www.thehistoryplace.org

North Carolina Seafood Festival

The second-largest festival in North Carolina and largest seafood fest presents dozens of seafood vendors, plus arts, live music, storytelling, fireworks, and tours of the state port. 907B Arendell St., Morehead City, NC 28557. Held the first weekend in Oct. Free. (252) 726-6273; www.ncseafoodfestival.org

Sample delicious seafood at the N.C. Seafood Festival. *N.C. Arts Council*

Sanitary Fish Market & Restaurant

This eatery is such a local fixture that you'll often see people sporting Sanitary Fish Market T-shirts all across the state. Enjoy fresh-caught fish and shellfish in a bright, casual, family-friendly atmosphere. 501 Evans St., Morehead City, NC 28557. Open daily, 11 A.M.–8:30 P.M. (252) 247-3111;www.sanitaryfishmarket.com

Shepard's Point

This "uptown steakhouse" features local seafood and produce, a contemporary martini bar, and an extensive wine selection. You can watch expert chefs prepare food in the open kitchen. The owners support the arts scene by displaying original

artwork. 913 Arendell St., Morehead City, NC 28557. (252) 727-0815; beaufortgrocery.com/spmain.html

Waterfront Junction

Customers come to Waterfront Junction for craft supplies, needlework, prints, crewel, embroidery, and nautical gifts. 103 S. Sixth St., Morehead City, NC 28557. Open Mon.–Sat. (252) 726-6283

New Bern/Craven County

The Accidental Artist

The Accidental Artist

Kids express their creativity by painting a pottery piece of their choice. Owner Donna Woodruff fires their one-of-a-kind masterpieces. 220 Craven St., New Bern, NC 28560. Tues.–Sat., 10 A.M.–6 P.M.; Sun., 1–5 P.M. (252) 634-3411; www.theaccidentalartistnc.com

Captain Ratty's Seafood Restaurant

Lively music floats out of this 1895 building. Inside, diners enjoy fresh seafood, steaks, burgers, and salads surrounded by original art and plenty of lore. 202 Middle St., New Bern, NC 28560. Mon.–Wed., 11 A.M.–9:30 P.M.; Thurs.–Sat., 11 A.M.–10:30 P.M.; Sun., noon–9 P.M. (252) 633-2088 or (800) 633-5292;www.captainrattys.com

Carolina Coastal Railroaders/Spring Train Show

You'll find model trains galore! The oldest and largest train show in the East is held in February. 2001-B S. Glen Burnie Rd., New Bern, NC 28562. Mon.–Thurs., 7–9 P.M.; Sat., 8:30 A.M.–noon. Free. (252) 723-2981; www.carolinacoastalrailroaders.org

FoxBern Manor

Carolina Creations Fine Art & Contemporary Craft Gallery

Owners Janet and Michael Francoeur display the works of over 250 artists—including potters, glassblowers, woodworkers, and jewelers—from North Carolina and across the country. 317-A Pollock St., New Bern, NC 28560. Mon.–Thurs. and Sat., 10 A.M.–6 P.M.; Fri., 10 A.M.–7 P.M.; Sun., 11 A.M.–4 P.M. (252) 633-4369; www.carolinacreations.com

Craven Arts Council & Gallery

The Chelsea

The Chelsea serves outstanding regional and international cuisine in a charming, casual atmosphere. Diners can enjoy art by regional artists such as Janet Francoeur, Doug Alvord, and Willie Taigliri. 335 Middle St., New Bern, NC 28560. Mon.–Sat., 11 A.M.–9 P.M. (252) 637-5469; www.thechelsea.com

Cow Café

Holy cow! Cow Café has over 200 funny cow-inspired items and toys, plus Uncle Mooford's old-fashioned shakes and Grandmoo Isla's wonderful cookies, sandwiches, and salads for lunch and supper. 319 Middle St., New Bern, NC 28560. (252) 672-9269

Craven Arts Council & Gallery/Bank of the Arts

The gallery's monthly exhibits showcase traditional and contemporary works. The great gift shop offers art, crafts, cards, and other original creations. 317 Middle St., New Bern, NC 28562. Mon.–Fri., 9 A.M.–5 P.M. (252) 638-2577; www.cravenarts.net

FoxBern Manor

This country B&B furnishes its suites with antiques and adorns its walls with local art. 935 Rollover Rd., New Bern, NC 28562. (252) 635-6697; www.foxbernmanor.com

FoxBern Manor

Holton Farm

Holton Farm has sweet, juicy strawberries to pick or purchase. Healthy, homegrown vegetables are sold, too. 1155 Olympia Rd., New Bern, NC 28560. (252) 633-0061

Meadows Inn B&B

Built in 1847 in the historic district, the inn features period furnishings. Bike tours, art classes, and other activities are offered. 212 Pollock St., New Bern, NC 28562. (252) 634-1776 or (877) 551-1776; www.meadowsinn-nc.com

Mitchell Hardware *NE Partnership*

Mitchell Hardware

Take a step back in time in one of the oldest hardware stores in the state. You'll find traditional pottery, bird-watching accessories, cast-iron cookware, and, yes, hardware. 215 Craven St., New Bern, NC 28560. Mon.–Sat., 8 A.M.–6 P.M. (252) 638-4261; www.mitchellhardwareonline.com

Moore Tree Farm

Gather up the family and visit an authentic tree farm of Virginia pine, Leyland cypress, white pine, Carolina sapphire, and cedar. 405 Parker Rd., New Bern, NC 28562. Open daily from the Sat. before Thanksgiving to Christmas Eve, 9 A.M.–5 P.M. (252) 638-4160; rickjonestreefarm@hotmail.com

MumFest

Mum's the word! Widely revered as one of the finest family festivals in the state, this event features jugglers, musicians, unicyclists, clowns, dance groups, arts and crafts, and flowers galore at Tryon Palace. PO Box 59, New Bern, NC 28563. Held on a mid-Oct. weekend. (252) 638-5781; www.mumfest.com

Mumfest *Tryon Palace*

New Bern Academy & Museum

This building housed the first school in North Carolina, established by law in 1776. Today, it's a museum featuring New Bern's history from 1710 through the Civil War. New St. and Hancock St., New Bern, NC 28560. Mon.–Sat., 1–4:30 P.M. Admission fee. (252) 514-4937; www.tryonpalace.org

New Bern Civic Theatre

This 1911 theater has found new life with musicals, dramas, and special events. It is open for viewing during business hours. 414 Pollock St., New Bern, NC 28560. Mon.–Thurs., 10 A.M.–4 P.M.; Fri., by appointment. (252) 633-0567; www.newberncivictheatre.org

New Bern Farmers' Market

Yummy pastries, golden honey, fresh produce, sparkling jams, and handmade crafts are for sale. Free-range chicken and lamb, delicious seafood, and fresh goat cheese are offered, too! Pony rides are available, and sometimes puppies are for sale. 421 S. Front St., New Bern, NC 28560. Sat., 7 A.M.–1 P.M. (252) 633-4403 or (252) 638-1696

New Bern Farmers' Market

New Bern Fireman's Museum

Here, you can admire antique firefighting equipment, including a wonderful collection of steam pumpers. Rare photographs and Civil War artifacts are also on display. 408 Hancock St., New Bern, NC 28562. Mon.–Sat., 10 A.M.–4 P.M. The cost is $5 for adults and $2.50 for children; kids six and under are free. (252) 636-4087; www.newbernmuseums.com

New Bern Fireman's Museum *NE Partnership*

Trent River Coffee Company

Enjoy coffee, tea, breakfast breads, and pastries in this former foundry with beautiful hardwood floors. Down East Folk Arts Society performances are held here, too. 208 Craven St., New Bern, NC 28560. Mon.–Fri.,

7 A.M.–5 P.M.; Sat., 8 A.M.–5 P.M.; Sun., 10 A.M.–late. (252) 514-2030

Tryon Palace Historic Sites & Gardens

Tryon Palace

Built between 1767 and 1770, Tryon Palace served as the first capital of North Carolina after the Revolutionary War. Today, you can see demonstrations of basket weaving, spinning, weaving, carding wool for thread, candle dipping, blacksmithing, and hearth cooking. 610 Pollock St., New Bern, NC 28562. (252) 514-4900 or (800) 767-1560; www.tryonpalace.org

Weavers Webb Gallery

Get those hands busy with a full selection of needlework supplies. Hand-woven textiles, including baby blankets and table linens, are for sale. 602 Pollock St., New Bern, NC 28562. (252) 514-2681

Newport/Carteret County

Carolina Rose offers a large selection of handmade quilts. *Karen A. Blum*

Carolina Rose

One of the largest craft malls on the Crystal Coast, Carolina Rose offers a great selection of handcrafted quilts. The unique "Crafty Kids" area sells arts and crafts made by local youth. 5568-B Hwy 70, Newport, NC 28570. Mon.–Sat., 9 A.M.–7 P.M. (252) 247-9992; carolinarose2005@earthlink.net

Clayton Garner Farm

Stop by for prepicked and pick-your-own berries, fruits, and vegetables. Rte. 4, Box 541-A, Newport, NC 28570. Apr. 25–July 30, Mon.–Fri., 7 A.M.–7 P.M.; Sat., 7 A.M.–5 P.M. (252) 223-5283

Oriental/Pamlico County

The Bean

Sip coffee at The Bean. *Towndock.net*

Rock on the porch with a cup of fresh coffee and a muffin, or try a cappuccino or an ice-cream cone while enjoying the view of the town dock and harbor. 304 Hodges St., Oriental, NC 28571. Mon.–Sat., 7 A.M.–9 P.M.; Sun., 7 A.M.–6 P.M. (252) 249-4918; thebeaninc@coastalnet.com

Brantley's Village Restaurant

This family-friendly restaurant offers a great lunch buffet. It's also known for its chicken and collard specials and its delicious homemade lemon, coconut, and chocolate pies. 900 Broad St., Oriental, NC 28571. Mon.–Thurs., 7 A.M.–8 P.M.; Fri.–Sat., 7 A.M.–8:30 P.M.; Sun., 11 A.M.–2 P.M. (252) 249-3509

Embrace the charm of the Cartwright House. *Towndock.net*

Cartwright House

This turn-of-the-century B&B has five wonderfully appointed rooms. Fresh muffins are delivered to guests in the morning. The innkeepers have bikes and kayaks for guests to explore the area. 301 Freemason St., Oriental, NC 28571. (252) 249-1337; www.cartwrighthouse.com

Charlotte Garrett Gallery & Studio

This gallery's brilliant watercolors of bird life, pets, and coastal scenes are vibrant and full of detail. Karen Meyer's baskets and McCabe Coolidge's pottery are sold here also. 502 Hodges St., Oriental, NC 28571. Open 10 A.M.–4 P.M. and by appointment. (252) 249-4942; www.garrettgallery.com

Circle Ten Art Gallery

The artwork here reflects Oriental's reputation as the state's sailing capital. Paintings, handmade jewelry, sculpture,

Circle Ten Art Gallery (p. 102)

Circle Ten Art Gallery

glass, and woodcarvings of the sea are featured. 1103 Broad St., Oriental, NC 28571-0634. Thurs.–Sat., 10 A.M.–5 P.M.; Sun., 1–4 P.M. (252) 249-0298

Croaker Festival

This fishy celebration features a parade, a street dance, the Croaker Queen pageant, free music, food, and arts. Oriental, NC 28571. Held the first weekend in July. (252) 675-1411; www.visitoriental.com/events.html

Croakertown

Croakertown has the perfect gift for everyone. *Towndock.net*

You'll find art, jewelry, weather vanes, books, and cards by artisans from near and far. 807 Broad St., Oriental, NC 28571. Mon.–Sat., 10 A.M.–5 P.M. (252) 249-0990

A Different Twist

Join the artists while you pick out an amazing piece of custom jewelry with exquisite beadwork and semiprecious stones, a hand-sewn sarong, or a pocketbook. 509 Broad St., Oriental, NC 28571. Tues.–Fri.,11 A.M.–6 P.M.; Sat., 11 A.M.–4 P.M. (252) 249-2498 or (877) 280-2255; www.differenttwist.com

Dragon Spokes

Park your car or moor your boat and discover the friendly village of Oriental on a rented bike. Hodges St., Oriental, NC 28571. (252) 670-8465

Get a unique sculpture created by Gary Gresko. *Towndock.net*

Gary Gresko Sculpture

Here, large outdoor public art, garden art, sculptural reliefs, wall hangings, and memorials come together with smaller works like *Inverted Pyramid*, a wonderful table of wood and metal. 119 Osprey Dr., Oriental, NC 28571. Open by appointment; the sculpture garden is accessible during daylight hours. (252) 249-1762; www.garygresko.com

Have a cozy stay at The Inn at Oriental B&B. *Towndock.net*

The Inn at Oriental B&B

This inn offers 12 guest rooms, a homemade American breakfast, and total relaxation by the fireplace or in the gardens. 508 Church St., Oriental, NC 28571. (252) 249-1078; www.innatoriental.com

Oriental Christmas

This maritime twist on Christmas finds boats competing for the best display of lights. Over 2,000 beautiful luminaries light the joyful parade. 507 Church St., Oriental, NC 28571. Held the second weekend in Dec. (252) 249-0555; www.visitoriental.com

Don't miss the harbor star during Oriental Christmas. *Towndock.net*

Oriental Harbor General Store, Deli & Bistro

Stop in for your trip snacks and check out the Dragon Duds, an exclusive line of clothing and gear featuring the signature Oriental Harbor dragon. 516 Water St., Oriental, NC 28571. Open daily. (252) 249-3783; www.orientalharbor.com

Oriental Rotary Club Annual Tarpon Tournament

This tournament has a unique photo contest. PO Box 205, Oriental, NC 28571. Held one weekend in July. (252) 249-1665; www.towndock.net/tarpon

Oriental Steamer Restaurant *Towndock.net*

Oriental Steamer Restaurant

This 1890s historic brick building is the place for terrific food. Local art adds a special touch. On occasion, you can enjoy live music while you dine. 401 Broad St., Oriental, NC 28571. Mon.–Thurs., 5–9 P.M.; Fri.–Sun., 11 A.M.–2 P.M. and 5–9 P.M. (252) 249-3557

Pirate Queen Paddling Tours

Pirate Queen Paddling Tours

This company offers eco-friendly paddling adventures and group overnight kayak trips for women over 50. PO Box 697, Oriental, NC 28571. (252) 341-2692; www.piratequeenpaddling.com

Spec Fever Guide Service

This guide service offers shallow-water fishing, light-tackle fishing, and fly-fishing for redfish, speckled sea trout, flounder, striped bass, giant red drum, tarpon, false albacore, and shad. Oriental, NC 28571. (252) 249-1520; www.specfever.com

Pine Knoll Shores/Carteret County

North Carolina Aquarium at Pine Knoll Shores

The setting for this outstanding facility is the beautiful Theodore Roosevelt Natural Area, bordering a tidal marsh. You can stroll the elevated walkways for a closeup view of the tidal basin's unique ecosystem. Inside the 35,000-square-foot facility, you can experience horseshoe crabs and other sea creatures through an exciting touch tank and a unique *Queen Anne's Revenge* tank with nurse sharks, delicate tigerfish, and other sea life. Located off Hwy 58 W., Pine Knoll Shores, NC 28512. Open daily, 9 A.M.–5 P.M.; open until 9 P.M. on Thurs. in July; closed Thanksgiving, Christmas, and New Year's. Admission fee. (252) 247-4003; www.ncaquariums.com

N.C. Aquarium at Pine Knoll Shores *Scott Taylor*

Salter Path/Carteret County

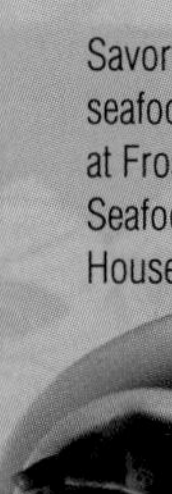

Frost Seafood House

Frost Seafood House is on the sound. Its specialties are soft-shell crabs and fresh seafood. Diners enjoy the local art on display. 1300 Hwy 58, Salter Path, NC 28575. Open daily, 7:30 A.M.–2 P.M. and 4:30–9 P.M. (252) 247-3202

Savory seafood at Frost Seafood House

Vanceboro/Craven County

Peace & Plenty Hunting Preserve *N.C. Wildlife Commission*

Peace & Plenty Hunting Preserve

The preserve features hunting for wild duck, deer, bear, and turkey on more than 2,000 acres. Hunts are also available for quail, pheasant, chukar, and duck. Lodging is available on-site. Oct.–March, Mon.–Sat. (252) 746-3106; www.peace-n-plenty.com

River Breeze Adirondack Chairs

These unique and comfortable chairs are hand-built by Bob and Susan Werner and brightly colored with special designs. 7801 Main St., Vanceboro, NC 28586. (252) 244-2452

White's Farm & Greenhouses

White's Farm & Greenhouses

You can pick your own or select fresh seasonal produce at White's Farm. Hanging baskets, plants, and perennials are also sold. 5200 US Hwy 17 N., Vanceboro, NC 28586. March–Dec., Mon.–Sat., 7 A.M.–7 P.M.; Sun., 10 A.M.–6 P.M. (252) 244-2428

Yoder's Farm & Garden Supply and The Dutch Oven

Old-fashioned ice cream, crafts, seed, implements, and handmade Amish furniture are for sale in this glorious store. The Dutch Oven serves up the best homemade desserts in the area. 4100 NC Hwy 118, Vanceboro, NC 28530. Mon.–Fri., 7:30 A.M.–5:30 P.M.; Sat., 7:30 A.M.–3 P.M. (252) 244-2992; yoderssupply@earthlink.net

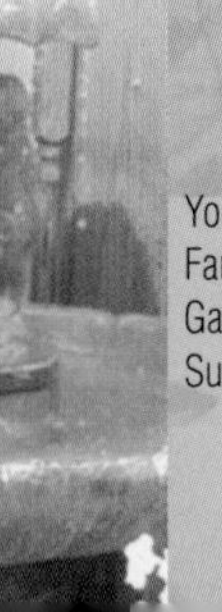

Yoder's Farm & Garden Supply

Red, White, and Blue

Duplin, Onslow, Pender, and Sampson Counties

Trot from turf to surf across this rambling trail. Take your pick of riding modes and settings: under the moonlight, down by the seaside, over a woodland trail, bouncing in a buggy, snuggled in a hayride. You can ride at working homesteads, annual fairs, riding stables, adventure parks, and cozy campgrounds along this trail. But riding, even in its many modes, is just one of the fun things to do on this colorful corridor.

This trail will have you seeing red for sure. You'll find it in luscious ripe strawberries, baskets of scarlet geraniums, lovely hand-painted pottery, and unique Christmas ornaments just right for gift giving (or a little self-indulgence).

White shows up in many shades: creamy Gouda cheese, pale scuppernong wine, slippery white oysters, fragrant homemade soaps, and the vanishing froth on an ocean wave.

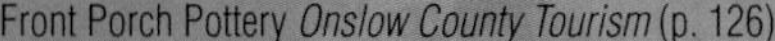
Front Porch Pottery *Onslow County Tourism* (p. 126)

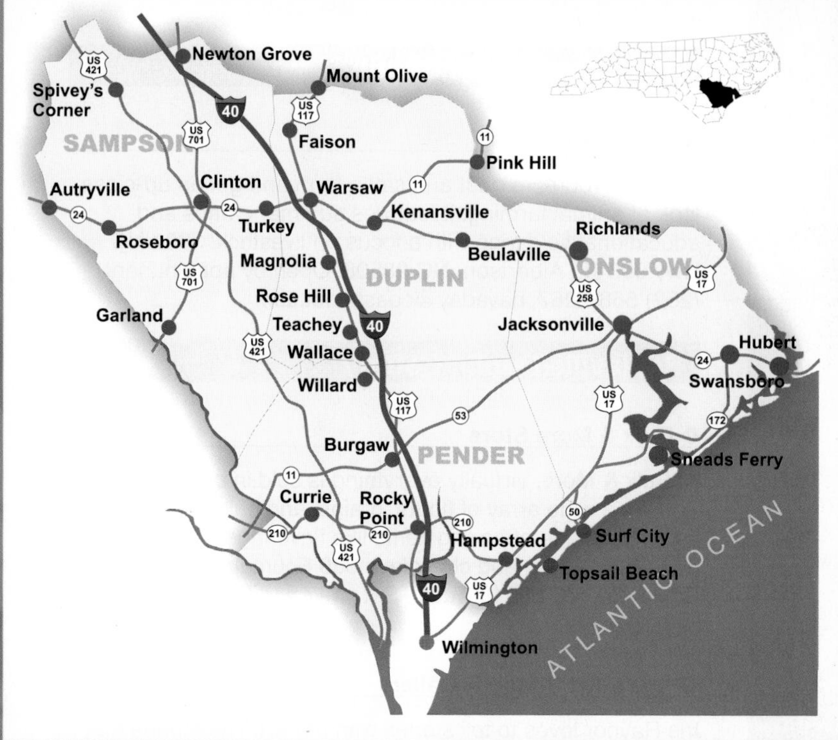

Maybe you prefer blues. Try them played as sassy notes at a local music festival, rolled around as a mouthful of plump blueberries, or splashed in designs on a handmade pitcher. See them stained deep into the grape stompers' feet at the harvest festival, or take the sparkling blue-green sea home with you in a local artist's original seascape.

And they all come together—the reds, whites, and blues—in places like the Missiles and More Museum, where you'll discover that the nation's rocket program began at Topsail Beach.

From hair-raising hollers at Spiveys Corner to seaside galleries at Surf City, you'll find experiences for every age and interest. Read on for town-by-town descriptions of the unique attractions that make up the "Red, White, and Blue" trail.

Albertson/Duplin County

Havaday Farms

Visit this 100-acre goat and cattle farm and get an up-close look at animal farming. It features summer camps and educational field trips with a focus on livestock. 3900 NC Hwy 903 N., Albertson, NC 28508. Open by appointment. (252) 568-2267; havaday@coastalnet.com

Beulaville/Duplin County

Bulk & More Store

At Bulk & More, virtually everything is sold in bulk sizes. There's a wide array of flours, grains, and bakery mixes and a complete line of baking items like flavorings, candy chips, dried fruit, yeast, and chocolate. 889 Fountaintown Rd., Beulaville, NC 28518. Tues.–Sat., 1–7 P.M. (910) 298-2183

Iris's Art Studio & Gallery

Iris Raynor loves to tell stories with her art. The stories may be about history, as in her prints of architectural structures, or about nature, especially her floral subjects. 493 Edmund Brinson Rd., Beulaville, NC 28518. Open by appointment. (910) 298-3793; www.irisraynor-artist.com

Tarkil Branch Farm's Homestead Museum *Duplin County Tourism*

Tarkil Branch Farm's Homestead Museum

The museum features a 1925 country store, a smokehouse, tobacco barns, farm equipment, and other artifacts, including 19th-century period furnishings. Wagon tours are available for groups. 1197 Fountaintown Rd., Beulaville, NC 28518. Sat., 9 A.M.–5 P.M.; open by reservation other days and for groups and bus tours. (910) 298-3804, (910) 296-4235, or (910) 290-0014; www.tarkilfarmsmuseum.com

Way Out Yonder

This country gift shop sells quilts, carved walking sticks, framed prints of original drawings, hand-crocheted doilies and afghans, tapestry wall hangings, wind chimes, spinners, bows, ornaments, and more. 2389 B Hwy 24 E., Beulaville, NC 28518. Open Tues.–Sat. (910) 298-8444

Burgaw/Pender County

Bannerman Vineyard/White Oak Farm

Bannerman Vineyard

This vineyard features six different varieties of native North Carolina muscadine grapes. Visitors can pick their own grapes from September 1 until mid-October. "Grape Day," held in mid-September, includes winemaking demonstrations, food, entertainment, and grape picking. 2624 Stag Park Rd., Burgaw, NC 28411. Mon.–Sat., 9 A.M.–6 P.M.; Sun., noon–6 P.M. (910) 799-4108 or (910) 259-5474

Dee's Drug Store

If you remember sitting at a soda fountain on a tall stool with your parents or friends, then you'll love Dee's Drug Store in downtown Burgaw. You can still have your choice of hand-dipped ice cream, orangeades, hot dogs, or one of Dee's famous grilled sandwiches. 111 S. Wright St., Burgaw, NC 28425. Open daily, 9 A.M.–2 P.M. (910) 259-2116; deesdr@bizec.rr.com

North Carolina Blueberry Festival

This celebration features everything from blueberry lip balm to blueberry smoothies. There's an antique car show, a pig cookoff, a beauty pageant, parades, and a blueberry recipe contest. Downtown Burgaw, NC 28425. Held the last Sat. in June. (910) 259-1235 or (888) 576-4756; www.ncblueberryfestival.com

Pender County Arts Council

Wonderful original art is on display in the historic depot, home of the Pender County Arts Council. Drop by and see the exhibits. 318 S. Cowan St., Burgaw, NC 28425. Thurs.–Sat., noon–4 P.M. (910) 259-4891

North Carolina Blueberry Festival

Pender County Spring Fest

This one-day fair is filled with vendors of all kinds, arts-and-crafts dealers, horse and buggy rides, music, food, and fun. It showcases local artists and heritage crafts. Burgaw, NC 28425. Held annually in May. Call for information. (910) 259-4844 or (888) 576-4756; www.visitpender.com

Clinton/Sampson County

Ashford Inn Bed and Breakfast

Listed on the National Register of Historic Places, this 1839 home was purchased by Confederate colonel John Ashford in 1869. A B&B since 1997, it features five guest rooms, each with a queen-sized bed and private bath. The inn also offers high-speed wireless Internet. 615 College St., Clinton, NC 28328. (910) 596-0961 or (888) 288-4346; www.ashford-inn.com

Comfort surrounds you at the Ashford Inn B&B.

Christopher's Restaurant

Christopher's is committed to supporting local farmers, using only locally grown pork and local vegetables in season. The pickup truck salad bar hints at the rural nature of the community the restaurant calls home. 8088 US Hwy 421 N., Clinton, NC 28328. Wed.–Thurs., 11 A.M.–8 P.M.; Fri.–Sat., 11 A.M.–9 P.M.; Sun., 11 A.M.–2 P.M. (910) 564-6942

The Courthouse Inn

Originally the courthouse for Sampson County, the inn features eight guest rooms, each with its own private bath, telephone, cable TV, and refrigerator. Several rooms open onto a wraparound porch. 102 E. Faison St., Clinton, NC 28328. (910) 592-3933; www.courthouseinnbb.com

Gracie's Grill

In business for 25 years, Gracie's is known for some of the best hot dogs in Sampson County. 123 Vance St., Clinton, NC 28328. Mon.–Sat., 6 A.M.–5 P.M. (910) 592-7782

Sampson Community Theatre

The theater has operated for more than 40 years. Productions include musicals, dramas, and comedies, all featuring local talent. 115 Fayetteville St., Clinton, NC 28328. Call for schedule and prices. (910) 592-8653; www.sampsontheater.com/index.html

Sampson County History Museum

The museum is located in the Best House (circa 1907), one of seven buildings on the premises. Another is the Bunting Log Cabin (circa 1750), one of the oldest structures in eastern North Carolina. 313 Lisbon St., Clinton, NC 28328. Wed.–Fri., noon–4 P.M.; Sat., 10 A.M.–4 P.M. (910) 590-0007; www.sampsonhmc.com

The Shield House Inn

This lovely Classic Revival home offers three bedrooms. One features queen-sized beds, one has two double beds, and one has a king-sized bed. Each has a TV, a VCR, a microwave, a mini-fridge, a coffee maker, a telephone, and a private bath. 216 Sampson St., Clinton, NC 28328. (910) 592-2634 or (800) 462-9817; www.shieldhouseinn.com

Currie/Pender County

Moores Creek National Battlefield

This Revolutionary War site has a museum, nature trails, a picnic area, and audiovisual programs. 200 Moores Creek Rd., Currie, NC 28435. Open daily, 9 A.M.–5 P.M.; closed on Christmas. (910) 283-5591; www.nps.gov/mocr

Moores Creek National Battlefield *Tim Boyd*

Faison/Duplin County

Cottle Farms, Inc.

Pick your own or get prepicked strawberries, potatoes, cabbages, onions, and squash. 192 Ned Cottle Ln. (off Hwy 403), Faison, NC 28341. Apr. 15–June 1, Mon.–Sat., 8 A.M.–7 P.M.; Sun., 1–6 P.M. (910) 267-4531; www.cottlefarms.com

Cottle Farms, Inc. (p. 111)

Faison Museum

Housed inside the town library, this unique museum holds the secrets of Faison's history—its people, churches, businesses, and schools. Shots taken by noted photographer Carson Boone adorn the walls. 106 Park Circle, Faison, NC 28341. Mon.–Fri., 2–6 P.M. (910) 267-0601

Southern Exposure

This restaurant features vegetables and greens produced by local farms. You'll also find fried green tomatoes with pimento cheese and corn salsa, the restaurant's signature appetizer. Artwork by local artists is on display and for sale. 202 W. Main St., Faison, NC 28341. Tues.–Sat., 11:30 A.M.–2 P.M. and 5–9 P.M.; Sun., 11:30 A.M.–10 P.M. (910) 267-0496

Garland/Sampson County

Old School Sorghum Festival

There's a lot to do at the Old School Sorghum Festival. You can see the 1880s cane press, vintage farm equipment, antique instruments, and the general store (circa 1900). You can also enjoy great food and live music and see how molasses is made. 5705 Old Mintz Hwy, Garland, NC 28441. Held the third Sat. in Oct. (910) 564-5069; www.members.aol.com/sorghumman

Godwin/Sampson County

Jackson Farm Guest House/Jan Mann Pottery

This 100-year-old, two-bedroom farmhouse is located in a private woodland setting on the 300-acre Jackson Farm. Ask about owner Jan Mann's porcelain pottery; she's known for her "Confederate Cup." 13902 Dunn Rd., Godwin, NC 28344. (910) 567-2978; www.jacksonfarm.com

Old School Sorghum Festival

Hampstead/Pender County

Coriander's Fine Foods and Catering

Coriander's serves dishes like "Mom's Meatloaf," marinated London broil, and homemade chicken pot pie. All are prepared with locally grown greens and produce. Be sure to ask about Coriander's cooking classes. 17011 US Hwy 17 N. and Cedar on the Green, Hampstead, NC 28443. Tues.–Fri., 11 A.M.–6 P.M.; Sat., 11 A.M.–3 P.M. (910) 270-3413; www.corianderscatering.com

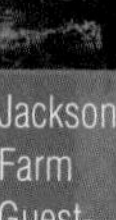

Jackson Farm Guest-house

Farmer Mac's Berries

If you want fresh berries, Farmer Mac's is the place to go. Blueberries are in season from mid-May through late June. Blackberries are available from June through July. 184 Berry Patch Rd., Hampstead, NC 28443. Mon.–Sat., 7 A.M.–dark; Sun., 1–6 P.M. (910) 270-4618; www.agr.state.nc.us/markets/gginc/store/ShowSite.asp?ID=2321

Pottery at the Jackson Farm

Hampstead Arts

This bright, teal-colored building houses pottery studios and a full line of art classes. Classes include pottery (thrown or hand-built), watercolors, oils, acrylics, drawing, stained glass, and "One-Stroke Painting." Children's classes are offered in art and pottery. Art supplies are sold on-site. 14663 US Hwy 17, Hampstead, NC 28443. Mon.–Sat., 10:30 A.M.–4:30 P.M. (910) 270-3003

Nature's Way Farm

Here, you'll find goat cheese, with and without herbs. You'll also discover homemade feta, bleu cheese, Gouda, and Caerphilly. Fresh clams, oysters, crabs, and squid are available in

Hampstead Arts

season. The farm also sells organic tomatoes, eggplants, greens, herbs, and homemade soaps. 115 Crystal Ct., Hampstead, NC 28443. Mon.–Sat., 8 A.M.–6 P.M.; call for Sunday hours. (910) 270-3036

Poplar Grove Plantation

This restored 19th-century plantation is anchored by a grand manor house featuring three floors of artifacts. There's also a tenant house, a smokehouse, a greenhouse, interpretive exhibits, and a blacksmith shop. 10200 US Hwy 17 N., Hampstead, NC 28443. Mon.–Sat., 9 A.M.–5 P.M.; Sun., noon–5 P.M. Admission fee. (910) 686-4868

Hubert/Onslow County

Rigg's Farm

The Red Barn Grill

This 32-seat diner overlooks the waterway. Local seafood—some of it caught by the owners—is the specialty. Everything on the menu is homemade. 107 Red Barn Rd., Hubert, NC 28539. Mon.–Thurs., 6 A.M.–9 P.M.; Fri.–Sun., 6 A.M.–10 P.M. (910) 326-1163

Rigg's Farm

At Rigg's Farm, you can pick your own produce, including strawberries, corn, tomatoes, watermelons, snap beans, butterbeans, peas, cantaloupes, cucumbers, squash, collards, and cabbages. 158 Old Hwy 24, Hubert, NC 28539. Apr. 15–Nov., Mon.–Sat., 7 A.M.–7 P.M.; Sun., 9 A.M.–6 P.M. (910) 326-4032

Nature's Way Farm (p. 113)

Jacksonville/Onslow County

Atelier Vesuvio

Atelier Vesuvio

Inside this sprawling studio and gallery, you'll find textile art on the walls, busts on pedestals, freestanding concrete creations with resin inserts, terra-cotta pieces, oil paintings, stained-glass windows, photography, and handcrafted one-of-a-kind jewelry. 1183 Canady Rd., Jacksonville, NC 28540. Open by appointment. (910) 346-8941; smhile@onslowonline.net

Botticelli Vineyards

Visit this pick-your-own and prepicked muscadine grape vineyard and make your own wine. The owners are retired art teachers, so ask about sketches and classes. 1195 Canady Rd., Jacksonville, NC 28540. Call for times. (910) 346-3131; botticellivineyards@earthlink.net

Botticelli Vineyards *Onslow County Tourism*

The Colonel's Lady Bed & Breakfast

This inn, located in the historic district of Jacksonville, has a lovely view of the New River. It was built in 1901 as a wedding present. Its three guest rooms feature period furnishings. 215 Mill Ave., Jacksonville, NC 28540. (910) 937-7718; www.bbonline.com/nc/colonelslady

Council for the Arts & Gallery

Here, you'll find a great gallery of original work from local and regional artists. 826 New Bridge St., Jacksonville, NC 28540. Mon.–Fri., 8:30 A.M.–4:30 P.M. (910) 455-9840;www.jaxarts.com

The Colonel's Lady Bed & Breakfast *Onslow County Tourism*

Council for the Arts & Gallery *Onslow County Tourism* (p. 115)

Hilda's Cooking & Catering Service

The boats docked behind this restaurant are a clue to something special. Hilda's brings in its own seafood and cooks it to perfection. 506 Bell Fork Rd., Jacksonville, NC 28540. Mon.–Wed., 11 A.M.–8 P.M.; Thurs.–Sat., 11 A.M.–9 P.M. (910) 347-8812

Justice Christmas Tree Farm

At this farm, you can select from white pine, Leyland cypress, and Fraser fir. Fresh wreaths, tree stands, and decorations are available, too. You can even get a tour of the farm and enjoy a hayride. 1325 Gould Rd., Jacksonville, NC 28540. Thanksgiving–Christmas Eve, 9 A.M.–dusk. (910) 346-6783

Kuumba Festival

It's pronounced Koo-oom-bah, and it means "creativity." Come to the Onslow County Fairgrounds for all-day fun, fellowship, education, food, and entertainment. Jacksonville, NC 28540. Held the third Sat. in Aug. (910) 346-6694, (910) 324-4291, or (910) 938-2491

Lynnwood Park Zoo *Onslow County Tourism*

Lynnwood Park Zoo

The Lynnwood Park Zoo contains more than 250 animals and 50 exhibits. Take the kids to see llamas, rheas, emus, foxes, antelopes, capybaras, wallabies, alligators, prairie dogs, and more. 1071 Wells Rd., Jacksonville, NC 28540. Mon.–Fri., 10 A.M.–5 P.M. Admission fee. (910) 938-5848

Onslow Farmers' Market

This market offers fresh fruits, vegetables, plants, and homemade products like jams and jellies. Pick up something to munch on your travels or to take home. 4024 Richlands Hwy, Jacksonville, NC 28540. Apr.–Nov., Tues.–Sat., 9 A.M.–3 P.M. (910) 455-5873;www.onslowcountyfarmersmarket.com

Justice Christmas Tree Farm

Slavin's Gallery

For more than a quarter of a century, Slavin's has exhibited fine art by North Carolina and national artists. It specializes in Civil War art. 201 C Country Club Rd., Jacksonville, NC 28540. Mon.–Sat., 10 A.M.–6 P.M. (910) 346-4105 or (800) 448-9517; www.slavinsgallery.com

Onslow Farmers' Market *Onslow County Tourism*

Thirty Acres and a Mule Farm

This family-friendly 30-acre farm features friendly ponies and other cuddly farm animals. You can taste old-fashioned dipped ice cream, root beer, sodas, and other confections at the snack and gift shop. 125 McGowan Rd., Jacksonville, NC 28540. Reservations are required. (910) 324-4499; www.30acremule.com

Whispering Dove Ranch

Tour this working goat ranch to observe farm animals in their natural environment. Visitors can participate in hands-on demonstrations and learn beekeeping skills. 689 Harris Creek Rd., Jacksonville, NC 28540. Mon.–Thurs., 10 A.M.–noon and 1–3 P.M., and by appointment. The cost is $5 per person. (910) 455-7123;ncagr.com/wclbgr.htm

Slavin's Gallery *Onslow County Tourism*

Kenansville/Duplin County

A Change of Venue Café, Inc.

The café features homemade soups, salads, sandwiches, and desserts and boasts a coffee bar with a big-screen TV. The works of local artists are for sale. 110 B Front St., Kenansville, NC 28349. Mon.–Fri., 8 A.M.–3 P.M. (910) 296-6200; venuecafe@earthlink.net

Thirty Acres and a Mule Farm *Onslow County Tourism*

Cowan Museum

Here, you'll find more than 2,000 artifacts that reflect the heritage of rural North Carolina. Farm implements, household items from the 18th and 19th centuries, a one-room log schoolhouse, a log tobacco barn, a log cabin, and a blacksmith shop are featured. 411 S. Main St., Kenansville, NC 28349. Tues.–Sat., 10 A.M.–4 P.M. (910) 296-2149; www.cowanmuseum.com

Cowan Museum

Graham House Inn

This landmark mid-1800s Greek Revival bed-and-breakfast is located in the historic district. You can relax on one of the three sheltered porches, sun on the deck, or stroll among the beautiful magnolia, oak, sycamore, and live oak trees dripping with Spanish moss. 406 S. Main St., Kenansville, NC 28349. (910) 296-1032 or (800) 767-9379; www.grahamhouseinn.com

Graham House Inn

Liberty Hall Plantation

This is the ancestral plantation of the Kenan family, for whom the town is named. Dating from the early 1800s, the plantation, considered a Southern landmark, features an elegant manor house and 10 outbuildings. 409 S. Main St., Kenansville, NC 28349. Tues.–Sat., 10 A.M.–4 P.M.; closed on major holidays. Admission fee. (910) 296-2175; www.itpi.dpi.state.nc.us/nchistorical.liberty.html

Murray House Country Inn Bed and Breakfast & Thomas Bennett Gallery

The Murray House Country Inn offers six guest rooms and suites with private baths. Most have Jacuzzis, desks, and private telephone and data lines. The house also features the Thomas Bennett Gallery. 201 NC Hwy 24/50, Kenansville, NC 28349. (910) 296-1000; www.murrayhouseinn.com

North Carolina Muscadine Festival

North Carolina is the home of the nation's first cultivated grapes. This festival celebrates the versatility of the muscadine with exhibits, cooking contests, tours of the vineyard and the plantation wine cellar, children's activities, and more. Exit 373 off I-40, Kenansville, NC 28349. Held in late Sept. (910) 296-2181; www.muscadineharvestfestival.com

Murray House Country Inn Bed & Breakfast

Star Jewelry

The jewelers here specialize in pendants, sliders, and earrings with hand-twisted silver. Many pieces incorporate semiprecious stones, shells, or even arrowheads. 1060 NC Hwy 11/903 N., Kenansville, NC 28349. Open by appointment. (910) 296-2015

Tree Spirit Studios

William Quinn's creations are carved from trees that have fallen due to storms or damage of some other kind. His "Tree Spirits" have unique personalities. 1060 NC Hwy 11/903 N., Kenansville, NC 28349. Open by appointment. (910) 296-2015; treespirit@gsiwave.com

Magnolia/Duplin County

Chestnutt Farms

Liberty Hall Plantation

This roadside stand's season starts in April with luscious strawberries, followed by cabbages and onions in spring. Next come blueberries, then watermelons, peanuts, and grapes. The season ends with pumpkins and mums in the fall. Poinsettias are available at holiday time. NC Hwy 11 at J. B. Stroud Rd., Magnolia, NC 28453. Opens at 10 A.M. (910) 296-7357 or (910) 296-0375

P ?

Maxwell Creek Hunting Preserve

Guided hunts for deer, quail, and dove are offered on 500 acres of undisturbed forestland preserved for wildlife. 309 Blind Bridge Rd. (Exit 373 off I-40), Magnolia, NC 28453. Open by appointment. (910) 289-2171

Mount Olive/Duplin County

Glenwood Farms

Glenwood Farms has crops, livestock, and an aquaculture display in the fish house. The attractions include a corn

maze in the fall and the "Spook Trail" hayride around Halloween. 413 NC Hwy 403, Mount Olive, NC 28365. Mon.–Fri., by appointment; Sat., 9 A.M.–dark; Sun., 1 P.M.–dark. The charge is $5 for everyone over three; special rates are offered for group tours. (919) 658-2288; www.glenwoodfarms.net

Glenwood Farms (p. 119)

Newton Grove/Sampson County

Old Mill Stream Nursery & Nature Adventures

The nursery offers picnic facilities, a barnyard, a fishpond, a beaver dam to inspect, and more than 70 acres to hike. 3224 Oak Grove Church Rd., Newton Grove, NC 28366. Apr.–June and Sept.–Nov., Mon.–Fri., 8 A.M.–5 P.M.; Sat., 9 A.M.–5 P.M.; Sun., 1–5 P.M.; July–Aug. and Dec.–March, Mon.–Fri., 8 A.M.–5 P.M.; open other times by appointment; closed holidays. (910) 567-2305 or (800) 307-3793; www.oldmillstream.com

Pink Hill/Duplin County

Cabin Lake County Park

The park features 180-plus acres, a 69-acre lake for swimming and fishing, a picnic pavilion, RV and primitive campsites, and opportunities for hiking. 220 Cabin Lake Rd., Pink Hill, NC 28572. Nov.–Feb., Fri.–Sun., 8 A.M.–6 P.M.; March and Oct., Thurs.–Sun., 8 A.M.–7 P.M.; Apr.–Sept., Thurs.–Sun., 8 A.M.–8 P.M.; open Memorial Day, July 4, and Labor Day. Admission fee. (910) 298-3648; http://www.duplincountync.com/qualityOfLife/recreation.html

Old Mill Stream Nursery & Nature Adventures

Maxwell's Mill Campground

Maxwell's Mill Campground is located on a beautiful 75-acre lake about 14 miles north of Kenansville. It offers full RV hookups, trailer rentals, boating, a pool, heated bathhouses, a laundry, a store, picnic tables, fire rings, nature trails, a game room, and great fishing. 142 Maxwell's Mill Campground Rd., Pink Hill, NC 28572. Memorial Day–Labor Day, 7 A.M.–7 P.M.; other months, 7 A.M.–5 P.M. (252) 568-2022

Richlands/Onslow County

Cabin Lake County Park *Duplin County Tourism*

Mike's Farm Strawberry Patch & Country Store

Take a hayride, dine at the family-style restaurant, or tour an old-fashioned country store and gift shop. You can also browse the on-site bakery or pick your own strawberries, lettuce, cabbages, potatoes, spring onions, and pumpkins in season. You can even pick out your own Christmas tree. 767 Luther Banks Rd., Richlands, NC 28518. Mon.–Sat., 8 A.M.–6 P.M. (910) 324-3422; www.mikesfarm.com

Mirey Creek

This shop features scented candles, bath and body products, goat-milk soaps, fudge, hand-painted gourds, and other items. 221 Haw Branch Rd., Richlands, NC 28518. Mon.–Tues. and Thurs., 9:30 A.M.–5 P.M.; Fri., 9:30 A.M.–6 P.M. (910) 324-3992

Museum Fest Annual Art and Craft Festival

Stroll the streets of Richlands to find the perfect gift or holiday item from the fabulous array of pottery, textiles, woodcrafts, and more. You'll find food, music, and lots of fun. 301 S. Wilmington St., Richlands, NC 28518. Held the first Sun. in Nov., 10 A.M.–5 P.M. (910) 324-5008; http://www.co.onslow.nc.us/museum/fest.aspx

Mike's Farm Strawberry Patch & Country Store *Onslow County Tourism*

Onslow County Museum

This museum offers displays on the colonial settlement period and artifacts of early trade and industry. There is a special focus on the agricultural tradition of the county. 301 S. Wilmington St., Richlands, NC 28518.

Tues.–Fri., 10 A.M.–4:30 P.M.; Sat.–Sun., 1–4 P.M. Admission is $1 for adults and teens. (910) 324-5008; www.co.onslow.nc.us/museum

Richlands Farmer's Day

Richlands Farmer's Day features live music, games, food, and street vendors, beginning with a parade at 9 A.M. Richlands High School, Richlands, NC 28574. Held in Sept. the Sat. after Labor Day, all day. (910) 324-7492; www.friendsoffarmers.org

Sara Margaret Inn

This beautiful old 19th-century home features three guest rooms. The inn is furnished with beautiful antiques and reproductions. 147 Beulaville Hwy, Richlands, NC 28574. (910) 324-1313; http://mywebpage.netscape.com/mustangcaddy/sara.html

Rocky Point/Pender County

Desperado Horse Farm & Trail Rides

You'll find people-friendly, calm horses and winding trails to ride either by day or night. There's even a petting zoo. 7214 NC Hwy 210, Rocky Point, NC 28457. Mon.–Sat., dawn–dusk; Sun., 2 P.M.–dusk. Trail rides cost $25 per hour per horse; call for other prices. (910) 675-0487; www.desperadohorsefarm.com

The Farm Market

Enjoy prepicked or pick-your-own strawberries, collards, onions, greens, and turnips. A fine selection of homemade jellies and jams is also available. 13538 NC Hwy 210, Rocky Point, NC 28457. Apr.–Oct., daily, 8 A.M.–6 P.M. (910) 675-9971

Desperado Horse Farm & Trail Rides

Rose Hill/Duplin County

The Bistro at Duplin Winery

The Farm Market

Executive chef William B. Fussell prepares a lunch menu of soups, salads, gourmet sandwiches, and daily entrées. Dinner, served on Friday, features a select menu created by Chef William. 501 N. Sycamore St., Rose Hill, NC 28458. Mon.–Thurs. and Sat., 11:30 A.M.–2 P.M.; Fri., 11:30 A.M.–2 P.M. and 6–9 P.M. (910) 289-4103; www.duplinwinery.com

Duplin Nursery & Garden Center

Duplin Nursery & Garden Center

The annuals sold here offer a beautiful canvas for the gardener and for all who appreciate a kaleidoscope of color. The dozens of greenhouses hold seasonal treasures like the nursery's famous geraniums, poinsettias, bedding plants, and houseplants. A gift shop is also on the premises. 276 Bay Rd., Rose Hill, NC 28458. Mon.–Fri., 8 A.M.–5 P.M.; Sat., 8 A.M.–noon; in Apr. and May, Sat. hours are extended until 3 P.M. (910) 289-2233

Duplin Winery

This is the oldest operating winery in North Carolina. It features daily tours and films, a museum, a gourmet-food sampling bar, a gift shop, and fine dining in the wonderful atmosphere of an original wine cellar. 501 N. Sycamore St., Rose Hill, NC 28458. Mon.–Thurs., 9 A.M.–5 P.M.; Fri.–Sat., 9 A.M.–6 P.M.; closed New Year's, Thanksgiving, and Christmas. (910) 289-3888 or (800) 774-9634; www.duplinwinery.com

Duplin Winery

Duplin Winery (p. 123)

Original Oil Paintings & Photos by Lin/Robert Dixon Farm

Linda Nichols works from photographs—either from your scrapbook or pictures she takes personally. The sitting room in Nichols's historic home on the Robert Dixon Farm is also the gallery. 128 Glenn Nichols Ln., Rose Hill, NC 28458. Tours of the home are available by appointment. (910) 289-4171;

Rose Hill Restaurant

Although steaks and seafood are always on the menu, the house specialty is chicken. The chickens are grown by local farmers, as are all the fresh vegetables and greens the restaurant serves. Don't leave without sampling the signature lemon pie or blueberry pie. 312 N. Sycamore St., Rose Hill, NC 28458. Mon.–Sat., 6 A.M.–8:30 P.M. (910) 289-2151

?

Six Runs Plantation

There are abundant populations of quail, duck, ring-necked pheasant, chukar partridge, and deer at Six Runs. The lodge has six spacious bedrooms. Guns, shells, and licenses are available. 2794 Register-Sutton Rd., Rose Hill, NC 28458. (910) 532-4810; www.iloveinns.com/bed_and_breakfasts/north_carolina/sixrunsplantationinc.htm

World's Largest Frying Pan

Used for community fundraising events, the frying pan weighs two tons, is 15 feet in diameter, and holds 200 gallons of cooking oil. The capacity is 365 chickens. 510 E. Main St., Rose Hill, NC 28458. (910) 289-3159; www.duplintourism.org/tourism_info.htm

Sneads Ferry/Onslow County

Dr. Rootbeer's Hall of Foam

Root beer is the main attraction here, but you'll also find ice cream, exotic citrus blends, and fountain favorites. There are wraps, dogs, and sandwiches to munch on while you peruse the memorabilia on the walls. 288 Fulcher Landing Rd., Sneads Ferry, NC 28460. Memorial Day–Labor Day, daily, 11:30 A.M.–9 P.M.; Labor Day–Christmas and March–Memorial Day, Wed.–Sun., 11:30 A.M.–7 P.M.; closed Christmas–Feb. (910) 327-7668; www.drrootbeer.com

World's Largest Frying Pan

The Green Turtle

Drive in or secure your boat at the dock and prepare to enjoy fresh local seafood. The walls are filled with local fishing art, photography, and sketches. Live music is featured on Friday and Saturday evenings. 310 Fulcher Landing Rd., Sneads Ferry, NC 28460. Open daily, 5 P.M.–closing. (910) 327-0262

Sneads Ferry Shrimp Festival

This annual festival features a Saturday-morning parade, Saturday-night fireworks, and a rollicking street dance. You'll find specialty foods, crafts, a carnival, a petting zoo, a boat show, military displays, a car show, a "Shrimperoo," a beer and wine garden, and a climbing wall. Sneads Ferry Community Center, Sneads Ferry, NC 28460. Held the second weekend in Aug. (910) 327-3335; www.sneadsferryshrimpfestival.com

The Green Turtle
Onslow County Tourism

Thurston Art Gallery

Sherry Williams Thurston is a prominent North Carolina artist especially well known along the coast for her landscapes, seascapes, and portraits. The gallery offers art classes. 328 Peru Rd., Sneads Ferry, NC 28460. Sat., 10 A.M.–5 P.M., and by appointment. Children's art classes are on Mon. and Tues. after school. (910) 327-1781 or (888) 327-1781; www.thurstonartgallery.com

Spiveys Corner/Sampson County

National Hollerin' Contest

Made famous by shows like *Late Night with David Letterman* and *The Tonight Show* with Jay Leno, the event welcomes all comers to test their skills in the nearly lost art of yelling at the top of one's lungs. Midway High School, Spiveys Corner, NC 28366. Held the third Sat. in June, noon–dusk. (910) 567-2600

Front Porch Pottery *Onslow County Tourism*

Surf City/Pender County

Topsail Art Gallery

Local and regional artists display their work in this gallery near the sea. Commissioned work is also available. 121 S. Topsail Dr., Surf City, NC 28445-9821. (910) 328-2138

Swansboro/Onslow County

Fish Trap

The Fish Trap offers a casual upscale setting and a menu that includes fresh seafood, steaks, chicken, and pasta. There's an extensive wine list, too. Works by local artists are displayed throughout the restaurant. 108 W. Corbett Ave., Swansboro, NC 28584. Mon.–Fri., 11 A.M.–2 P.M. and 5–9 P.M.; Sat.–Sun., 11 A.M.–9 P.M. (910) 326-1433

Front Porch Pottery

Bob and Lou Ayers sell an impressive array of North Carolina pottery. You'll find easy conversation and charming pottery. Bowls, pitchers, plates, and other pieces for everyday use are on display. 105C Church St., Swansboro, NC 28584. Mon.–Fri., 11 A.M.–5 P.M. (910) 326-7900

 Phil Shivar Gallery

Stop by, meet Phil Shivar in person, and see his work. Shivar paints acrylic landscapes and waterside scenes including the birds, boats, and docks of eastern North Carolina. 105E Church St., Swansboro, NC 28584. Mon.–Sat., 11 A.M.–6 P.M. (910) 326-2526

River Grille

This delightful eatery in Old Town Square serves up high-quality coffee, homemade sausage, and great homemade fries, along with down-home pancakes and unique specials. 108-A Corbett Ave., Swansboro, NC 28584. Mon.–Fri., 11 A.M.–10 P.M.; Sat.–Sun., 8 A.M.–10 P.M. (910) 325-0111

Phil Shivar Gallery *Onslow County Tourism*

White Oak River Bistro

Visitors enjoy casual waterfront dining, inside or outside. The bistro features North Carolina wines and local seafood and produce. Local artwork and photography are displayed throughout. 206 W. Corbett Ave., Swansboro, NC 28584. Memorial Day–Labor Day, Mon.–Fri., 8 A.M.–10 P.M. (910) 326-1696; heath10219@coastalnet.com

Yana's Ye Olde Drug Store Restaurant

Yana's is famous for fresh apple, banana, peach, and strawberry fritters. This authentic 1950s drugstore turned restaurant also offers cheeseburgers, old-fashioned milk shakes and malts, and other homemade goodies. 9 Front St., Swansboro, NC 28584. Open daily, 6 A.M.–4 P.M.; breakfast is served all day. (910) 326-5501; www.yanamamas.com

Yana's Ye Olde Drug Store Restaurant *Onslow County Tourism*

Teachey/Duplin County

McMillan Victorian Inn

The home was built in 1908 and restored in 1998 into an appealing and comfortable bed-and-breakfast inn. It has four tastefully decorated bedrooms, each with a private bath, a TV, and a telephone. 109 N. West Ave., Teachey, NC 28464. (910) 285-5747; www.mcmillanvictorianinn.com

Topsail Beach/Pender County

McMillan Victorian Inn *Duplin County Tourism*

Blue Gecko

The Gecko is hard to beat for great deli items, sandwiches, meats, salads, and other favorites. Local seafood is always featured. Customers like to browse the original artwork, gifts, glassware, hand creams, and sundries on sale. 808 S. Anderson Blvd., Box 3439, Topsail Beach, NC 28445. May–early Sept., 9 A.M.–8 P.M. (910) 328-1022; alucien@attglobal.net

Missiles and More Museum

Did you know that one of the nation's rocket programs was launched at Topsail Beach? Exhibits show the 1940s research and testing involved in early United States rocketry. 720 Channel Blvd. (off NC Hwy 50), Topsail Beach, NC 28445. Apr.–mid-Oct., Mon.–Tues. and Thurs.–Sat., 2–4 P.M. Free. (910) 328-4722; www.topsailmissilesmuseum.org

Blue Gecko

Turkey/Sampson County

B&B Pecan Processors of North Carolina

Here, you'll find pecans of all descriptions for all tastes. Try the new Elizabeth's Exceptional Pecan Brittle, which is softer than most brittle, with a delicious buttery taste. 107 Thomson Ave., Turkey, NC 28393. Mon.–Fri., 10 A.M.–5 P.M.; Sat., 10 A.M.–4 P.M. (910) 533-2229 or (866) EAT-PECANS

Wallace/Duplin County

Art of Hope

Artist Hope Smith displays and sells her paintings, prints, and small pieces of artfully painted furniture and also holds private art classes for small groups. Custom framing is offered, too. 107 S. Teachey Rd., Wallace, NC 28466. Open most weekdays; call before visiting. (910) 285-4940; www.hopegsmith.com

Lake Leamon Campground

Sites with power hookups are available, as are more rustic sites suitable for primitive camping. Swimming, paddleboats, and canoes are among the attractions. 5357 NC Hwy 41 S., Wallace, NC 28466. Open daily; the swimming area is open 10 A.M.–6 P.M. Sites with full RV hookups are $20; primitive sites and tent sites with power and water are $5 per person. Fees are charged for swimming, fishing, and Jet Ski rentals. (910) 284-2785

The Mustard Seed

The Mustard Seed

This garden café features soups, sandwiches, and pastas in a unique setting. Hand-painted murals decorate the walls. The gift shop is filled with handmade items from local artisans. 127 W. Main St., Wallace, NC 28466. Café, Mon.–Sat., 11 A.M.–2:30 P.M.; gift shop, Mon.–Sat., 10 A.M.–4 P.M. (910) 285-8375; bettysurf@hotmail.com

Stone Leaf Café

The restaurant is located in a building listed on the National Register of Historic Landmarks. Chef John Tyler Fussell handpicks fresh produce and seafood weekly from local providers. 110 W. Main St., Wallace, NC 28466. Tues.–Sat., 11 A.M.–3 P.M. and 5 P.M.–closing; Sun., 10 A.M.–3 P.M. (910) 285-8600; stoneleafcafe@earthlink.net

Warsaw/Duplin County

The Country Squire Restaurant and Winery

The Country Squire Restaurant and Winery

Since 1961, this restaurant has offered a unique style of Old English candlelight dining. The menu features continental selections of pork, poultry, and vegetables. Steak and seafood are the specialties. 748 NC Hwy 24/50, Warsaw, NC 28398. Sun.–Fri., 11:30 A.M.–2 P.M. and 5:30–10 P.M.; Sat., 5:30–11 P.M. (910) 296-1727 or (877) 830-1602; www.countrysquireinn.com

Gary's Pottery

Here, you'll find a large variety of poured concrete yard ornaments, ironwork, woodcrafts, and even low-cost headstones. 1245 Carrolls Rd., Warsaw, NC 28398. (910) 293-9900; www.garyspottery.com

L. P. Best House/Warsaw Veterans' Museum

This restored 1894 Queen Anne–style house is the home of Duplin County's veterans' museum. Exhibited in different rooms are photos, artifacts, military displays, uniforms, and other memorabilia donated by veterans. 119 E. Hill St., Warsaw, NC 28398. Thurs.–Fri., 1–5 P.M.; Sat., 2–4 P.M. (910) 293-2190; www.duplintourism.org/tourism_info.htm

Sheffield's Daylily Garden

This lovely and lavish garden is perhaps the largest daylily garden in southeastern North Carolina. Around 2,000 varieties produce a rainbow of petals. Stop by and enjoy this colorful setting. 162 E. Meadowbrook Ln., Warsaw, NC 28398. Mon.–Sat., 9 A.M.–7 P.M.; Sun., 2–6 P.M. Free. (910) 293-4615

Gary's Pottery

Willard/Pender County

Penderlea Homestead Museum, Inc.

Penderlea Homestead Museum, Inc.

The Penderlea Homestead Museum tells the story of the federal government's attempt to help people build self-sufficient communities during the Great Depression. Under the arrangement, Penderlea residents leased their homes from the government for $60 a year. In the 1940s, they began buying their houses. About 100 of the original 300 homes remain. You'll find photographs, documents, furnishings, and artifacts, all dating to around 1934. 284 Garden Rd., Willard, NC 28478. Sat., 1–4 P.M., and by appointment. Admission fee. (910) 285-3490;www.penderleahomesteadmuseum.org

Creeks, Cooking, and Culture

Greene, Jones, Lenoir, and Wayne Counties

The slow, strong current of rural life flows throughout this trail. You'll find it in a field full of cattle or an antique tractor museum. You'll see its quirky side at a pickle festival. You'll be calmed by the rhythm of paddling on an ancient creek or amused by a hike where whiskey stills were once federally operated.

Capture this trail's essence in its hearty cuisine—tender buttermilk biscuits made fresh each morning at a local diner, a plate of succulent pork barbecue, or a golden orange sweet potato dripping rich juices and melting butter. Greens and beans and corn arrive fresh

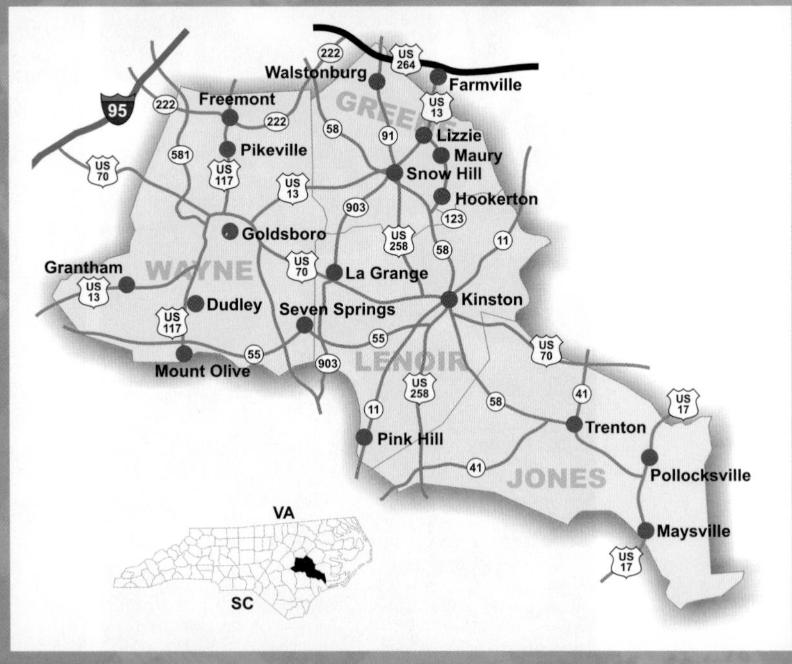

Baskets by local artists at Greene County Museum
Greene County Musuem (p. 148)

in season from local growers to small diners and unique restaurants where food nourishes more than the body.

Rural at its core, "Creeks, Cooking, and Culture" highlights the icons cherished in country life, but often with a twist. Hunting includes traditional English foxhunts. You'll find quilters and chainsaw sculptors, as well as model ship builders and internationally acclaimed seascape painters. A wooded setting reveals a rustic gift shop full of fine gold and silver jewelry alongside other handcrafted items from around the globe. Nationally known jazz artists play on the same stage as country fiddlers.

This trail has the recipe for the best stew of the necessary, the beautiful, and the just plain fun. Plan your visit today by reading the following town-by-town descriptions of the unique attractions that make up the "Creeks, Cooking, and Culture" trail.

Dudley/Wayne County

Teri-Jim's Christmas Trees

Grady's Barbecue

This joint really cooks. Its hot pit-cooked barbecue and short orders have packed locals and visitors in for nearly 20 years. 3096 Arrington Bridge Rd., Dudley, NC 28333. Mon.–Fri., 5:30 A.M.–2 P.M.; Sat., 5:30 A.M.–6 P.M. (919) 735-7243

Teri-Jim's Christmas Trees

Find just the right tree to put the presents under. Teri-Jim's also has a large selection of Christmas accessories and wreaths. 350 Ruskin Rd., Dudley, NC 28333. Thanksgiving–Christmas Eve, 9 A.M.–dusk. (919) 735-8140

Charles B. Aycock Birthplace

Fremont/Wayne County

Charles B. Aycock Birthplace

Elected in 1900, Charles B. Aycock is remembered as "the education governor" because of his many efforts to revitalize education in the state. The site features the Aycock home (circa 1846), outbuildings, and a newly relocated 1893 schoolhouse. All are fine examples of rural life around the turn of the last century. 264 Governor Aycock Rd., Fremont, NC 27830. Apr.–Sept., Mon.–Sat., 9 A.M.–5 P.M.; Sun., 1–5 P.M.; Nov.–March, Tues.–Sat., 10 A.M.–4 P.M.; Sun., 1–4 P.M. (919) 242-5581; www.nchistoricsites.org/aycock

Daffodil Festival *Wayne County Travel & Tourism*

Daffodil Festival

This annual festival coincides with the blooming of thousands of colorful daffodils. Events include the arts-and-crafts show and sale, horse-drawn trolley rides, tours of the Fremont Heritage Museum, and a daffodil exhibit. 120 Main

St., Fremont, NC 27830. Held the last Sat. in March, 10 A.M.–5 P.M. Free. (919) 242-5151; kpeeden@ncisp.net

Fremont Heritage Museum

Exhibits and displays tell the story of rural life during the 1800s and 1900s in Fremont, formerly named Nahunta. The town honors S. L. Fremont, an early chief engineer of the Wilmington-Weldon Railroad. 112 E. Main St., Fremont, NC 27830. Sun., 2–5 P.M. (919) 242-5319

Alton's Barbecue *Wayne County Travel & Tourism*

Goldsboro/Wayne County

Alton's Barbecue

In addition to locally renowned 'cue and its accompanying sauce, Alton's serves Brunswick stew and banana pudding. Diners enjoy the locally painted tobacco pictures and farm scenes on the walls. The owners use locally grown vegetables. 257 Combs Rd., Goldsboro, NC 27530. Thurs.–Sat., 7 A.M.–8:30 P.M. (919) 734-4332

Annual Eastern Carolina Regional Horse Festival

Annual Eastern Carolina Regional Horse Festival

For all things equine, this festival is hard to beat! Presenters and clinicians cover animal health, equipment and products, barn safety, body-condition scoring, and hunter gymnastics. Then there's hunt seat equitation, showmanship, stock seat equitation, and trail clinics for youths and amateurs. Wayne Regional Fairgrounds, Goldsboro, NC 27533. Held in March. (919) 731-1525; eileen_coite@ncsu.edu

Arts Council & Gallery of Wayne County *Wayne County Travel & Tourism*

Arts Council & Gallery of Wayne County

This vital organization exhibits the art of local artists and offers many programs to introduce children to the arts. It also has art studios, a children's studio and gallery, and restored gardens. 2406 E. Ash St., Goldsboro, NC 27534. Mon.–Fri., 9 A.M.–5 P.M. Free. (919) 736-3300; www.artsinwayne.org

Benjamin Gufford Pottery

The potter reinterprets masterworks of the abstract impressionist period by adding textural surfaces to altered forms, using the raku method of glazing and firing. Stop by for a visit or demonstration. 171 Charlie Braswell Rd., Goldsboro, NC 27530. Open by appointment; summer, Mon.–Sat., 8 A.M.–7 P.M.; fall–spring, Mon.–Fri., 5–9 P.M.; Sat.–Sun., 8 A.M.–7 P.M. (919) 735-1130; benjamingufford.freeservers.com

Berry Towne Crafts

You'll find wonderful handmade crafts on the campus of the O'Berry Center, a cluster of group homes serving people with physical and mental challenges. Participants benefit from developing skills, and customers enjoy crafts including By Nature Soap, pottery, dried flowers, and textiles. 400 Old Smithfield Rd., Goldsboro, NC 27530. Mon.–Fri., 9 A.M.–4 P.M. (919) 581-4073; www.berrytownecrafts.com

Central Lunch

Treat yourself to Southern home-style cooking—including tender, homemade buttermilk biscuits—at one of the last real diners in town. 103 N. Center St., Goldsboro, NC 27530. Mon.–Fri., 6 A.M.–3 P.M. (919) 735-7979

DC Western

Need a saddle . . . or just want to look at some beautiful leatherwork? You'll find it here, at one of the largest saddle shops east of the Mississippi. 1968 Rosewood Rd., Goldsboro, NC 27530. (888) 735-2313

Elroy Farms

Elroy Farms has pick-you-own and fresh strawberries, as well as tomatoes, beans, melons, pumpkins, and corn. In the fall, you'll find beautiful mums and big pumpkins for sale. Come back just before the holidays and pick out a Christmas tree! 170 Woodpeck Rd., Goldsboro, NC 27534.

Mon.–Sat., 8 A.M.–6 P.M.; Sun., 1–6 P.M. (919) 778-6303

McCall's BBQ & Seafood

Locals come here for the great food, the great service, and a view that includes a landing field at Seymour Johnson Air Force Base. Try the banana pudding. 139 Millers Chapel Rd., Goldsboro, NC 27534. Open daily, 11 A.M.–9 P.M. (919) 751-0072

Narrated Historic Horse-Drawn Trolley Tours

Enjoy the historic sites of downtown Goldsboro via a horse-drawn trolley accompanied by a narrator. The tour includes wonderful architecture. 218 E. Walnut St., Goldsboro, NC 27533. Tours are usually scheduled for one Sun. each in Apr., Sept., Oct., and Nov. The cost is $30 per person. (919) 735-4959; www.dgdc.org

Narrated Historic Horse-Drawn Trolley Tours
Wayne County Travel & Tourism

Plum Tree Gardens B&B

What was once the intimate and gracious Daniels-Stenhouse home now operates as a four-room B&B. The original exterior of the 1888 Victorian gem includes a wraparound porch, a copper roof, wood siding painted gray with violet, and copper and ivory trim. 109 S. George St., Goldsboro, NC 27530. (919) 736-9412 or (919) 736-3356; www.plumtreegardens.com

Stomp Johnson's Produce Market

Take home prepicked cabbages, onions, potatoes, corn, beans, cucumbers, tomatoes, peas, and collards. Don't forget some prepicked (or pick-your-own) strawberries for dessert. Flower and vegetable plants and hanging baskets are available, too! 3226 US Hwy 13 N., Goldsboro, NC 27534. Apr. 21–Nov. 24, Mon.–Sat., 8 A.M.–5 P.M. (919) 738-2685

Stomp Johnson's Produce Market

Wayne Regional Agricultural Fair *Wayne County Travel & Tourism*

Wayne Regional Agricultural Fair

One of the bigger regional fall fairs in eastern North Carolina promises fun for the whole family, plus, as always, a tribute to agriculture. PO Box 1100, Goldsboro, NC 27533. Held late Sept.–early Oct. Admission fee. (919) 635-7277; www.waynefair.com

Waynesboro Historical Village

Experience barrel hoop racing, sack racing, checkers, hopscotch, horseshoes, tug of war, and other games enjoyed by children and adults in the 19th century. This annual event also features period music, Civil War cannon fire, and raids on the village. 801 US Hwy 117 S., Goldsboro, NC 27533. Held one weekend in July. (919) 731-1653; www.waynesboroughhistoricalvillage.com

Waynesboro Historical Village *Wayne County Travel & Tourism*

Wilber's BBQ & Restaurant

If you see a parking lot crammed with cars, it must be breakfast time, the lunch hour, or dinnertime at this local bastion of 'cue and other Southern victuals. 4172 US Hwy 70 E., Goldsboro, NC 27530. Open daily, 6 A.M.–10 P.M. (919) 778-5218

Hookerton/Greene County

Quail Ridge Preserve

Quail, pheasant, dove, chukar, and deer abound in over 500 acres of superb forest and cleared land at this preserve. There's also a skeet range. Lodging and meals are available for up to four guests at a time. 784 Morris BBQ Rd., Hookerton, NC 28538. Oct.–March, Mon.–Sat.; also open for dove season. (252) 747-5210

Quail Ridge Preserve *N.C. Wildlife Resources Commission*

Kinston/Lenoir County

The Arts Center

Approximately 500 artists show their work here each year. Works in all media are available for sale, as are a variety of handcrafted items in the Arts Center Gift Shop. 400 N. Queen St., Kinston, NC 28502. Tues.–Fri., 10 A.M.–6 P.M.; Sat., 10 A.M.–2 P.M. Free. (252) 527-2517; www.kinstoncca.com

Caswell No. 1 Fire Station Museum

Barnet Park Disc Golf Course

It's like golf . . . in the woods . . . with your hands. It's disc golf! The course features 18 holes with a par of 66. Using the short tees, the course is 4,383 feet. Sand Clay Rd., Kinston, NC 28504. Open during daylight hours. Free. (252) 939-3332

Caswell Center Museum and Visitor Center

The 1800s Stroud House became the Caswell Center in 1911; it was the first facility to serve mentally disabled patients in North Carolina. Today, it's a museum focusing on the early years of the facility. 2415 W. Vernon Ave., Kinston, NC 28504. Mon.–Fri., 8 A.M.–5 P.M. Free. (252) 208-3780; www.caswellcenter.org

Caswell No. 1 Fire Station Museum

Get a glimpse of what it was like to fight fires in bygone days. You'll see a 1922 American LaFrance pumper, along with a collection of helmets, nozzles, ladders, fire extinguishers, and other memorabilia spanning 100 years. 118 S. Queen St., Kinston, NC 28504. Tues., Thurs., and Sat., 10 A.M.–4 P.M. Free. (252) 522-4676

CSS *Neuse* State Historic Site
N.C. Division of State Historic Sites

CSS *Neuse* State Historic Site/ Richard Caswell Memorial

The CSS *Neuse* was one of 22 ironclads commissioned by the Confederate navy. When Union troops occupied Kinston in March 1865, the ship was burned and sunk by its crew. At the ship's raising in 1963, its nearly 15,000 artifacts comprised one of the largest collections ever discovered aboard a Confederate naval vessel. A portion of the collection is on display in the visitor center, along with the skeleton of the original ship. The site also honors Kinston resident Richard Caswell, the state's first elected governor. 2612 W. Vernon Ave. (US Hwy 70 Bus.), Kinston, NC 28504. Mon.–Sat., 10 A.M.–5 P.M. Free. (252) 522-2091; www.cssneuse.nchistoricsites.org

Cultural Heritage Museum

Located in the renovated Peoples Bank, a 1924 two-story brick-veneer building in the Classical Revival style, the museum has three distinct themes: United States colored troops in the Civil War, African-Americans in military service, and local African-American heroes. 242 S. Queen St., Kinston, NC 28502. (866) 324-5339

Festival on the Neuse

The aroma of spicy pork draws visitors to the big barbecue contest, where the competition is as hot as the meat. Try homemade ice cream, funnel cakes, and other favorites. Live music, a street dance, children's rides, vendors, an art tent, an amateur dog show, a car show, and the annual duck race round out the events. Kinston, NC 28502. Held one weekend in late Apr. (252) 523-2500; www.festivalontheneuse.com

Grainger-Hill Performing Arts Center

This renovated gem is home to premier dramas, pageants, performances by the North Carolina Symphony, and more. The building is one of the best examples of Classical Revival architecture in North Carolina. 300 Park Ave., Kinston, NC 28502. (252) 527-1131; www.ghpac.com

Harmony Hall

Harmony Hall

First owned by Richard Caswell, the state's first elected governor, Harmony Hall later served as a hospital during the Civil War. Today, it is as majestic as ever. The house was remodeled around 1790 and again in 1835; the most recent restoration was completed in 1984. 109 E. King St., Kinston, NC 28501. Mon. and Wed., 10 A.M.–1 P.M.; Fri., 10 A.M.–12:30 P.M. Free. (252) 522-0421; www.lenoircountyhistorical.com

King's Restaurant

King's Restaurant

A local favorite since 1936, King's is well known for its barbecue, chicken, and seafood. You can also buy King's special barbecue sauce, seafood breading mix, biscuit mix, grits, and hushpuppy mix. 405 E. New Bern Rd., Kinston, NC 28504. Mon.–Fri., 10:30 A.M.–9 P.M.; Sat.–Sun., 7 A.M.–9 P.M.; closed Christmas. (252) 527-2101

Kinston Area Railroad Modelers Association

See the trains, the scenery, and the setup that have taken hundreds of hours to create. Thomas the Tank Engine is here, too! It's all in the basement of the Arts Center. 400 N. Queen St., Kinston, NC 28502. Sat., 10 A.M.–2 P.M.; the model trains run the first and fourth Sat. of each month, 11 A.M.–2 P.M. Free. (252) 527-2517; www.kinstoncca.com/community.htm

Kinston Winter Bluegrass Festival

This annual event brightens up a winter weekend with lively music. Past performers have included the Lonesome River Band, Mountain Heart, Mac Wiseman, and many more. Lenoir Community College Gym, US Hwy 70 E., Kinston, NC 28501. Held the third weekend in Feb. (252) 522-1066 or (252) 559-0778; www.kinstonwinterbluegrass.com

Monthly Eastern NC Bluegrass Association Show

This show has been featuring great bluegrass fun since 1982. King's Restaurant hosts a preshow of the three-band lineup, and

there's often room for jammers! Lenoir Community College, Kinston, NC 28501. Held the second Sat. of each month; the doors open at 6 P.M. Admission fee. (252) 522-1066; www.encbluegrass.freeservers.com

Neuseway Planetarium, Health & Science Museum

Neuseway Nature Park & Planetarium/Health & Science Museum

At the nature park, check out the native and non-native animals. You'll also enjoy the interactive health and science museum and the planetarium, with its 32-foot dome and its projector that displays stars, constellations, and video shows. 401 W. Caswell St., Kinston, NC 28504. Tues.–Sat., 9:30 A.M.–5 P.M.; Sun., 1–5 P.M. Admission fee for individuals; group rates apply. (252) 939-3367

Noble's Tree Farm

Here's a great place to select your Christmas tree. White pines, Virginia pines, and red cedars are available. Preselect your tree by the Saturday before Thanksgiving. 1919 Winter Forest Dr., Kinston, NC 28504. Nov. 27–Dec. 22, Sun.–Fri., 1–5 P.M.; Sat., 9 A.M.–5 P.M. (252) 523-9421

Unique Boutique

This giant shopping bazaar features handmade jewelry, paintings, pottery, baskets, handbags, and lots more. Clothing and food vendors also participate. 400 Queen St., Kinston, NC 28501. Held one day in Sept. (252) 527-2517

LaGrange/Lenoir County

Garden Spot Festival

This festival starts off with a street dance on Friday night. Saturday brings more live music, dancing, rides, games, a Rotary Club auction, a charity softball game, vendors, and fireworks. Downtown LaGrange, NC 28551. Held the second weekend in Sept. Free. (252) 566-9691; tinsurance@earthlink.net

Lizzie/Greene County

Greene County Hounds

The owners stage a mounted hunt following the protocol and traditions of a typical English foxhunt. The small, private foxhunting pack is mostly crossbred and English. Visitors are welcome, but hunting is by permission of the huntsman. Shades of England! 922 Friendship Church Rd., Lizzie, NC 27828. Held Nov.–March. (252) 753-4931; jcoop@esn.net

Maury/Greene County

Maury Supply

One trip to this practical yet fun place will get you just about everything you need for your day's activities, including fishing tackle and bait, snacks and sodas, beer, penny candy, rubber boots, rain gear, paint and hardware, plumbing supplies, fertilizer and farm chemicals, hunting licenses, and burning permits. Hwy 123 and Hwy 903, Maury, NC 28554. Mon.–Fri., 6 A.M.–6 P.M.; Sat., 6:30 A.M.–1:30 P.M. (252) 747-7490

Garden Spot Festival

Mount Olive/Wayne County

Holly Grove Farms

Holly Grove Farms makes specialty goat cheeses right on the farm, where the farmers hand-raise their goats. 1183 Grantham School Rd., Mount Olive, NC 28365. (919) 689-2031; www.hollygrovecheese.com

Mt. Olive Pickle Company Gift Shop

Here at the gift shop of the regionally famous pickle maker, you'll find pickle T-shirts, golf putters, Christmas tree ornaments, and lots of other unique items. Corner of Cucumber and Vine, Mount Olive, NC 28365. Mon.–Fri., 8 A.M.–5 P.M. (919) 658-2535 or (800) 672-5041; www.mtolivepickles.com

North Carolina Pickle Festival

This "dilly" of a festival celebrates pickles with three days

North Carolina Pickle Festival *Wayne County Travel & Tourism* (p. 143)

of rides, a golf classic, a photo contest, classic cars, games, and food for every taste (just as long as it can be garnished with a pickle). 123 N. Center St., Mount Olive, NC 28365. Held the last weekend of Apr. (919) 658-3113; www.ncpicklefest.org

Pikeville/Wayne County

Nahunta Farm Sausage Store

Check out one of the largest displays of pork products in the nation. You'll find custom-ordered sausages, cured hams, and other fresh pork cuts produced from locally grown hogs. Nahunta Farm Rd., Pikeville, NC 27863. Mon.–Sat., 8 A.M.–5 P.M. (919) 242-4852

Northern Wayne Heritage Museum/North Carolina Cotton Museum

Visitors can explore this large collection of artifacts, photographs, and printed materials documenting the life of cotton farmers. Mill St., Pikeville, NC 27863. Tues.–Fri. and Sun., 1–5 P.M. (919) 242-2166

A Secret Garden Winery

This winery features all-natural muscadine and fruit wines handcrafted the old way, using no chemicals or added sulfites—only fruit, sugar, and water. 1008 Airport Rd., Pikeville, NC 27863. Thurs.–Sat., 9 A.M.–6 P.M.; Sun., 1–6 P.M. (919) 734-0260; www.asecretgardenwinery.com

Northern Wayne Heritage Museum *Wayne County Travel & Tourism*

Pink Hill/Lenoir County

Tyndall Tractor Museum

Pink Hill's very own Wilbur Tyndall presents the history of the John Deere tractor and of farming in Lenoir County, bringing the past to life. 409 N. Front St., Pink Hill, NC 28501. Open by appointment. Free. (252) 568-6261 or (252) 568-3261

Pollocksville/Jones County

Tyndall Tractor Museum

Country Dreams B&B

In addition to comfortable accommodations, this B&B boasts a crafts shop where local crafters and artists display and sell stained glass, quilts, and other creations. 362 Lee's Chapel Rd., Pollocksville, NC 28573. Crafts shop, Mon.–Sat., 9 A.M.–6 P.M. (910) 221-7494; www.countrydreamsnc.com

Foscue Plantation House

Foscue Plantation House

Two centuries ago, Foscue Plantation sprawled over 10,000 acres. During the Civil War, it served as a hospital for Union troops. Today, the 200-year-old building, which still retains some of its original furnishings, is open for public viewing. 7509 US Hwy 17 N., Pollocksville, NC 28573. Thurs., 10 A.M.–4 P.M., and by appointment. (910) 743-5531 or (252) 224-9881; carolfoy@earthlink.net

Moore's Hide-a-way Cottage

Escape the bustle of everyday life at this romantic little cabin on a 60-acre farm with horse trails beside the beautiful Trent River. The cottage sleeps four and has two baths. 8541 US Hwy 17, Pollocksville, NC 28573. (252) 670-3040 or (252) 224-4281; www.co.jones.nc.us/recreation.htm

Parker Produce

During strawberry season, you can pick lots of juicy, ripe berries for all those spring-fresh desserts. Try not to eat them all before you get back to the car! 903 Goshen Rd., Pollocksville, NC 28573. Apr.–early June, Mon.–Fri., noon–5 P.M.; Sat., 10 A.M.–1 P.M. (252) 224-0010

Moore's Hide-a-way Cottage

Pollocksville Town Hall

This 1893 Atlantic Coastline train station on the banks of the Trent River was given

Pollocksville Town Hall (p. 145)

to the town in 1993. The old waiting rooms have been renovated for office space, and the building is open to the public. 103 Main St., Pollocksville, NC 28573. Mon.–Fri., 9 A.M.–4 P.M. (252) 224-9831; www.co.jones.nc.us/PollockA.htm

Seven Springs/Wayne County

Mae's Restaurant

Delicious, spicy beef and chicken and popular Southern dishes make this restaurant a favorite among locals and visitors alike. 300 Main St., Seven Springs, NC 28578. Mon. and Thurs.–Sat., 6 A.M.–2 P.M.; Tues.–Wed., 5–8 P.M. (252) 569-1779

Seven Springs Restaurant

Seven Springs Restaurant

Although the restaurant is famous for its delicious, locally grown collards, turnip greens, and okra served up family-style, there's music in the air, too. Gospel, country, and bluegrass are featured on Thursday nights. 400 Main St., Seven Springs, NC 28578. Sun.–Wed., 5 A.M.–2 P.M.; Thurs.–Sat., 5 A.M.–8 P.M. (252) 569-1521

WorkArts Chainsaw Sculptor

WorkArts Chainsaw Sculptor

Jeff Lee says he likes to let the chips fall where they may . . . and they fall everywhere when this creative chain-saw artist gets to work! Sometimes, he even creates chain-saw art from damaged trees for yards and gardens. Jeff sells his own creations and works on commission, too. 8028 Hwy 55 W., Seven Springs, NC 28578. (252) 569-8261; www.workarts.com/index.htm

Snow Hill/Greene County

Benjamin W. Best Country Inn & Carriage House

Built in 1850 by Benjamin Williams Best, a prominent farmer in Greene County, this historic Greek Revival structure was moved to its present location on this working farm in 1998. 2193 Mewborn Church Rd., Snow Hill, NC 28580. (252) 747-5054 or (866) 633-0229

Contentnea Creek Paddle Trails

Native Americans of the Tuscarora tribe named this creek Contentnea, meaning "as fish go by." The Greene County section of this ancient creek trail meanders through nearly 50 miles of farmland and undeveloped creek-side land. There are five sections especially recommended for paddling. Snow Hill, NC 28580. (252) 258-0916

Contentnea Creek Shooting Preserve

This preserve is ideally situated in one of North Carolina's best bird habitats. It features professional guides, fine dogs, and an abundance of game, including quail, pheasant, duck, and deer. 450 Gray Rd., Snow Hill, NC 28580. Oct.–March, Mon.–Sat., and by appointment. (252) 747-5982; www.contentneacreekhunting.com

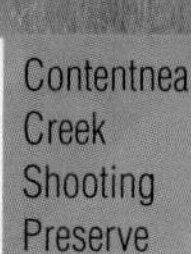

Contentnea Creek Shooting Preserve

Corbett Town Hunting Preserve

Few hunters leave this place empty-handed because the owners have taken steps to ensure high concentrations of game on their land. You'll find pheasant, chukar, quail, and dove. Deer are plentiful, too. 884 Corbett Town Rd., Snow Hill, NC 28580. (252) 747-3630

Dail Family Farms

Dail Family Farms

This farm sells tomatoes, sweet corn, melons, potatoes, peas, okra, butter beans, and other healthy and full-of-flavor vegetables, freshly picked and ready for you to enjoy. Don't forget a fresh-cut bouquet. Or you can pick your own blooms to dress up the table. 336 Pridgen Rd. (Hwy 258 S.), Snow Hill, NC 28580. Mon.–Sat., 8 A.M.–6 P.M. (252) 560-8315; dailfamilyfarm@aol.com

Greene County Museum

At this museum, you can learn about the unique cultural and historical heritage of Greene County and, if you've got local kin, do some genealogical research while you're here. There are also displays of art by local artists and students and a gift shop featuring many locally inspired items. 107 N.W. Third St., Snow Hill, NC 28580. Tues.–Fri., 10 A.M.–5 P.M.; Sat., 10 A.M.–1 P.M. Free. (252) 747-1999; www.rootsweb.com/~ncgcgrr/

Greene County Museum

Johnson Marsh Hunting Preserve & Bird Dog Training Facility

The preserve has a five-stand clay-target range and offers guided and unguided quail, pheasant, and chukar partridge hunting. Its lodge features fine dining. 1329 Jesse Hill Rd., Snow Hill, NC 28580. Oct.–March, Mon.–Sat. (252) 747-8657 or (800) 378-7299; www.johnson-marsh.com

La Flama

Snow Hill's first Mexican restaurant serves lunch and dinner . . . and you may even see a mariachi band. Enjoy the wall murals, painted by a local artist, as you feast on a variety of Mexican dishes, including choices for vegetarians and children. 111 S.E. Second St., Snow Hill, NC 28580. Mon.–Sat., 11 A.M.–9 P.M. (252) 747-4333

Moody Farm

This small, family-owned farm has gourds, gourd art, and gourd birdhouses for sale. Gourd types include bushel, martin, bottle, mini, ornamental, canteen, and dipper. They're usually ready for harvest after the first frost each fall. 690 Jesse Hill Rd., Snow Hill, NC 28580. Open by appointment. (252) 747-1132; www.moodyfarm.com

Panache Mosaics

Kim Barrow's mosaics are inspired by nature and her family's farm. Her works include stained glass, vitreous glass, and pique assiette. Her substrates are as varied as wedi, hardibacker, old window frames, terra cotta, bowling balls, and even concrete! 4084 Hull Rd., Snow Hill, NC 28580. Open by appointment. (252) 747-7317; home.earthlink.net/~panachemosaics/

Johnson Marsh Hunting Preserve *N.C. Wildlife Resources Commission*

Rainbow Meadow Farms

The farmers sell pasture-raised organic lamb and pork, as well as free-range chicken, eggs, turkey, duck, pheasant, and rabbit. 3181 Grays Mill Rd., Snow Hill, NC 28580. Open by appointment. (252) 523-0298; www.rainbowmeadowfarms.com

Ribeyes Steakhouse

Owner Calvin Watson serves up Omaha rib-eye steaks, chicken breasts, and shrimp and stocks his salad bar with locally grown produce. Diners can also choose a locally grown baked sweet potato to go with their meal. 1012 Kingold Blvd., Snow Hill, NC 28580. Tues.–Sun., 5–10 P.M. (252) 747-7006

Rosenwald Center for Cultural Enrichment, Inc.

Thousands of white frame Rosenwald schools, named after philanthropist Julius Rosenwald, once dotted the landscape of the South. By 1928, one in every five rural schools for black students in the South was a Rosenwald school. Today, the Rosenwald Center works to preserve and reuse Rosenwald schools as centers for community activities. Greene County has six such sites. 108 Kingold Blvd., Snow Hill, NC 28580. Mon.–Fri., noon–5 P.M.; Sat., by appointment. Free. (252) 747-4912 or (252) 560-6221

Snow Hill Hardware

If you're traveling with kids, be sure to let them experience the friendly smiles and personal attention of this downtown Snow Hill delight. Owner Terry Thomas has just about anything you can imagine, from paint to livestock feed. You can pick up some fishing tackle and bait, walk a block to the creek, and drop your line. 119 S.E. Second St., Snow Hill, NC 28580. Mon.–Fri., 7:30 A.M.–5 P.M.; Sat., 7:30 A.M.–noon. (252) 747-3811

Stoney Creek Hunting Preserve

Stoney Creek Hunting Preserve
N.C. Wildlife Resources Commission

This preserve stages specialized hunts such as a season-opening dove hunt. You'll find a variety of packages including dove, chukar, deer, duck, pheasant, and quail hunts. 1273 Lloyd Harrison Rd., Snow Hill, NC 28580. Oct.–March, Mon.–Sat. (252) 747-8463 or (252) 560-1151; www.stoneycreekonline.net

Strickland-Dail Dining and Catering

This popular country buffet owes its beginnings to a backyard pool house in Farmville. When the original restaurant burned, the business relocated to Snow Hill. Today, it features the great recipes of Greene County prepared with locally produced food, just like before. Be sure and save room for the heavenly desserts! 416 Kingold Blvd., Snow Hill, NC 28580. Tues.–Wed., 11 A.M.–2:30 P.M. and 4–7:30 P.M.; Thurs.–Fri., 11 A.M.–2:30 P.M. and 4–8:30 P.M. (252) 753-4550

Sugg Farms & Produce

Nothing beats a fresh, juicy watermelon on a hot summer day—and Sugg Farms has some of the biggest around. In March, Sugg starts the melons in the greenhouses from its own seed. Around the first of May, it moves the small plants to the field, where the vines grow and run until harvest time in July and August. 4948 Hwy 58 S., Snow Hill, NC 28580. Harvest season, 8 A.M.–5 P.M., or by appointment. (252) 747-5737

Trenton/Jones County

Annual Community Auction

This eagerly anticipated event showcases farm equipment, vehicles, tools, antiques, general merchandise, and occasional "junk"! There's also a flea market on the grounds and lots of down-home barbecue and chicken. American Legion Grounds, S. King St. Ext., Snow Hill, NC 28580. Held the second Sat. in Jan., 8:30 A.M.–5 P.M. (252) 448-3481; www.co.jones.nc.us/Trenton.htm

Zaks

This surprising find offers beautiful, handmade gold and silver jewelry in a highly rustic setting. Other gifts imported from around the world are also on display. You might even see some wildlife wandering around the property! 1552 Ten Mile Fork Rd., Trenton, NC 28585. Sat., 10 A.M.–5 P.M. (252) 448-1920

Walstonburg/Greene County

Jones Fruit Farm

Stop by for fresh fruit and produce that you can pick yourself or buy prepicked. Strawberries are available from April through June; peaches from June through August; cantaloupes and peaches from July through August; cabbages in May; and blueberries from June through July. 7094 Beaman Old Creek Rd., Walstonburg, NC 27888. Mid-Apr.–Aug., Mon.–Sat., 8 A.M.–6 P.M.; Sun., 2–6 P.M. (252) 747-3989

Relyea's Produce Patch & Crazy Prawns

Fresh peas, butter beans, tomatoes, squash, sweet corn, melons, and other tender, juicy vegetables and fruits are sold here. Relyea's also has shelled peas and butter beans, along with homemade jams, jellies, pickles, and prawns in season. 831 Meadow Rd., Walstonburg, NC 27888. Mon.–Fri., 7 A.M.–6 P.M.; Sat., 7 A.M.–1 P.M. (252) 753-3227; nrelyea@geeksnet.com

Soggy Bottom Hunting Preserve

This preserve in the heart of North Carolina hunting country features acres of cropland, forests, swamps, and creeks that attract enough fowl to delight any hunter. Birds include quail, pheasant, chukar, and duck. The deer are abundant, too! 930 Meadow Rd., Walstonburg, NC 27888. (252) 413-9851 or (252) 753-5620

Cliffs of the Neuse State Park
N.C. Division of Parks and Recreation

Lights . . . Waves . . . Action!

Brunswick, Columbus, and New Hanover Counties

Trip the lights fantastic along this trail. You'll think you're on the set of a movie (and you could be, given the area's impressive film and TV production capabilities) because the views are so breathtaking: ocean sunsets, picturesque lighthouses, sun-dappled pathways under graceful live oaks, fragrant fields of flowers and herbs, and even some planetarium stargazing.

Savor a succulent seafood dinner on a romantic riverboat. Get a new perspective from a battleship's bridge. Tackle the waves straight from the beach, or contemplate the ripples in an arboretum pond. Pack a picnic basket full of road-stand goodies: ripe, juicy berries, fresh herb-infused cheeses, a luscious tomato sandwich, and a bottle

Silver Coast Winery tasting bar *Silver Coast Winery* (p. 161)

of sparkling local wine. Now paddle down a black-water creek for a lunch you won't forget!

Looking for action? Pick your type, laid-back or lively. Stop in at a nursery and plant your own salad bowl, complete with herbs and edible flowers. Take in a concert at elegant Thalian Hall. Witness a "NASPig" race (you did a double-take on that one, didn't you?). Feel the cool fall breeze from a hayride around the farm. Stomp your feet and make wine, or clog a double-toe step at a bluegrass festival. In fact, the festivals on this trail cover the map in food, fun, agriculture, and art. Take in the EUE Screen Gems studio, the largest movie and television production facility east of California. Celebrate everything from azalea blossoms, strawberries, oysters, watermelon, and yams to jazz, blues, films, and American Indian culture. You get the picture!

Read on for town-by-town descriptions of the unique attractions that make up the "Lights . . . Waves . . . Action!" trail and plan your trip today.

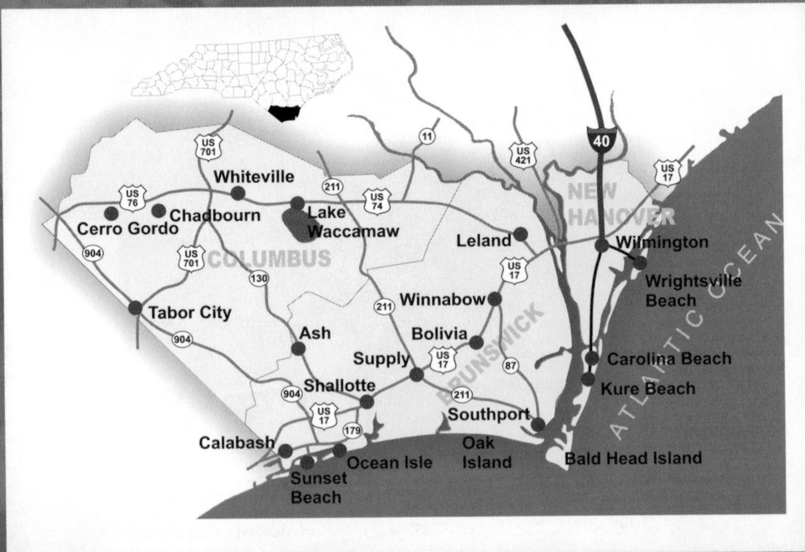

Bolivia/Brunswick County

Faircloth Exotic Animal Zoo

This private zoo has Siberian tigers, African lions, bears, buffalo, New Guinea singing dogs, wolves, and a wide variety of exotic chickens, peacocks, and pheasants. There are Zebu cows, Texas longhorns, Scottish Highland bulls, Watusi cows, ducks, geese, horses, and donkeys. Children and adults can feed lambs and goats in the petting zoo. 544 McKay Rd., Bolivia, NC 28461. Open daily, 10 A.M.–dusk. The cost is $6 for adults and $4 for children. (910) 253-6820

Roans Branch Hunting Preserve

The preserve specializes in quail, pheasant, and chukar (Indian partridge) hunting. It offers licensed fishing guides, a skeet range, and campsites with RV hookups. 4288 US Hwy 17 Bus. E., Bolivia, NC 28461. Oct.–March, Mon.–Sat. (910) 253-4785; www.roansbranch.com

Bolton/Columbus County

Waccamaw-Siouan Powwow

"The People of the Fallen Star" have an autumn powwow with a traditional march and dance on sacred ground in honor of elders and heroes. The festivities include competitions in dance, music, drums, and song. Beautiful handmade regalia with striking intricate beadwork is worn for these ceremonies. Native crafts and food (cornbread!) are a don't-miss. 7275 Old Lake Rd., Bolton, NC 28423. Held the third weekend in Oct. (910) 655-8778; siouan@aol.com

Lake Waccamaw State Park *N.C. Division of Parks & Recreation*

Calabash/Brunswick County

Captain Nance's Calabash Seafood Restaurant

This family-style seafood restaurant on the Calabash River has been in operation for nearly 30 years. Captain Nance's uses seafood caught on its shrimp boats. Diners enjoy a

Indigo Farms

great view. 9939 Nance St., Calabash, NC 28467. Open daily, 11 A.M.–9 P.M. (910) 579-2574

Indigo Farms and Heritage Day

Stop here for fresh-farm produce, bakery goods, and plants. You can see a "NASPig" race, wool spinning, antique tractor displays, a horse-powered cane mill, Civil War reenactments, and more on Farm Heritage Day, held the first Saturday in October. Or you can take a hayride on Pumpkin Day, held the third Saturday of that same month. 1542 Hickman Rd. N.W., Calabash, NC 28467. Open seasonally, Mon.–Sat., 8 A.M.–5:30 P.M. Free. (910) 287-6794; www.localharvest.org/farms/M3808

Sunset River Marketplace

Sunset River Marketplace

Delicate blown glass, unique sculpture, contemporary and traditional art, meticulously crafted jewelry, and textiles by talented local artists are available here. Art classes are offered in painting, basket making, pottery, and photography. 10283 Beach Dr. S.W., Calabash, NC 28467. (910) 575-5999; www.sunsetrivermarketplace.com

Cerro Gordo/Columbus County

Betty Strickland Farm

Do fresh strawberries bring a smile to your face? At this farm, you can pick your own or get them prepicked. 2780 Cedar Grove Church Rd., Cerro Gordo, NC 28430. Open Apr.–May; the farm store is open Mon., Wed., and Fri. (910) 654-3646

Grady Strickland Farm

Grady Strickland Farm

Prepicked and pick-your-own berries and produce are sold here. Greenhouse produce is available from August through October. 30040 Cedar Grove Rd., Cerro Gordo, NC 28430. Mon.–Sat., daylight hours. (910) 654-3976

Chadbourn/Columbus County

Atlantic Coastline Depot Museum

Atlantic Coastline Depot Museum
NC Echo

Here, you'll discover the story of railroading and of the North Carolina Strawberry Festival. There are model railroads, Audubon prints, period furnishings, and fashions from the early 1900s. Colony St. and Railroad St., Chadbourn, NC 28431. Tues., 10 A.M.–5 P.M.; Fri., 10 A.M.–4 P.M.; Sun., 2–5 P.M. Free. (910) 654-4590; www.discovercolumbus.org

North Carolina Strawberry Festival

"The Strawberry Capital of the World" has celebrated the juicy fruit since the 1940s. The three-day festival includes bands, clowns, beauty queens, and, of course, strawberry shortcake. US Hwy 74/76 and Hwy 410, Chadbourn, NC 28431. Held the first weekend in May. (888) 533-7196; www.ncstrawberryfestival.com

Fair Bluff/Columbus County

Fair Bluff Depot Museum

This 1897 Atlantic Coastline Railroad passenger and freight depot offers a glimpse of community life during the height of the railway era. The memorabilia collections date from the 1700s to the 1940s. 339 Railroad St., Fair Bluff, NC 28430 Tues., 10 A.M.–4 P.M.; Sun., 2–4 P.M. Free. (910) 649-7707

Fair Bluff Depot Museum
NC Echo

North Carolina Watermelon Festival

Can a watermelon grow to over 100 pounds? See them yourself and enjoy food, fun, and entertainment for the whole family at this festival on the downtown riverfront. Fair Bluff, NC 28430. Held the last weekend in July. Free. (910) 212-0013; www.ncwatermelonfestival.com

River Bend Outfitters

River Bend offers guides for canoeing, kayaking, and fishing the nationally designated Wild and Scenic Lumber River. 1206 Main St., Fair Bluff, NC 28439. Fees are charged for boat rentals and guide services. (910) 649-5998; www.whitevillenc.com/rbo/

Hallsboro/Columbus County

Honey Hill Hunting Preserve

This preserve has been called "a wing shooter's paradise." If being on a hunt in the crisp autumn air is your favorite pastime, call Honey Hill. The facility offers guided quail and pheasant hunts. 3535 Honey Hill Rd., Hallsboro, NC 28442. (910) 640-7806; www.honeyhillhuntingpreserve.com/

Kure Beach/New Hanover County

Fort Fisher Civil War Museum *N.C. Division of State Historic Sites*

Fort Fisher Civil War Museum/ State Historic Site

Fort Fisher, the last major stronghold of the Confederacy, was the South's largest Civil War earthwork fortification. It kept the port of Wilmington and the Cape Fear River open to blockade runners, which delivered vital armaments and supplies to the Confederacy. It saw two major battles before falling to the Union army in January 1865. 1610 Fort Fisher Blvd. S., Kure Beach, NC 28449. Apr.–Oct., Mon.–Sat., 9 A.M.–5 P.M.; Sun., 1–5 P.M.; Nov.–March, Tues.–Sat., 10 A.M.–4 P.M.; Sun., 1–4 P.M. Free. (910) 458-5538; www.fortfisher.nchistoricsites.org

N.C. Aquarium at Fort Fisher

North Carolina Aquarium at Fort Fisher

This 93,000-square-foot facility features the Shark Tooth Ledge, the Moray Eel Cave, alligators, and many freshwater wonders.

Outside are nature trails, garden boardwalks, nearby beach access, and pond-side observation decks with telescopes to view the creatures in the estuary. 900 Logger Head Rd., Kure Beach, NC 28449. Open daily, 9 A.M.–5 P.M. The cost is $8 for adults, $7 for seniors and active military, and $6 for children six–17. (866) 301-3476; www.ncaquariums.com/ff/ffindex.htm

Lake Waccamaw/Columbus County

Lake Shore Lodge

Lake Waccamaw Depot Musuem *N.C. Arts Council*

Nestled on the waterfront in a quiet village, this colonial inn with its great sun porch is an artist's delight. Although the rooms are filled with antique furniture, they also offer all the modern conveniences. 2014 Lake Shore Dr., Lake Waccamaw, NC 28450. (910) 646-3748; www.bbonline.com/nc/lakeshore/index.html

Lake Waccamaw Depot Museum

This remarkable 1904 Atlantic Coastline Railroad depot is listed on the National Register. The highlights are a 300-year-old American Indian canoe, marine fossils, exhibits on the turpentine industry, and railroad memorabilia. 201 Flemington Ave., Lake Waccamaw, NC 28450. July–Aug., Tues.–Fri., 1–5 P.M.; Sat.–Sun., 3–5 P.M. Free. (910) 646-1992

Lake Waccamaw Girls and Boys Home Exhibition Center

Jazz, Big Band, swing, spirituals, gospel, piano performances by groups and individual artists, horse shows and exhibitions, rodeos, kennel club shows, cookoffs, and more are regular features here. 400 Flemington Dr., Lake Waccamaw, NC 28450. Fees are charged for some events. (910) 646-3083; www.boysandgirlshomesofnc.com

Lake Waccamaw Girls and Boys Home Exhibition Center *N.C. Arts Council*

Wacca Country Gift Shop *N.C. Arts Council*

Wacca Country Gift Shop

This Native American gift and souvenir shop features Waccamaw-Siouan quilts, pottery, and other handmade items. 557 Carver Moore Rd., Lake Waccamaw, NC 28450. Mon., Wed., and Fri., 10 A.M.–5 P.M. (910) 646-3871

Leland/Brunswick County

Shelton Herb Farm

Over 800 varieties of herbs are grown at Shelton Herb Farm, one of the largest in North Carolina. Culinary herbs, edible flowers, and medicinal herbs are available. Delightful fragrances waft from Ponderosa lemons, limes, Mayer lemons, Calamondon oranges, kumquats, and grapefruits. You can take classes like "Planting a Salad Bowl Garden" and "Christmas Herbs—Legends and Lore." Located just off US Hwy 17 S. at 340 Goodman Rd., Leland, NC 28451. Mon.–Sat., 8 A.M.–5 P.M. Free. (910) 253-5964; www.ncagr.com/NCproducts/ShowSite.asp?ID=2514

Shelton Herb Farm

Oak Island/Brunswick County

Oak Island Senior Citizens Craft Shop & Center

This shop offers a variety of arts and crafts, from baskets to photographs of local landmarks to beautiful watercolors. 5918 E. Oak Island Dr., Oak Island, NC 28465. Mon.–Sat., 10 A.M.–5 P.M. (910) 278-5224

Pottery by Bob Furr

Learning to cane a chair at the Oak Island Senior Citizens Craft Shop & Center

At this fully operational pottery studio and hand-painted furniture gallery, look for award-winning designs in dinnerware, fish platters, serving bowls, and vases.

8501 E. Oak Island Dr., Oak Island, NC 28465. Tues.–Sat., 9 A.M.–5 P.M. (910) 278-5991; www.theyaupontree.com

Ocean Isle/Brunswick County

Museum of Coastal Carolina

Museum of Coastal Carolina *NC Echo*

The entire family will enjoy waterfowl, swamp, and forest dioramas, extensive shell and antique fishing collections, and the "Reef Room." Kids' activities are offered daily in summer. 21 E. Second St., Ocean Isle, NC 28467. Summer, Mon. and Thurs., 9 A.M.–9 P.M.; Tues.–Wed. and Fri.–Sat., 9 A.M.–5 P.M.; Sun., 1–5 P.M.; winter, Fri.–Sat., 9 A.M.–5 P.M.; Sun., 1–6 P.M. The cost is $8 for adults, $6 for seniors and students, and $4 for children 3–5. (910) 579-1016; www.museumofcc.org

Silver Coast Winery and Gallery

Silver Coast Winery and Gallery

The helpful Silver Coast family will guide you through the fermentation room and explain the steps in the winemaking process. Certainly not to be missed are the art gallery's metal and clay sculptures and wine gifts. Monthly festivals with music and food are offered. 6680 Barbeque Rd., Ocean Isle, NC 28469. March–Dec., Mon.–Sat., 11 A.M.–6 P.M.; Sun., noon–5 P.M.; Jan.–Feb., Thurs.–Sun., noon–5 P.M. Tasting fees. (910) 287-2800; www.silvercoastwinery.com

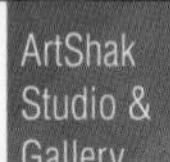

Southport/Brunswick County

ArtShak Studio and Gallery

ArtShak Studio & Gallery

Don't miss this unusual art gallery. The "yellow room" has painted glassware, while the "lavender room" has painted furniture ranging from impressionistic to funky to cool. You'll also enjoy the freestanding, wall-hung, and mobile sculptures in aluminum, brass, copper, and steel, some finished with textures, patinas, or paints. 822 N. Howe St., Southport, NC 28461. (910) 457-1757; artshak@bellsouth.net

Franklin Square Art Gallery

Franklin Square Art Gallery

The gallery houses Brunswick County's largest collection of oils, watercolors, and sculptures by local and state artists. Frequent juried photography, quilt, and art shows attract artists from Maine to Florida. 130 E. West St., Southport, NC 28461. Mon.–Sat., 10 A.M.–5 P.M. Free. (910) 457-5450; www.franklinsquaregallery.org

North Carolina Maritime Museum at Southport

The nautical history of the Lower Cape Fear is this museum's subject. Its collections include 100 ship models, a 2,000-year-old canoe fragment, Civil War artifacts recovered from sunken blockade runners and offshore wrecks, and items such as sharks' teeth and fishing gear. An extensive research library, films, and programs are offered year-round. 116 N. Howe St., Southport, NC 28461. Tues.–Sat., 9 A.M.–5 P.M. Admission is free. (910) 457-0003; http://www.ncmaritime.org/branches/southport_default.htm

North Carolina Maritime Museum at Southport *NC Echo*

The Provision Company

This waterside eatery is accessible by boat, car, and foot. Ask for "Thee Special"—one-half pound of steamed local shrimp, a crab cake, and a homemade cucumber salad. Diners enjoy live music and one of the best views in Southport! 130 Yacht Basin Dr., Southport, NC 28461. March 17–Nov. 15, daily, 11 A.M.–9 P.M. (910) 457-0654

Ricky Evans Gallery

The Ricky Evans Gallery exhibits his well-known lighthouse paintings, in addition to a series of paintings of historic Southport landmarks and a new coastal waterfront series. 211 N. Howe St., Southport, NC 28461. Mon.–Fri.,

10 A.M.–5 P.M.; Sat., 10 A.M.–4 P.M. (910) 457-1129; www.rickyevansgallery.com

Ricky Evans Gallery

Southport Visitor Center

Tourist information and a display of artifacts are featured here. 113 W. Moore St., Southport, NC 28461. Summer, Mon.–Sat., 10 A.M.–5 P.M. (800) 388-9635; www.southport-nc.com

Sunset Beach/Brunswick County

Blue Heron Gallery

For nearly 30 years, Jo Ann Johnston's gallery has been a showcase for more than 200 American and Canadian artists. As Jo Ann says, "The only thing mass-produced here is originality!" 1780-10A Chandlers Ln., Sunset Beach, NC 28468. Mon.–Sat., 10 A.M.–5 P.M. (910) 575-5088; www.blueherongallery-nc.com

Crabby Oddwaters

This popular restaurant is located above a seafood market in a historically significant building. Local seafood is grilled and steamed to your delight. Antiques and art are available for purchase. 310 Sunset Blvd., Sunset Beach, NC 28468. Late March–Labor Day, daily, 5–9 P.M. (910) 579-6372

Diving mask at the Southport Visitor Center

The Ingram Planetarium and Science Center

The Ingram Planetarium and Science Center has hands-on exhibits and a 360-degree sound and light experience. Visitors can view the universe as our planet travels through space and time. Hwy 904 and Hwy 179, Sunset Beach, NC 28467. Show times, Thurs.–Sat., 3, 4, 6, and 7 P.M. Admission fee. (910) 575-0033; www.ingramplanetarium.org

Twin Lakes Seafood

Twin Lakes Seafood has served fresh, local seafood since 1970. After perusing the 22-page menu, enjoy the local artwork on display. 102 Sunset Blvd., Sunset Beach, NC 28468. Open daily, 4:30–9 P.M. (910) 579-6373

Supply/Brunswick County

Brunswick Community College Performing Arts Series

This series showcases everything from magic shows to the down-home music of the Carolinas. 50 College Rd. N.W., Supply, NC 28462. Seasonal. (800) 754-1050, ext. 416; www.bccowa.com

Tabor City/Columbus County

Four Rooster Inn

This quaint inn built in 1949 features four beautiful rooms. You'll find lots of camellias and azaleas, afternoon tea, turndown service, and in-room morning coffee, along with a full Southern gourmet breakfast. 403 Pireway Rd. (Hwy 904), Tabor City, NC 28463. (910) 653-3878;www.travelassist.com/reg/nc1346.html

North Carolina Yam Festival

This annual celebration of the area's most famous agricultural product is held the fourth week in October. It features a parade, live entertainment, arts and crafts, and great food! 103-D E. Fifth St., Tabor City, NC 28463. (910) 653-2031; www.taborcitync.org

Strickland's Farm Produce and Corn Maze

This farm operation sells fresh spring Dixie peas and tasty fall butter beans. 8229 Swamp Fox Hwy W., Tabor City, NC 28463. Mon.–Sat., 8 A.M.–7 P.M.; Sun., 2–6 P.M.; corn maze and hayrides, mid-Sept.–Oct., Fri., 6–10 P.M.; Sat., 10 A.M.–10 P.M.; Sun., 2–6 P.M. The cost is $7 for adults and $5 for children. (910) 649-7921; stricklandproduce@yahoo.com

The Todd House

The Todd House has been in Tabor City since 1923, when Mary Todd offered meals and rooms for quail hunters and traveling salesmen. Today's homemade meals still include red velvet cake, sour cream pound cake, and homemade relishes and jellies! 102 Live Oak St., Tabor City, NC 28463. Sun. and Tues.–Fri., 11 A.M.–2:30 P.M.; Mon., 11 A.M.–2:30 P.M. and 5–7:30 P.M. (910) 653-3778; toddhouse@earthlink.net; www.toddhouse.net/index.htm

Robe Mr. Carter wore at UNC-CH when receiving his honorary degree. *NC Echo*

W. Horace Carter Newspaper Museum

The W. Horace Carter Newspaper Museum honors the publisher and editor of the *Tabor City Tribune,* best known for editorials denouncing the Ku Klux Klan. In 1953, Carter won the first-ever Pulitzer Prize for a weekly paper. *Tabor-Loris Tribune* Office, 1108 E. Fifth St., Tabor City, NC 28463. Open during office hours. Free. (910) 653-3153

Whiteville/Columbus County

Columbus County Arts Council

Stop by this gallery to see its impressive array of exhibits by local artists and its gift shop. 822 S. Madison St., Whiteville, NC 28472. Tues.–Fri., 9 A.M.–5 P.M. (910) 640-2787; www.columbuscountyarts.com

Coval L. Formy-Duval Farm

Pick your own or buy fresh-picked fruits and vegetables at this roadside market. 2766 New Britton, Whiteville, NC 28472. Apr.–June, 7 A.M.–8 P.M. (910) 642-5323

Columbus County Arts Council *N.C. Arts Council*

The Madison House Bed & Breakfast Inn

Innkeepers Jack and Yvonne Ellis capture the elegance and serenity of the Victorian era at this inn featuring a garden and pool. The on-site chef prepares delicious full-service meals. 101 N. Madison St., Whiteville, NC 28472. Room rates start at $95. (910) 640-2132; www.whitevillenc.com

North Carolina Museum of Forestry

Celebrate the rich natural history and cultural heritage of North Carolina's forests at this 17,226-square-foot museum featuring fascinating interpretive and interactive exhibits and exciting educational programs. 415 S. Madison St., Whiteville, NC 28472. Mon.–Fri., 9 A.M.–5 P.M.; Sat., 1–4 P.M.; Sun., 2–5 P.M. Free. (910) 914-4185; www.naturalsciences.org/visinfo/forestry

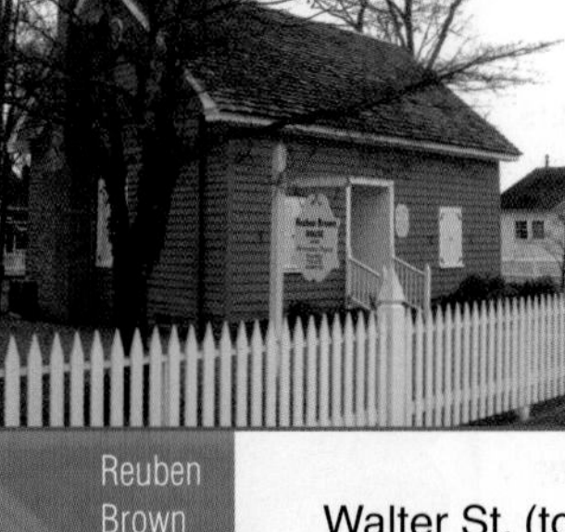

Reuben Brown House *N.C. Arts Council*

Reuben Brown House

This historic home of the former principal of White Academy reflects the simple life of an early-19th-century schoolmaster. 104 E. Walter St. (tourism bureau), Whiteville, NC 28472. Open by appointment. Free. (800) 845-8419

Wilmington/New Hanover County

Airlie Gardens

An enchanted place of fine Southern gardens, Airlie Gardens is a stroller's delight, especially wonderful when the azaleas and camellias are in bloom. Visitors enjoy live jazz and movies near the lake in summer and the Cape Fear Folk Fest in April. 300 Airlie Rd., Wilmington, NC 28403. Tues.–Sun., 9 A.M.–5 P.M. The cost is $8 for adults and $3 for kids six–12. (910) 798-7700; www.airliegardens.org

Airlie Gardens

Battleship *North Carolina*

Discover how the *North Carolina* fought and survived every major naval offensive in the Pacific during World War II, becoming the most decorated United States battleship. The battleship stands as a prime example of the sea power of her time and is preserved almost exactly as she was on active duty. You can step aboard where history took place and explore nine decks, the crew's quarters, gun turrets, and much more. 1 Battleship Rd. (US Hwy 17/74/76/421), Wilmington, NC 28402. Open daily, 8 A.M.–8 P.M. Admission fee. (910) 251-5797, ext. 3004; www.battleshipnc.com

Bellamy Mansion

The Bellamy Mansion is one of the state's most spectacular examples of antebellum architecture. Built by free and enslaved black artisans, it features 14 massive Corinthian columns. The house is a fitting stage for their stories and those of occupying Union soldiers at the close of the Civil War. 503 Market St., Wilmington, NC 28401.Tues.–Sat., 10 A.M.–5 P.M.; Sun., 1–5 P.M. The cost is $8 for adults and $4 for children five–12. (910) 251-3700; www.bellamymansion.org

Bellamy Mansion

Burgwin-Wright House

The lovely 1770 Georgian Burgwin-Wright House was built for a merchant, planter, and colonial official. Its elegant antique furnishings are by the National Society of the Colonial Dames of America. An open-hearth cooking demonstration is offered one Saturday each month, when various menus are prepared to reflect the colonial period. 224 Market St., Wilmington, NC 28401. Tues.–Sat., 10 A.M.–4 P.M.; closed in Jan. Admission fee. (910) 762-0570; www.museumsusa.org/data/museums/NC/108957.htm

Burgwin-Wright House *NC Echo*

C. W. Worth House B&B

This gracious B&B recaptures the lifestyle of an 1893 Victorian home in the historic district. Innkeepers Margi and Doug Erickson offer lush gardens with a relaxing waterfall and ponds. The house is just a short stroll down tree-lined streets from the Cape Fear riverfront. 412 S. Third St., Wilmington, NC 28401. Rates range from $140 and include a full breakfast. (800) 340-8559; www.worthhouse.com

C. W. Worth House B&B

Caffe Phoenix

This popular restaurant offers a tempting variety of selections, including vegetarian specials. It is also known for its exhibits featuring the work of local artists. In addition, it sponsors a local farmers' market in the parking lot on

Caffe Phoenix (p. 167)

Wednesday and Saturday. 9 S. Front St., Wilmington, NC 28401. (910) 343-1395

Cape Fear Blues Festival

The premier all-blues event in eastern North Carolina is held the fourth weekend of July at selected venues. It is presented by the Blues Society of the Lower Cape Fear. Some events take place at area attractions, others at restaurants and bars. PO Box 1487, Wilmington, NC 28402-1487. (910) 350-8892; www.capefearblues.org

Cape Fear Museum of History and Science

Where can you find the Michael Jordan Discovery Gallery, handcrafted bridal dolls, the story of regional foods, and an ancient sloth? The Cape Fear Museum has thousands of artifacts and photographs. 814 Market St., Wilmington, NC 29401. Memorial Day–Labor Day, Mon.–Sat., 9 A.M.–5 P.M.; Sun., 1–5 P.M. Admission fee. (910) 798-4350; www.capefearmuseum.com

Children's Museum of Wilmington *NC Echo*

Charles Jones African Art

In business for more than 25 years, Charles Jones African Art carries an extensive and varied inventory of traditional African art. It offers appraisal and research services and collects and purchases early photographic archives, books on African art, and vintage postcards from Africa. 311 Judges Rd., 6-E, Wilmington, NC 28405. (910) 794-3060; www.cjafricanart.com

Children's Museum of Wilmington

Stimulating, imaginative, and, yes, just good fun, this museum inspires curiosity and the innate love of learning that youngsters possess. Exhibits on nautical themes, circus experiences, animals, and nature are designed for infants to children age 11. 116 Orange St., Wilmington, NC 28401. Mon.–Fri., 10 A.M.–5 P.M.; Sat., 10 A.M.–6 P.M.; Sun., 1–6 P.M. Admission fee. (910) 254-3534; www.playwilmington.org

Louise Wells Cameron Art Museum (p. 171)

CLW Pottery

Cindy L. Weaver showcases her unusual wood-smoked porcelain at her studio, shared with husband Tracy Weaver, a trompe l'oeil artist. 1501 Amhearst Ct., Wilmington, NC 28412. Open by appointment. (910) 452-4962; www.clwpottery.com

Giant sloth skeleton at the Cape Fear Museum of History and Science *NC Echo*

The Cotton Exchange

A landmark warehouse is now a showcase for artists and craftspeople. Plan lots of time to stroll through this great place. During the summer months, you can have lunch on the porch. 321 N. Front St., Wilmington, NC 28401. Mon.–Sat., 10 A.M.–5:30 P.M.; many shops are also open Sun., 1–5 P.M. (910) 343-9896; www.shopcottonexchange.com

Cucalorus Film Festival

A cucalorus is a film set that creates a dappled effect. And since 1994, it's also an extraordinary March film festival. Nearly 100 films are presented over five days, attracting indie artists and film fans from around the world. 815 Princess St., Wilmington, NC 28402-2763. (910) 343-5995; www.cucalorus.org

Deluxe

Deluxe offers a casual upscale menu of French, Asian, Italian, New Southern, and Caribbean delights by award-winning chefs, served in a historic building. There's art on the walls for viewing and purchase, live music during Sunday brunch, and a children's menu. The restaurant won *Wine Spectator*'s Award of Excellence from 2001 to 2004. 114 Market St., Wilmington, NC 28401. Mon.–Sat., 5:30 P.M.–close; Sun., 10:30 A.M.–2:30 P.M. and 5:30 P.M.–close. (910) 251-0333; www.deluxenc.com

The Cotton Exchange

EUE Screen Gems Studios

Take a walk through Wilmington's two-decade film history with a tour of the picturesque 48-acre film lot that has been home to more than 400 productions. The one-hour walking tour includes visits to the sets of the hit show *One Tree Hill*. 1223 N. 23rd St., Wilmington, NC 28405. Memorial Day–Labor Day, Sat.–Sun., noon and 2 P.M.; Sept.–May, Sat., noon and 2 P.M. Admission fee. (910) 343-3433; tours@screengemsstudios.com; www.screengemsstudios.com

Deluxe (p. 169)

A Frame of Mind

This charming gallery of paintings, crafts, and lots and lots of baskets is set in a lovely old home in a historic area of Wilmington. 1903 Princess St., Wilmington, NC 28405. Mon., 10 A.M.–3 P.M.; Tues.–Fri., 10 A.M.–6 P.M.; Sat., 10 A.M.–5 P.M. (910) 251-8854

Latimer House & Archives

Latimer House & Archives

This 1852 home of Wilmington's historical society is an exceptional example of upper-class life during the Victorian period. Its 14 rooms contain more than 600 historic objects, including furniture, jewelry, tableware, tools, and more. 126 S. Third St., Wilmington, NC 28401. Mon.–Fri., 10 A.M.–3:30 P.M. Admission fee. (910) 762-0492; www.latimerhouse.org

Lewis Strawberry Nursery & Farms

Buy fresh-picked strawberries or pick your own—blueberries and blackberries, too. Homemade ice cream, plants, and flowers are also available. 6517 Gordon Rd., Wilmington, NC 28411. Apr.–July, Mon.–Sat., 8 A.M.–6 P.M.; Sun., 1–6 P.M. (910) 452-9659

Lewis Strawberry Nursery & Farm

Louise Wells Cameron Art Museum

This state-of-the-art facility features a permanent collection of North Carolina and American art from the 18th century to the present. A sculpture garden, computer-generated art, pottery, and even wooden decoys are on display, as are works by Mary Cassatt. Visitors can dine at The Forks and shop for baskets, pottery, fine art, handcrafted jewelry, and children's toys. 3201 S. 17th St., Wilmington, NC 28412. Tues.–Thurs. and Sat., 10 A.M.–5 P.M.; Fri., 11 A.M.–9 P.M.; Sun., 10:30 A.M.–4 P.M. Admission fee. (910) 395-5999;www.cameronartmuseum.com

Michele Tejuola Turner—Grandma Nettie *Permanent Collection, Louise Wells Cameron Art Museum*

New Elements Gallery

Located in the heart of historic downtown Wilmington, New Elements Gallery has been showcasing regional and national fine art and crafts since 1985. 216 N. Front St., Wilmington, NC 28401. Tues.–Sat., 11 A.M.–5:30 P.M. (910) 343-8997; www.newelementsgallery.com

NoFo Café

NoFo (North of Fourth) is a café serving favorites such as shrimp and grits. It is also a gourmet and art gift shop. Look for the giant metal fish. 1125 Military Cutoff Rd., Wilmington, NC 28408. Mon.–Sat., 10 A.M.–3 P.M. and 5–9 P.M.; Sun., 10 A.M.–3 P.M. (910) 256-5565; www.nofo.com/tour_forum.php

New Elements Gallery

North Carolina Azalea Festival

Wilmington's signature festival, begun in 1947, includes a three-hour parade, home tours, garden tours, street fairs, and lots of great music. PO Box 3275, Wilmington, NC 28406. Held in mid-Apr. (910) 794-4650; www.ncazaleafestival.org

North Carolina Jazz Festival

This three-day event celebrates music from swing to Dixieland. Begun in 1979, it's one of the longest-running classic jazz festivals on the East Coast. Wilmington Hilton Riverside, 301 N. Water St., Wilmington, NC 28401. Held in late Jan. or Feb. (910) 793-1111; www.capefearjazz.com

Old Wilmington City Market

This established landmark of old Wilmington is the perfect place to stroll. You'll find fresh fruit and steaming coffee to enjoy on the waterfront. 119 S. Water St., Wilmington, NC 28401. Tues.–Fri., 10 A.M.–5 P.M.; Sat., 8 A.M.–5 P.M.; Sun., noon–5 P.M. (910) 343-0042

Old Wilmington City Market

Pictures and Things

This shop features framed prints and paintings and items depicting African-American culture. 1109 Princess St., Wilmington, NC 28401. Tues.–Fri., 10 A.M.–6 P.M. (910) 762-9594

Pinehurst Pottery

Pottery, baskets, grapevine wreaths, prints, sculpture, wind chimes, metal yard ornaments, artificial trees, silk flowers and arrangements, candles, and lamps are available here. 7222 Market St., Wilmington, NC 28411. (910) 686-0338

The Racine Center for the Arts

Visitors can meander in a marketplace for fine art and crafts, then relax with a latte in the open-air sculpture garden. 203 Racine Dr., Suite 100, Wilmington, NC 28403 Mon.–Wed. and Fri., 10 A.M.–6 P.M.; Thurs., 10 A.M.–7 P.M.; Sat., 10 A.M.–5 P.M.; Sun., 1–5 P.M. (910) 452-2073;www. racinecenter.com

Riverfront Farmers' Market

Riverfront Farmers' Market

This terrific curbside market has produce, herbs, cut flowers, seafood, and more. On the third Saturday of the month, local artisans and crafters offer their works. Visitors enjoy special events and live musical entertainment monthly. N. Water St. between Princess and Market, Wilmington, NC 28401. Mid-Apr.–mid-Dec., Sat., 8 A.M.–12:30 P.M. (910) 520-6875; www.wilmingtonfarmers.com

Thalian Hall Center for the Performing Arts

Thalian Hall is one of the oldest and most beautiful theaters in America. In continuous use since 1858, it forms the east wing of Wilmington City Hall. 310 Chestnut St., Wilmington, NC 28402-0371. (910) 343-3664 or (800) 523-2820; www.thalianhall.com

Thalian Hall
NC Echo

Tidal Creek Co-op, Café & Deli

This is one of the best salad bars in the area, with locally grown organic produce, cheeses, and health-food products. 5329 Oleander Dr., Wilmington, NC 28403. Mon.–Sat., 8 A.M.–8 P.M.; Sun., 10 A.M.–6 P.M. (910) 799-2667; www.tidalcreek.coop/

University of North Carolina Wilmington

The university's collections, housed in 16 buildings on campus, include clothing, textiles, jewelry, pottery, furniture, figures, drawings, photographs, prints, and scrolls from all over the world. 601 S. College Rd., Wilmington, NC 28403. (800) 732-3643; www.uncw.edu/arts

The University of North Carolina Wilmington
NC Echo

Walls Gallery

Nestled among trees in the center of town, this small gallery houses works by local, national, and international artists, as well as a gilding studio and a conservation framing facility. 2173 Wrightsville Ave., Wilmington, NC 28403. Tues.–Sat., 10 A.M.–6 P.M. (910) 343-1703; www.wallsgallery.com

Water Street Restaurant & Sidewalk Café

Water Street Restaurant & Sidewalk Café

Located in the 1835 Quince Building, a former peanut warehouse, the restaurant evokes a bygone era in Wilmington. The emphasis is on fresh-caught seafood, generous vegetables, Black Angus beef, homemade dressings, and soup specials. The restaurant features live jazz, bluegrass, Dixieland, and flamenco weekly. 5 S. Water St., Wilmington, NC 28401. (910) 343-0042; www.5southwaterstreet.com

Wilmington Gallery at New Castle

A co-op gallery with juried works of members of the Wilmington Art Association, this is the place for affordable original fine art, pottery, and gifts. Featuring rotating exhibits by some of the area's finest artists, it is located in the arts and antiques district. 616 B Castle St., Wilmington, NC 28401. Mon.–Sat., 10 A.M.–6 P.M.; Sun., 1–5 P.M. (910) 343-4370; www.wilmingtongallery.com

Wilmington Railroad Museum

Looking for something new and exciting to do with the kids? Come by to climb aboard a steam locomotive or check out a red caboose. The museum has model train displays and a hands-on corner. Visitors learn about the history of railroads and people like Edison and Pullman. 505 Nutt St., Wilmington, NC 28401. Oct.–March, Mon.–Sat., 10 A.M.–4 P.M.; Apr.–Sept., Mon.–Sat., 10 A.M.–5 P.M.; Sun., 1–5 P.M. Admission fee. (910) 763-2634; www.wrrm.org

Wilmington Railroad Museum
NC Echo

Winnabow/Brunswick County

Brunswick Town/Fort Anderson State Historic Site

Brunswick Town/Fort Anderson State Historic Site *NC Echo*

Founded in 1726, Brunswick Town was the site of the famous Stamp Act Rebellion. During the Civil War, the Confederates there protected the entrance of the Cape Fear River. Today, excavations and the remains of old buildings reveal much about life during these two distinct periods of American history. Demonstrations are held each Saturday in summer. 8884 St. Phillips Rd. S.E., Winnabow, NC 28479-5035. Tues.–Sat., 10 A.M.–4 P.M. Free. (910) 371-6613; www.nchistoricsites.org/brunswic

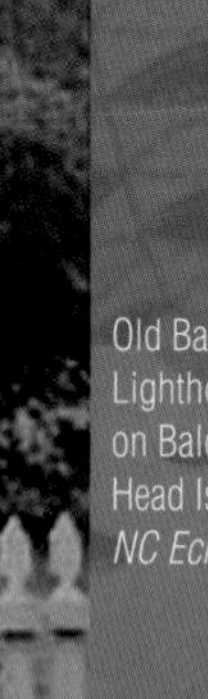

Old Baldy Lighthouse on Bald Head Island *NC Echo*

Hushpuppies, Pimento Cheese, and Sweet Tea

Caswell, Franklin, Granville, Person, Vance, and Warren Counties

Yearning for a soul-satisfying, natural experience? Create your own by taking in these organic farms, handmade crafts, and lush, rolling landscapes.

Get closer to your food sources with a walk along pastures of free-range chickens, goats, or cattle. Take in the waves of color at nurseries, gardens, and greenhouses.

Watch in fascination as a piece of wood becomes a lyrical dulcimer. Enjoy tasty treats made from the marriage of goat's milk and fresh herbs. Delight to the fragrance of handmade soaps or to

Art Studio 205/Fine Portraits, Franklinton (p. 180-81)

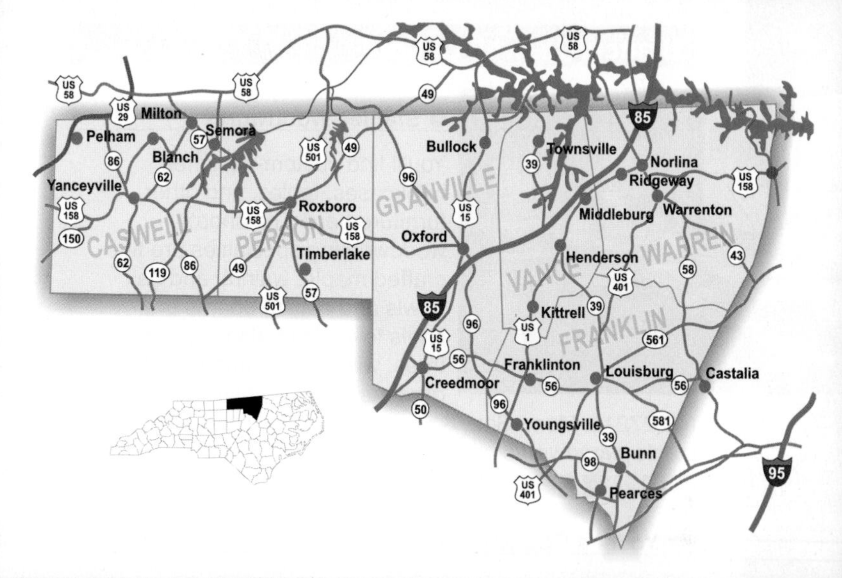

the simple life stories illustrated in colorful folk art or graceful Native American pottery.

Pack a pimento cheese sandwich, some hand-selected berries, and a jug of sweet tea and head off to find the perfect picnic spot. That's not easy on this trail simply because there are so many: lakeside landscapes, farm paths, panoramic gardens by the pond, and more. Don't forget the camera! You might want to prove that you saw a pumpkin slingshot or a herd of the world's smallest cattle.

As you trace the journey from gifted growers to inspired artisans, you'll wonder at the resourcefulness and creativity of each. You'll want to extend your experience by taking home an original work of art or a basket filled with mouth-watering goodies.

Read on for town-by-town descriptions of the unique attractions that make up the "Hushpuppies, Pimento Cheese, and Sweet Tea" trail.

Blanch/Caswell County

Stanley Woodworks

Stanley Woodworks

You'll find custom-designed bookcases, tables, and other furniture here. The shop's woodworking specialties are fine-crafted maple, walnut, and oak bowls and cutting boards that chefs love. You'll also enjoy the trees, wildflowers, and rare iris gardens. 7657 Blanch Rd., Blanch, NC 27212. Mon.–Sat., 8 A.M.–5 P.M. (336) 234-9320; www.stanleywoodworks.net

Yoder's Country Market

This Amish-style store offers hard-to-find items like whole-wheat berries and spelt, Amish-made furniture, meats and cheeses, wonderful pastries, and relishes and jams. Natural personal-care products and homeopathic remedies, herbs, minerals, and vitamins add up to a one-of-a-kind place. 6827 Blanch Rd., Blanch, NC 27212. Mon.–Sat., 9 A.M.–5:30 P.M. (336) 234-8072; www.yodersmart.com

Bullock/Granville County

Christmas Place Farms

Here, you can pick your own strawberries, pumpkins, and sweet potatoes and enjoy hayrides, children's activities, and a petting zoo. The farm is located two miles off Hwy 15. 3627 Harry Davis Rd., Bullock, NC 27507. Mon.–Fri., 8 A.M.–8 P.M.; Sat., 8 A.M.–6 P.M.; Sun., 11 A.M.–5 P.M. (919) 693-4496; christmasplacefarms2002@yahoo.com

Pick your own strawberries at Christmas Place Farms *Bob Radcliffe*

Triple B Farms

Triple B carries free-range eggs and meats—chickens, turkeys, grass-finished beef, and pasture-raised pork. All animals are raised in a natural environment. Visitors are welcome to see the farm by appointment. 3564 Harry Davis Rd., Bullock, NC 27507. (919) 693-4246; triplebfarms@gloryroad.net

Bunn/Franklin County

Jeffreys' Strawberry Patch

The Jeffreys have grown strawberries for 15 years. This site with a playground and picnic area turns strawberry picking (or purchasing) into a real outing. Save room for "Strawberry Slush"—a Jeffreys' favorite. 69 Berry Ln., Bunn, NC 27508. Mon.–Fri., 7 A.M.–dark; Sat., 7 A.M.–6 P.M. (919) 496-4626; www.ncagr.com/ncproducts/ShowSite.asp?ID=1774

Franklin County Farm Tour

Vollmer Farm

Vollmer Farm, "America's country playground," is more than a strawberry and pumpkin haven. It's a true agri-cultural experience. Fresh lettuce and veggies, ice cream, and sandwiches plus artwork, crafts, gifts, and the unique "Back Forty" family entertainment area are offered in a farm setting. 617 NC Hwy 98 E., Bunn, NC 27508. Apr. 15–July 31, Mon.–Sat., 8 A.M.–7 P.M.; Sun., 1–6 P.M.; mid-Sept.–Oct. 31, farm and market café, Mon.–Sat., 9 A.M.–6 P.M.; Sun., 1–6 P.M.; Back Forty, Sat., 10 A.M.–5 P.M. During the fall, admission to the Back Forty is $7 a person, which includes a hayride, an underground slide, the pumpkin slingshot, two playgrounds, fish and duck ponds, animals, a nature trail, and more. (919) 496-3076; www.vollmerfarm.com

Castalia/Franklin County

Rare Bird Nursery

This nursery caters to gardeners interested in wildlife. It offers a comprehensive selection of plants that provide food and shelter for animals. Children researching school projects (and parents!) love the resource center. 252 Collie Rd., Castalia,

Find treats for birds at the Rare Bird Nursery *Karen A. Blum*

NC 27816. Thurs.–Sat., 10 A.M.–6 P.M. (919) 853-2716; www.rarebirdnursery.com

Creedmoor/Granville County

Cedar Creek Gallery

You'll find this award-winning gallery tucked back into the edge of the woods near the little town of Creedmoor. Sid and Pat Oakley started Cedar Creek in 1968 on what used to be an old tobacco field. The gallery has grown from one building to more than 10; it carries the works of over 200 of America's most accomplished craftspeople. Many of the artisans represented have works in the permanent collections of the Smithsonian, the Corning Museum, the Mint Museum, and the Chrysler Museum. Their work has also been collected by heads of state, royalty, ambassadors, and big companies. Cedar Creek guarantees all its merchandise. 1150 Fleming Rd., Creedmoor, NC 27522. Daily, 10 A.M.–6 P.M.; closed Thanksgiving and Christmas. (919) 528-1041; www.cedarcreekgallery.com

Cedar Creek Gallery

Lyon Farms

Here, you can pick your own luscious strawberries . . . or have blueberries, blackberries, melons, okra, squash, onions, beets, asparagus, beans, cucumbers, tomatoes, greens, or corn picked and waiting for you. 1549 Northside Rd., Creedmoor, NC 27522. Apr. 15–July, Mon.–Sat., 8 A.M.-8 P.M.; Sun., 1–6 P.M.; Aug.–Sept., Mon.–Sat., 9 A.M.–6 P.M. (919) 528-3263

Art Studio 205/ Fine Portraits

Franklinton/Franklin County

Art Studio 205

M. Theresa Brown and Stephen Filarsky specialize in portrait painting of pets, places, and people, too. Art Studio 205 offers art classes that combine creativity and knowledge to go beyond the basics. Franklinton, NC 27525. Fees are charged. (919) 528-9703; www.portraitsnc.com

Henderson/Vance County

Art House

This art studio specializes in commissioned artwork, including hand-painted furniture and murals. Art lessons and classes are also available. 424 Dabney Dr., Henderson, NC 27536. Mon.–Fri., 10 A.M.–5 P.M. (252) 438-8383; ArtHousejag@hotmail.com

Franklin Brothers Nursery & Greenhouse

Franklin Brothers Nursery & Greenhouses

Figs, grasses, roses, trees, baskets, and bulbs—these experts have everything you need, and great advice, too. The fall festival for kids includes pumpkin decorating, hayrides, and a mini-maze. 3193 Vicksboro Rd., Henderson, NC 27537. Mon.–Sat., 8 A.M.–5 P.M. (252) 492-6166; www.franklinbrothers.com

Henderson Institute Historical Museum

Henderson Institute Historical Museum *NC Echo*

The museum houses many interesting historical items from the Henderson Normal and Industrial Institute, a United Presbyterian school established in 1887. The school, operated primarily to educate black teachers, is listed on the National Register of Historic Places. Beckford Dr. and W. Rockspring St., Henderson, NC 27536. Call before visiting. (252) 438-7392; www.ncecho.org

Henderson Rec Players

The players offer music, drama, and comedy in the summer. Henderson, NC 27536. Call for schedule. (252) 492-9400

July Fourth and Parade of Lights on Water *Vance County Tourism*

July Fourth and Parade of Lights on Water

Satterwhite Point Park on beautiful Kerr Lake is the place to be for the Fourth! Live entertainment, food, fireworks, and a lighted boat parade provide illuminating fun. Picnic tables and grills are available on a first-come basis. Kids will enjoy the "Tot Lot." No alcohol is allowed. Satterwhite Point Park, Henderson, NC 27536. (252) 438-2222 or (866) 438-4565; www.kerrlake-nc.com

Kerr Lake State Recreation Area

Kerr Lake is a 50,000-acre man-made lake that extends 39 miles up the Roanoke River along 800 miles of wooded and cove-studded shoreline. The lake boasts bass, catfish, and crappie; seven state parks and nearly 700 campsites; and two marinas with concessions. 6254 Satterwhite Point Rd., Henderson, NC 27537. Nov.–Feb., 8 A.M.–6 P.M.; March and Oct., 8 A.M.–7 P.M.; Apr. and Sept., 8 A.M.–8 P.M.; May–Aug., 8 A.M.–9 P.M. Fees are charged. (252) 438-7791; www.ncsparks.net/kela

Kerr Lake State Recreation Area *N.C. Division of Parks and Recreation*

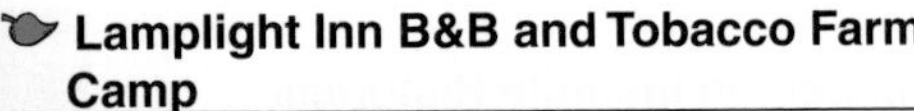

Lamplight Inn B&B and Tobacco Farm Camp

Part of an 1850s tobacco farm near Kerr Lake, the restored farmhouse has all the modern amenities and lots of atmosphere in each beautiful guest room. Restored tobacco-barn cabins offer a rustic setting. A farm implement museum, a craft shop, a corncrib, a gazebo, and an RV camp are on the five-acre grounds. Flemingtown Rd. (Exit 220 off I-85), Henderson, NC 27537. (877) 222-0100; www.lamplightbandb.com

Mistletoe Villa

The architect who designed the Executive's Mansion in Raleigh was commissioned to build the Queen Anne–style Mistletoe Villa (circa 1883), now on the National Register.

The house, lawn, and gardens are available for rent. 144 E. Young Ave., Henderson, NC 27536. (252) 438-7219; www.mistletoevilla.com

The Peanut Roaster

Oh, nuts! Spicy, orange-flavored, chocolate, or just plain roasted North Carolina–grown peanuts are sure to suit your taste buds. The family recipes used here were developed in 1949. Sample a few to find your favorite. 394 Zeb Robinson Rd., Henderson, NC 27536. Mon.–Fri., 8 A.M.–6 P.M.; Sat., 8:30 A.M.–5 P.M.; Sun., 11 A.M.–5 P.M. (252) 431-0100 or (800) 445-1404; www.peanut.com

Ruth Russell Williams, Folk Artist

Her family were sharecroppers. Ms. Williams raised a family, started painting, and is now an internationally recognized American folk artist. 45 Williams Ln., Henderson, NC 27537. (252) 492-2662; www.ruthsart.com

Show, Shine, Shag, and Dine Show

Here, you'll find antique cars, classic cars, hot rods, muscle cars, and nostalgic drag cars . . . over 600 cruisin' engines! A barbecue cookout and a shag dance contest add to the fun. East Coast Drag Times Hall of Fame honors are presented on Sunday. Downtown Henderson, NC 27536. Held the third weekend in Oct. (252) 438-2222 or (866) 438-4565; www.kerrlake-nc.com

Show, Shine, Shag, and Dine Show *Vance County Tourism*

The Silo Restaurant

A favorite among locals for more than 20 years, the Silo is designed to resemble an old dairy barn. The 100-year-old wood used to construct the restaurant was salvaged from a tobacco barn. Guests here enjoy fine dining including steaks, seafood, and a salad bar. 2002 Graham Ave., Henderson, NC 27536. Mon.–Sat., 4:30–10 P.M.; Sun., 11:30 A.M.–2:30 P.M. and 4:30–9 P.M. (252) 492-6772

Supply Line Country Market and Provisions and Baskets

Stop here to make a picnic lunch of fresh deli meats and cheeses and to buy gourmet coffees, nuts, wines, and produce. Gift baskets are offered. 235 Raleigh Rd., Henderson, NC 27536. Mon.–Sat., 8 A.M.–7 P.M. (252) 438-2836; www.provisionsandbaskets.com

Vance County Regional Fair

This local fair, which debuted in 1917, offers live entertainment, puppet shows, midway rides, a petting zoo, food vendors, and agricultural and heritage exhibits. US Hwy 1 Bypass and NC Hwy 39, Henderson, NC 27536. Held in Sept. (434) 348-3378; www.vancecountyfair.com

Vance County Regional Fair *Vance County Tourism*

Wildflower Café

Fine food meets local art in a restored historic building. Salads and sandwiches are offered for lunch and steaks, seafood, and pasta for dinner. 200 S. Garnett St., Henderson, NC 27536. Mon.–Wed., 10:30 A.M.–2:30 P.M.; Thurs.–Fri., 10:30 A.M.–2:30 P.M. and 5:30–9 P.M. (252) 430-1775

Kittrell/Vance County

Buffaloe Milling Company, Inc.

This unique retailer and wholesaler sells flour and a large variety of cornmeal, hushpuppy, and biscuit mixes. It also stocks feed for dogs, horses, goats, chickens, birds, fish, cows, hogs, and rabbits. Buffaloe Mill Rd., Kittrell, NC 27544. Mon.–Fri., 7 A.M.–noon and 1–4 P.M. (252) 438-8637; buffaloemilling@yahoo.com

Corner Oaks Farm & Greenhouse

Come start your spring garden here, or stop for fresh produce in the summer. 3031 Dick Smith Rd., Kittrell, NC 27544. (252) 492-8069

Kittrell Confederate Cemetery

This is the final resting place of 52 casualties of the Petersburg Campaign who died between August 1, 1864, and April 15, 1865, at the Kittrell Springs Hotel, which had been converted into a hospital. Off US Hwy 1 Bypass, West Chavis Ln., Kittrell, NC 27544. vctourism@gloryroad.net

Melvin's Gardens

Melvin's Gardens offers painted glass and furniture, birdhouses, and over 100 varieties of herbs just right for every taste! It is located off NC Hwy 39 north of Louisburg. 2863 Sims Bridge Rd., Rocky Ford, NC 27544. (252) 432-9118; www.ncagr.com/ncproducts/showsite.asp?ID=2710

Louisburg/Franklin County

Double "D" Equestrian Center

Double "D" Equestrian Center, LLC

Double "D" has 20 miles of trails over rolling countryside, boarding options for your best friend, equestrian clinics, trailer campsites—everything you want! Riding trails wind through 200-year-old cypress stands. There's an outdoor arena for exercising and jumping, as well as camping on the hillside overlooking the Tar River. Amenities include restrooms with shower facilities and a lounge built in one of the old milking parlors. 733 Egypt Church Rd., Louisburg, NC 27549. (919) 496-6564; www.doubledequestrian.com

Freedom Farms

These "Little Cattle with Big Futures" are Dexter cattle, an endangered breed classified as "watched" by the American Livestock Breeds Conservancy. They're the smallest breed of cattle in the world. In addition to cows, the farmers raise free-range Muscovy ducks and a wide variety of free-range chickens. 17 Lloyd's Way, Louisburg, NC 27549. Call

Freedom Farms

ahead. (252) 432-4200; www.FreedomFarmDexters.com

Leonard Family Farm

In business since 1919, this farm features pasture-based, "Beef Quality Assurance Certified" natural Angus beef raised without hormones or antibiotics. It offers 45-minute tours on farm life, past and present, along with a hayride and free pumpkins. 571 Leonard Farm Rd., Louisburg, NC 27549. Open Sept.–Nov. Call to schedule. (919) 496-4852; www.leonardfarm.com

Louisburg College Art Gallery

The traveling exhibitions gallery hosts seven shows during the academic year; the permanent exhibitions gallery features African masks, 20th-century prints and drawings, and a selection of North Carolina pottery. 501 N. Main St., Louisburg, NC 27549. Mon.–Fri., 9 A.M.–5 P.M. (919) 497-3238; www.louisburg.edu

Lynch Creek Farm & Antiques

Lynch Creek Farm & Antiques

Lynch Creek Farm displays 18th-, 19th-, and 20th-century French and English furniture, art, and accessories. During your visit, you will also see grass-fed cows, chickens, and honeybees. Lynch Creek sells fresh herbs, honey, eggs, cut flowers, and living wreaths. A picnic area is provided. 1973 Rocky Ford Rd., Louisburg, NC 27544. (252) 492-2600; www.LynchCreek.com

Mae Farm

Mae Farm

Mae Farm is a free-range hog operation where hogs are raised antibiotic- and hormone-free. A nature trail and hayrides are available. Located off NC Hwy 39 N., 57 Mitchell Baptist Church Way, Louisburg, NC 27549. Call ahead. (252) 430-1988; michae61017@earthlink.net

May Franklin County Farm, Foods & Crafts Tour

The tour of farms, gardens, and studios is organized by the North Carolina Cooperative Extension. Live music is provided by Ridgeway Opry House. Maps are provided to tour participants. Franklin County Cooperative Extension, 103 S. Bickett Blvd., Louisburg NC 27549. Held the third weekend in May, 1–5 P.M. Admission is $5 for adults; children are free. (919) 496-3344; www.franklin.ces.ncsu.edu

May Franklin County Annual Farm, Foods, & Crafts Tour

North Carolina Meat Goat Producers Co-op

This cooperative of 40 Chevron and Cabrito goat producers offers high-quality meat and goats. Halal (Muslim-blessed) meat is available as well. All meat is antibiotic- and medicinal residue–free. 103 S. Bickett Blvd., Louisburg, NC 27549. Mon.–Fri., 9–5 P.M. (919) 496-2280; www.ordergoat.com

Middleburg/Vance County

Middleburg Steak House

Middleburg Steak House dates to 1934, when it opened as a community center built by the Civil Works Administration. The hand-cut log building remains essentially the same—a rustic but cozy place for dinner. US Hwy 1 N. and US Hwy 158 E. (Exit 220 off I-85), Middleburg, NC 27556. Wed.–Sat., 5:30–10 P.M.; Sun., 5:30–9 P.M. (252) 492-7088

Milton/Caswell County

Cadmus Pottery

This workshop features wheel-thrown pottery and raku by Shirley Cadmus, who uses pit-fired and wood-fired kilns to create her distinctive stoneware vessels. 532 Snatchburg Rd., Milton, NC 27305. Mon., Wed., and Sat., 10 A.M.–5 P.M. (336) 234-9429; www.potsnpixels.com

Cadmus Pottery

Norlina/Warren County

Creations by Mike

This shop features oil paintings on canvas and . . . saw blades! 984 US Hwy 158 Business W., Norlina, NC 27563. (252) 456-4040 or (252) 213-1366; creations4040@yahoo.com

Holtzmann's Farm Produce

Holtzmann's offers genuine Ridgeway cantaloupes, watermelons, and honeydews. 364 US Hwy 1 S., Norlina, NC 27563. Open spring–summer. (252) 456-2033

Dining car turned museum *Norlina Museum*

Norlina Junction Park and Museum

The Norlina Train Museum is a converted Seaboard Coastline Railroad dining car that served hungry soldiers in World War II. Today, it houses artifacts and historical displays of the town and surrounding area from pre-colonial times to the present. Hyco St., Norlina, NC 27563. Open daily. Call ahead to visit the museum. (252) 456-2406; www.norlina.com

Roost Crossroads Antiques & Collectors Mall

Here, you can browse home furnishings, china, crocks, clocks, knickknacks, and books. Intersection of US Hwy 1 and US Hwy 158, Norlina, NC 27563. Mon.–Sat., 10 A.M.–5 P.M.; Sun., 1–5 P.M. (252) 456-2406; www.roostx.com

Roost Crossroads Antiques & Collectors Mall

Oxford/Granville County

Granville County Museum

Located in the 1946 "freezer locker" (a.k.a. county jail), this museum offers exhibits that explore the Oxford-China connection, history, science, and the arts. While the cells are gone, the flavor remains!1 Museum Ln., Oxford, NC 27565. Wed.–Fri., 10 A.M.–4 P.M.; Sat., 11 A.M.–3 P.M. (919) 693-9706; gcmuseum@earthlink.net

Wright's Farm

Fresh produce is for sale here. 1700 Oak Hill Rd., Oxford, NC 27565.Open daily, May–Sept. Call to find out what's in season. (919) 693-7667

Pearces/Franklin County

Flying Pig Farm

Garlic—eight field-grown varieties—garlic butter and dips, organic shiitake mushrooms, specialty cut flowers, and plenty of flying pigs add up to a delightful spot to visit. 55 Cabin Hill Rd., Pearces, NC 27597. Sat.–Mon., 9 A.M.–5 P.M. Call ahead. (919) 404-2493; www.flyingpigfarm.net

Enjoy organic mushrooms at the Flying Pig Farm.

Pelham/Caswell County

SleepyGoat Farm

Retired physicians turned farmers have transformed a tobacco farm into a unique goat farm that makes hard and soft cheeses. At the spring open houses, there's usually a baby goat or two to cuddle. 7215 Allison Rd., Pelham, NC 27311. May–Aug., second Sun. of each month, 3–5 P.M. (336) 388-5388; www.sleepygoatfarm.com

Ridgeway/Warren County

Oakley Hall

Built in 1855, Oakley Hall is attributed to master builder Jacob Holt and is one of Warren County's premier plantation homes. 195 Joe Jones Rd., Ridgeway, NC 27570. (252) 257-2411

Ridgeway Cantaloupe Festival

One of the most exquisite tastes ever to come out of North Carolina is the Ridgeway cantaloupe. The festival honors this little melon during a daylong event packed with fun, games, arts and crafts, country music, and plenty of Southern cooking. 668 US Hwy 1 S., Ridgeway, NC 27570.

Held the third Sat. in July, 10 A.M.–4 P.M. (252) 456-2601; liamtheluthier@vance.net

Ridgeway Dulcimer Shoppe and Opry House

Billy Jarrell makes and sells handcrafted, custom-made, and specially designed dulcimers. When he's not making dulcimers, Billy turns his property into a weekly venue for performances by country music acts. 704 US Hwy 1 S., Ridgeway, NC 27570. (252) 456-3890; www.users.vance.net/liamtheluthier

Ridgeway Dulcimer Shoppe

Roxboro/Person County

Barrister's Bed & Breakfast

This 1921 Georgian Revival structure has hand-painted murals, family-crest panels, lace tablecloths, and billiards. Wireless Internet, a stocked fridge, and a full Southern breakfast are offered, too! 400 N. Main St., Roxboro, NC 27573. (336) 597-2848; www.barristersbedbreakfast.com

Clarksville Station

Barrister's Bed & Breakfast

Here, you can dine in an authentic restored railroad depot and train (or maybe in the station's water tower) on prime rib, a salad bar, and homemade cheesecake! 4080 Durham Rd., Roxboro, NC 27573. Tues.–Fri., 11:30 A.M.–2 P.M. and 5:30–9 P.M.; Sat.–Sun., 5:30–9 P.M. (336) 599-9153; personcountytda@personcounty.com

Cornerstone Cabin

This completely furnished lakefront two-story log cabin sleeps 10. It features a fireplace in the family room, screened porches, and two full baths. Mayo Lake (Hwy 49 and Neal's Store Road), Roxboro, NC 27574. (919) 676-8897; www.collegeshoppe.com/cornerstonecabin

Cottage on Reams 518

Those who prefer town living to country life might find this furnished two-bedroom cottage in historic uptown Roxboro to their liking. 518 Reams Ave., Roxboro, NC 27573. (919) 676-8897; www.collegeshoppe.com/518reams

Cottage on Reams 518

Fifth Row Farm

This farm offers fresh produce. Turn right off Highway 57 onto Morton-Pulliam Road and go 3.8 miles. The farm is on the left; signs are posted. 3825 Morton-Pulliam Rd., Roxboro, NC 27573. May–Oct., daily, 7 A.M.–8 P.M. (336) 599-4835

Hinterland Media, Inc.

Artist George Buchanan paints outdoor scenes and specializes in portraiture. His video on how to be a "portable artist" is an inspiration. 315 Yarborough Rd., Roxboro, NC 27574. (336) 599-1895; www.georgebuchanan.com

The Kirby Gallery

The gallery showcases and sells art in all mediums from artists in the region. Monthly artist receptions are held on the first Sunday. 213 N. Main St., Roxboro, NC 27573. Mon.–Tues. and Thurs.–Fri., 1–5 P.M. (336) 597-1709; www.ArtsinPerson.com

Cornerstone Cabin

Our Pride Foods

Stop! Pimento cheese ahead! This family-owned business makes much-loved pimento cheeses and spreads. 1128 N. Main St., Roxboro, NC 27573. Tues.–Wed., 9 A.M.–noon; call for other times. (336) 597-4978; ourpride@earthlink.net

Our Pride Foods *Karen Browning*

Person County Museum of History

Sapony Indian maps, documents, drawings, and photos depict more than 400 years of the tribe's life. Among the highlights are stories about Hall of Famer Enos Slaughter and the 300 antique and contemporary dolls in the Dorothy Brooks Doll Collection. 309 N. Main St., Roxboro, NC 27573. Tours, Wed.–Sat., 10 A.M.–2 P.M. The cost is $5 for adults, $4 for seniors (55 and up), and $3 for groups; children 12 and under are free. (336) 597-2592; www.visitroxboronc.com

318 South Main Street

This 1920s two-story brick home has four furnished bedrooms. Guests can play the piano or sit a spell on the porch! 318 S. Main St., Roxboro, NC 27573. (919) 676-8897; www.collegeshoppe.com/318southmain

Semora/Caswell County

McGhee's Mill Produce

McGhee's offers fresh produce. 9550 McGhee's Mill Rd., Semora, NC 27343. May–July, Fri.–Sun., 8 A.M.–6 P.M. (336) 597-2973

Timberlake/Person County

Brooks Farms

To reach this produce stand from Durham, go north on US Highway 501 about 17 miles and watch for the signs. From Roxboro, go south on US Highway 501 for eight miles and watch for the signs. From Hillsborough, take Highway

57 North and watch for the signs. 545 Tom Oakley Rd., Timberlake, NC 27583. Late Apr.–Oct., Sun., 1–8 P.M. (336) 364-2114

P ?

Flat River Nursery

To reach this farm stand and plant nursery, follow US Highway 501 North from Durham to Timberlake. Turn left onto Dick Holeman Road. Go approximately two miles to the third road on the right. Turn right and go 1.5 miles. The farm is on the right. 1548 Holeman-Ashley Rd., Timberlake, NC 27573. Apr.–Oct., Mon.–Fri., 8 A.M.–5 P.M.; call for Sun. hours. (336) 364-2460

P ?

Free Spirit Retreat and Equine Center

Located on 50 acres just north of Durham, the center offers special experiences in horse-human connections and is home to a breeding program of straight Egyptian Arabian horses. Overnight accommodations are available for horse and nature lovers seeking a unique retreat experience. 6929 Oxford Rd., Timberlake, NC 27583. Open daily; reservations are needed for special retreat programs. Fees vary with the type of program. (336) 597-7359; www.freespiritretreat.net

Person County Museum of History *NC Echo*

Mayo Lake Guide Service

This service provides fishing guides to enhance your bass and crappie fishing experience—and your luck. 186 Jim Moore Rd., Timberlake, NC 27583. Open by appointment. A half-day guided bass trip costs $65 for up to two people; a full-day guided bass trip costs $125 for up to two people; a half-day guided crappie trip costs $75 for up to five people; a full-day guided crappie trip costs $135 for up to five people. (336) 364-1431; jah2524@yahoo.com

P ?

Townsville/Vance County

Nancy Knott Studio

Artist Nancy Knott specializes in tobacco crafts, oils,

watercolors, pastels, and handmade paper. 14 Rockchurch Rd., Townsville, NC 27537. Open by appointment. (434) 252-0662

Warrenton/Warren County

Ivy Bed and Breakfast

The Ivy is an elegant bed-and-breakfast in the historic district. Guest rooms are named after the ladies who lived here throughout the years. All rooms feature queen-sized beds, beautiful heart-pine floors, lovely window treatments, and interesting antiques. The Ivy has four bedrooms and three baths. 331 N. Main St., Warrenton, NC 27589. (252) 257-9300 or (800) 919-9886; www.ivybedandbreakfast.com

The MaeB Farm

The MaeB Farm features 10 acres planted with old and new fruit trees. Duane and Alice Putnam are reviving and renewing an old orchard that includes pecans, apples, pears, peaches, apricots, plums, cherries, and grapes. 1031 Warren Plains Rd., Warrenton, NC 27589. (540) 878-1099; MaeBFarm@hotmail.com

The MaeB Farm

Magnolia Manor Plantation Bed & Breakfast

Guests enjoy true Southern hospitality in the simple elegance of this circa 1815 plantation manor house. The remarkable Italianate overbuild by Jacob Holt included a ladies' parlor and a gentlemen's parlor, a grand hall with a magnificent staircase, an enlarged upstairs room, and two large chimneys. The appearance became that of a house within a house. The current owners replaced the home's old floors with flooring milled from an 1880s cotton mill. They acquired 13 adjoining acres with old outbuildings and an orchard of 21 mature pecan trees and a massive white oak believed the be the fifth-largest in the United States. The home is listed on the National Register of Historic Places. 128 Pet Burwell Rd., Warrenton, NC 27589. (252) 257-6055 or (800) 390-8552; www.magnolia-manor.com

Oakley Hall Antiques & Art Gallery

This is the second-oldest brick store in Warrenton, built in 1882. In addition to antiques, the shop features an art gallery specializing in the works of noted painter Marjorie Rose Powell. 102 S. Main St., Warrenton, NC 27589. (252) 257-2411; okhall@mindspring.com

The Scarlet Rooster

This one-of-a-kind shop offers unique accessories for home and entertaining, including works by local artists. Some of the handcrafted items are made by local woodworkers or woven by weavers of the North Carolina Blue Ridge Mountains. Custom items are also available. 116 N. Main St., Warrenton, NC 27589. Mon.–Sat., 10 A.M.–5 P.M. (252) 257-1993

Senora Richardson Lynch

Senora Lynch is nationally known for her decorative style of bichrome pottery featuring plant and animal patterns that have significance in Sapony Indian traditions. Senora uses a special technique to scratch patterns through a white clay surface to reveal the red clay underneath. Many of her works are in highly respected American art collections, including the Smithsonian Institution. Her life and work are the subject of a book, *The Contemporary Southeastern Indian Pottery of Haliwa-Saponi Artist Senora Lynch*, by Christopher Everett. 123 E. Haliwa Dr., Warrenton, NC 27589-8861. (252) 257-5771

Yanceyville/Caswell County

Baldwin Family Farms

The farm is a multigenerational, sustainable Charolais cattle operation owned and operated on 750 acres by the Baldwin family. The Baldwins founded their farm in 1969 when they purchased two registered Charolais heifers. Their beef is sold at retail outlets and at the farm, which is open to visitors. 5341 NC Hwy 86 S., Yanceyville, NC 27379. Mon.–Sat., 9 A.M.–5 P.M. (336) 694-4218 or (800) 896-4857; www.baldwinfamilyfarms.com

Rare Bird Nursery *Karen A. Blum* (p. 179-80)

Caswell Council for the Arts/Civic Center

The council's gallery features the work of local artists. 536 E. Main St., Yanceyville, NC 27379. Mon.–Fri., 9 A.M.–5 P.M. (336) 694-4591; ccarts@caswell.k12.nc.us

Gatewood House and History Museum

This is the former home of artist Maud Gatewood. The primary focus of the museum is Thomas Day, "Chicken" Stephens, and the Kirk-Holden War, as well as the old Caswell County Courthouse, local agricultural history, and local family history. 15 Main St., Yanceyville, NC 27379. Mon.–Fri., noon–4 P.M. (336) 694-4965

"Celestial Tabby Cat" by Louellen Vernon-White

Hall's Strawberry & Vegetable Farm

Here, you can pick your own or buy from the roadside market. Visitors love the fall corn maze! From Reidsville, take Highway 87 South to Burlington to Cherry Grove Road. 179 Oakus Page Rd., Yanceyville, NC 27320. May–Aug., Mon.–Sat., 7 A.M.–7 P.M.; Oct., Sat., 10 A.M.–6 P.M.; Sun., 1–6 P.M. (corn maze). (336) 421-0693 or (336) 634-9088; www.cornfieldmaze.com

Louellen Vernon-White, Printmaker

Charming etchings of "guardian angel" cats and dogs are featured at this working printmaking studio in Blanch, near Yanceyville. Call ahead. (336) 234-7394; www.louellenvernonwhite.com

"Dog Story" by Louellen Vernon-White

September Brightleaf Hoedown

The hoedown offers music, street dances, food, and more music! This area is a haven for artists. You'll find 80 arts-and-crafts booths, plus plenty of barbecue and Brunswick stew. The event takes place on a September weekend. Historic Town Square, Yanceyville, NC 27379. Sat., 9:30 A.M.–sundown; Sun., 1–6 P.M. (336) 694-6106; www.caswellcountync.gov/ainterest/festivals.htm

Youngsville/Franklin County

Cajun Canoes

Cajun Canoes offers custom-made pirogues (Cajun canoes), built by hand from plywood. 137 Bethlehem Church Rd., Youngsville, NC 27596. Daily, 8 A.M.–5 P.M. Call ahead. (919) 496-1507; jbsharley03@aol.com

Hill Ridge Farms

This 55-acre recreational farm is one of the Triangle's best destinations for old-fashioned, educational family fun. It offers a petting barn, a fish-feeding pond, picnic grounds, gemstone panning, and a country store. One of the farm's newest attractions is Big John, a 16-gauge, 100-passenger steam engine. 703 Tarboro Rd., Youngsville, NC 27596. Open seasonally. (919) 556-1771 or (800) 358-4170; www.hillridgefarms.com

Hill Ridge Farms

Red Barn Trading Post

The owner is a purveyor of reclaimed materials and a designer of eclectic home furnishings. He builds birdhouses, potting tables, bird feeders, and sheds. You'll find antiques and collectibles—and fresh produce, too. 106 N.W. Railroad St., Youngsville, NC 27596. Thurs.–Fri., 10 A.M.–6 P.M.; Sat., 8 A.M.–6 P.M.; Sun., 2–5 P.M. (919) 818-7375

What's pimento cheese?

Like dropping peanuts in a cold bottle of Pepsi, there's no more Southern concoction—except perhaps tomato pie—than pimento cheese, a cool, satisfying dish that folks make "just the way Mama did."

Our friend Staci offers a fine take on the old standard:

Staci's Pimento Cheese

1 lb. colby, medium cheddar, or colby jack, shredded
8 oz. pimentos, chopped
1 cup Duke's mayonnaise or other lemony mayo
1 tsp. Worcestershire

Mix together using a potato masher or a large slotted spoon. Chill awhile. Savor on crackers, as a sandwich with cold tea, or just on a spoon.

Hushpuppies

How does a simple batter of cornmeal, sugar, flour, milk, egg, and a dash of seasoning become the stuff of legend? The tale is oft told that hunters and fishermen would fry up thumb-sized nuggets over their campfires and toss them to their yapping dogs with the cry, "Hush, puppy." Today's versions sometimes show off with a bit of added onion. The cook's secret? Refrigerate the dough before cooking for a just-right crispy flavor. They're served up with flair before any meal, especially barbecue.

Heart of the East

Edgecombe, Nash, Pitt, and Wilson Counties

Visitors who want the quintessential eastern North Carolina experience should plan a trip to this region. This is where the Piedmont gives way to the coastal plain and where long, wide farm fields, often bordered on the horizon by a line of hardwood trees, start to dominate the landscape.

Strawberries, blueberries, melons, pumpkins, and the magnificent collards—those green, leafy vegetables with a flavor between cabbage and kale—are found in abundance at produce stands and farmers' markets. Connoisseurs also travel to this area in order to sample the fabled barbecue of eastern North Carolina—smoked and flavored with a spicy vinegar sauce.

Residents in these parts value arts and culture. This trail is rich with galleries, art centers, and music venues reflecting the vitality and the spirit of the "Heart of the East." Rocky Mount's old Imperial Tobacco Factory, a massive brick structure dating from the early 20th century, has been transformed into beautifully designed spaces that are perfect for visual arts exhibitions, theater performances, classroom studios, and a children's museum and science center. Greenville, home to East Carolina University, has year-round offerings in the performing and visual arts.

Be sure to check out local arts councils. Their venues include a classic vaudeville theater house, a renovated Baptist church, and a 1903 bank building. They have an array of outstanding artists.

History buffs should wend their way to historic Tarboro to tour the 1808 Blount-Bridgers House, which

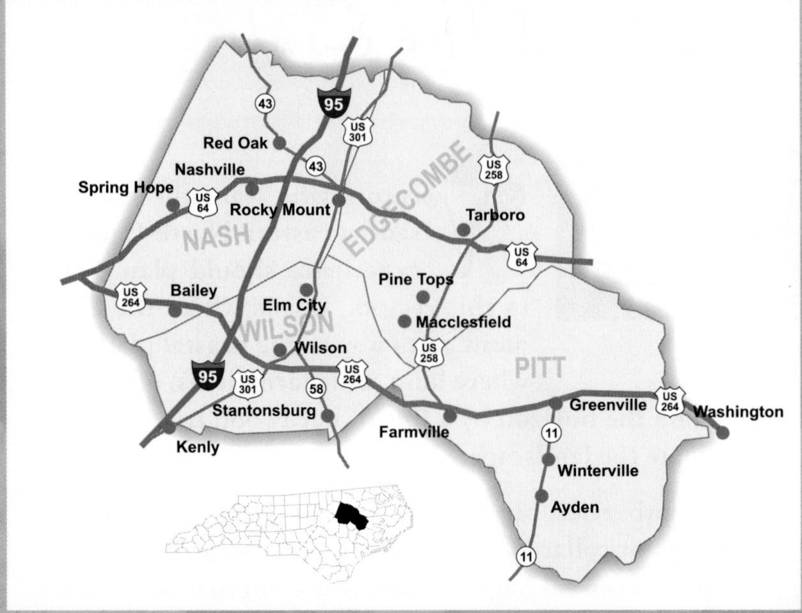

features a collection of furniture, artifacts, and artwork that documents 200 years of Edgecombe County history and culture. Another unique resource is the Country Doctor Museum in Nash County. Founded as a tribute to the contributions of rural physicians, the museum preserves thousands of medical artifacts and historic texts gathered from across the nation. In Pitt County, Colonial- and Victorian-style homes and buildings are preserved in the historic districts of the small towns of Ayden and Farmville.

The dark waters of the Tar River run through this region and provide ample recreational opportunities for fishing, canoeing, and kayaking. Read on for town-by-town descriptions of the unique attractions that make up the "Heart of the East" trail.

Ayden/Pitt County

The Country Doctor Museum

Shiloh Farm

This experience is sure to bring memories for those who grew up on a farm. This proud family farm has educational and wholesome activities for adults and children of all ages—old-fashioned hayrides, an animal viewing area, a playground, a picnic shelter, a barbecue pit, and bonfire areas. 7280 County Home Rd., Ayden, NC 28513. (252) 746-8017; shilohfrm@aol.com

Bailey/Nash County

Bailey's Berry Farm

Here, you'll find luscious strawberries and blueberries—and a name and location that are easy to remember: Bailey's Berry Farm in Bailey, North Carolina! 5645 Strickland Rd., Bailey, NC 27807. Mid-Apr.–mid-June, Mon.–Sat., 7 A.M.–7 P.M.; Sun., 1–6 P.M. (252) 235-4131; wbailey@bbnp.com

The Country Doctor Museum

Classic cars, buggies, portable apothecary chests that doctors used on house calls, and interesting medical instruments from the 1800s depict rural health care. The "Art of Nursing" exhibit is a tribute to TLC. Docents offer one-hour tours, and the gift shop has functional, fun, and instructional merchandise. 6642 Peele Rd., Bailey, NC 27807. Tues.–Sat., 9 A.M.–5 P.M.; closed Christmas week and major holidays. Admission is $5 for adults, $4 for seniors, and $3 for students. (252) 235-4165: www.CountryDoctorMuseum.org

Finch Blueberry Nursery, Pottery & Home for Bluebirds & Open House

Over 50 years ago, Jack Finch found his blueberry hill. Son Dan—a potter, artist, farmer, and entrepreneur—now runs this

Finch Pottery

"bluesy" place. Tour the nursery, watch Dan at work, take a pottery class, or shop for handcrafted bluebird houses, nesting supplies, and other treats for your feathered friends. An open house, held the second Sunday in November, welcomes 60 artists with artistic creations, demonstrations, hot cider, and lots of fun. 5526 Finch Nursery Ln., Bailey, NC 27807. Mon.–Fri., 8 A.M.–5 P.M.; the pottery and bluebird shop are open weekends by appointment. (252) 235-4664 or (800) 245-4662; www.danfinch.com

Elm City/Nash County

Gibson Pottery, Sculpture & Fine Woodworking

Working from his ceramic and woodworking home studio, artist Matt Gibson designs and creates unique pottery, sculpture, and fine woodworks. 6196 Bones Acres Rd., Elm City, NC 27822. Open by appointment. (252) 937-7956

Farmville/Pitt County

The Buzz Around

The buzz about this restaurant isn't just over the good food or the locally grown honey featured in several delightful dishes. It's also about the artwork, the live music Friday nights, and the quaint charm of a two-story historic building. The locals' favorite is the "Sautéed Pepper Jack–Cheese Grit Squares," topped with black bean salsa. Honey butter produced by bees raised by the chef and made in-house is a staple. 3750 S. Main St., Farmville, NC 27828. Wed., 11 A.M.–2 P.M.; Thurs.–Fri., 11 A.M.–2 P.M. and 5:30–10 P.M.; Sat., 5:30–10 P.M. (252) 753-3959; info@thebuzzaround.com

Ceramic tray created by Deborah Kornegay, Artist.

Farmvillearts Gallery

The Arts Council Gallery in the historic Art Deco Paramount Theatre features something new each month except July and August—photography, collectibles, perhaps a new painter. Four theatrical productions and visiting performers—pianists and jazz and choral groups—are on the calendar. April's Dogwood Festival features arts, crafts, and concerts. 3723 N. Main St., Farmville, NC 27828. Mon.–Thurs., noon–5 P.M. (252) 753-3832; www.farmvillearts.org

May Museum & Park

Housed in an 1860s-era home on the National Register of Historic Places, the museum has an extensive collection of 19th- and early-20th-century quilts, which are displayed on a rotating basis. It chronicles the cultural and commercial heritage of Farmville and western Pitt County from colonial times to the present with exhibits from its 40,000 photos, artifacts, and records. 3802 S. Main St., Farmville, NC 27828. Mon.–Fri., 8 A.M.–5 P.M. (252) 753-6725; www.farmville-nc.com

Greenville/Pitt County

Artisan's Market

This market offers more than 50 exclusive shops for decorative accessories and fine gifts, including arts and crafts by local and regional artists. Browse around—you'll find fanciful and fun things for kids and moms, from T-shirts to silver to coffee to beads and bags. 150 Plaza Dr., Greenville, NC 27858. Mon.–Sat., 10 A.M.–6 P.M.; Sun. afternoon. (252) 355-5536 or (800) 537-5564; www.visitgreenvillenc.com

Carolina Seasons Nursery

Exceptional-quality perennials from coneflowers to daylilies, shrubs, trees, annuals, and potted and cut flowers are sold by a family with 25 years' experience. 549 Hwy 903 N., Greenville, NC 27834. Spring–summer, Mon.–Sat., 9 A.M.–6 P.M.; Sun., noon–5 P.M.; fall–winter, Mon.–Sat., 9 A.M.–5:30 P.M. (252) 758-1280; www.carolinaseasons.com

College View Historic District

Take a walking tour through the historic district, which features over 250 Craftsman Bungalow, American Foursquare, and Spanish Revival structures. North side of

Fifth St., Greenville, NC 27858. (252) 329-4200 or (800) 537-5564; www.visitgreenvillenc.com

East Carolina University Theater Series

ECU is an arts and cultural powerhouse year-round. There's a Saturday-afternoon theater series for the young and young-at-heart. Top entertainment ranging from Wynton Marsalis to the Bolshoi Ballet, summertime musicals, comedy, and classics are offered by the School of Theatre and Dance. Wright Auditorium, ECU Campus, Greenville, NC 27858-4353. (252) 328-4788 or (800) ECU-ARTS; www.ecuarts.com

Wall mural by an Emerging Artist *Emerge Gallery & Art Center*

Emerge Gallery & Art Center

This hot new gallery operated by North Carolina artists and students features ceramics, jewelry, painting, and sculpture. The dynamic exhibition space shows professional artists, student work, and community favorites like "The Tiny Art Show." Monthly poetry readings, film nights, and concerts are offered. Artists work in upstairs studios. 404 S. Evans St., Greenville, NC 27858. Tues.–Sat., 11 A.M.–6 P.M.; Sun., 1-4 P.M.; summer, Tues.–Sat., 11 A.M.–6 P.M. (252) 551-6947; www.emergegallery.com

Encourage your budding artist at Emerge Gallery & Arts Center.

Greenville Museum of Art

Nineteenth- and 20th-century American landscapes and contemporary paintings complement one of the largest public collections of North Carolina Jugtown pottery. 802 S. Evans St., Greenville, NC 27858. Tues.–Fri., 10 A.M.–4:30 P.M.; Sat.–Sun., 1-4 P.M. Free. (252) 329-4200 or (800) 537-5564; www.visitgreenvillenc.com

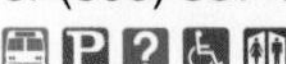

Hollingsworth Farms

Boer goats of top quality and in great health are for sale on this farm. 3119 Ivy Rd., Greenville, NC 27858. Mon.–Fri., 5–9 P.M.; Sat., 9 A.M.–6 P.M.; Sun., 3–6 P.M. (252) 355-2808; thforbes57@hotmail.com

Ledonia Wright African-American Cultural Center

The center features an interesting and rare 150-piece collection of artworks by the Kuba people of Zaire. Bloxton House, ECU Campus, Greenville, NC 27858-4353. Mon.–Thurs., 8 A.M.–8 P.M.; Fri., 8 A.M.–5 P.M. Free. (252) 328-6495; www.ecu.edu/lwcc/

Science & Nature Center

Learn about waterfowl of the Atlantic flyway, turtles, and seashells. Interactive displays interest kids and adults. 1000 Mumford Rd., Greenville, NC 27834. Tues.–Sat., 9:30 A.M.–5 P.M.; Sun., 1-5 P.M. Small admission fee. (252) 329-4561 or (800) 537-5564; www.visitgreenvillenc.com

Sunday in the Park

The Greenville Summer Pops Orchestra plays on the banks of the Tar River. Town Common, Greenville, NC 27834. Sun., 7 P.M. Free. (252) 329-4200 or (800) 537-5564; www.visitgreenvillenc.com

Wellington B. Gray Gallery

Internationally known contemporary artists present crafts, fine art, graphics, video, and installation art. Student *oeuvre* and faculty exhibitions are regularly offered. Fifth St., ECU Campus, Greenville, NC 27858. Mon.–Wed. and Fri., 10 A.M.–4 P.M.; Sat., 10 A.M.–2 P.M.; summer, Mon.–Thurs., 10 A.M.–3 P.M. (252) 328-6336; www.ecu.edu/graygallery

Grifton/Pitt County

Grifton Historical Museum of Area Culture

The museum features prehistoric and Tuscarora Indian artifacts, tobacco and farming tools, fossils, and natural history and Civil War exhibits. The Shad Festival Room and an exhibit on the world's first polyester plant are unique to the museum. 202 Creekshore Dr., Grifton, NC 28530. (252) 329-4200 or (800) 537-5564; www.visitgreenvillenc.com

Classes for kids at Emerge Gallery & Arts Center

Nashville/Nash County

Nash Arts Center

Stained-glass windows filter the light in this lovely gallery. The former Baptist church provides an inspirational setting for regional visual and performing arts, including Barbershop Showcases. 100 E. Washington St., Nashville, NC 27856. Mon.–Fri., 10 A.M.–4 P.M. (252) 459-4734; www.nasharts.org

Nash Arts Center

The Nashville Exchange Steakhouse & Café

The 1913 Jones & May Company dry-goods store is now a cool regional restaurant. Local produce and meats are on the menu; artworks by local and regional artists are on the walls. 229 W. Washington St., Nashville, NC 27856. Mon.–Wed., 7:30 A.M.–3 P.M.; Thurs.–Fri., 7:30 A.M.–3 P.M. and 5:30–9 P.M.; Sat., 5:30–9 P.M. (252) 459-6275; nashex@earthlink.net

The Nashville Exchange Steakhouse & Cafe

Red Oak/Nash County

Stover Pottery

Hand-built coiled stoneware baskets, platters, and wall reliefs with seasoned cedar, grapevines, bamboo, and driftwood are available here. Wheel-thrown pieces influenced by Asian and Indian cultures mix with contemporary thrown, altered, and carved work. 6257 Moore Rd., Red Oak, NC 27868. Open by appointment. (252) 443-5598; www.stoverpottery.com

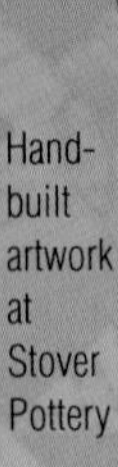

Hand-built artwork at Stover Pottery

Rocky Mount/Nash County

Down East October Festival

Nash and Edgecombe counties are proud cosponsors of this fest of live bands, art, crafts, dance, entertainment, and food. Downtown Rocky Mount, NC 27802. Held the second Sat. in Oct., 10 A.M.–6 P.M. (252) 972-1151; www.rockymountnc.gov/parks/def.html

Dunn Center for the Performing Arts

Mims Galleries presents everything from fine arts to photos and computer and acrylic arts. Wesleyan Theatre, the Tar River Orchestra, and choral groups perform here. 3400 N. Wesleyan Blvd., Rocky Mount, NC 27804-8699. Mon.– Fri., 9 A.M.–5 P.M. (252) 985-5197 or (800) 303-5097; www.dunncenter.com

Dunn Center for the Performing Arts

Farmers' Market and Strawberry Jazz

Strawberry Jazz is held in the historic Mill Village area on the second Saturday in May. It offers live jazz music as well as chocolate-covered, ice-cream-laden, or just plain berries. 1006 Peachtree St., Rocky Mount, NC 27804. Apr.–Dec., Sat., 8 A.M.–1 P.M. (252) 407-7920; jgwinters@coastalnet.com

Fisher Pumpkin Farm

The name says it all! In addition to pumpkins, you can find gourds, fall squash, and Indian corn. Family Farm Day has sheep shearing, horse shoeing, cow milking, wool spinning, and butter making. Fun! 7413 Red Oak Blvd., Rocky Mount, NC 27804. Sept. 25–Nov. 5, Mon.–Sat., 9 A.M.–6 P.M.; Sun., 1-6 P.M. (252) 443-4439

Four Sisters Gallery

Four Sisters Gallery of Self-Taught Visionary Art

Coastal-plain folk art shines here. The gallery is located at the Pearsall Building on the North Carolina Wesleyan College campus. 3400 N. Wesleyan Blvd., Rocky Mount, NC 27804. Mon.–

Fri., 9 A.M.–5 P.M.; Sat., 9 A.M.–noon. (252) 985-5268; www.ncwc.edu/arts/lynch/

Pleasant Hill Cheese

"Great things from pleasant cows," say the makers of Pleasant Hill cheese, yogurt, butter, and soaps. Hwy 11, Box 474, Rocky Mount, NC 27801. Mon.–Sat., 7 A.M.–6 P.M.; Sun., 1-5 P.M. Please call ahead. (252) 446-2914; jt047@aol.com

Rocky Mount Arts Center

Find interesting artwork at the Rocky Mount Arts Center like this piece by Clyde Jones.

Cultural travelers love to stop at the beautiful Imperial Centre. The arts center houses nine galleries, a theater, and a gift shop. Comprehensive programs of concerts and visual arts are featured, along with textiles, paintings, photography, and sculpture. 270 Gay St., Rocky Mount, NC 27804. Tues.–Wed. and Sat., 10 A.M.–5 P.M.; Thurs.–Fri., 10 A.M.–9 P.M.; Sun., 1-5 P.M. (252) 972-1163; www.rockymountnc.gov/artscenter

Rocky Mount Children's Museum & Science Center

The Imperial Centre is the result of a massive restoration of old brick warehouses. The children's museum rocks with hands-on exhibits to encourage science and technology understanding. 100 Imperial Plaza, Rocky Mount, NC 27802. (252) 972-1154; www.rockymountnc.gov/artscenter

Smith's Red & White

You'll find country sausage (hot or mild, links or patties), country ham, and other pork products, all made on-site by this local family business. 3635 N. Halifax Rd., Rocky Mount, NC 27804. Mon.–Fri., 8 A.M.–7 P.M.; Sat., 8 A.M.–6 P.M. (252) 443-4323; virginiaprice@earthlink.net

Stonewall Manor

Harris Acres Farm

This outstanding example of late Federal architecture, built around 1830 by Bennett Bunn and operated as a museum by the Nash County Historical Association, is listed on the National Register of Historic Places. 1331 Stonewall Ln., Rocky Mount, NC 27804. Open the second Sun. of each month, 2–4:30 P.M. Admission is $5 for adults, $3 for seniors, and $2 for kids under 12. (252) 442-6695; http://stonewallmanornc.org

Tarboro/Edgecombe County

Billy's Family Enterprises

Barbecue and cocktail sauces with a taste distinctive to eastern North Carolina vinegar-based recipes are featured. Gift baskets are available, too. 247 S. Shiloh Farm Rd., Tarboro, NC 27886. 6 A.M.–10 P.M. (252) 823-4931; www.billyssauces.com

Blount-Bridgers House

Blount-Bridgers House

This restored, fully furnished historic plantation house was built around 1810 for United States representative Thomas Blount (1759–1812). The house includes 19th-century decorative arts, an arboretum, and a permanent collection of 20th-century oils, pastels, and drawings by Hobson Pittman, Thomas Sully, and Thomas Landseer. 130 Bridgers St., Tarboro, NC 27886-3686. Mon.–Fri., 10 A.M.–4 P.M.; Sat.–Sun., 2–4 P.M.; closed on Sat., Jan.–March. Admission fee. (252) 823-4159; www.edgecombearts.org

Edgecombe County Veterans Military Museum

This museum honors Edgecombe County's sons and daughters who answered their nation's call to defend and preserve the freedoms that citizens now enjoy. 106 W. Church St., Tarboro, NC 27886. Thurs.–Sat., 10 A.M.–4 P.M. Free. (252) 823-0891; banksies@earthlink.net

Hobson Pittman Gallery/Edgecombe Arts

This contemporary gallery of art and history features new exhibits bimonthly. An art fair is held the third Saturday in May; heritage reenactments are offered the last weekend in September. Blount-Bridgers House, 130 Bridgers St., Tarboro, NC 27886. Tues.–Fri., 10 A.M.–4 P.M.; Sat.–Sun., 2–4 P.M. Donations are accepted. (252) 823-4159; www.edgecombearts.org

Deans Farm Market

Wilson/Wilson County

Deans Farm Market

Deans has everything for your picnic—veggies, fruits, pumpkins, and hayrides. It also has a place to get lost—the cotton maze! 4231 NC Hwy 42 W., Wilson, NC 27893. Mon.–Sat., 8 A.M.–5 P.M. (252) 237-0967; www.deansfarmmarket.com

Landscape Source

Yard-art statuary and nursery and landscaping materials can be found here. 541 N. Goldsboro St., Wilson, NC 27893. Mon.–Sat., 8 A.M.–5 P.M. (252) 243-0078

Raleigh Road Nursery & Garden Center

This garden center offers full service, from fountains to furniture and all the greenery you'll need for indoors and out. 4175 US Hwy 264 (Raleigh Rd. Pkwy.), Wilson, NC 27893. Mon.–Sat., 9 A.M.–5 P.M. (252) 291-0114

Raleigh Road Nursery & Garden Center

The Whitehead Inn

Step into the charmed life! Named "One of the Best Places to Stay in the South," this inn is comprised of four historic homes. The pre–Civil War main house and the turn-of-the-century cottages have all the amenities, as well as beautiful décor

and lush gardens. 600 W. Nash St., Wilson, NC 27893. (252) 243-4447; www.whiteheadinn.com

The Whitehead Inn

Wilson Arts Center/Wilson Arts Council

The downtown Wilson Arts Center features exhibitions of regional artists. The arts council also manages the productions at the Boykin Center. 124 W. Nash St., Wilson, NC 27893. Mon.–Fri., 9 A.M.–5 P.M.; Sat., 9 A.M.–3 P.M. (252) 291-4329; www.wilsonarts.com

Wilson Botanical Gardens

Come relax in these formal gardens featuring native plant species and plenty of trees, ornamental grass collections, lilies, and mixed plantings. Bring a picnic! 1806 S.W. Goldsboro St., Wilson, NC 27893. Mon.–Fri., 8 A.M.–5 P.M. (252) 237-0113; www.wilson-co.com/arboretum.html

Wilson Botanical Gardens

Wilson Visitors Bureau

Visitor information is available here. 124 E. Nash St., Wilson, NC 27893. Mon.–Fri., 9 A.M.–5 P.M. (800) 497-7398; www.wilson-nc.com

Winterville/Pitt County

A. W. Ange House

This 1901 Victorian house, listed on the National Register of Historic Places, has a collection of more than 1,000 artifacts. 2543 Church St., Winterville, NC 28530. Open during daylight hours. (800) 537-5564; www.visitgreenvillenc.com

Simpson Whirligig at the Wilson Arts Center

Wilson Visitors Bureau (p. 211)

Pitt County Farmers' Market

Baked goods, jams, jellies, handmade crafts, and all the veggies, fruits, and plants a person could want can be found here. County Home Rd., Winterville, NC 28590. Tues., Thurs., and Sat., 8 A.M.–1 P.M.; Fri., 8 A.M.–3 P.M. (800) 537-5564

Renston Homestead

Here, you can have an agricultural adventure in the heart of a thriving farm community listed on the National Register of Historic Places. Historical and modern farm tours are offered for groups. Picnic lunch areas are available. 4064 NC Hwy 903 S., Winterville, NC 28590. Strawberry season, Mon.–Fri., 7:30 A.M.–6 P.M.; Sat., 7:30 A.M.–4 P.M.; Sun., 1-5 P.M. (252) 321-3204 or (252) 714-3838; mlskinner@mail.com

Homes for Bluebirds (p. 201)

Crossroads, PatriArts, and Native Ways

Bladen, Cumberland, Harnett, Johnston, Robeson, and Wake Counties

Travelers cruising through North Carolina's southern Piedmont on I-95 might not realize that they're traversing a region of flourishing farmlands. In fact, this gentle undulating countryside is considered by many to be the agricultural heartland of the state. Farm hamlets here often sprang up where two rural roads intersected. These crossroads communities still exist, often just a few miles off the interstate.

Farms on this trail produce some of the world's finest strawberries, blackberries, blueberries, tomatoes, corn, peppers, cantaloupes, melons, and squash. Visitors can shop for these fruits and vegetables at a multitude of farms, produce stands, and farmers' markets in all seven counties. Farmers here are also famous for their skill at curing hams. Stop in at a ham shop and take home smoked, honey-glazed, and even wine-glazed products.

If agricultural history piques your interest, you'll note that this is one of the South's top tobacco-producing regions. It's been that way for many generations, and the history and traditions associated with this industry are presented at sites like the Tobacco Farmlife Museum in Johnston County.

This trail encompasses some of the most ethnically diverse communities in the Southeast. Beginning in the 1730s, Highland Scots and Irish settled along the beautiful Cape Fear and Lumber rivers. Both freed blacks and runaway slaves also lived here. Before that, native peoples inhabited the territory. The Lumbee, Tuscarora, and Waccamaw Siouan tribes still call this area home. Attend the outdoor drama *Strike at the Wind* to learn the story of Henry Berry Lowrie, a Lumbee who sought justice for American Indian people after the Civil War.

Although the predominant character of the region is rural, urban areas are also important transportation and cultural crossroads. In the state's early history, the town of Fayetteville

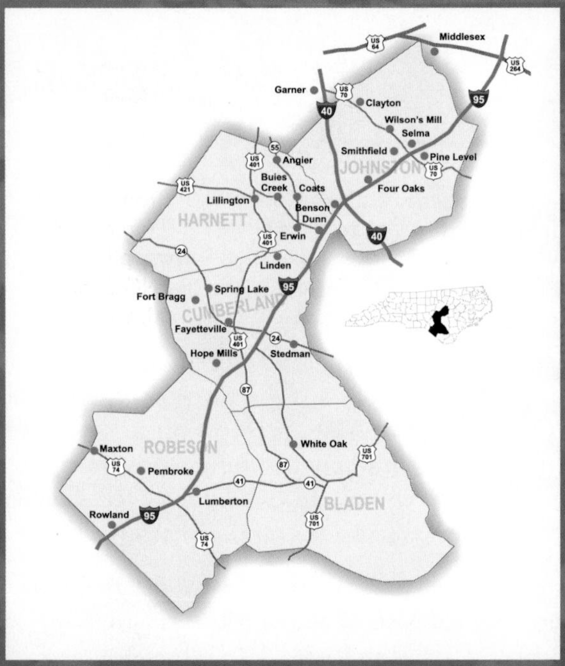

served as an inland port, the hub of a major plank road, and North Carolina's first capital. During the Civil War, Fayetteville housed an important arsenal that drew Union general William T. Sherman to North Carolina. Fort Bragg, the largest military installation in the world, began in 1918 and has trained military personnel from across the nation and the globe. Take in the Airborne & Special Operations Museum, which tells the history of the army's elite forces from World War II to today through Smithsonian-quality exhibits.

Today, places like Fayetteville and Smithfield embrace a diverse mixture of cultures and traditions. You can enjoy an impressive array of offerings from artists' studios, museums and galleries, regional theaters, and performance venues presenting music and dance.

Outdoor enthusiasts should experience Raven Rock high above the Cape Fear River or the nine distinctive natural areas found at Howell Woods Environmental Learning Center. Plan your own itinerary by reading the following town-by-town descriptions of the unique attractions that make up the "Crossroads, PatriArts, and Native Ways" trail.

Angier/Harnett County

Bike Fest at Angier Depot Square

This annual motorcycle festival draws visitors from across the state. A bike show features more than 100 motorcycles. The festival offers live music, food, and vendors, plus activities for children. 19 W. Depot St., Angier, NC 27501. Held the first Sat. in June. Free. (919) 639-2500; www.angierchamber.org

Crepe Myrtle Celebration *Angier Chamber of Commerce*

Crepe Myrtle Celebration

For more than 30 years, Angier, also known as "the Town of Crepe Myrtles," has welcomed fall with a festival that celebrates the town's heritage and small-town life. Live music and entertainment, festival food, handmade crafts, rides, and games and activities for children are featured. 19 W. Depot St., Angier, NC 27501. Held the second weekend of Sept. Free. (919) 639-2500; www.angierchamber.org

Benson/Johnston County

Benson Mule Days

Benson Mule Days *N.C. Division of State Historic Sites*

Celebrate the hardworking farm mules that were replaced by modern equipment in the 1950s. Friday is dedicated to the mule, with a judging contest, jumping, pulling, and racing events. Saturday's large parade features more than 2,000 horse and mule entries. There are also rodeo events, carnival rides, arts-and-crafts vendors, food, and live entertainment. Downtown and Chamber Park, Benson, NC 27504. Held the fourth weekend in Sept. Fri.–Sat., 9 A.M.–11 P.M.; Sun., 1–5 P.M. Free. (919) 894-3825; www.benson-chamber.com

Crepe Myrtle Celebration

Benson Museum of Local History

Benson Museum of Local History

Retrace Benson's roots with a collection of railroad memorabilia, antiques, quilts, hardware, and farming artifacts. 303 E. Church St., Benson, NC 27504. Wed., 2–4 P.M., or by appointment. Free. (919) 894-3825

Benson Singing Convention

The oldest Southern gospel convention in the nation includes three days of music ranging from concerts to competitions. The event is held outdoors. Blankets and lawn chairs are encouraged. Benson Singing Grove, Main St., Benson, NC 27504. Fri., 7–10 P.M.; Sat., 9 A.M.-10 P.M.; Sun., 11 A.M.–5 P.M. Free. (919) 894-6051

Meadow Village Grill

Meadow Village's 100-item buffet features true Southern cuisine. Be sure to leave room for the large selection of homemade desserts! 7400 NC Hwy 50 S., Benson, NC 27504. Thurs.–Sat., 11 A.M.–9 P.M.; Sun. and Tues.–Wed., 11 A.M.–2:30 P.M. (919) 894-5430

Northlake Christmas Trees

Cut your own at Northlake Christmas Trees. Enjoy the delightful fragrance. Get energized by a crisp walk outdoors along several roads and paths on the farm. 7326 Meadowbrook Rd., Benson, NC 27504. Open the first week of Dec. Call for times. (919) 894-3524

The Pound Cake Company

Featured in *Southern Living*, Jan Matthews Hodges opened this bakery after winning several blue ribbons at the North Carolina State Fair. The rest is history. 101-A N. Market St., Benson, NC 27504. Wed. and Fri., 6:30–9 P.M.; Sat., noon–5 P.M. (919) 894-8448; www.thebestcake.com

Preston Woodall House Bed & Breakfast

This Queen Anne residence (circa 1910) has been beautifully restored into a bed-and-breakfast. Three cottages consisting of three bedrooms each, a living area, and a kitchen are located on the adjoining street. The house is on the National Register of Historic Places. 201 E. Hill St., Benson, NC 27504. (919) 894-7025; www.woodallhouse.com

Preston Woodall House Bed & Breakfast

Smith's Nursery and Strawberry Farm

Smith's is open year–round for seasonal plants and produce. Strawberry season is from mid-April to early June, blueberry season from June to July, and blackberry season from June to August. School field trips are offered. 443 Sanders Rd., Benson, NC 27504. Mon.–Sat., 8 A.M.-6 P.M.; Sun., 1–5 P.M. (919) 934-1700; www.smiths-nursery.com

Stephensons' Bar-B-Q

The Stephensons are "good people," as they say in the South, and they're keeping alive the traditional way of cooking pork. Pork shoulders are smoked each day! 11964 NC Hwy 50 N., McGees Crossroads, Benson, NC 27504. Mon.–Sat., 10 A.M.–9 P.M. (919) 894-4530

W. J. Barefoot Auditorium

W. J. Barefoot Auditorium

This historic structure, once the K-12 school for Benson, now houses a 350-seat auditorium, Benson Town Hall, the Benson Chamber of Commerce, and the Benson Museum of Local History. 303 E. Church St., Benson, NC 27504. Mon.–Fri., 8:30 A.M.–5 P.M. Rental fees are charged. (919) 894-5117; www.townofbenson.com

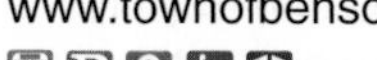

White Swan Bar-B-Q

White Swan Bar-B-Q

Cooking pork over a slow fire, seasoning it with spices, and adding a vinegar sauce is an eastern North Carolina tradition. White Swan Bar-B-Q has been doing it right for more than 40 years. 105 N. Honeycutt St., Benson, NC 27504. Daily, 10 A.M.–9 P.M. (919) 894-4446

Buies Creek/Harnett County

Lundy-Fetterman Museum and Exhibit Hall

This location features 175 revolving exhibits of animal and marine wildlife. The museum is located in the Lundy-Fetterman School of Business on the Campbell University campus. The collection was donated to Campbell by the Lundy family. 165 Dr. McKoy Rd., Buies Creek, NC 27506. Mon.–Tues., 10 A.M.–3 P.M.; other times by appointment. Free. (910) 814-4398; www.campbell.edu/business/museum.html

Banks Miniature Horse Farm

Clayton/Johnston County

Banks Miniature Horse Farm

Home to more than 40 beautiful miniature horses from outstanding bloodlines, the farm provides an atmosphere where horses are admired and respected. 2667 Peele Rd., Clayton, NC 27520. Mon.–Fri., 9 A.M.–5 P.M. Call for an appointment. (919) 412-1684; www.banksminiaturehorsefarm.com

Beasley's Berries

Pick your own strawberries from mid-April to mid-June. Bring the whole family to enjoy the outdoors and the red ripeness of strawberries. 2914 Peele Rd., Clayton, NC 27520. Mon.–Sat., 8 A.M.–7 P.M.; Sun., 1–6 P.M. (919) 553-6923

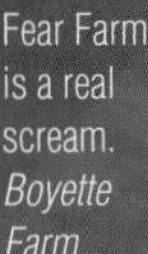

Fear Farm is a real scream. *Boyette Farm*

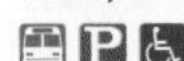

Boyette Farm

After the fall harvest, Glenn Boyette prepares to scare everyone at the "Fear Farm" event the three weekends before Halloween. The event includes hayrides, haunted houses, games, and a gift shop. From Thanksgiving to New Year's, the farm features "Lights on the Neuse." 1620 Loop Rd., Clayton, NC 27527. (919) 553-4094; www.claytonfearfarm.com

The Clayton Center

The Clayton Center features a 600-seat performing-arts auditorium. The Palladian Concert Series brings national and regional performing-arts, dance, comedy, and theater groups to the area each year. 111 E. Second St., Clayton, NC 27520. Box office, Mon.–Fri., 10 A.M.–noon and 1–5 P.M. (919) 553-1737;www.theclaytoncenter.org

Clemmons Educational State Forest

Well-marked trails plus exhibits and displays make learning fun and easy at Clemmons Educational State Forest. "Talking" trees and rocks are a favorite with children. 2411 Old US Hwy 70 W., Clayton, NC 27520. Mid-March–late Nov., Tues.–Fri., 9 A.M.–5 P.M.; Sat.–Sun., 11 A.M.–8 P.M. (daylight savings time), 11 A.M.–5 P.M. (Eastern time). Free. (919) 553-5651; www.dfr.state.nc.us

Visit the talking trees at Clemmons Educational State Forest.

The Coffee Mill

The Coffee Mill offers coffees and light fare, as well as a location for artists to display their work. The Flip Side features local performers every Friday and Saturday night. 105 S. Lombard St., Clayton, NC 27520. Mon., 7 A.M.–8 P.M.; Tues., 7 A.M.–10 P.M.; Wed.–Fri., 7 A.M.–9 P.M.; Sat., 8 A.M.–9 P.M.; Sun., 8 A.M.–2 P.M. (919) 550-0174; www.thecoffeemill.com

Check out local artwork at the Coffee Mill.

G. O. Designs

Bright, color still lifes and unique abstracts characterize the oils, acrylics, and mixed-media work of Gail O'Neil. Handmade jewelry, photography, pottery, silk scarves, and original creations by other North Carolina women artists are here, too. 401 E. Main St., Suite 105, Clayton, NC 27520. Tues. and Thurs., 10 A.M.–7 P.M.; Wed. and Fri., 10 A.m.–6 P.M.; Sat., by appointment. (919) 553-6188; www.gailoneildesign.com

Johnston County Arts Council

Johnston County Arts Council

231 E. Second St., Clayton, NC 27520. (919) 553-1930; www.johnstoncountyarts.org

McCall's Bar-B-Cue & Seafood

If you love a buffet with lots of country cooking, salads, and desserts, McCall's Bar-B-Cue & Seafood is just the place. 10365 US Hwy 70 W., Clayton, NC 27520. Daily, 11 A.M.–9 P.M. (919) 550-3877

Morning Glory Inn

The Morning Glory Inn Bed & Breakfast is a charming historic home with five guest rooms, each with a full bath. Guests enjoy the public parlor and dining area for complimentary breakfast, as well as the exercise room. 507 E. Second St., Clayton, NC 27520. (919) 550-8547; www.morning-glory-inn.com

Morning Glory Inn

Neuse Adventures Canoe & Kayak Rentals

Spend two hours drifting down the Neuse River in a canoe or kayak with guide Johnny House. The slow-moving river passes beavers, cranes, and wildlife, accompanied by the sweet smell of honeysuckle. 2975 Covered Bridge Rd., Clayton, NC 27520. (919) 553-3295; www.neuseadventures.com

Riverwood Street Festival

Fred Smith Company hosts the annual Riverwood Street Festival in late April. The festival includes a Friday-night concert and a full day of activities on Saturday. Music, food, crafts, and free rides for the kids are featured. 400 Riverwood Dr., Clayton, NC 27520. Free. (919) 550-8086; www.fredsmithcharity.com

The Village Farmers' Market

The Village Farmers' Market, located at the planned community known as Flowers Plantation, offers fresh produce, home-baked pies, cakes, and fudge. 4684 NC Hwy 42 E., Clayton, NC 27520. (919) 550-0765; www.flowersplantation.com/village

Farm-fresh produce at The Village Farmers' Market

Coats/Harnett County

Annual Coats Farmer's Day

Farmer's Day has been around since 1910 and still celebrates the agricultural heritage of Harnett County. It has grown to include a golf tournament, a tractor show, entertainment, a kids' park, sack races, pole climbing, marble shoots, and an antique car show. Main St., Coats, NC 27521. Held on a Sat. in Oct., 9 A.M.–5 P.M.; street dance, 8–11 P.M. A fee is charged for the dance. Call for specific date. (910) 897-6213; www.CoatsChamber.com

Coats Heritage Museum

The museum has military, 4-H, historic furnishings, and aviation displays; books, articles, and art by local citizens; a display of farm implements; and the Cotton Museum, depicting an entire process from seed to finished product. 109 S. McKinley St., Coats, NC 27521. Sun., 2–5 P.M., and by appointment. Free. (910) 897-2525; www.coatsmuseum.com

Coats Heritage Museum

Noah's Landing

This nonprofit nature center features more than 40 different exhibits showcasing llamas, coatimundi, kinkajou, and much more. Interactive tours allow visitors to touch and even feed the animals. 1489 Live Oak Rd., Coats, NC 27521. Mon.–Fri., by appointment; Sat., 10 A.M.–5 P.M.; Sun., 1–5 P.M. Admission fee. (910) 897-NOAH; www.noahslanding2x2.com

Dunn/Cumberland County

Averasboro Battlefield Complex *Fayetteville Area Convention & Visitors Bureau*

Averasboro Battlefield Complex

The complex includes the site of the March 15, 1865, Battle of Averasboro, three plantation homes, Chicora Cemetery, and a museum that features detailed dioramas and artifacts. The site is marked with signage highlighting key locations. The battle's anniversary is held in mid-March, and Heritage Living History is celebrated on the last Saturday in October. 3300 NC Hwy 82, Dunn, NC 28334. Tues.–Sat., 10 A.M.–4 P.M.; Sun., 1–4 P.M. Free. (910) 891-5019; www.averasboro.com

The Barrington House

The Barrington House *Dunn Chamber of Commerce*

This charming B&B is located in a restored historic home. Details include mahogany paneling, sliding pocket doors, white marble–encased fireplaces, and crystal chandeliers. The location also has six acres of beautiful gardens, a huge porch, an outdoor patio with a fireplace, a copper-roofed round pavilion, an eight-foot fountain, and garden statuary. 608 W. Barrington St., Dunn, NC 28334. (910) 892-6980 or (800) 719-1674; www.barringtonhousenc.com

Cottle Farms

Home of General William C. Lee

Delicious, juicy strawberries are a North Carolina favorite. This farm offers an opportunity to pick fresh strawberries between April 15 and June 1. Come out with the family and enjoy some wholesome outdoor fun in the sunshine! Located between Dunn and Erwin on US Hwy 421. Mon.–Sat., 8 A.M.–7 p.m.; Sun., 1–6 P.M. (910) 892-4248

General William C. Lee Airborne Museum

Listed on the National Register of Historic Places, this was the home of Dunn native William C. Lee, the major general remembered as "the Father of the U.S. Army Airborne." 209 W. Divine St., Dunn, NC 28335. Mon.–Fri., 8:30 A.M.–4 P.M.; Sat., 11 A.M.–4 P.M. Tours are offered on Sat. and by appointment. Free. (910) 892-1947; www.visitDunn.com

Harnett Regional Theatre

Harnett Regional Theatre

This venue provides community-theater presentations from September through May and children's theater workshops in June. 114 N. Wilson Ave., Dunn, NC 28335. (910) 892-8142; www.onlinehrt.org

The Howard House

The Howard House

The Howard House, which operates as the Dunn Woman's Club House, is a Colonial Revival mansion built between 1908 and 1909 that is listed on the National Register of Historic Places. The house is available for rent for receptions, meetings, exhibits, and other social events. 402 S. Layton Ave., Dunn, NC 28335. (910) 892-3282

Johnson Strawberry Farm

Berry-licious! This family farm features prepicked and pick-your-own strawberries. Other produce available on a seasonal basis includes squash, Irish potatoes, corn, cantaloupes, watermelons, cabbages, and onions. 2901 Hobson Rd. (Hwy 301 N.), Dunn, NC 28334. Mon.–Sat., 7 A.M.–7 P.M. (910) 892-4926

An original watercolor by artist Joanna McKethan

"Originals" Art Studio

This gallery located in the heart of downtown Dunn features Joanna McKethan's winning watercolors. It also exhibits her original oil paintings and collages. Lessons are available. 126 E. Broad St., Dunn, NC 28334. Mon.–

Thurs., 10 A.M.–7 P.M.; Fri., 10 A.M.–5 P.M.; Sat. and other times by appointment. (910) 892-7062; www.joriginals.net

Tart's Produce Stand

Tart's Produce Stand

This produce stand features a variety of seasonal farm-fresh fruits and vegetables. A second stand carries a complete nursery selection of plants and flowers. Harnett Crossing Shopping Center, 2008 W. Cumberland St., Dunn, NC 28334. The flower stand is open daily; produce stand, Fri.–Sat., 8 A.M.–7 P.M.; Sun., 10 A.M.–6 P.M. (910) 892-1324

Touchstone Energy NC Cotton Festival

This local festival, which draws more than 8,000 each year, offers something for everyone—family fun, entertainment, and education about cotton. It includes tours of a cotton gin; arts and crafts; a pig cookoff; music; a classic car, truck, tractor, and Harley-Davidson show; midway rides; and a petting zoo. Downtown Dunn, NC 28335. Held the first weekend in Nov. Fri., 6–10 P.M.; Sat., 10 A.M.–4 P.m. Free. (910) 892-3282; www.nccottonfestival.com

Touchstone Energy NC Cotton Festival *Dunn Chamber of Commerce*

Fayetteville/Cumberland County

Airborne & Special Operations Museum

The museum traces the heroic history of Airborne and Special Operations forces. Displays, life-sized dioramas, audiovisual displays, a motion simulator, and a large-screen theater all help visitors appreciate the courage and patriotism demonstrated by these extraordinary soldiers. 100 Bragg Blvd., Fayetteville, NC 28301. Tues.–Sat., 10 A.M.–5 P.M.; Sun., noon–5 P.M. Free. (910) 483-3003; www.asomf.org

Airborne & Special Operations Museum *Fayetteville Area Convention & Visitors Bureau*

Arsenal Park

Arsenal Park *Fayetteville Area Convention & Visitors Bureau*

The four-and-a-half-acre site contains the remnants of the United States Arsenal, built in 1836 to store arms and manufacture ordnance goods. The state of North Carolina seized the arsenal at the beginning of the Civil War. On March 11, 1865, Union forces destroyed the facility. Tours of the site are given by the Museum of the Cape Fear Historical Complex. 801 Arsenal Ave., Fayetteville, NC 28305. Tues.–Sat., 10 A.M.–5 P.M.; Sun., 1–5 P.M. Free. (910) 486-1330; www.ncmuseumofhistory.org

Art & Soul

This downtown gallery features original works of art by both regional and national artists. 231 Franklin St., Fayetteville, NC 28301. Mon.–Fri., 10 A.M.–6 P.M.; Sat., 10 A.M.–4 P.M. (910) 485-7812; margoj@theartscouncil.com

Arts Council of Fayetteville/Cumberland County

301 Hay St., Fayetteville, NC 28301. (910) 323-1776; www.theartscouncil.com

Art & Soul Gallery

Campbellton Landing

This site is named after the old ferry landing at Campbellton Village, which became the first settlement in the area in 1730. It is where the king of England granted landowner Peter Lord a license to keep a public ferry in 1764. Confederate breastworks were placed here in 1865. 1122 Person St., Fayetteville, NC 28301. Free. (910) 483-1649 or (800) 255-8217

Campground United Methodist Church

Campground Methodist Church was organized in 1862. However, regular camp meetings of several days' duration were held on this spot beginning in the early 1840s. The nearby cemetery contains graves dating back to 1838. 4625 Campground Rd., Fayetteville, NC 28314. Open Sun.–Fri.; call ahead for church escort. (910) 867-9436; www.campgroundumc.com

Campbelton Landing *Fayetteville Area Convention & Visitors Bureau* (p. 225)

Cape Fear Botanical Garden

Cape Fear Botanical Garden is beautiful year-round. Located on 79 acres, it features a large urban forest with nature trails, a natural amphitheater, and terrain ranging from open pine forest to lush riverbank. Adults and children can study pioneer life by viewing an authentic 1886 farmhouse. 536 N. Eastern Blvd., Fayetteville, NC 28301. March–Dec., Mon.–Sat., 10 A.M.–5 P.M.; Sun., noon–5 P.M.; Jan.–Feb., Mon.–Sat., 10 A.M.–5 P.M. Admission is $5 for adults and $4 for military; children under 12 are free; admission is free on the first Sat. of each month and during the month of Apr. (910) 486-0221; www.capefearbg.org

Cape Fear Regional Theatre

Founded in1962, Cape Fear Regional Theatre presents an annual series of plays, performances, and special events that entertain, enlighten, inspire, and educate both performers and audiences. 1209 Hay St., Fayetteville, NC 28305. Theater office, Mon.–Fri., 9 A.M.–5 P.M. (910) 323-4234; www.cfrt.org

Cape Fear Studios

Cape Fear Studios

Here, you can watch artists working in studio spaces and enjoy changing exhibitions in the galleries. Functional and decorative pottery by local potters is featured. Select from paintings in oil, acrylic, pastel, and watercolor. Fabrics and hand-dyed silks, jewelry, primitives, sculpture, glass, and hand-woven baskets are also available. 148 Maxwell St., Fayetteville, NC 28301. Tues.–Fri., 11 A.M.–5 P.M.; Sat., 10 A.M.–4 P.M.; Sun., 1–5 P.M. Free. (910) 433-2986; www.capefearstudios.com

City Center Gallery & Books

Located in the former Ray Building, one of the few turn-of-the-century Victorian buildings left downtown, City Center

Gallery & Books includes an art gallery and a used bookstore. A limited selection of new books about Fayetteville and gift items such as jewelry and handmade items by local crafters are also available. 112 Hay St., Fayetteville, NC 28301. Mon.–Sat., 10 A.M.–5 P.M. (910) 678-8899; www.citycentergallery.com

City Center Gallery & Books *Fayetteville Area Convention & Visitors Bureau*

Cross Creek Cemetery

This is the oldest public cemetery in Fayetteville. It features monuments dating from 1786 to 1964 and exhibits nearly every major type of grave marker found in North Carolina. The cemetery has the first Confederate monument erected in the state. N. Cool Spring and Grove streets, Fayetteville, NC 28301. Open daily. (910) 483-5311 or (800) 255-8217; www.visitfayettevillenc.com

E. E. Smith Monument

This monument honors Dr. E. E. (Ezekiel Ezra) Smith, a respected African-American educator who headed Fayetteville State University for 50 years. He also served as ambassador to Liberia and founded North Carolina's first African-American newspaper. 1200 Murchison Rd., Fayetteville, NC 28301. (910) 483-5311 or (800) 255-8217; www.visitfayettevillenc.com

E. E. Smith Monument *Fayetteville Area Convention & Visitors Bureau*

1897 Poe House

Not to be confused with the famous writer, Fayetteville's Edgar Allen Poe was a prominent businessman. Poe's home stands upon land that was part of the United States Arsenal destroyed by General William T. Sherman at the end of the Civil War. Guides are available through the Museum of the Cape Fear Historical Complex. 206 Bradford St., Fayetteville, NC 28305. Tues.–Sat., 10 A.M.–5 P.M.; Sun., 1–5 P.M. Free. (910) 486-1330; www.ncmuseumofhistory.org

1897 Poe House

Fascinate-U Children's Museum *Fayetteville Area Convention & Visitors Bureau*

Fascinate-U Children's Museum

This museum features safe, interactive exhibits, displays, and classroom space. The hands-on displays represent a mini-city where children can explore their world the way they know best—through creative role-playing, manipulation, and interaction. 116 Green St., Fayetteville, NC 28302. Tues. and Thurs., 9 A.M.–5 P.M.; Wed., 9 A.M.–7 P.M.; Sat., 10 A.M.–5 P.M.; Sun., noon–5 P.M. Admission is $3 for children and $1 for adults. (910) 829-9171; www.fascinate-u.com

Fayetteville Area Convention & Visitors Bureau

245 Person St., Fayetteville, NC 28301. Mon.–Fri., 8 A.M.–5 P.M.; Sat. and holidays, 10 A.M.–4 P.M. (910) 483-5311 or (800) 255-8217; www.visitfayettevillenc.com

Fayetteville Museum of Art

Occupying the first building in North Carolina designed and built as an art museum, the museum offers exhibitions, concerts, workshops, and special events. Two galleries, classrooms, studio space, an art reference and slide lending library, and a museum store are also located here. 839 Stamper Rd., Fayetteville, NC 28303. Mon.–Fri., 10 A.M.–5 P.M.; Sat.–Sun., 1–5 P.M. Free. (910) 485-5121; www.fayettevillemuseumart.org

Fayetteville Rose Garden

The Fayetteville Rose Society's rose beds display more than 35 types of roses and more than 1,000 individual rose bushes. 2201 Hull Rd., Fayetteville, NC 28303. Open during daylight hours. Free. (910) 678-8400; www.faytechcc.edu

Fayetteville Rose Garden *Fayetteville Area Convention & Visitors Bureau*

Fayetteville State University Planetarium

The planetarium's programming centers around sky phenomena and connections with historical events. The planetarium features a projector with 2,354 stars. It offers five programs geared to specific grade-level curricula or K-12 school groups, including astronomy and space science programs for Boy and Girl scouts. General programs are

Fayetteville State University Theatre Company *Fayetteville Area Convention & Visitors Bureau*

offered to the public when time permits. 1200 Murchison Rd., Fayetteville, NC 28301. Open by appointment. For groups of 20 or more, please call to schedule. Free. (910) 672-1652; http://astro.uncfsu.edu/planetarium

Fayetteville State University Theatre Company

The theater program provides four to five shows per academic year—two shows in the fall, two in the spring, and an optional Christmas performance. Butler Bldg., 1200 Murchison Rd., Fayetteville, NC 28301. Performances, Thurs.–Sat., 7-10 P.M. Admission is $8 for adults and $5 for seniors. (910) 672-1006 or (800) 222-2594; www.uncfsu.edu/speech&theatre/fsu_drama_guild.htm

Freedom Memorial Park

This military memorial park commemorates the service of those who gave their lives for their town and country. It also stands as a testament to those in service today. 101 Bragg Blvd., Fayetteville, NC 28301. Open daily during daylight hours. Free. (910) 867-7776; www.freedommemorialpark.com

Freedom Memorial Park

The Gilbert Theater

The Gilbert Theater is a nonprofit, award-winning theater with a mostly volunteer staff and a company of artists. It provides contemporary, socially relevant, and entertaining theater, as well as the classics and original works by local playwrights. (910) 678-7186; www.gilberttheater.com

Gillis Hill Farm

One of the oldest family farms in North Carolina, Gillis Hill Farm offers exciting and educational farm tours that include wagon rides, agricultural seminars, farm animal exhibits, and antique farm equipment and structures. 2701 Gillis Hill Rd., Fayetteville, NC 28306. Open by appointment. (910) 867-2350; jdgillis2@aol.com

Gregs!

Gregs! is a fine-art, pottery, and gift gallery located in the heart of historic downtown Fayetteville. It features watercolors and pottery by artist Greg Hathaway. Other artists are represented in a changing exhibition schedule. Gregs! also has gifts, candles, retro goodies, and a paint-your-own pottery studio. 122 Maxwell St., Fayetteville, NC 28301. Mon.–Sat., 10 A.M.–6 P.M. (910) 483-8355; greg@schoollink.net

Find unique gifts at Gregs!

Griffin's Coffee Shop

This small, neighborhood coffee shop serves a delicious Italian espresso, which is also available for resale. Local art by Mary Nan Thompson and North Carolina pottery from Seagrove are on display. 1225 Fort Bragg Rd., Fayetteville, NC 28305. Mon.–Thurs., 6:30 A.M.–8 P.M.; Fri., 6:30 A.M.–9 P.M.; Sat., 7 A.M.–9 P.M.; Sun., 8 A.M.–6 P.M. (910) 484-5860; kmcelhiney@visitfayettevillenc.com

Griffin's Coffee Shop *Fayetteville Area Convention & Visitors Bureau*

Jambbas Ranch

Enjoy a leisurely visit and see buffaloes, llamas, elk, cows, deer, camels, and a whole ranch full of friendly domestic and exotic birds and animals. The attractions include a welcome center, a covered bridge, Fort Rest, the No Chance Gold Mine, a swinging bridge, and the Cape Fear River. 5386 Tabor Church Rd., Fayetteville, NC 28312. Mon.–Sat., 9:30 A.M.–5 P.M.; Sun., 1–5 P.M. Admission is $6 for adults, $4 for children over two and students, and $4 for groups; children under two are free. (910) 484-4808; www.jambbas.com

Jambbas Ranch *Fayetteville Area Convention & Visitors Bureau*

Just Claying Around

Just Claying Around is a paint-your-own pottery studio. Paints, brushes, and other tools are supplied. The shop owners glaze and fire their guests' pieces and have them ready in one week. 201 S. McPherson Church Rd., Fayetteville, NC 28303. Wed.–Thurs., 10 A.M.–6 P.M.; Fri.–Sat., 10 A.M.–8 P.M.; Sun., noon–5 P.M. (910) 487-9242; kmcelhiney@visitfayettevillenc.com

Just Claying Around

Lazy Acres Campground

The campground owners will try to make your stay, whether it's overnight or for several days, an enjoyable one. Whether you are visiting friends and family or just getting away, the area has a lot to offer. Tent and RV campers are welcome. 821 Lazy Acres St., Fayetteville, NC 28306. (910) 425-9218; www.lazyacrescampground.net

Market House

The Market House sits on the spot where in 1789 North Carolina both ratified the United States constitution and chartered the University of North Carolina. On May 29, 1831, a fire broke out and destroyed over 600 structures in Fayetteville, including the old statehouse. In 1832, the Market House was rebuilt on the site. In 1907, it was saved in what was probably one of the earliest examples of historic preservation in the state. At the intersection of Person, Hay, Green, and Gillespie streets, Fayetteville, NC 28301. Free. (910) 483-5311 or (800) 255-8217; www.visitfayettevillenc.com

The Mash House Restaurant & Brewery

A fully operational brewery, the Mash House offers up to nine handcrafted beers made on site. Tours of the brewery are available upon request. The Mash House has a large steak selection, homemade pizzas fired in a brick oven, fresh fish, and a variety of pastas and sandwiches. 4150 Sycamore Dairy Rd., Fayetteville, NC 28303. Mon.–Thurs., 11:30 A.M.–midnight; Fri.–Sat., 11:30 A.M.–2 A.M.; Sun., 10:30 A.M.–10 P.M. (910) 867-9223; www.themashhouse.com

Market House

Museum of the Cape Fear Historical Complex

Exhibits chronicle American Indians, European settlements, slavery, plank roads, steam boating, industry, and the Civil War. The museum features permanent exhibitions and a special exhibit gallery, as well as topical exhibits on early-19th-century domestic life, transportation, and the traditions of folk potters. 801 Arsenal Ave., Fayetteville, NC 28305. Tues.–Sat., 10 A.M.–5 P.M.; Sun., 1–5 P.M. Free. (910) 486-1330; www.ncmuseumofhistory.org

Museum of the Cape Fear Historical Complex (p. 231)

Not Quite Antiques

This shop carries vintage and antique furniture, works by local artists and artisans, unique items from Africa and India, Polish pottery, and candles. It features a serene tearoom providing samples of interesting teas. 108 Roxie Ave., Fayetteville, NC 28304. Tues.–Sat., 10 A.M.–6 P.M. (910) 323-0300; nqantiques@aol.com

Rude Awakening Coffee House

Rude Awakening is located in a renovated 1914 building. It serves organic, fair-trade, shade-grown coffees with a variety of origins. Coffee is served within five days of being roasted. A full espresso-based coffee menu with decaf and soy substitutions is available. The gift selection includes limited-edition T-shirts and framed vintage Fayetteville postcards. 227 Hay St., Fayetteville, NC 28301. Mon.–Sat., 8 A.M.–noon. (910) 223-7833; www.rudeawakening.net

Rude Awakening Coffee House
Fayetteville Area Convention & Visitors Bureau

Smith Farms

This is authentic farming, unadorned for tourists. You'll see goats and organic produce being raised on a small farm that sells directly to consumers and sometimes to farmers' markets as well. 2844 Custer Ave., Fayetteville, NC 28301. Open by appointment. (910) 323-3780

St. Andrews United Methodist Church

St. Andrews was built in 1848. Early members of the church built the traditional frame structure with center-aisle poles separating men from women. St. Andrews was one of the only churches in Fayetteville to maintain a Sunday school during the Civil War. 121 Lofton Dr., Fayetteville, NC 28311. Mon.–Fri., 9 A.M.–4 P.M.; Sun., 8 A.M.–6 P.M. (910) 488-4648; www.standrewsfayetteville.org

The Stage Door Theatre

This intimate community theater features the award-winning *That Improv Show* and produces scripted performances as well. 934 Cambridge St., Fayetteville, NC 28303. Fri.–Sat., 8 P.M. Admission fee. (910) 433-2900; www.thestagedoortheatre.org

The Stage Door Theatre *Fayetteville Area Convention & Visitors Bureau*

Fort Bragg/Cumberland County

82nd Airborne Division War Memorial Museum

The museum honors the heroes of America's first airborne division. The 82nd has served as a strategic deployment force since 1942, ready to deploy worldwide within 18 hours. Bldg. C-6841, Ardennes St., Fort Bragg, NC 28310. Tues.–Sat., 10 A.M.–4:30 P.M.; closed Thanksgiving, Christmas, and New Year's. Free. (910) 432-3443; www.bragg.army.mil/18abn/

Iron Mike

Iron Mike was created in 1961; his stance is that of an airborne soldier who has completed a combat jump. The statue was inspired by Private First Class Michael A. Scambellure, an 82nd Airborne Division soldier who received the Silver Star for his heroic actions in Sicily. Randolph and Armistead streets, Fayetteville, NC 28301. Located on the Fort Bragg military installation; visitors must enter through a public entrance and present photo I.D. and vehicle registration. (910) 483-5311 or (800) 255-8217; www.visitfayettevillenc.com

Four Oaks/Johnston County

Barbara A. Keen Studio

Visitors are welcome at the fine-arts studio of Barbara Keen, who specializes in stained glass and original paintings. 309

Barbara A. Keen Studio (p. 233)

N. Main St., Four Oaks, NC 27524. Mon–Fri., 10 A.M.–5 P.M., or by appointment. (919) 963-3190; bakeen@earthlink.net

Bentonville Battlefield State Historic Site

The Battle of Bentonville in 1865 was the largest Civil War battle on North Carolina soil. You can walk the fields where 80,000 Union and Confederate soldiers fought and tour the Harper House, which served as a makeshift hospital for the wounded from both armies. The museum displays many artifacts from the battle. 5466 Harper House Rd., Four Oaks, NC 27524. Apr.–Oct., Mon.–Sat., 9 A.M.–5 P.M.; Sun., 1–5 P.M.; Nov.–March, Tues.–Sat., 10 A.M.–4 P.M.; Sun., 1–4 P.M. Free. (910) 594-0789; www.bentonvillebattlefield.nchistoricsites.org

The Harper House at Bentonville Battlefield State Historic Site

The Dwelling Place

This charming farmhouse offers visitors a smoke-free environment, four guest rooms, complimentary breakfast, and a quiet alternative to I-95 traffic. 6734 US Hwy 301 S., Four Oaks, NC 27524. (919) 963-4088

Four Oaks Auction House

Antique shoppers from around the country travel to Four Oaks every other Monday and the fourth Saturday of each month for auctions. Visit on-line to see what Four Oaks Auction House has available for serious dealers and antique buyers. 201 Main St., Four Oaks, NC 27524. Mon. auction schedule, 3:30 P.M., box lots; 6 P.M., glass; 7 P.M., furniture; Sat. auction schedule, 5 P.M. (919) 963-3482; www.4oaksauction.com

Howell Woods Environmental Learning Center

Howell Woods consists of more than 2,800 acres featuring nine natural communities and diverse flora and fauna.

The Dwelling Place

Facilities include a classroom for 36 to 50 people, an exhibit hall, an amphitheater, and a natural-resources library available to the public. Programs are offered through Johnston Community College. 6601 Devil's Racetrack Rd., Four Oaks, NC 27524. Mon.–Fri., 8 A.M.–5 P.M.; the hiking trails are open daily. Free. (919) 938-0115; www.johnstoncc.edu/howellwoods

Garner/Wake County

Ribs R Us

Cooking ribs is a skill, one that the folks at Ribs R Us have definitely mastered. Ribs are cooked to perfection with a rich red sauce that has a wonderful spicy taste. Ashley Turner Shopping Center, 5638 NC Hwy 42 W., Garner, NC 27529. Tues.–Thurs., noon–2 P.M. and 5–9 P.M.; Fri.–Sat., noon–9 P.M.; Sun., 2–9 P.M. (919) 662-9900

Strawberry Festival

Held the last weekend in April, the Strawberry Festival draws thousands of visitors to enjoy great fair foods, strawberries from area farmers, rides for the kids, community vendors, and local artists. Exit 312 off I-40 (Technology Dr.), Garner, NC 27529. Sat., 10 A.M.–5 P.M. Free. (919) 773-8448; www.greaterclevelandchamber.com

Hope Mills/Cumberland County

McNeill Strawberry Farm

This pick-your-own strawberry operation also offers other produce for sale at the farm stand. It is open from early April through the end of May. Located two miles southeast of I-95 at Exit 41 on Chickenfoot Rd., Hope Mills, NC 28348. Mon.–Sat., 7:30 A.M.–5:30 P.M. A picking fee is charged. (910) 425-7354; mcneillfarm@earthlink.net

Lillington/Harnett County

Cape Fear River Trail

Canoe enthusiasts will enjoy this multiuse recreational river trail. The Cape Fear River, a brown-water river, is the longest river contained entirely in the state of North Carolina. Along its path, the river produces a number of rapids and falls. Raven Rock State Park, Lillington, NC 27546. Free. (910) 893-4888; ravenroc@foto.infi.net

Farmer's Strawberry and Produce

Delicious homegrown strawberries are available in April and May. Onions, snap beans, tomatoes, potatoes, cabbage, and squash are available between April and June. 209 Holder Rd., Lillington, NC 27546. Open daily. (910) 893-6076

Just A Growing Produce

Fruits and vegetables available in-season include greenhouse cucumbers, tomatoes, and spring squash; onions from mid-April through June; blackberries and blueberries in June and July; and cantaloupes and watermelons in July. 5689 US Hwy 421 N., Lillington, NC 27546. Mid-Apr.–mid-July, Tues.–Sat. (910) 893-2989

Homegrown goodies at Just A Growing Produce

Lillington Chamber of Commerce

827½ Eighth St., Lillington, NC 27546. Mon.–Thurs., 9 A.M.–5 P.M. (910) 893-3751; www.lillingtonchamber.org

Lillington Farmers' Market

This year-round farmers' market features fresh local produce and other homegrown and handmade treats. 401 N. Lillington, Lillington, NC 27546. Tues., 3–6 P.M.; Sat., 8 A.M.–12:30 P.M. (910) 893-8206

Linden/Cumberland County

North Carolina Work Horse & Mule Association Annual Corn Planting Day

Lillington Chamber of Commerce

This event is held every spring on an April Saturday to showcase demonstrations of farming in the early 1900s. Other activities include wagon rides, campfire cooking demonstrations, corn shelling, and performances of bluegrass music. 5489 Indian Ridge Farm Rd., Linden, NC 28356. Free. (910) 980-0066; ridgeriders4@earthlink.net

Middlesex/Johnston County

Triple S Ranch

In the same family for five generations, Triple S Ranch provides farm tours, hayrides, a nature trail, a playground, a cookout area, a fishing pond, a basketball court, a softball field, a horseshoe-pitching area, patch gardens, and a stage for performances. 533 Barnes Lake Rd., Middlesex, NC 27557. Fees are charged. (919) 202-4991; www.sssranch.com

Pembroke/Robeson County

Givens Performance Arts Center

Seating 1,600 plus, this facility is home to three professional performing-arts series, as well as other events. Whether they like Broadway, pop, American Indian, or children's productions, visitors will find something special at the Givens. UNC-Pembroke, Pembroke, NC 28372. (910) 521-6287 or (800) 367-0778; www.uncp.edu/gpac

The Museum of the Native American Resource Center

This museum features exhibits of authentic American Indian artifacts, as well as arts and crafts from Indian people across North America, from Abenaki to Zuni. Many items come from North Carolina Indians, with special emphasis on Robeson County. UNC-Pembroke, Pembroke, NC 28372. Mon.–Fri., 8 A.M.–5 P.M. Free. (910) 521-6282; www.uncp.edu/nativemuseum

Hinnant Family Vineyards and Winery

Pine Level/Johnston County

Hinnant Family Vineyards and Winery

Hinnant Family Vineyards is the largest muscadine vineyard in the state, covering 62 acres. The vineyards were initially planted in 1971 to provide North Carolina wineries with wine grapes. In 2001, the Hinnant family started producing its own varieties of wine. 826 Pine Level–Micro Rd., Pine Level, NC 27568. Mon.–Fri., 11 A.M.–5 P.M.; Sat., 10 A.M.–6 P.M.; Sun., 1–5 P.M. Free tours are available. Tastings cost $4 per person. (919) 965-3350; www.hinnantvineyards.com

Parkside Café

If you're looking for traditional Southern fare, a trip to Parkside Café is definitely in order. The specials—ham, fried chicken, beef stew, chicken pastry, or seafood—vary daily. 2176-A US Hwy 70A, Pine Level, NC 27568. Daily, 7 A.M.–8:30 P.M. (919) 965-4100

American Music Jubilee

Rowland/Robeson County

Border Belt Farmers' Market

Early tobacco warehouses and farming equipment are on display in this converted Atlantic Coastline Railway depot. You can explore the early years of other Lumberton industries, such as railroads, timber, and turpentine. Old Train Depot, Main St., Rowland, NC 28383. Mon., Wed., and Fri., 11 A.M.–3 P.M. Free. (910) 628-9216; www.fairmontnc.com

Selma/Johnston County

Chosse your favorite handmade soap at Anderson Street Soap Company.

American Music Jubilee

Great American music and sidesplitting comedy delight audiences every weekend in Selma. Musical productions feature '50s rock-and-roll and classic and contemporary country. The Down Home Southern Christmas Show starts in early November and runs through the week of Christmas. 300 N. Raiford St., Selma, NC 27576. Matinees, 1:40 P.M.; evening shows, 7:40 P.M. (919) 202-9927 or (877) 843-7839; www.amjubilee.com

Anderson Street Soap Company

The Anderson Street Soap Company creates Royal Honey Glyercin and many handmade soaps, gifts, and lotions. It is located in the Uptown Selma Antique District. 103 E. Anderson St., Selma, NC 27576. Mon.–Fri., 9 A.M.–5 P.M.; Sat., 9 A.M.–6 P.M. (919) 975-1155; www.andersonstsoapnnutritionco.com

Atkinson's Milling Company

The mill has been in continuous operation for more than 250 years. The stone-ground cornmeal is noted for its quality. Products include hush-puppy mix, biscuit mix, funnel cake mix, seafood breading, and chicken breading. 95 Atkinson Mill Rd., Selma, NC 27576. Mon.–Fri., 8 A.M.–5 P.M. (919) 965-3547; www.atkinsonmilling.com

Atkinson's Milling Company

DeWayne's Home & Garden Showplace

This is the place for flowers, plants, trees, and much more. The gift shop offers everything for the avid gardener, including a wide selection of small and large concrete fountains. The Christmas shop on the second floor has year-round deals on holiday collectibles. 1575 Industrial Park Dr., Selma, NC 27576. Mon.–Sat., 9 A.M.–6 P.M.; Sun., 10 A.M.–6 P.M. (919) 202-8471; www.dewaynes.com

Historic Selma Union Station

Selma was founded in 1867 by Colonel John W. Sharpe, a Confederate veteran and native of Selma, Alabama. The current Selma Union Station was built in 1924 and completely restored in the fall of 2003. Visitors enjoy exhibits on the history of Selma and the role of the railroad in Johnston County. Daily Amtrak service from New York and Miami is available. 500 Railroad St., Selma, NC 27576. The station opens 30 minutes before Amtrak arrivals and departures. Free. (919) 965-9841; www.selma-nc.com

DeWayne's Home & Garden Showplace

Selma East Coast Antique Show

With more than 100 dealers lining the streets of the Uptown Selma Antique District each September, this event is a great shopping experience for amateur and professional antique hunters. In addition to street vendors, shoppers can enjoy Selma's more than 15 antique shops and malls. Uptown Selma Antique District, Selma, NC 27576. Sat., 8 A.M.–5 P.M.; Sun., 10 A.M.–5 P.M. (919) 965-9841; www.selma-nc.com

Caboose at Historic Selma Union Station

Sweetwater's Grille & Cheesecake Co.

This locally owned restaurant is decorated with historic postcards, photos, and antiques. It serves salads, sandwiches, steaks, and seafood. Live entertainment is offered on Thursdays. But most of all, leave room after a delicious meal for Sweetwater's own cheesecake. One of the 12 flavors will tempt you! "Triple Chocolate Cheesecake" is a local favorite. 112 S. Raiford St., Selma, NC 27576. Mon.–Wed., 11 a.m.–9 P.M.; Thurs.–Sat., 11 A.M.–10 P.M.; Sun., 11 A.M.–3 P.M. (919) 202-0145; www.sweetwatersrestaurant.com

Smithfield/Johnston County

Ava Gardner Festival

The Ava Gardner Museum hosts an arts and film festival each year in late September or early October. The festival starts on Friday night with an opening gala for a new exhibition themed especially for the festival. Saturday features an art show and sale by local artists, jazz music, Ava's movies at the Historic Howell Theatre, and heritage tours around Smithfield and to the Brogden community, where Ava was raised. 325 E. Market St. and downtown, Smithfield, NC 27577. Fri., 7 P.M.–10 P.M.; Sat., 10 A.M.–5 P.M. Call for dates. Admission is $5; movies and heritage tours are also $5. (919) 934-5830; www.avagardner.org

Ava Gardner Museum

Ava Gardner Museum

This 6,400-square-foot museum is home to original scripts, photos, costumes, and personal effects of Ava Gardner, who went from local country girl to one of Hollywood's film goddesses. Ava's friends and costars included Mickey Rooney, Clark Gable, Frank Sinatra, and Gregory Peck. Her gravesite is located in nearby Sunset Memorial Gardens, approximately one mile from the museum. 325 E. Market St., Smithfield, NC 27577. Mon.–Sat., 9 A.M.–5 P.M.; Sun., 2–5 P.M. Admission is $5 for adults, $4 for seniors and groups, and $3 for children three–12; children under three are free. (919) 934-5830; www.avagardner.org

Festival of Trees

Starting the first weekend of December, you can enjoy a display of Christmas trees decorated by local groups in unique and whimsical themes that relate to the season. A variety of entertainment is provided throughout the two-

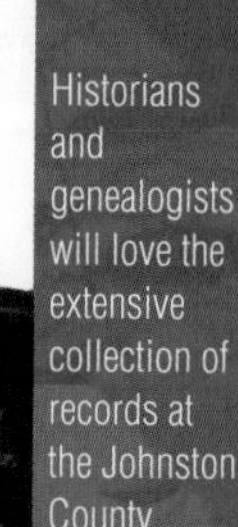

Historians and genealogists will love the extensive collection of records at the Johnston County Heritage Center.

week event. Johnston Medical Mall, Bright Leaf Blvd., Smithfield, NC 27577. Free. (919) 989-5380

Holt Lake BBQ & Seafood

Holt Lake BBQ & Seafood

Family-style service ensures that you will enjoy a taste of barbecue, flounder, shrimp, and Brunswick stew with vegetables and hush puppies. You won't leave the table hungry! 3506 US Hwy 301, Smithfield, NC 27577. Mon., 11 A.M.–2 P.M.; Tues.–Sat., 11 A.M.–9 P.M. (919) 934-0148

Jan's Strawberries & Peach Farm

For more than 30 years, Jan's has sold strawberries, peaches, and other farm produce and served up homemade strawberry ice cream to visitors and locals along rural Brogden Road. Strawberries are available from mid-April to mid-June and peaches at the end of June. 3188 Stevens Sausage Rd., Smithfield, NC 27577. (919) 934-2989

Johnston County Heritage Center

The Johnston County Heritage Center has assembled an extensive collection of public records, manuscripts, family histories, photographs, newspapers, and artifacts for scholars, amateur historians, genealogists, and students to explore the history and culture of Johnston County. 241 E. Market St., Smithfield, NC 27577. Mon.–Sat., 9 A.M.–5 P.M. Free. (919) 934-2836; www.johnstonnc.com/heritage

Memory Lane Frame Studio specializes in shadow boxes.

Lazy O Farm

Seasonal events include Easter Egg Dayz, Summer Dayz, Maze Dayz, and Turkey Dayz. You can enjoy a millet maze, farm animals, hayrides, and picnic areas on this working farm. Visits are for groups of 10 or more by appointment only. 3583 Packing Plant Rd., Smithfield, NC 27577. (919) 934-1132; www.ncagr.com/ncproducts/showsite.asp?ID=2121

Memory Lane Frame Studio

Local framer Tara Dunn supports artists from around Johnston County and throughout the state. Stop by to visit the frame-shop gallery and to enjoy original works and new miniatures by Leslie Macon. 307 S. Third St., Smithfield, NC 27577. Wed.–Fri., 10 A.M.–6 P.M.; Sat., 10 A.M.–2 P.M.; and by appointment. (919) 938-2900; www.home.earthlink.net/~memorylaneframes

Riverside Coffee Company

Riverside Coffee in downtown Smithfield is popular with both locals and visitors. It features a variety of coffees, sandwiches, salads, and desserts. Local artists display their works for viewing and for sale. 227 E. Market St., Smithfield, NC 27577. Mon.–Sat., 6 A.M.–5 P.M. (919) 209-0066

Riverside Coffee Company

Smithfield Ham & Yam Festival

Held the first weekend in May, the festival has ham biscuits, barbecue, and sweet potatoes galore. It also features local artists, craft vendors, and activities and games for the kids, including a hog trot and a piglet race. Visitors enjoy an *American Idol*–type singing contest and local bands throughout the day. A national artist closes out Saturday's events. Downtown Smithfield, NC 27577. Sat., 9 A.M.–10 P.M.; Sun., noon–5 P.M. Free. (919) 934-0887; www.downtownsmithfield.com

Hickory-smoked Johnston County hams

Smithfield Ham Shop

Country hams reach their flavorful best as a result of a meat-preserving process called curing. Johnston County hams are cured in the traditional manner, using dry salt and a selective aging process over three months. The Smithfield Ham Shop features authentic country ham, spiral honey hams, turkeys, and dry-cured bacon. 204 N. Bright Leaf Blvd., Smithfield, NC 27577. Mon.–Fri., 9 A.M.–5 P.M. (919) 934-8054 or (800) 543-4267; www.countrycuredhams.com

White Swan Bar-B-Q

The original White Swan Bar-B-Q was built in Smithfield along the US Hwy 301 corridor. Today, you can find six locations around Johnston County. Cooking pork shoulders, adding "secret" seasonings, and using a vinegar-based sauce are eastern North Carolina traditions—ones that White Swan is proud to uphold. 3198 US Hwy 301 S., Smithfield, NC 27577. Daily, 10 A.M.–9 P.M. (919) 934-8913

Spring Lake/Harnett County

West Produce

This third-generation farm features strawberries and spring vegetables in April. From May through August, sweet corn, tomatoes, squash, cucumbers, peppers, butter beans, and melons are in season. From September through October, the farm features tours, classes on American agriculture, hayrides, pumpkins, fall vegetables, and jams and jellies. In November, greens, collards, cabbage, broccoli, and sweet potatoes are available. 2026 Hayes Rd., Spring Lake, NC 28390. Apr. 15–Nov. 24, Mon.–Sat., 10 A.M.–6 P.M.; Sun., 1–5 P.M. (910) 497-7443; www.ncfarmfresh.com

Stedman/Cumberland County

Bunce Brothers Farms

Here, you can pick your own strawberries in season. The following produce is offered in season: pumpkins, greens, tomatoes, watermelons, and cantaloupes. 6267 Blake Rd., Stedman, NC 28391. Mon.–Fri., 8 A.M.–6 P.M.; Sat., 8 A.M.–noon. (910) 483-5007; tmb81235@aol.com

White Oak/Bladen County

Harmony Hall Plantation

One of the oldest plantation sites in southeastern North Carolina, this historic home was built around 1760. Harmony Hall Heritage Day takes place in early May, and the Christmas open house is in early December. Both events feature 18th- and 19th-century exhibits, oxcart rides, colonial crafts, blacksmithing, music, food and drink, and fun. 1615 River Rd., White Oak, NC 28399. Sat., 10 A.M.–2 P.M.; Sun., 2–4 P.M.; and by appointment. A $1 donation is requested. (910) 866-4844; www.Harmonyhallnc.com

Wilson's Mills/Johnston County

Pumpkin Festival

Held the second weekend of October, the festival is a sure bet for family fun with music, dance performances, arts-and-crafts vendors, pumpkin-cooking and pumpkin-carving contests, and more. It kicks off the weekend with a pageant on Friday night. Town Hall, Wilson's Mills, NC 27593. Sat., 10 A.M.–4 P.M. Free. (919) 938-3885

Wilson's Mills Farm Market & Greenhouse

It you don't have time to grow it or pick it yourself, plan to visit Wilson's for locally grown produce, plants, flowers, and homemade baked items such as cakes, breads, and pies. You'll also enjoy the pick-your-own strawberries, available from mid-April to mid-June; the pick-your-own field peas in mid-summer; and the pumpkin patch in the fall. 5494 Wilson's Mills Rd., Wilson's Mills, NC 27520. (919) 934-6918

Potters' Wheels and Organic Fields

Alamance, Chatham, Guilford, Lee, Orange, and Randolph Counties

Ah, the rich earth. In North Carolina's Piedmont region, coarse clay soil serves as inspiration for potters. For nearly 200 years, master potters have forged a unique tradition and style of pottery making, crafting local clay into incredible forms and colors.

The Seagrove area attracts visitors from around the country. Here, generations of potters have perfected a salt-glazing technique developed by their European ancestors. The results are beautiful works that are functional, yet masterful, works of art. It's fitting that the North Carolina Pottery Center makes its home in Seagrove and that two major pottery festivals are held in this region each year. Opportunities abound to tour quaint galleries and working artists' studios in this region. (More great Seagrove potters are found in the "Scenes of the Sandhills Trail.")

The rich soil that produces beautiful pottery also contributes to a thriving agricultural community. Vineyards roll across the hills. One of the state's two wine trails meanders through here. Farmers' markets overflow with heirloom tomatoes, cut flowers, lavender and basil, arugula and other leafy greens, berries, figs—nearly every fruit and vegetable you can imagine.

In fact, this area has the largest concentration of organic farms in North Carolina. You can visit many farm operations and enjoy hands-on experiences while you sample the tasty goat cheeses, herb breads, and fresh fruits and vegetables.

A quote by popular author Barbara Kingsolver on the Chatham County Cooperative Extension's Web site for organic and sustainable farming sets the stage for what you might expect on this trail: "Recall that whatever lofty things you might accomplish today, you will do them only because you first ate something that grew out of dirt."

It seems fitting to add that the beautiful pottery you are eating from may have also come from the same place.

Plan your trip by reading the following town-by-town descriptions of the unique attractions that make up the "Potters' Wheels and Organic Fields" trail.

Apex/Chatham County

Red Moon Imaging & Gallery M

You can view and purchase art by talented local artists. The gallery also exhibits the photos of resident artist Michael Mayo. 1434 Farrington Rd., Unit E, Apex, NC 27502. Mon.–Fri., 10 A.M.–6 P.M., and by appointment. (919) 363-1811; www.redmoonimaging.com

Worthington Studios

The artist's bold strokes and color create vibrant likenesses of landscapes, flowers, and animals. 1434 Farrington Rd., Unit C, Apex, NC 27523. Mon.–Fri., 10:30 A.M.–9 P.M. (919) 362-8686; www.worthingtonstudios.com

Archdale/Randolph County

J. F. Hudson Studio

Artist Joanna Frazier Hudson creates and displays a wide range of drawings, stone lithographs, and photographs. 202 Stratford Rd., Archdale, NC 27263. (336) 434-5543; jhudson_art@northstate.net

Asheboro/Randolph County

A. R. Britt Pottery

Aaron Britt makes hand-turned, traditional Seagrove-style pottery featuring original-formula glazes. His shop showcases other potters' work, too! 5650 US Hwy 220 S., Asheboro, NC 27205. Spring–fall, Mon.–Sat., 9 A.M.–5 P.M.; Sun., noon–5 P.M. (336) 873-7736 or (800) 240-1283; www.seagrovepottery.net

Asheboro Fall Festival

Fall Festival

Spend a fall weekend shopping for crafts and food from more than 400 vendors! The stages showcase gospel, bluegrass, and contemporary musical performers.

Downtown Asheboro, NC 27204. Held the first weekend in Oct. Fri. night, kickoff parade; Sat., 10 A.M.–6 P.M.; Sun., 1–6 P.M. Free. (336) 629-0399; www.randolphartsguild.com

Latham's Pottery

The potters create hand-turned stoneware in 10 beautiful, lead-free glazes. Pie plates, mugs, pitchers, candle cups, and casseroles are available. 7297 US Hwy 220 S., Asheboro, NC 27205. Mon.–Sat., 9 A.M.–5 P.M. (336) 873-7303; www.discoverseagrove.com

Mid-State Tractor Parade and Show

Paying tribute to that iconic farm vehicle has never been so much fun! People come for the tractor games and kiddie tractor pull, as well as the bluegrass, gospel music, and clogging. 151 Sunset Ave., Asheboro, NC 27205. Held one Sat. in mid-Oct.; the parade begins at 11 A.M. Free. (336) 736-7103

Moring Arts Center

This is a funky, functional, hilarious, artsy, bold, daring, and just plain fun gift shop and gallery! It offers ten exhibitions a year, too. 123 Sunset Ave., Asheboro, NC 27204. Mon.–Fri., 9 A.M.–5 P.M.; Sat., 10 A.M.–2 P.M. (336) 629-0399; www.randolphartsguild.com

North Carolina Aviation Museum & Air Show

Discover the story of aviation through helmets, flight suits, armaments, medals, and items confiscated from enemy airmen. 2222-G Pilot's View Rd., Asheboro, NC 27204. Mon.–Sat., 10 A.M.–5 P.M.; Sun., 1–5 P.M. Admission fee. (336) 625-0170; www.ncairmuseum.org

North Carolina Zoological Park

More than 1,000 animals from Africa, North America, and Australia live in environments that simulate their natural habitats. 4401 Zoo Pkwy., Asheboro, NC 27205. Open daily except Christmas; Apr.–Oct., 9 A.M.–5 P.M.; Nov.–March, 9 A.M.–4 P.M. Admission fee. (336) 879-7000 or (800) 488-0444; www.nczoo.org

Southern Randolph Country Days

Arts, crafts, pottery, food, music . . . and lots of it! Add a parade and you've got two full days of fun. Downtown Seagrove, NC 27203. Held the third weekend in Sept. Sat., 10 A.M.–6 P.M.; Sun., noon–6 P.M. Free. (336) 629-5015; jerrykingsurveying@earthlink.net

Toms Creek Farm & Nursery

April's Farm Fest and July's Pickin' by the Pond have music, food, and kids' games. Customer Appreciation Day in September features workshops, arboretum walks, food, and music. Breakfast with Santa is the first Saturday in December. 6454 Old NC Hwy 49, Asheboro, NC 27239. Mon.–Fri., 9 A.M.–5 P.M.; Sat., 9 A.M.–4 P.M. (336) 857-2131; www.tomscreeknursery.com

Trash and Treasures Antiques

Shop here for antiques, quality used furniture, collectibles, and decorator items. 230 Sunset Ave., Asheboro, NC 27203. Wed.–Sat., 10 A.M.–6 P.M. (336) 625-4870; epollardjr@yahoo.com

Bennett/Chatham County

Bluebird Hill Farm

Free-range fowl provide natural fertilizer for a variety of herbs, flowers, and produce. Vinegars, preserves, and crafts are sold, too. 421 Clarence Phillips Rd., Asheboro, NC 27208. May–Nov., open Sun.–Mon. by appointment. (336) 581-3916; www.ces.ncsu.edu/chatham/ag/SustAg/farmphotoaugust2905.html

Burlington/Alamance County

Alamance Battleground State Historic Site

Here, you can walk through an original pre–Revolutionary War battlefield. Two monuments mark the site of the May 16, 1771, battle. 5803 NC Hwy 62 S., Burlington, NC 27215. Mon.–Sat., 9 A.M.–5 P.M. Free. (336) 227-4785; www.alamancebattleground.nchistoricsites.org

Burlington-Alamance International Cultural Festival

Alamance Battleground State Historic Site *N.C. Division of State Historic Sites*

The festival includes dance performances, live bands, plays, clowns, children's rides, exhibits that show the history of Alamance County, and foods from around the world. Downtown Burlington, NC 27216. Held Labor Day weekend. Fri.–Sun., 10 A.M.–10 P.M. Free. (336) 570-0284; baicfest1@netzero.net

Burlington Carousel Festival

Experience the Dentzel Menagerie Carousel and the splendid works of a great array of carousel artists and craftsmen, plus live entertainment. 1333 Overbrook Rd., Burlington, NC 27215. Held the third weekend in Sept. Sat., 10 A.M.–6 P.M.; Sun., 1–6 P.M. Free. (336) 222-5030; www.burlingtonnc.gov/festival

"Paths of the Past" Historic Architecture Walking Tour

Follow the markers to discover everything from Art Deco to Gothic Revival. Brochures are available at 200 S. Main St., Burlington, NC 27216. Mon.–Fri., 8 A.M.–5 P.M. Free. (336) 222-5002; www.burlingtondowntown.com

Sunset Rhythms Concert Series

Sunset Rhythms Concert Series *Burlington Downtown Corporation*

Musicians perform everything from classic rock-and-roll to beach, jazz, and swing. 200 S. Main St., Burlington, NC 27216. Mid-May–June, Fri., 6:30–8:30 P.M. Free. (336) 222-5002; www.burlingtondowntown.com

Textile Heritage Museum

Photos, artifacts, and maps bring the heritage of the mills to life. A special area highlights Alamance County's current textile industry. 2406 Glencoe St., Burlington, NC 27217. Sat.–Sun., 1–4 P.M., and by appointment. Free. (336) 260-0038; www.TextileHeritageMuseum.org

Carrboro/Orange County

BenchChicks Jewelers

Come to the co-op studio, meet the seven women artists, and browse the collection of exclusive designs. 300-G E. Main St., Carrboro, NC 27510. Open by appointment. (919) 542-6399; fran_schultzberg@yahoo.com

Carrboro Farmers' Market

Produce, flowers, cheeses, meats, jams, pickles, baked goods, bedding and landscape plants, herbs, honey, soap, and craft items are sold. 301 W. Main St. (on the town commons), Carrboro, NC 27510. Apr.–Oct., Wed., 3:30–6:30 P.M.; Sat., 7 A.M.–noon; March and Nov.–Dec., Sat., 7 A.M.–noon. (919) 932-1641; www.carrborofarmersmarket.com

The Clay Centre

The Clay Centre

Here, you can observe artists working their clay. Their work includes hand-built and wheel-thrown functional and decorative clay wares. 402 Lloyd St., Carrboro, NC 27510. Mon.–Fri., 10 A.M.–4 P.M. (919) 967-0314; www.claycentre.com

Nested

This gift and home furnishings shop focuses on fine crafts and high design, much of it from North Carolina. 118 B E. Main St., Carrboro, NC 27510. Tues.–Wed., 10 A.M.–6 P.M.; Thurs.–Sat., 10 A.M.–8 P.M. (919) 338-8023; www.nestedhome.com

Panzanella at Weaver Street Market

The community-owned eatery has a diverse menu, including vegan dishes from locally grown vegetables. It also offers local art and music. Carr Mill Mall, 100 N. Greensboro St., Carrboro, NC 27510. Mon., 11:30 A.M.–2 P.M.; Tues.–Thurs., 11:30 A.M.–2 P.M. and 5:30–9 P.M.; Fri.–Sat., 11:30 A.M.–2 P.M. and 5:30–10 P.M.; Sun., 10:30 A.M.–2 P.M. and 5:30–9 P.M. (919) 929-0010, ext. 132; www.panzanella.com

Chapel Hill/Orange County

Genesis Farm

On the self-guided tour, you can visit edible flower gardens, fragrance gardens, and kitchen herb gardens. You can also learn about native medicinal plants and shop for produce, flowers, herbs, and eggs. 1841 Jo Mac Rd., Chapel Hill, NC 27516. Open seasonally, Tues.–Sun., 1–5 P.M. (919) 968-4759; www.genesisfarmnc.com

Negative Space Sculpture

Howard Schroeder sculpts mahogany, walnut, and cherry to create flowing, graceful art with unending lines. 2115 Copeland Way, Chapel Hill, NC 27517. (919) 933-0293; www.howardaschroeder.com

Niche Gardens

You'll find perennials, trees, shrubs, grasses, and a gallery for garden art by North Carolina artists. 1111 Dawson Rd., Chapel Hill, NC 27516. Spring and fall, Mon.–Sat., 9 A.M.–5 P.M.; Sun., 10 A.M.–5 P.M.; summer, Mon.–Sat., 9 A.M.–5 P.M.; winter, Mon.–Fri., 9 A.M.–5 P.M.; closed the last two weeks of Dec. A garden tour is offered at 10 A.M. on Sat. in spring and fall. (919) 967-0078; www.nichegardens.com

North Carolina Botanical Garden

Native plants in natural settings reflect North Carolina's diverse geographic regions. Old Mason Farm Rd. and US Hwy 15/501 Bypass, Chapel Hill, NC 27599. Mon.–Fri., 8 A.M.–5 P.M.; Sat., 9 A.M.–5 P.M.; Sun., 1–5 P.M. Free. (919) 962-0522; www.ncbg.unc.edu

Spence's Farm

Come visit a 200-year-old family farm transformed into a teaching environment built around life on a working farm. Special camps, programs, and a self-guided tour are offered. 6407 Mill House Rd., Chapel Hill, NC 27516. Fees are charged. (919) 968-8581; www.spencesfarm.com

Spence's Farm

Womancraft Fine Handcrafted Gifts

This artist-owned gallery shop sells jewelry, pottery, fiber art, glass, photography, and fine handcrafted items. Eastgate Shopping Center, 1800 E. Franklin St., Chapel Hill, NC 27511. Mon.–Sat., 10 A.M.–7 P.M.; Sun., noon–5 P.M. (919) 929-8362; www.womancraftgifts.com

Colfax/Guilford County

A. B. Seed, Inc.

A. B. Seed offers one of the largest selections of plants in the Piedmont. The staff specializes in plant containers for indoor and outdoor display. 2914 Sandy Ridge Rd., Colfax, NC 27235. Spring–summer, Mon.–Sat., 8 A.M.–6 P.M.; Sun., 10 A.M.–6 P.M.; fall–winter, Mon.–Sat., 9 A.M.–5 P.M.; Sun., 10 A.M.–5 P.M. (336) 393-0214; www.abseedco.com

A.B. Seed, Inc.

Piedmont Triad Farmers' Market

People come here for fresh vegetables and fruits right off the farm. If you get hungry, you can fill up at the Farmer's Kitchen Restaurant. 2914 Sandy Ridge Rd., Colfax, NC 27235. Open daily, 6 A.M.–6 P.M. (336) 605-9157; www.triadfarmersmarket.com

Efland/Orange County

Fickle Creek Farm B&B

Come enjoy this working farm by day, then relax in the B&B's comfortable accommodations at night. 4122 Buckhorn Rd., Efland, NC 27243. (919) 304-6287; www.home.mebtel.net/~ficklecreek

Franckearts

Louise Francke paints pictures of animals, both from her imagination and on commission. She also creates hand-pulled etchings. 3200 Elizabeth Walters Rd., Efland, NC 27243. Open by appointment. (919) 563-0330; www.franckearts.com

Elon/Alamance County

Creek Side Winery

Tour the vineyards, visit the tasting room, and enjoy the works of local artists in rotating exhibitions. 3515 Stoney Creek Church Rd., Elon, NC 27244. Mon. and Thurs.–Sat., noon–6 P.M.; Sun., 1–6 P.M. Tasting fees. (336) 584-4117; www.creeksidewinery.com

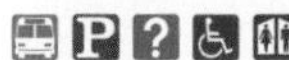

Gibsonville/Alamance County

Grove Winery

This small artisan winery specializes in Cabernet Sauvignon, Chardonnay, Merlot, Norton, Nebbiolo, Traminette, and Sangiovese. 7360 Brooks Bridge Rd., Gibsonville, NC 27249. Fri.–Sat., noon–5 P.M.; Sun., 1–5 P.M. Tasting fees. (919) 584-4060; www.grovewinery.com

Fickle Creek Farm B&B

Glencoe/Alamance County

Glencoe Mill Village & Museum

Drive through this 105-acre site along the Haw River for a glimpse of a mill complex, including 32 houses, a mill store, an office, a lodge, and other buildings. A self-guided walking tour is available. River Rd. and NC Hwy 62, Glencoe, NC 27216. Sat.–Sun., 1–4 P.M. Free. (336) 228-6644; www.glencoemill.com

Graham/Alamance County

Captain James & Emma Holt White House/Alamance County Arts Council

The 1873 house is home to the Alamance County Arts Council's permanent collection, touring exhibitions, and a gift shop. 213 S. Main St., Graham, NC 27253. Mon.–Sat., 9 A.M.–5 P.M. Free. (336) 226-4495; www.artsalamance.com

Original Hollywood Horror Show

Emmy Award–winning filmmakers Dean and Starr Jones create spooky sets perfect for the Halloween season. Their show is not for the shy, timid, or physically challenged. Bass Mountain Rd., Graham, NC 27253. The box office opens at 7:30 P.M. (336) 513-6938; www.originalhollywoodhorrorshow.com

Greensboro/Guilford County

Center for Visual Artists Greensboro

The center promotes the advancement and development of visual art. 200 N. Davie St., Greensboro, NC 27401. Tues. and Thurs.–Sat., 10 A.M.–5 P.M.; Wed., 10 A.M.–7 P.M.; Sun., 2–5 P.M. Free. (336) 333-7485; www.greensboroart.com

Fun Fourth Festival

The festival features the Freedom Run and Walk, a block party, Heritage Day at the 19th-century Blandwood Mansion, a street festival and parade, a concert, and a huge fireworks show. Greensboro, NC 27429. Held on the Fourth of July weekend. Most events are free. (336) 274-4595; www.aroundthepiedmonttriad.com

Kathleen Clay Edwards Library

You'll find exquisite murals in this library, set in the midst of a scenic 98-acre park. 1420 Price Park Dr., Greensboro, NC 27410. Mon.–Thurs., 9 A.M.–9 P.M.; Fri.–Sat., 9 A.M.–6 P.M.; Sun., 2–6 P.M. (336) 373-2923; www.greensboro-nc.gov/departments/library/branches/KCEFB

High Point/Guilford County

Angela Peterson Doll & Miniature Museum

Visitors discover over 2,500 dolls, miniatures, and dollhouses and enjoy special exhibits of African-American heritage dolls and Shirley Temple dolls. 101 W. Green Dr., High Point, NC 27260. Apr.–Oct., Mon.–Fri., 10 A.M.–5 P.M.; Sat., 9 A.M.–5 P.M.; Sun., 1–5 P.M.; Nov.–March, Tues.–Fri.,

10 A.M.–5 P.M.; Sat., 9 A.M.–5 P.M.; Sun., 1–5 P.M. Admission fee. (336) 885-DOLL or (336) 887-2159

High Point Museum and Historical Park

Trace the development of this vibrant city from a small Quaker village to the capital of the furniture and textile industries. Guided tours of two colonial houses and a blacksmith shop are offered. 1859 E. Lexington Ave., High Point, NC 27262. Museum, Tues.–Sat., 10 A.M.–4:30 P.M.; Sun., 1–4:30 P.M.; park, Sat., 10 A.M.–4 P.M.; Sun., 1–4 P.M. Free. (336) 885-1859; www.highpointmuseum.org

Hillsborough/Orange County

Alexander Dickson House/Orange County Visitors Center

The Alexander Dickson House is a restored 18th-century Quaker-plan farmhouse. 150 E. King St., Hillsborough, NC 27278. Mon.–Fri., 8:30 A.M.–5 P.M.; Sat., 10 A.M.–4 P.M.; Sun., 1–4 P.M. Free. (919) 732-7741; www.historichillsborough.org

The Bookmark Used Bookstore and Gallery

In addition to selling used books and CDs, the store has a gallery that features local artists. 102 N. Churton St., Hillsborough, NC 27278. Tues.–Sat., 11 A.M.–6 P.M. (919) 384-5424; thebookmark@gmail.com

Burwell School Historic Site

The Reverend and Mrs. Robert Burwell operated a school for young women here from 1837 to 1857. Restored to its 19th-century appearance, the two-room brick music building is the site of the first school. Docent-led tours are available. 319 N. Churton St., Hillsborough, NC 27278. Wed.–Sat., 11 A.M.–4 P.M.; Sun., 1–4 P.M.; and by appointment. Free. (919) 732-7451; www.burwellschool.org

Orange County Visitors Center

Churton Street Realty Gallery

Locally created sculpture, fabrics, woodwork, pottery, photography, oils, acrylics, watercolors, and even finger paintings are on display. 121 N. Churton St., Suite 1-C, Hillsborough, NC 27278. Mon.–Fri., 9 A.M.–5 P.M. Free. (919) 732-1855; www.churtonstreetrealty.com

Hillsborough Arts Council

The council offers exhibits, visual arts, events, and music from classical and jazz to folk and gospel. 102 W. King St., Hillsborough, NC 27278. (919) 643-2500; www.hillsboroughartscouncil.org

Hillsborough Candlelight Tour

Jennifer E. Miller Artist's Studio

On these horse-drawn carriage rides through downtown Hillsborough, owners of historic homes open their doors, offering music and a glimpse into the past. Downtown Hillsborough, NC 27278. Admission fee. (919) 732-8156; www.candlelighttour.com

Hillsborough Farmers' Market

Take home a bounty of vegetables, baked goods, artisan cheeses, meats, nursery plants, crafts, baskets, jams, and jellies! 128 N. Churton St. (on Sat.) and 144 E. Margaret Ln. (on Wed.), Hillsborough, NC 27278. Apr.–May and Labor Day–Nov., Sat., 8 A.M.–noon; June–Labor Day, Sat., 8 A.M.–noon; Wed., 4–7 P.M.; Dec.–March, first and third Sat., 10 A.M.–noon. (919) 732-8315; www.hillsboroughfarmersmarket.org

Hillsborough Hog Day

In addition to three tons of pork, visitors enjoy an antique car show, games and rides for kids, crafts, and live music. Downtown Hillsborough, NC 27278. Held the weekend of the third Sat. in June. Fri., 6–9 P.M.; Sat., 9 A.M.–6 P.M. (919) 732-8156; www.hogdays.com

Historic Hillsborough Tour Services

Discover Hillsborough through walking, bus, and seasonal guided theme tours. 150 E. King St., Hillsborough, NC 27278. Mon.–Sat., 10 A.M.–4 P.M.; Sun., 1–4 P.M.; closed Thanksgiving, Christmas, and New Year's. Fees are charged. (919) 732-7741 or (877) 732-7748; www.historichillsborough.org

Jennifer E. Miller—Artist's Studio

The artist specializes in watercolors and oil paintings. She also does commissions and lessons. 102 W. King St. (above Tupelo's Restaurant), Hillsborough, NC 27278. Open by appointment. (919) 644-8637; www.waveoverwave.com

Melissa Designer Jewelry

Award-winning jewelry artist Melissa Booth makes one-of-a-kind creations in gold. 112 S. Churton St., Hillsborough, NC 27278. Tues.–Fri., 11 A.M.–6 P.M.; Sat., 11 A.M.–4 P.M. (919) 643-2600; www.jewelrybymelissa.com

Melissa Designer Jewelry showcases graceful lines. *Melissa Booth*

Orange County Historical Museum

You'll find over 1,500 artifacts and photos covering subjects from the first American Indian settlements through the 20th century. 201 N. Churton St., Hillsborough, NC 27278. April–Dec. 24, Tues.–Sat., 11 A.M.–4 P.M.; Sun., 1–4 P.M.; Dec. 26–March, Tues.–Sat., noon–3 P.M.; Sun., 1–4 P.M.; closed on major holidays. Free. (919) 732-2201; www.orangecountymuseum.org

TerraChic Jewelry Design

One-of-a-kind handmade fine silver and glass jewelry is sold here, along with unique, chic, trendy, and distinctive necklaces, earrings, rings, and broaches. 117 W. King St., Suite 5, Hillsborough, NC 27278. Open by appointment. (919) 644-2278; sinderamy@yahoo.com

Vera Pottery & SecondWind Farm

A unique blend of art and agriculture, this pottery features a farm with fresh fruits, flowers, and vegetables! 308 Southwind

Ln., Hillsborough, NC 27278. Open by appointment. (919) 245-1014; www.verapottery.com

Sunshine Lavendar Farm *Annie Baggett*

Hurdle Mills/Orange County

Sunshine Lavender Farm and Festivals

Annie Baggett grows lavender for bath salts, powder, bouquets, candle tins, eye pillows, hand and body cream, lip balm, samplers, and soap. 4104 Millstone Rd., Hurdle Mills, NC 27541. June and Sept. events are offered. (919) 732-5533; www.sunshinelavenderfarm.com

Jamestown/Guilford County

Castle McCulloch

In 1832, Charles T. McCulloch built the McCulloch Gold Mill. Using locally quarried granite, he created an enduring engine house out of rock. The mill operated continuously for over 30 years. 3925 Kivett Dr., Jamestown, NC 27282. Apr.–Oct., open Sun., and by appointment. (336) 887-0706; www.castlemcculloch.com

Castle McCulloch

Julian/Guilford County

The Barn Dance

This G-rated nightclub serves up dinner, dancing, and fun. 6341 Thillippi Rd., Julian, NC 27283. Sat., doors open at 6:30 P.M., show starts at 7:30 P.M. Admission fee. (336) 865-9200; www.thebarndanceinc.com

Homeland Creamery

This family-run dairy farm makes and sells hormone-free milk, butter, and ice cream. Tours are available. 6506 Bowman Dairy Rd., Julian, NC 27283. Winter, Mon.–Sat., 9 A.M.–6 P.M.; Sun., 1–6 P.M.; summer, Fri.–Sun., 9 A.M.–9 P.M. (336) 685-6455; www.homelandcreamery.com

Mebane/Alamance County

Art on the Vine at Iron Gate Winery

Be sure to discover this art, music, and wine festival featuring area artists. 2540 Lynch Store Rd., Mebane, NC 27302. Held one weekend in mid-May. Free. (919) 304-9463; www.artonthevinenc.com

Craftique

Craftique offers a full line of handmade mahogany bedroom and dining-room pieces, as well as accent items. 1257 W. Center St., Mebane, NC 27302. Mon.–Sat., 9 A.M.–4 P.M.; free tours are offered Tues. and Thurs. at 11 A.M. (919) 563-1212; www.craftiquefurn.com

Iron Gate Winery

Everhope Farms and Studio

This business sells free-range, hormone-free meat, yarn from its sheep, asparagus, blueberries, lavender, and hay. The studio features stained and fused glass, jewelry, and mosaics. 7106 Hebron Church Rd., Mebane, NC 27302. Open by appointment. (919) 563-1781; everhope@mebtel.net

Falcon Lane Pottery

Functional wheel-thrown stoneware is sold here. The artisans' pots make use of altered forms, carving, brushwork, and other hand-applied details. 108 Falcon Ln., Mebane, NC 27302. Open by appointment. (919) 304-2086; www.falconlanepottery.com

Favorite Designs—Custom Designs in Ironwood

Designer-craftsman Larry Favorite works with ironwood to create boxes, bowls, vases, and sculpture. 951 S. Fifth St., Mebane, NC 27302. Mon.–Fri., 8 A.M.–5 P.M. (919) 563-5864; www.silverhawk5.com/favorite

Osprey Studio

Jude Lobe's paintings are her way of preserving the endangered landscape. Music is another theme of her work. 303 S. Eighth St., Mebane, NC 27302. Open by appointment. (919) 260-9889; www.judelobe.com

Solgarden

This shop features home accents, silver jewelry, garden accessories, and unique gifts. North Carolina artists sell their pottery, metalwork, stained glass, woodwork, and paper goods here. 115 N. Fourth St., Mebane, NC 27302. Mon.–Sat., 10 A.M.–7 P.M. (919) 563-5031; auditori@mebtel.net

Moncure/Chatham County

Piedmont Biofuels Cooperative Refinery and Research Farm

Members make their own fuel from recycled fryer oil and train people to do the same. 4783 Moncure Pittsboro Rd., Moncure, NC 27559-9338. One-hour tours are offered Sun. at 1 P.M. Donations are encouraged. (919) 321-8260; www.biofuels.coop/

New Hill/Chatham County

New Hope Valley Railway

Experience the heritage of the Bonsal community by viewing historic railroad equipment, an operating train, and a locomotive exhibition. 5121 Daisey St., New Hill, NC 27562. Fees are charged for train rides. (919) 362-5416; www.nhvry.org

Vase by wood artist Larry Favorite *Favorite Designs*

Oak Ridge/Guilford County

Old Mill of Guilford

This working water-powered gristmill, listed on the National Register of Historic Places, has a gift shop that sells stone-ground meal, honey, ham, and North Carolina pottery and crafts. 1340 NC Hwy 68 N., Oak Ridge, NC 27310. Open daily, 9 A.M.–6 P.M. Free. (336) 643-4783

Pittsboro/Chatham County

Blue Horizon Farm

This family farm specializes in organic produce and eggs. It also custom-grows organic vegetables and cut-flower transplants in the greenhouse. 430 Otis Johnson Rd., Pittsboro, NC 27312. Open by appointment. (919) 545-9478; www.bluehorizonfarm.com

Carnivore Preservation Trust

This sanctuary provides homes to carnivores in need of rescue and educates the public. 1940 Hanks Chapel Rd., Pittsboro, NC 27312. Tours, Sat.–Sun., 10 A.M. and 1 P.M., and by appointment. Fees are charged. (919) 542-4684; www.cptigers.org

Chatham Arts Gallery

Visitors can view paintings, sculpture, jewelry, furniture, recordings, and other works by area artists. 115 Hillsboro St., Pittsboro, NC 27312. Tues.–Sat., 11 A.M.–5 P.M.; first Sun. of the month, noon–5 P.M. (919) 542-0394; www.chathamarts.org

Chatham Marketplace

This full-service grocery store and café is committed to offering sustainable, locally grown, and locally produced food. 480 Hillsboro St., Suite 320, Pittsboro, NC 27312. Open daily, 8 A.M.–8 P.M.; Sun. brunch, 10 A.M.–2 P.M. (919) 704-6491; www.chathammarketplace.coop

Carnivore Preservation Trust

Forrest Dweller Sculpture Garden

Here, you'll find the work of Forrest Greenslade, a sculptor who creates whimsical creatures that he calls "Forrest Dwellers." 149 Tinderwood (Fearrington Village), Pittsboro, NC 27312. Open by appointment. (919) 545-9743; www.forrestgreenslade.com

Fusions Art and Fine Craft Gallery

The gallery includes the work of over 25 area artists in all media. The store sells raw glass materials and offers classes. 53 Hillsboro St., Pittsboro, NC 27312. Wed.–Fri., 10:30 A.M.–5:30 P.M.; Sat., 10 A.M.–4 P.M.; first Sun. of the month, noon–4 P.M. (919) 260-9725; www.pittsboroshops.com

General Store Café

A blend of down-home and hip, this café offers an art gallery, a bookstore, and live music Thursday through Saturday evenings. The menu includes soups, salads, sandwiches, burritos, and a quiche of the day. 39 West St., Pittsboro, NC 27312. Mon.–Wed., 7:30 A.M.–9 P.M.; Thurs.–Sat., 7:30 A.M.–10:30 P.M.; Sun., 9 A.M.–4 P.M. (919) 542-2432; www.thegeneralstorecafe.com

The Goathouse Gallery

This is the home and workplace of Italian sculptor and potter Siglinda Scarpa. 680 Alton Alston Rd., Pittsboro, NC 27312. Open by appointment. (919) 542-6815; www.siglindascarpa.com

Melody Troncale Pottery

You'll find colorful handmade stoneware, functional pottery, sculpture, and tiles. 353 Beaumont Ln., Pittsboro, NC 27312. Mon.–Fri., 1–5 P.M. Call for tours and fees. (919) 837-2942; www.melodytroncale.com

Forrest Dweller Sculpture *Forrest Greenslade*

Nu Horizons Farm Country Market

The market has free-range pork, chicken, and beef; homemade jams, jellies, breads, and pies; local produce; local arts and crafts; and Amish quilts and crafts. 975 Pittsboro Goldston Rd., Pittsboro, NC 27312. Wed.–Sat., 10 A.M.–6 P.M. Admission fee. (919) 542-4007

Orchids by Hanks Chapel Greenhouses

Thousands of orchid hybrids and species are the attraction here. Repotting and decorative containers are offered—orchid rentals, too! Wholesale and retail sales are available. 2698 Hanks Chapel Rd., Pittsboro, NC 27312. Tues.–Fri., 10 A.M.–5 P.M.; Sat., 10 A.M.–3 P.M. (919) 542-6887; www.orchidsbyhankschapel.com

Rosemary House B&B

This gracious 1912 Colonial Revival home offers five guest rooms with private baths, some with fireplaces and double whirlpool tubs. 76 West St., Pittsboro, NC 27312. (919) 542-5515 or (888) 643-2017; www.rosemary-bb.com

Shakori Hills Grassroots Festival

Rosemary House B&B

The festival features country, Cajun, zydeco, bluegrass, African, and old-time music. Dance styles include contra, square, shag, Latin, and swing. Kids' activities, workshops, crafts, and a poetry slam are all part of the fun. 1439 Henderson Tanyard Rd., Pittsboro, NC 27312. Held the third weekend of Apr. and the first weekend of Oct. Fees are charged. (919) 542-8142; www.shakorihills.org

Twin Birch Products Co.

Birch is the ideal wood for needlework tools. The artisans' knitting and other needles are warm to the eye and touch, lightweight, well balanced, quiet, and flexible. 191 Arrowhead Loop, Pittsboro, NC 27312. Fri.–Sat., 10 A.M.–3 P.M., and by appointment. (919) 545-0098; www.twinbirchproducts.com

Randleman/Randolph County

New Salem Pottery

New Salem's slip-decorated earthenware reproduces the Quaker forms and designs of potter William Dennis (circa 1790–1820). German, English, and original designs are available, too. 789 New Salem Rd., Randleman, NC 27317. Wed.–Sat., 10 A.M.–5 P.M., and by appointment. (336) 498-2178; www.newsalempottery.com

Sanford/Lee County

Brookshire Artist Gallery

New Salem Pottery

The gallery features art created in North Carolina, with a focus on Sanford. 102 S. Steele St. (first floor, Shops of Steele Street), Sanford, NC 27330. Mon.–Sat., 10 A.M.–5 P.M. (919) 777-6959 or (919) 776-6909; BrookshireArtist@yahoo.com

Brush and Palette Club Annual Art Show

The show features paintings, sculpture, pottery, and carvings by county artists. Typically, 500 works are on display and for sale. McIver St., Sanford, NC 27332. Held one week in late Oct., daily, 10 A.M.–8 P.M. (919) 498-2731; vickigregghogan@yahoo.com

Chana's Art Market

The original work by award-winning artist Chana Meeks available here includes wheel-thrown, hand-sculpted mugs, hand-painted rocks, and vinyl floor mats. Shops of Steele Street, Sanford, NC 27330. Mon.–Sat., 10 A.M.–5 P.M., and by appointment. (919) 663-4550; chanas_art_market@yahoo.com

Craftibarb

You'll find one-of-a-kind fabric handbags with beads and fancy fringes for dazzling displays of colors and textures. Shops of Steele Street, Sanford, NC 27330. Mon.–Sat.,

10 A.M.–5 P.M. (919) 777-6959; www.craftibarb.com

Dale's Greenhouse and Garden Center

Dale's is stocked with nursery-grown annuals, perennials, shrubs, and trees, as well as tools and yard art. US Hwy 1, Sanford, NC 27332. March–Oct., Mon.–Sat., 8 A.M.–6 P.M.; Sun., 1–6 P.M.; Nov.–Feb., Mon.–Sat., 8 A.M.–5 P.M.; Sun., 1–5 P.M. (919) 776-9013; lsm19622003@yahoo.com

Down on the Farm

Here, you can indulge in bedding plants, daylilies, peonies, and produce in season. 1314 Bragg St., Sanford, NC 27332. Thurs.–Fri., 8 A.M.–5 P.M.; Sat., 8 A.M.–noon. (919) 770-2461; fharrington1050@msn.com

Garden of Eden Specialty Soaps

"Clean" is the fragrance you'll notice when you walk in. Skin-nurturing handmade soaps, homemade lotions, lip balms, and salves are sold. Shops of Steele Street, Sanford, NC 27332. Mon.–Sat., 10 A.M.–5 P.M. (919) 777-6959; www.gardenofedenspecialtysoaps.com

Gary Thomas Farms

Select from hothouse tomatoes, cucumbers, asparagus, lettuce, onions, and sweet potatoes at this seasonal stand. You can pick your own strawberries or buy them prepicked. 443 Thomas Rd., Sanford, NC 27332. Apr.–June, Mon.–Sat., 7:30 A.M.–7 P.M. (919) 258-3262; pdt2@alltel.net

Griffin Evergreens

Add a festive experience to your holidays by choosing and cutting your own Christmas tree or purchasing fragrant wreaths. Near the intersection of Broadway Rd. and Avent Ferry Rd., Sanford, NC 27332. Thanksgiving–Dec. 24, 1–7 P.M. (919) 258-3587; grapevine@alltel.net

Griffin Vineyard

If you pick your own muscadine grapes in season, you'd better hope these juicy snacks aren't gone before you can get them home! Thomas Rd., Sanford, NC 27332. Sept., Sat., 8 A.M.–3 P.M. (919) 258-3587; grapevine@alltel.net

Gross Farms

The produce barn opens in mid-April with fresh strawberries ready for the picking. Jams, jellies, relishes, syrups, ciders, and homemade ice cream are sold, too. 1606 Pickett Rd., Sanford, NC 27332. Apr.–Aug., Mon.–Sat., 7:30 A.M.–6:30 P.M.; Sun., 1–6 P.M.; Sept.–Oct., Mon.–Thurs., by appointment; Fri.–Sat., 7 A.M.–10 P.M.; Sun., 1–6 P.M. (919) 498-6727; www.grossfarms.com

Hart Studios

Artist C. J. Hart does decorative painting on-site and also offers classes. 112 W. Second St., Sanford, NC 27344. Studio, Wed. and Fri.–Sat., 10 A.M.–4 P.M.; classes, Sat., 10 A.M.–12:30 P.M. and 1:30–4 P.M. (919) 774-9813 or (919) 770-2042

Jackson Brothers Produce

Featured products include apples, greenhouse tomatoes, homegrown vegetables, homemade jelly and preserves, hoop cheese, and side meat. 2424 Jefferson Davis Hwy, Sanford, NC 27332. Mon.–Sat., 7 A.M.–7 P.M.; Sun., 8 A.M.–6 P.M. (919) 776-6632; www.jacksonbros.com

Old Timey Fig Bushes

Available cultivars include Celeste, brown turkey, and magnolia. The on-site Fig Demonstration Garden includes 12 or more cultivars grown throughout the South. 3519 Wicker St. Ext., Sanford, NC 27330. Open by appointment. (919) 776-9687; donandjeanne@alltel.net

Railroad House Historical Museum

The museum, constructed by the Raleigh and Augusta Airline Railroad in 1872, displays artifacts, documents, and pictures. 110 Charlotte Ave., Sanford, NC 27331. Sat., 11 A.M.–4 P.M.; Sun., 1:30–5 P.M., and by appointment. Free. (919) 776-7479; www.downtownsanford.com/railroad_house.htm

Sanford Farmers' Market

In addition to seasonal produce, look for homemade soaps and bath products, baked goods, jams, jellies, and farm-fresh eggs. Lions Club Fairgrounds, Colon Rd., Sanford, NC 27332. Apr.–Oct., Wed., 3–6 P.M.; Sat., 8 A.M.–noon. (919) 775-5624; susan_condlin@ncsu.edu

Sanford Pottery Festival

The largest pottery festival in North Carolina brings together traditional and contemporary potters. Dennis A. Wicker Civic Center, 1801 Nash St., Sanford, NC 27330. Held the weekend before Mother's Day. Sat.–Sun., 9 A.M.–4 P.M. Admission fee. (919) 776-4351; www.sanfordpottery.com

The Tree Patch

Choose and cut your own tree or purchase one already cut. The farm grows Leyland cypress, red cedar, Virginia pine, and white pine. 1747 Henley Rd., Sanford, NC 27330. Thanksgiving–Dec. 24, Mon.–Fri., 3 P.M.–dark; Sat., 9 A.M.–dark; Sun., 1 P.M.–dark. (919) 776-6475; jhall@wave-net.net

Out of the Fire (p. 270)

Saxapahaw/Alamance County

Benjamin Vineyards & Winery

The vineyard grows muscadines, as well as French grapes and French hybrids. Free tastings and tours, a gift shop, and local art exhibitions are offered. 6516 Whitney Rd., Saxapahaw, NC 27253. Thurs.–Sun., noon–5 P.M. (336) 376-1080; www.benjaminvineyards.com

Out of the Fire

You'll find vessels carved in a style inspired by ancient Mexican art and the work of Southwestern Native Americans. Sculpted animals, garden spirits, and botanical tiles are available, too! 6035 Church Rd., Saxapahaw, NC 27253. Open by appointment. (336) 376-9091; cbiles@triad.rr.com

Seagrove/Randolph County

Anita's Pottery and Dogwood Gallery

The potter makes incredible miniature pieces, using just her fingers for shaping. The gallery also offers water gardens, wind chimes, baskets, stained glass, and art glass. 2513 NC Hwy 705, Seagrove, NC 27341. Mon.–Sat., 10 A.M.–5 P.M. (336) 879-3040; www.anitaspottery.com

Avery Pottery & Tileworks

Blaine Avery's pieces take function to the next level with his use of animal additions and slip decorations. Laura Avery creates sculptural pieces, individual tiles, and mosaic pieces. 1423 NC Hwy 705, Seagrove, NC 27341. Tues.–Sat., 10 A.M.–5 P.M.; Sun.–Mon., by appointment. (336) 873-7923; www.discoverseagrove.com

Kings Pottery *Terry King* (p. 272)

Blue Moon Gallery and Ole Fish House Pottery

You'll find contemporary and traditional pottery by North Carolina potters and artists from across the United States. Crafts include jewelry, glass, metalwork, candles, and soap. 1387 NC Hwy 705 S., Seagrove, NC 27341. Mon.–Sat., 10 A.M.–5 P.M. (336) 879-3270; www.blue-moon-gallery.com

Daniel Johnston Pottery

The potter studied in England and Thailand. He makes functional and decorative pieces using ashes and salt glazes, as well as celadon.

He digs his own clay locally. 6199 Sugg Dr., Seagrove, NC 27341. Open by appointment; kiln openings, Sat., 9 A.M.–5 P.M.; Sun., noon–5 P.M. (336) 629-6388; paulaes11@earthlink.net

Dixieland Pottery

Rooted in family traditions, the potters adapt heritage shapes in their work. Utilizing local clay, they specialize in custom dinnerware. 1162 Cagle Loop Rd., Seagrove, NC 27341. Mon.–Sat., 9:30 A.M.–5 P.M. (336) 873-8463; mrmsdixieland@wmconnect.com

The Duck Smith House B&B

Sisters Barbara and Suzanne Murphy operate this charming inn. They serve a full breakfast on fine china each morning in the breakfast room. 465 N. Broad St., Seagrove, NC 27341. (336) 873-7099 or (800) 869-9018; www.ducksmithhouse.com

Fork Creek Mill Pottery

This little pink pottery will make you want to stop and look. Inside, you'll find a focus on raku and cat creations in clay. 246 Old Plank Rd., Seagrove, NC 27341. Tues.–Sat., 9 A.M.–5 P.M. (336) 873-7258; www.seagrovepotteries.com

Fork Creek Mill Pottery

The Great White Oak Gallery

This gallery features distinctive hand-decorated stoneware and porcelain, as well as high-fired stoneware with oxblood and other unusual glazes. 437 N. Broad St. (US Hwy 220 Alt.), Seagrove, NC 27341. Mon.–Sat., 9 A.M.–4:30 P.M. (336) 873-8066; greatwhiteoakgallery@triad.rr.com

Johnston and Gentithes Art Pottery

This pottery features one-of-a-kind pieces crafted using local clay and English porcelain, then salt-glazed and fired in a wood kiln. 249 E. Main St., Seagrove, NC 27341. Mon.–Sat., 10 A.M.–5 P.M.; Sun., 1–5 P.M. (336) 873-9176; www.johnstonandgentithes.com

Kings Pottery

Kings is one of the oldest potteries in the Seagrove area. The potters love making sculptural folk pottery, as well as functional everyday wares. 4905 Reeder Rd., Seagrove, NC 27341. Mon.–Sat., 9 A.M.–5 P.M. (336) 381-3090; www.kingspottery.com

Museum of North Carolina Traditional Pottery

The museum supports and promotes local potters by providing visitor maps that highlight the location of 112 pottery shops and include colored pictures of pottery. 122 Main St. (NC Hwy 705), Seagrove, NC 27341. Mon.–Fri., 10 A.M.–2 P.M.; Sat., 9 A.M.–3 P.M. Free. (336) 873-7887; www.seagrovepotteryheritage.com

North Carolina Pottery Center

The center provides maps, samples of pottery, and assistance in locating the more than 100 pottery studios and galleries of Seagrove. 250 East Ave. (NC Hwy 705), Seagrove, NC 27341. Tues.–Sat., 10 A.M.–4 P.M.; closed on major holidays. Admission fee. (336) 873-8430; www.ncpotterycenter.com

Phil Morgan Pottery

Phil Morgan is one of only a handful of crystalline potters across the country who still create the glaze the old-fashioned way. Check out the salt-glazed face jugs and chickens, too! 966 NC Hwy 705, Seagrove, NC 27341. Mon.–Sat., 9 A.M.–5 P.M. (336) 873-7304; philmorg@asheboro.com

Vivid red pottery at Kings Pottery *Terry King*

Potts Pottery

Stop by Potts Pottery and browse the delightful selection of products ranging from traditional plates, cups, and saucers to lamps and vases. 630 E. Main St. (NC Hwy 705), Seagrove,

NC 27341. Tues.–Sat., 9 A.M.–5 P.M. (336) 873-9660; www.visitrandolphcounty.com/pottery.php?id=58

Seagrove Pottery Festival

This is the largest event with Seagrove potters in one place. It features only Seagrove potters, as well as more than 50 folk and heritage artists from across the state. Seagrove School, Seagrove, NC 27341. Held the weekend before Thanksgiving. (336) 873-7887

Tom Gray Pottery

Full kiln awaits firing at the North Carolina Pottery Center.

Here, you'll find the right pot for breaking bread, as well as serving bowls, colanders, trays, spoon jars, teapots, mortar and pestle sets, dinnerware, and Communion sets. 1480 Fork Creek Mill Rd., Seagrove, NC 27341. Tues.–Sat., 10 A.M.–5 P.M. (336) 873-8270; www.n2clay.com

Uwharrie Crystalline Pottery

This pottery specializes in crystalline, the art of growing crystals on vases during firing. Visitors can glaze a vase and watch as it is fired. 112 East Ave., Seagrove, NC 27341. Mon.–Sat., 9 A.M.–5 P.M.; Sun., noon–5 P.M. (336) 873-7532;

Whynot Pottery

The potters specialize in high-fired stoneware utilizing a variety of shapes and glazes. 1013 Fork Creek Mill Rd., Seagrove, NC 27341. Tues.–Sat., 9 A.M.–5 P.M. (336) 873-9276; www.whynotpottery.com

Sedalia/Guilford County

Charlotte Hawkins Brown Museum

This state historic site honors the work of Dr. Brown and the Palmer Institute and showcases the contributions of African-Americans to North Carolina's educational and social history.

6136 Burlington Rd., Sedalia, NC 27342. Free. (336) 449-4846; www.chbrownmuseum.nchistoricsites.org

Famed educator Charlotte Hawkins Brown *N.C. Division of State Historic Sites* (p. 273)

Siler City/Chatham County

Allred Pottery

The husband-and-wife potters delight in creating whimsical and functional pottery, turned or hand-built and decorated with the potters' own nontoxic glazes. 4908 Pleasant Hill Church Rd., Siler City, NC 27344. Feb.–Dec., daily, 10 A.M.–5 P.M. (919) 663-2819; www.allredpottery.com

Bed & Breakfast at Laurel Ridge

Chef and owner David Simmons spoils guests with his trademark culinary delights, served on the area's distinctive pottery. 3188 Siler City–Snow Camp Rd., Siler City, NC 27344. (919) 742-6049 or (800) 742-6049; www.laurel-ridge.com

Darrel Tracy, Ceramic Sculptor

This ceramic arts studio specializes in hand-built tree house sculptures. Collections exhibited include nightlights, lamps, and special urns. 112 W. Second St., Siler City, NC 27344. (919) 704-5216; quakercrafts@earthlink.net

Horizon Cellars Winery & Vineyard

The winery and vineyard offer wine tastings, tours, art and music events, and sales. 466 Vineyard Ridge, Siler City, NC 27344. Mon.–Tues. and Thurs.–Fri., 11 A.M.–5 P.M.; Sat., 11 A.M.–6 P.M.; Sun., noon–5 P.M. Fees are charged for some events. (919) 742-1404; www.horizoncellars.com

The Inn at Celebrity Dairy

The eight-room B&B hosts special events. Activities include spring and fall "Open Barn" events and gourmet dinners on the third Sunday of each month. 144 Celebrity Dairy Way, Siler City, NC 27344. (919) 742-5176 or (877) 742-5176; www.celebritydairy.com

Karen Poetzinger, Fiber Artist

This artist makes one-of-a-kind fiber art pieces with traditional rug-hooking methods. Flannel is hand-dyed, cut into strips, and hooked through a loosely woven linen foundation. 138 N. Chatham St., Siler City, NC 27344. Open Fri. 11 A.M.–6 P.M. and by appointment. (919) 663-2072

Lori LaBerge, Fiber Artist

Original fiber art is created by traditional rug hooking. Each piece is hand-dyed, hand-hooked, and either hand-finished or framed with care. 227 N. Chatham St., Siler City, NC 27344. Open by appointment. (919) 663-2072; www.lorilaberge.com

Murals: *Farmer's Alliance, History of Chatham Hospital,* and *Our Hardware Heritage*

Three outdoor murals by Stacye Leanza feature scenes from the community's past. Sites include Ace Hardware (119 E. Raleigh St.), the Farmer's Alliance co-op (134 S. Chatham Ave.), and Chatham's first and only hospital (125 W. Raleigh St.). (919) 545-0479; sleanza@blast.com

NC Arts Incubator Gallery

Visit the only business incubator in North Carolina focused on the arts. 138 N. Chatham Ave., Siler City, NC 27344. Jan.–March, Wed.–Sat., 11 A.M.–2 P.M.; Apr.–Dec., Wed.–Fri., 11 A.M.–4 P.M.; Sat., 11 A.M.–2 P.M. (919) 663-2072; ncartsgallery@earthlink.com

Oakmont Nursery

The nursery offers ornamental trees and shrubs. 9985 US Hwy 64 W., Siler City, NC 27344. March–June and Sept.–Nov., Mon.–Fri., 8 A.M.–noon and 1–5 P.M.; Sat., 9 A.M.–1 P.M.; July–Aug. and Dec.–Feb., Mon.–Fri., 8 A.M.–noon and 1–5 P.M. (919) 663-3607; oakmont@centernet.net

Person to Person Art Studio & Gallery

Roger Person's art is filled with humor and color in a mixture of mediums, including glass, metal, ceramics, wood, and acrylics. 210 N. Chatham Ave., Siler City, NC 27344. Open by appointment. (919) 663-0982; person@charter.net

Red Dirt Girl

Clay artist Cheryl Essex's work ranges from traditional to whimsical. 138 N. Chatham St., Siler City, NC 27344. Mon.–Sat., 10 A.M.–4 P.M. (919) 777-9621; www.reddirtgirl.com

Sculpture Department at Central Carolina Community College

This is a working studio for local students. At different times of the year, you can experience a wood firing, a salt-kiln firing, blacksmithing, or a bronze pour. 138 N. Chatham Ave., Siler City, NC 27344. Mon.–Thurs., 8 A.M.–9 P.M.; Fri., 8 A.M.–4 P.M.; Sat., 10 A.M.–2 P.M. (919) 742-4156; www.cccc.edu/Programs/Sculpture.html

Stacye Leanza

The artist works in oil and acrylics, focusing on industrial and electrical themes, as well as portraits and outdoor murals. Chatham Ave. and E. Second St., Siler City, NC 27344. Open by appointment. (919) 663-2072; sleanza@blast.com

Snow Camp/Alamance County

Bass Mountain Bluegrass Festival

Two times a year, top local and national bluegrass acts perform. Jam sessions run 24 hours a day. Food and crafts are sold. 1256 Longest Acres Rd., Snow Camp, NC 27349. Memorial Day weekend, Thurs.–Sun.; Labor Day weekend, Fri.–Sun. Admission fee. (336) 229-9055; www.bassmountain.com

Mural by Stacye Leanza

Snow Camp Outdoor Theater

Sword of Peace is about Quakers during the Revolutionary War. *Pathway to Freedom* is about the Quaker role in the Underground Railroad. The multi-building historic site includes a restaurant. 801 Drama Rd., Snow Camp, NC 27349. Productions, Wed.–Sat. beginning at dusk; historic sites and museums, summer, 8 A.M.–8 P.M.; winter hours are by appointment. Fees are charged. (336) 376-6948; www.snowcampdrama.com

Sophia/Randolph County

Mosaic Human Sundial of Peace—*Reflections of Peace on Earth*

The mosaic pieces for this sundial—more than 2,000 tiles—were made by hand by over 500 children at New Market Elementary School and in the surrounding community. New Market Elementary School Playground, 6096 US Hwy 311 S., Sophia, NC 27317. Accessible daily during daylight hours. (336) 495-7742 or (336) 495-3340; linda3@northstate.net

Stokesdale/Guilford County

Sadie's Herbal Garden

Delightful soaps are made on-site, along with creams, lotions, skin-care products, candles, herbal teas, and related products. 8406 Hwy 158 (Main St.), Stokesdale, NC 27357. Mon.–Sat., 9 A.M.–6 P.M. (336) 644-7627; www.sadiesherbalgarden.com

Trinity/Randolph County

Homethrown Pottery

Stop in for hand-turned stoneware pottery, soy candles, soy lotions, potpourri, herbal products, all-natural pet treats, and more. 408 Gray Rock Rd. S., Trinity, NC 27370. Wed.–Sat., 10 A.M.–6 P.M., and by appointment. (336) 476-8452; www.homethrownpottery.com

Scenes of the Sandhills

Anson, Hoke, Montgomery, Moore, Richmond, and Scotland Counties

From small-town charm to life on the farm, "Scenes of the Sandhills" offers quiet relaxation amid longleaf pines, the rolling greens of world-class golf courses, peach orchards, and quaint shops that present the best of North Carolina.

Although the Sandhills area is recognized as the home of the Pinehurst Resort—one of the most prestigious golfing destinations in the world—the region offers a unique combination of activities that blend art, tranquil beauty, and robust agriculture.

This trail also highlights the artistic importance of the North Carolina pottery tradition. Honoring roots that

Lumber River, Scotland County

trace back to the mid-18th century, potters in Moore County still use local clay, wood-fired kilns, and ash, salt, and alkaline glazes. Works by contemporary potters including the Owens family demonstrate the tradition and longevity of materials, techniques, and even forms of North Carolina pottery. (More great Seagrove-area potters are found in the "Potters' Wheels and Organic Fields" trail.)

Visit pottery studios where works vary in shape, color, and size, where each pot is sculptural—a work of art—in its form and composition. Take part in a pottery, painting, or woodworking workshop. Indulge your taste buds with fresh-from-the-farm produce and delicious home-baked dishes and goodies. The area's rich soil and moderate climate produce juicy peaches. Orchards offer yummy peach products, from homemade ice cream to preserves.

Create beautiful jewelry at a beading workshop in Wadesboro, or learn how to plant a tree at one of the local nurseries. Touch handspun yarn, taste fresh goat-milk cheeses and homemade ice cream, or pick up soybean candles and emu-oil lotions for aromatherapy at home.

Whether you visit for the day or a long weekend, you'll find the Sandhills an off-the-beaten-path treasure that features home-cooked, hand-cut, homegrown fun. Read on for town-by-town descriptions of the unique attractions that make up the "Scenes of the Sandhills" trail.

Aberdeen/Moore County

Artists League of the Sandhills

This former storage terminal of the Aberdeen & Rockfish Railroad houses the studios of 40 artists-in-residence, a gallery, and classrooms. Art classes for kids and adults include drawing, mixed media, pastels, watercolors, oils, and acrylics. 129 Exchange St., Aberdeen, NC 28315. Mon.–Fri., 9 A.M.–5 P.M.; gallery, noon–3 P.M. (910) 944-3979; www.artistleague.org

Pressley Farms Corn Maze

Inn at Bryant House

A National Historic Register property, the nine-bedroom inn has been completely restored to its original 1913 splendor. 214 N. Poplar St., Aberdeen, NC 28315. (919) 944-3300 or (800) 453-4019; www.innatbryanthouse.com

The Malcolm Blue Farm and House

This antebellum farm, built around 1825 and listed on the National Register of Historic Places, features barns, a gristmill, and 100-year-old Darlington oaks. It sponsors the Malcolm Blue Historical Crafts and Farm Skills Festival in September and a bluegrass festival in the summer. A Christmas open house is held the second Sunday in December. 1177 Bethesda Rd. (Hwy. 5 and E. L. Ives Dr.), Aberdeen, NC 28315. Museum, Wed.–Sat., 11 A.M.–2 P.M., and by appointment. A fee is charged for tours. (910) 944-7558; www.malcolmbluefarm.com

Cameron/Moore County

Cameron Historic District and Antiques Fair

Born of a plank road and a railroad and spurred on by the turpentine and dewberry industries, Cameron prospered in the late 19th and early 20th centuries. The Fayetteville plank road arrived in the area in the 1850s. With the arrival of the railroad in 1875, a town was planned. Cameron still retains its turn-of-the-century character and the charm of a quiet village. Carthage St., Carthage, NC 28326. Held the first Sat. of the month, May–Oct. (910) 245-1185; www.antiquesofcameron.com

Ferguson Farms

Ferguson Farms

Brake for ice cream! Fresh vegetables and fruits—especially summer plums and figs—also await. This is a North Carolina Farm Fresh Certified Roadside Farm Market. 172 US Hwy 1 Bus., Cameron, NC 28326. May–Sept., Mon.–Fri., 8 A.M.–6 P.M.; Sun., noon–6 P.M. (910) 245-2936

Pressley Farms Corn Maze

Fall means hayrides, a pumpkin patch, and an amazing corn maze. The farm is two miles off US Hwy 15/501. 1051 Union Church Rd., Cameron, NC 28326. Sept.–Oct., Fri., 6–10 P.M.; Sat., noon–10 P.M.; Sun., 1–6 P.M.; other times by appointment. (910) 947-4891; www.sandhillsagriculture.com

Yarborough's Greenhouses

Nursery plants are available at this greenhouse one-half mile east of US Hwy 1. 1939 Cranes Creek Rd., Cameron, NC 28326. March–Oct., open daily. (910) 245-7681

Candor/Moore County

Bruton's Vineyard

Want to make your own wine? Come pick muscadine grapes and succulent blackberries. 547 Hwy 211, Candor, NC 27229. June–Nov., Mon.–Sat., 7:30 A.M.–6 P.M.; also open Sun. during grape season. (910) 673-2757; www.sandhillsagriculture.com

Pick your own at Bruton's Vineyard.

Cow Run Farm Hunting Preserve

This is a casual, yet challenging, hunting experience on a 660-acre family-owned farm specializing in quail, chukar, and pheasant. All hunts are conducted in open fields and standing timber and are limited to one party at a time to ensure safety and quality. Guides are available. 107 Tabernacle Church Rd., Candor, NC 27229. Open Oct. 31–March 31. Reservations are required. (910) 974-4455; www.cowrunfarmhunting.com

Craven's Produce and Flowers

You'll find fresh, delicious fruits and vegetables, as well as an ample selection of plants and flowers for your garden. 362 Capel Mill Rd., Candor, NC 27229. Apr.–Oct., Mon.–Fri., 8 A.M.–5 P.M. (910) 652-5957

Johnson Farm

Johnson Farm is country at its best. Stop to savor the ice cream and peach dumplings, or browse the gift shop. 4009 US Hwy 220 S., Candor, NC 27229. June–Oct., daily, 8:30 A.M.–6 P.M. (910) 974-7730

Parsons Farm

Piedmont residents love ice cream! It's never fresher than at this farm stand, which also features seasonal produce to take home. Hwy 211 E., Candor, NC 27229. Apr.–Oct. and Dec., Mon.–Sat., 8 A.M.–7 P.M.; Sun., 1–7 P.M. (910) 974-9755; parsonsfarm5@earthlink.net

Carthage/Moore County

The Blacksmith Inn

Four spacious rooms, each with a fireplace, await golfers and cultural travelers. Located in Carthage's historic district,

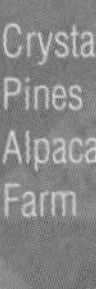

Crystal Pines Alpaca Farm

the inn is listed on the National Register of Historic Places. 703 McReynolds St., Carthage, NC 28327. (910) 947-1692 or (800) 284-4515; www.homeofgolf.com/visitors/bandbs

P

Crystal Pines Alpaca Farm

This working alpaca farm features hayrides, a petting zoo, educational programs, fresh farm eggs, and plant sales. 200 Holly Ridge Rd., Carthage, NC 28327. March–June and Sept.–Nov., Tues. and Thurs., 9 A.M.–5 P.M. Some fees are charged. (910) 947-6649

P ?

The Old Buggy Inn

Lovingly restored, this Queen Anne Victorian home is minutes from golf in Pinehurst and Southern Pines; antiques in Cameron, Vass, and Aberdeen; and over 70 nationally recognized potters in Seagrove. The rooms have carved fireplaces, huge windows, and beautiful antiques. 301 McReynolds St., Carthage, NC 28327. (910) 947-1901 or (800) 553-5247; www.oldbuggyinn.com

P

Persimmon Hill Farm

From azaleas to soaps, live music, farm demonstrations, and crafts—there's something sure to charm you here. Stop in the coffee and tea room, too. 4680 US Hwy 15/501 S., Carthage, NC 28327. Tues.–Sat., 9 A.M.–6 P.M.; Sun., 1–6 P.M. (910) 947-6033; www.sandhillsagriculture.com

P ?

Pressley Farms Berry Patch

This is the home of the world's largest strawberry! And how is that measured? Come find out. And take home berries or sweet melons. Fall features pumpkins, a petting zoo, and hayrides. 444 Bryant Rd., Carthage, NC 28327. Mon.–Sat., 7 A.M.–6 P.M. (910) 947-4891; www.sandhillsagriculture.com

P ?

Eagle Springs/Moore County

Carter Farms

Bask in the warmth of the sun as you pick fresh strawberries at this friendly farm. Carter Farms is fun for the whole family. 673 Eagle Springs Rd., Eagle Springs, NC 27242. Apr.–June, Mon., Wed., and Fri.–Sat., 8 A.M.–5 P.M. (910) 673-7730; www.sandhillsagriculture.com

Fireshadow Pottery

You'll find potters and sculptors at work in a landscape of abundant flowers and a soothing water garden. Browse the showroom, take a tour, request a demonstration, or simply soak up the serenity of this special place. 244 Falls Dr., Eagle Springs, NC 27242. Tues.–Sat., 10 A.M.– 5 P.M.; call for special Christmas hours. (910) 673-8317; www.fireshadow.com

Freeman Pottery

The old farmhouse sparkles! You'll find functional pieces with graffito artwork of trees, fences, barns, log cabins with outhouses, and country churches. The artwork depicts seasonal and nighttime motifs. A large array of miniatures (up to six inches) is available, too. 1147 McDuffie Rd., Eagle Springs, NC 27242. Tues.–Sat., 9 A.M.–5 P.M. (910) 673-2044; bfoushee@triad.rr.com

Inn at Eagle Springs

This secluded B&B is just 20 minutes west of Pinehurst. It offers six charming rooms, two friendly dogs, and plenty of ice cream and fruit for lazy afternoons. It's a great place for a reunion. 1813 Samarcand Rd., Eagle Springs, NC 27242. (910) 673-2722; www.innateaglesprings.com

Nichols Pottery

This shop is known for its "Women of Faith" biblical pieces. Cooks will like the cornbread pans, apple bakers, and cake pans. Check out the birdhouses, candlesticks, vases, and pitchers. Hwy 705, Eagle Springs, NC 27242. Mon.–Sat., 10 A.M.–6 P.M.; Sun., 1–5 P.M. (910) 948-4392; www.discoverseagrove.com

David's Produce and Plant Farm

Ellerbe/Richmond County

Bynum Farm and Nursery

Peaches, plums, and nectarines are the specialties at this orchard in the historic Windblow area. Abundant watermelons, cantaloupes, and nursery stock are available, too. 123 Gallimore Rd. (Hwy 73), Ellerbe, NC 28338. July and Aug., daily, 7:30 A.M.–6 P.M.; trees are sold mid-Dec.–early Apr. by appointment. (910) 652-2204; www.bynumfarm.com

David's Produce and Plant Farm

How about a banana split or a sundae while you check out the wrought-iron garden accessories? Over the years, the stand has added jams, dressings, country ham, hot roasted peanuts, hoop cheese, and honey to go with 32 creamy flavors of ice cream. 2940 US Hwy 220 N., Ellerbe, NC 28228. Spring–summer, daily, 8 A.M.–6 P.M.; fall, daily, 9 A.M.–5 P.M. (910) 652-6413; www.davidsproduce.com

Bynum Farm and Nursery

DeWitt's Outdoor Sports

Group hunts, sporting clays, lodging, meals, and game birds are available here. DeWitt's is located four miles northwest of Ellerbe. 443 Jimmy Carriker Rd., Ellerbe, NC 28338. Mon.–Fri., 10 A.M.–6 P.M.; Sat., 9 A.M.–6 P.M.; Sun., 1–6 P.M. (910) 652-2926; gamebirds@etinternet.net

Ellerbe Springs Inn and Restaurant

This National Register inn, built in 1906, features 13 guest rooms decorated with Victorian antiques, a full-service restaurant, a springhouse, and a two-suite historic guest cottage that overlooks a lake and tennis courts. Visitors can enjoy nearby walking trails and historic sites. 2537 US Hwy 220 N., Ellerbe, NC 28338. (910) 652-5600; www.ellerbesprings.com

Ellerbe Springs Inn and Restaurant

Ellerbe Springs Nursery, Inc.

The home of the one-dollar azalea, this large nursery offers an ample selection of garden and landscaping varieties. 2408 US Hwy 220 N., Ellerbe, NC 28338. Mon.–Sat., 8 A.M.–5 P.M. (910) 652-3361

Gibson's Nursery

Azaleas, field-grown collards, cabbages, tomatoes, and other varieties of plants are sold at Gibson's. 342 Gibson Nursery Rd., Ellerbe, NC 28338. Mon.–Sat., 8 A.M.–5 P.M. (910) 652-6254; www.sandhillsagriculture.com

Hill's Horn of Plenty

Hill's Horn of Plenty

Hill's is the home of the "Sweet Corn King" and the "Ice Cream Caboose." You'll also find jams, jellies, pickles, relishes, and cool drinks. 1930 US Hwy 220, Ellerbe, NC 28338. May–Sept., daily, 8 A.M.–6 P.M. (910) 652-6147; yhwarrior@aol.com

Lizzie's Produce and Restaurant

Hungry? Lizzie's features an on-site restaurant with delicious home-cooked meals. 3974 US Hwy 220 N., Ellerbe, NC 28338. Mon.–Sat., 7 A.M.–10 P.M. (910) 652-3914; www.sandhillsagriculture.com

McAuley Plant Farm

With 25 greenhouses, this family-owned business offers a large variety of bedding, vegetables, and potted plants, including hanging baskets. In the fall, the farm holds a mum and pansy event featuring mule and donkey tours. 1311 Haywood Parker Rd., Ellerbe, NC 28338. March–June and Sept.–Oct., daily, 8 A.M.–5 P.M. (910) 652-3071; www.sandhillsagriculture.com

Rankin Museum of American and Natural History

Recognized for its diverse and unique collections, this museum explores the history and cultures of early America with an impressive collection of artifacts, farm tools, fossils, and American Indian exhibits. 131 W. Church St., Ellerbe, NC 28338. Mon.–Fri., 10 A.M.–4 P.M.; Sat.–Sun., 2–5 P.M.

(910) 652-6378; www.rankinmuseum.com

Rickie DeWitt Farm

Sweet—as in potatoes and watermelons—is the word here. Pick your own if you like. Seasonal produce is available. 641 Jones Springs Church Rd., Ellerbe, NC 28338. Open year-round, Mon.–Sat. (910) 652-5621; www.sandhillsagriculture.com

Triple L Farm

Does the name stand for "lush, lovely, and lively"? Triple L has old-fashioned hand-dipped ice cream—just the thing to go with its peaches, strawberries, watermelons, and cantaloupes. 2205 Derby Rd., Ellerbe, NC 28338. May–Aug., daily, 7 A.M.–6:30 P.M. (910) 417-0438; marcielambeth@carolina.net

The Webb Farm, Quail Grounds, and Lodge

Nestled in the heart of 1,200 acres of prime quail habitat, The Webb Farm offers comfortable accommodations, gourmet dining, and a great room with a fireplace where guests sit and share tales. Saddle the horses and head to the milo field and open pinewoods to experience one of North Carolina's finest wing-shooting destinations. 522 John Webb Rd., Ellerbe, NC 28338. (910) 652-6563

The Webb Farm, Quail Grounds, and Lodge

Wilson Farms

Ready for supper? Come pick your berries, corn, okra, cucumbers, and other veggies and fruits. 303 Gold Leaf Farm Rd., Ellerbe, NC 28379. Apr.–Sept., daily, 7 A.M.–7 P.M. (910) 417-1636

Ether/Montgomery County

Floyd's General Store

Find some yesteryear at this old-time general store. For 90 years, the family has brought everyday country to life with its selection of hardware, groceries, stoves, case knives, and cast-iron cookware. Toys, games, books, and unique collectibles will make new memories for you. 1145 Cagle Rd., Ether, NC 27247. Mon.–Sat., 7 A.M.–6 P.M. (910) 428-2008; www.floydsgeneralstore.com

Hamlet/Richmond County

Hamlet Passenger Depot

Historic Hamlet is a rare reminder of the glory days of passenger rail activity on the Eastern Seaboard. Built in 1900, the depot still functions as a passenger site. Model trains, a model railroad town, and several restored rail cars are on display. 2 Main St., Hamlet, NC 28345. Tours, Sat.–Sun., 1–4 P.M., and by appointment. Free. (910) 582-2651; www.micropublishing.com/railroad

Hamlet Passenger Depot

National Railroad Museum and Hall of Fame, Inc.

Exhibits help visitors explore the history of the Eastern Seaboard Air Line Railway and discover interesting facts about the town of Hamlet and Richmond County. Artifacts, photos, books, and documents lend historic authenticity. 23 Hamlet Ave., Hamlet, NC 28345. Sat., 11 A.M.–4 P.M., and by appointment. Free. (910) 582-2383; www.micropublishing.com/railroad/

The Robert L. and Elizabeth S. Cole Auditorium and Community Center

Performances include regional and national touring artists, musical productions, and plays. US Hwy 74, Richmond Community College Campus, Hamlet, NC 28345. Office, Mon.–Fri., 9 A.M.–5 P.M. (910) 582-7950; www.richmond.cc.nc.us/ColeIndex.html

The Robert L. and Elizabeth S. Cole Auditoriium and Community Center

Seaboard Festival

The event features model train displays, the Conductor's Call Contest, live music, and rides on the kiddie train. Artists, crafters, food vendors, and local organizations have booth displays and items for sale. Main St., Hamlet, NC 28345. Held the last Sat. in Oct., 9 A.M.–5 P.M. Free. (910) 582-2651

Hoffman/Richmond County

McKinney Lake State Fish Hatchery

This 18-acre warm-water hatchery grows channel catfish from fingerling size (three to four inches) to harvestable size (eight to 12 inches) for the North Carolina Wildlife Resources Commission's Community Fishing Program. 220 McKinney Lake Rd., Hoffman, NC 28347. Mon.–Fri., 8 A.M.–4 P.M. Tours are available by appointment. Free. (910) 895-5330

Seaboard Festival

Laurinburg/Scotland County

Art by Design

This full-service studio and shop in the historic downtown offers pottery, paintings, jewelry, and glassware by local artisans. 131 Main St., Laurinburg, NC 28352. Tues.–Fri., 9 A.M.–5:30 P.M.; Sat., 9 A.M.–3 P.M. (910) 610-1133; artbydesign@carolina.net

John Blue House and Cotton Gin

Visit a restored and operational pre–Civil War cotton gin, authentic log cabins, and the Cotton Blossom Railroad, all on the grounds of the John Blue House. 13040 X-Way Rd., Laurinburg, NC 28353. Mon.–Sat., 10 A.M.–noon and 1–4 P.M. Tours are available. Free. (910) 276-7238 or (910) 277-7860; www.johnbluecottonfestival.com

Laurinburg After Five Concerts

Concerts are held on the campus of St. Andrews Presbyterian College the second Thursday of each month from May through September. 606 S. Atkinson St., Laurinburg, NC 28353. Free. (910) 276-7420; www.laurinburgchamber.com

Locklear Produce

Laurinburg After Five Concerts *Laurinburg Chamber of Commerce* (p. 289)

Choose juicy, fresh fruits and vegetables in season here and you'll be buying a little history as well. Locklear Produce is one of Laurinburg's longest-running produce markets. 13020 X-Way Rd., Laurinburg, NC 28352. In season, daily, 7 A.M.–7 P.M.; off-season, 10 A.M.–5 P.M. (910) 277-1736

McNair Town and Country Store

This old-time hardware store recaptures another era even as it features seeds and goods for today's homes and fields. 121 Fairly St., Laurinburg, NC 28352. Mon.–Fri., 8 A.M.–5 P.M.; Sat., 8 A.M.–1 P.M. (910) 276-2812

Quality Produce

Locally made canned goods include hot and mild chow-chow. In season, you can buy fresh-from-the-field peas, greens, tomatoes, squash, butter beans, potatoes, cukes, and melons. 9300 Johns Rd., Laurinburg, NC 28352. Open daily, 8 A.M.–7 P.M. (910) 276-4983; bettyj@gmail.com

Scotland County Museum

The museum includes local Civil War memorabilia and a collection of vintage vehicles and machinery, such as early steam engines, antique cars, tractors, and farm equipment. 13043 X-Way Rd., Laurinburg, NC 28352. Mon.–Fri., 10 A.M.–4 P.M., and by appointment. Free. (910) 277-6875

Scottish Heritage Center

St. Andrews Pipe Band *Scottish Heritage Center*

Located in the DeTamble Library at St. Andrews Presbyterian College, the center houses old and rare books on Scottish and Scottish-American history, genealogy, and culture, as well as current scholarly titles and periodicals. The center also contains exhibits of the area's Scottish settlement and artifacts about Scottish heroine Flora MacDonald, who resided briefly in the region in the late 18th century. You'll also find the largest collection of Celtic music in the United States and the Fiona Ritchie Radio Archive for *The Thistle and Shamrock*, a radio program. 1700 Dogwood Mile, Laurinburg, NC 28352. Free. (910) 277-5236 or (800) 763-0198; www.sapc.edu/shc/shc/index.php

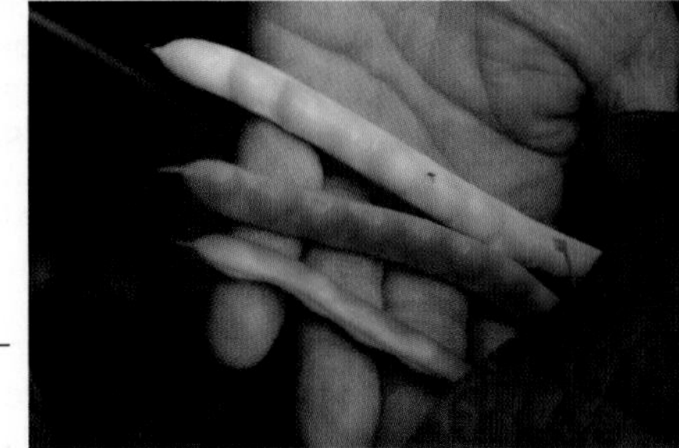

Quality Produce

Thomas Walton Manor B&B

Savor the restful elegance of one of Laurinburg's most gracious residences, now featuring beautiful guest rooms, individually designed bedrooms, and manicured grounds. 400 Church St., Laurinburg, NC 28352. (910) 276-0551; www.thomaswaltonmanor.com

Lilesville/Anson County

Pee Dee Orchards

Pee Dee Orchards offers a variety of Sandhills peaches that ripen at different times, as well as delicious homemade ice cream. US Hwy 74 about 1 mile west of the Pee Dee River, Lilesville, NC 28091. May–Oct., daily, 8 A.M.–7 P.M. (704) 848-4801; www.discoveranson.com

Pee Dee Orchards *Anson County Tourism*

Maxton/Scotland County

First Presbyterian Church of Maxton

The people of Shoe Hill village, now known as Maxton, requested that the Fayetteville Presbytery build a church for them. And so it was that in 1878 a new church was formed. The building remains standing in the middle of Maxton. 303 N. Patterson St., Maxton, NC 28364. Mon.–Thurs., 9 A.M.–4 P.M. (910) 844-5515

Maxton Museum

Built in the 1880s, the building has housed a number of businesses, including a smithy. It was moved to North Patterson Street in the 1890s and was used as the law office of Gilbert B. Patterson until 1922. The building moved to its present location in 1972. Since 1982 the home of the Maxton Historical Society, it houses collections of educational, social, industrial, and genealogical interest. Graham St., Maxton, NC 28364. Sun., 2–4 P.M., or by appointment. Free. (910) 844-2377; www.ci.maxton.nc.us/librarymuseum.htm

Morris Plant Farm

Bulbs and seasonal plants add fresh color to your life. Stop by Morris Plant Farm and pick your favorite shades! 19441 Old Maxton Rd., Maxton, NC 28364. (910) 276-0515

Morven/Richmond County

Pauline's Pride Greenhouses

Container-grown broadleaf evergreens are sold here, as are vegetable, bedding, annual, and perennial plants. You'll find Pauline's between Highway 145 (Old Plank Road) and Cason Oldfield Road. 701 Sandy Ridge Church Rd., Morven, NC 28119. Open year-round, Tues.–Sat., 8 A.M.–5 P.M. (704) 851-3636; www.sandhillsagriculture.com

Mount Gilead/Montgomery County

Town Creek Indian Mound State Historic Site

This unusual phenomenon offers visitors a glimpse of pre-Columbian life in the Piedmont. Town Creek, situated on the Little River (a tributary of the Great Pee Dee), has a program of archaeological research. Interpretive exhibits, audiovisual programs, self-guided tours of the rebuilt structures and mound, and group activities bring alive a rich cultural heritage from the buried past. The reconstructed ceremonial center includes the mound and major temple, the minor temple, and the burial house, or mortuary. 509 Town Creek Mound Rd., Mount Gilead, NC 27306. Tues.–Sat., 10 A.M.–4 P.M.; Sun., 1–4 P.M.; closed on major holidays. The Native American Heritage Festival is held in Sept. Free. (910) 439-6802; www.towncreek.nchistoricsites.org

Town Creek Indian Mound State Historic Site

Peachland/Anson County

ArtrageousFolk

You'll find copper-enameled mermaids, Madonnas, banjos, angels, clocks, and critters made by Denny Maloney, an antiquities collector turned artist. Spring openings are announced each year. 979 Savannah Rd. (Rte. 1414), Peachland, NC 28133. Open by appointment; open houses are held in the spring and fall. (704) 272-0851; www.artrageousfolk.com

The John Tucker Store

An antique collector's delight, this was once a general store. Glass-topped cases and a Hoosier cabinet hold collectible glassware, tools, toys, and one-of-a-kind treasures. The "dining room" features an assortment of glassware and china in breakfront cabinets, in corner cabinets, and on drop-leaf tables, which are also for sale. A Christmas open house is held the first weekend in December. On NC Hwy 218 north of Peachland, NC 28133. Fri.–Sat., 10 A.M.–4 P.M.; Sun., 2–6 P.M. (704) 272-9357 or (704) 519-6843; johntuckerstore@alltel.net

7KidsFarm

Patricia Cabrera, who started 7KidsFarm, was raised on a farm in Brazil. Now, Patricia, her husband, and their seven children grow vegetables, raise livestock, and make products. They sell homemade jams, goat-milk cheese, butter soaps and lotions, hand-spun yarn, handmade pottery, and eco-friendly soybean candles. 945 Horne Rd., Peachland, NC 28133. (704) 624-4051; www.7kidsfarm.com

The John Tucker Store *Anson County Tourism*

Pinehurst/Moore County

Broadhurst Gallery and Garden

Browse this lovely art gallery and lush sculpture garden to see original art created by nationally recognized artists. 2212 Midland Rd., Pinehurst, NC 28374. Tues.–Fri., 11 A.M.–5 P.M.; Sat., 1–4 P.M., and by appointment; gallery talks, Fri., 4 P.M. (910) 295-4817; www.broadhurstgallery.com

Pinehurst Harness Track

Come observe horses put through their paces in the early morning from October to May. Try the trackside restaurant for breakfast. Events include annual spring matinee races, horse shows (from May to October), and polo matches. 200 Beulah Hill Rd. (NC Hwy 5), Pinehurst, NC 28374. Open year-round, Mon.–Sat., 8 A.M.–dusk. Tickets are on sale for events. (910) 295-4446 or (800) 433-TROT; www.pinehurstharness.com

Sandhills Horticulture Gardens

The Ebersole Holly Garden, the largest accessible holly collection on the East Coast, joins with the Rose, Conifer, Sir Walter Raleigh, Hillside, Fruit and Vegetable, and Desmond Native Wetland Trail gardens to cover 27 acres. The site is an educational adventure to anyone with an interest in plants, nature, and design composition—and a fitting tribute to Frederick Law Olmsted, who designed Pinehurst. Sandhills Community College, Pinehurst, NC 28374. Open year-round, daylight–dark. Free. (910) 695-3882; www.sandhills.cc.nc.us/lsg/hort.html

Raeford/Hoke County

Carolina Horse Park

This one-of-a-kind, 250-acre park has flat fields perfect for show jumping, dressage, and racing, as well as expansive wooded areas for cross-country courses and obstacles. Gorgeous hardwoods, longleaf pines, and other plant varieties have been carefully preserved. This site for national equestrian competitions—including steeplechase, eventing, and dressage—is unique in North Carolina. 2814 Montrose Rd., Raeford, NC 28376. (910) 246-9808 or (888) 615-4520; www.carolinahorsepark.com

North Carolina Turkey Festival

This September festival, originally named the Hoke Heritage Hobnob, promotes turkeys—the area's number-one commodity—and attracts more than 60,000 visitors a year. Along with the traditional cooking competition, you'll find games, crafts, music, and more. McLaughlin Park, Raeford, NC 28376. (910) 875-5929 or (910) 904-2424; www.hoke-raeford.com/index2.htm

Raft Swamp Farms

Here, you'll see North Carolina's first organic farm incubator. Small tracts of land are available for lease. The farmers specialize in vegetable and blueberry production, beekeeping, and establishing muscadine vineyards and peach orchards. Hiking and bird watching are also available to visitors. The farm offers on-site use of equipment, training for farmers, and on-site composting. Hwy 211 at Andrews Rd., Raeford, NC 28376. Open during daylight hours by appointment. (910) 977-0950; www.raftswampfarms.org

Robbins/Moore County

From the Ground Up

Meditation bells call you to this pottery in a barn. Functional burnished wood-fired pieces include plates, bowls, bells, and soul and love pots. You can stroll to the "fairy forest" through pines. In the 1890s, this was a still. 172 Crestwood Rd., Robbins, NC 27325. Mon.–Sat., 9 A.M.–5 P.M.; often open Sun. (910) 464-6228; mahanpots@rtmc.net

Williams Pottery

This pottery shop produces functional stoneware that features hand-painted designs and multicolored glazes. Dinnerware, lamps, platters, square plates, and oval dishes can be made to order. The Civil War farmhouse property has been family-owned since the 1940s. 2170 Dan Rd., Robbins, NC 27325. Tues.–Sat., 10 A.M.–5 P.M. (910) 464-2120; williamspottery@earthlink.net

Rockingham/Richmond County

Arts Richmond Center for the Creative Arts

This local arts-council facility in two historic 1890s buildings houses visual arts spaces, studios, galleries, and an indoor/outdoor gallery for festivals and small performances. 123 E. Washington St., Rockingham, NC 28380. Mon.–Fri., 10 A.M.–5 P.M.; Sat., 10 A.M.–2 P.M. Call for special exhibits information. (910) 997-6008; rcc@etinternet.net or artsrich@carolina.rr.com

Bountiful Gardens Greenhouses

This garden nursery four miles south of Rockingham offers a wonderful assortment of bedding plants, geraniums, poinsettias, garden mums, pansies, and shrubs. 134 Thompson Farm Rd., Rockingham, NC 28379. Mon.–Sat., 8 A.M.–5 P.M. (910) 997-3233; www.sandhillsagriculture.com

Emily's Sandbox Garden Center

This gift shop carries unique local garden crafts and commercial and handmade items, too. Take home some of its organic produce, jams, and jellies. 503 Rockingham Rd., Rockingham, NC 28379. Tues.–Fri., 9 A.M.–5:30 P.M.; Sat., 9 A.M.–2 P.M. (910) 997-7311; www.sandhillsagriculture.com

Ford's Bluegrass Mill

You'll experience a good old-fashioned country time here every Friday, with talented musicians playing authentic bluegrass. Bring the whole family. Snacks are available; smoking and alcohol are not allowed. 134 City Lake Dr., Rockingham, NC 28379. Fri., 7:30 P.M. Admission is $3; kids under 12 are free.

Leak Wall House

A historic landmark in downtown Rockingham, the house was built in 1853 for a businessman and Confederate officer, then later served as a bank. It's now owned by the Richmond County Historical Society. Washington St., Rockingham, NC 28380. Call for an appointment and a tour schedule. (910) 895-9057

Richmond Community Theatre

This charming community theater has been producing top-notch entertainment for nearly three decades. Since 2003, the theater has also featured children's movies during the "Arts and Agriculture" events held each Saturday morning in front of the facility. 111 E. Washington St., Rockingham, NC 28380. Fees are charged for performances; free movies are shown on Sat. during the "Arts and Agriculture" summer events. (910) 997-3765

Richmond County Tourism Development Authority/ Chamber of Commerce

Up-to-the-minute information on the best the county has to offer is available here. 505 Rockingham Rd., Rockingham, NC 28379. (910) 895-9057 or (800) 858-1688; www.richmondcountychamber.com

Rockingham Farmers' Market

This community farmers' market features produce, crafts, and baked goods produced within 50 miles. Harrington Square, Rockingham, NC 28379. May–Oct., Sat., 8 A.M.–noon. (910) 997-8255; www.sandhillsagriculture.com

Smith Berry Farm

Here, you'll find both pick-your-own and fresh-picked produce options. Seasonal produce includes strawberries, greenhouse tomatoes, and blackberries. 247 Terry Bridge Rd., Rockingham, NC 28379. Apr.–July, daily, 8 A.M.–7 P.M., and by appointment. (910) 895-4560

Thursday Plaza Jam

The free concerts held outdoors on Cole Plaza (next to Rockingham City Hall) are great fun for the whole family. Performers vary in style and genre. 514 Rockingham Rd., Rockingham, NC 28379. May–Oct., first Thurs. of the month, 6:30–8:30 P.M. Free. (910) 997-5546; www.gorockingham.com

Rockingham Farmers' Market

Seagrove/Randolph County

Ben Owen Pottery

Located in the community of Westmoore, this renowned potter specializes in wood-fired, traditional, and contemporary works that are prized in many museums and public and private collections. The pieces feature a wide range of vibrant colors. Special kiln openings are offered. 2199 S. Pottery Hwy (NC Hwy 705), Seagrove, NC 27341. Tues.–Sat., 10 A.M.–5 P.M.; closed during Jan. Call ahead for groups. (910) 464-2261 or (336) 879-2262; www.benowenpottery.com

Bulldog Pottery

Contemporary artists Bruce Gholson and Samantha Henneke make distinctive ceramic pieces with unique glazes and graceful forms. Bulldog Pottery carries unusual and iridescent molybdenum crystalline glazes with a distinctive luster. 3306 US Hwy 220 Alt., Seagrove, NC 27341. Tues.–Fri., 1–5 P.M.; Sat., 10 A.M.–5 P.M.; call ahead for Sunday or group tours. (910) 428-9728 or (336) 302-3469; www.bulldogpottery.com

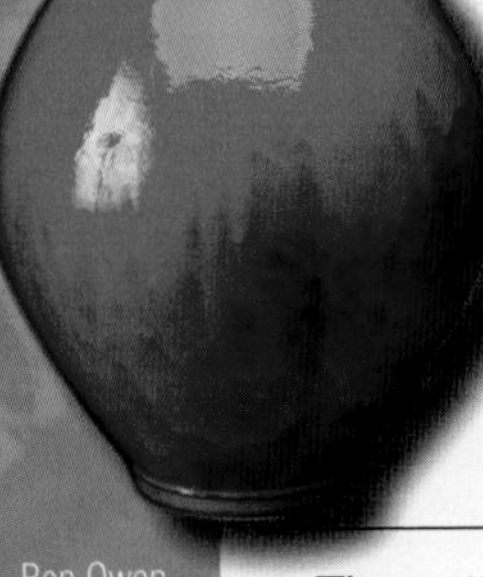

Ben Owen Pottery *Ben Owen III* (p. 297)

Cady Clay Works

John Mellage's elegant forms are accented by Beth Gore's richly layered glazes. Firing in the large wood kiln accents each piece with melted ash and flashing from the flame's path. The pottery made here includes decorative and functional pieces such as dinnerware, serving pieces, lamps, and vases. Bring a picnic. 3883 Busbee Rd., Seagrove, NC 27341. Tues.–Sat., 10 A.M.–4 P.M.; open weekends only during Jan. and July. (910) 464-5661; www.cadyclayworks.com

Hickory Hill Pottery

The potters make traditional stoneware in friendly, functional forms like baking dishes with periwinkle and jade-colored glazes. 4539 Busbee Rd., Seagrove, NC 27341. Mon.–Sat., 9 A.M.–5 P.M.; usually closed for two weeks after Christmas. (910) 464-3166

JLK Jewelry at Jugtown Pottery

Pottery cabochons are layered with glazes to create stones full of depth, dimension, and color. Artisan Jennie Lorette Keatts offers a full jewelry line including many one-of-a-kind handmade pieces set in sterling silver and accented with semiprecious stones, gold, and copper. 330 Jugtown Rd., Seagrove, NC 27341. Tues.–Sat., 8:30 A.M.–5 P.M. (910) 464-2653; www.jlkjewelry.com

Jugtown Pottery and Museum

Revered potters Vernon and Pam Owens feature their traditional pottery in this working studio and American crafts shop. Vernon is a recipient of the North Carolina Folk Heritage Award and the National Heritage Fellowship. The couple produces pieces ranging from traditional jugs and candlesticks in wood-fired salt glaze and frog skin to vases, bowls, and jars in glazes made with wood ash. The shop also houses a museum that explores the history of local pottery traditions from the early 1900s to the present. Picnic tables are available, so bring lunch or a snack to enjoy after browsing the shop. 330 Jugtown Rd., Seagrove, NC 27341. Tues.–Sat., 8:30 A.M.–5 P.M. (910) 464-3266; www.jugtownware.com

Luck's Ware

A fifth-generation potter and the recipient of the 1994 Living Treasure of North Carolina Award, Sid Luck produces the traditional churns, crocks, face jugs, and pitchers of his ancestors. Visitors can experience the ancient art of wheel-thrown pottery from the mixing of the clay to the finished product. Son Matt, a sixth-generation potter, continues the tradition. 1606 Adams Rd., Seagrove, NC 27341. Mon.–Sat., 9 A.M.–5 P.M. (336) 879-3261

Ray Pottery

At this potter's shop, you'll find high-quality gas-fired stoneware featuring a palette of sublime glazes including ox blood (copper red), rutile blue, tenmoku, and various ash glazes. All glazes used here are mixed from scratch by the potters. Browse the gallery to find a unique handmade piece to purchase for display in your home. 460 Cagle Rd., Seagrove, NC 27341. Tues.–Sat., 10 A.M.–5 P.M.; call for Sun.–Mon. hours. (336) 879-6707; paul@rtmc.net

Rockhouse Pottery

The decorative designs of grapes, dogwoods, pines, tulips, and Noah's Ark really rock! All pottery is hand-turned on a wheel, carved, glazed, and fired on-site. Come browse the shop and observe the talented potters at work. 1792 NC Hwy 705 S., Seagrove, NC 27341. Mon.–Sat., 9 A.M.–5 P.M. (336) 879-2053

JLK Jewelry at Jugtown Pottery

Westmoore Pottery

This pottery specializes in the production of wares that recall pieces crafted in the 17th, 18th, and 19th centuries. The potters' historically accurate work is displayed in museums and living-history sites around the country and is occasionally used in period movies. Visitors can observe the potters at work. 4622 Busbee Rd., Seagrove, NC 27341. Mon.–Sat., 9 A.M.–5 P.M.; closed July 17–31 and Dec. 24–Jan. 17. (910) 464-3700; www.westmoorepottery.com

Southern Pines/Moore County

Arts Council of Moore County

The arts council is located in the Campbell House, which features three spacious exhibit areas. Original paintings and pottery by local artists are for sale. 482 E. Connecticut Ave., Southern Pines, NC 28388. Mon.–Fri., 9 A.M.–5 P.M.; each third Sat.–Sun. of the month, 2–4 P.M. (910) 692-4356; www.artscouncil-moore.org

Convention and Visitors Bureau of Pinehurst, Southern Pines, and Aberdeen Area

The bureau has information on the area's 43 golf courses and its many restaurants and hotels, as well as details about concerts and live theatrical performances, historical reenactments, equestrian events, street festivals, and antique fairs. 10677 US Hwy 15/501, Southern Pines, NC 28388. Mon.–Fri., 9 A.M.–5 P.M. (910) 692-3330 or (800) 346-5362; www.homeofgolf.com

Knollwood House B&B

This luxurious English manor house stands among five acres of longleaf pines, dogwoods, azaleas, towering holly trees, and 40-foot magnolias. Knollwood's lawns roll down to the 15th fairway of a famous Donald Ross golf course. Breakfast and complimentary refreshments are served. 1495 W. Connecticut Ave., Southern Pines, NC 28387. (910) 692-9390; www.knollwoodhouse.com

Necklace from JLK Jewelry at Jugtown Pottery (p. 300)

Literary Hall of Fame at Weymouth Center

The North Carolina Literary Hall of Fame is housed in the Weymouth Center for the Arts & Humanities, the home of the late James Boyd, who wrote the critically acclaimed historical novel *Drums*. The home has long been a gathering place for writers, including F. Scott Fitzgerald and Thomas Wolfe. 555 E. Connecticut Ave., PO Box 939, Southern Pines, NC 28388. (910) 692-6261; www.weymouthcenter.org

Midland Road Manor B&B

Located in the heart of the Sandhills, this charming B&B is a peaceful place to get away. It's on the road once described as "the Park Avenue of the Sandhills," where tall pines and beautiful homes line the avenue from Southern Pines to Pinehurst. 1625 Midland Rd., Southern Pines, NC 28387. (910) 693-7979; www.midlandroadmanor.com

Moore County Historical and Heritage Tours

Historic Shaw House is an example of the antebellum homes constructed after the cabins of the early Sandhills settlers. The homes that may be seen by appointment include the 1829 Bryant House; the Joel McLendon Cabin, the oldest house in Moore County still on its original location; the early-19th-century Garner House; and the Britt Sanders Cabin, an example of the early Sandhills settlers' one-room cabins. This organization promotes awareness and appreciation of the heritage of Moore County. Southern Pines, NC 28388. The Shaw House properties are open Tues.–Fri., 1–4 P.M. (910) 692-2051; www.moorehistory.com

The Sunrise Theater

Built in 1898 as a hardware store, the building became a movie theater in the 1940s. The Arts Council of Moore County restored the theater as a performing-arts center for concerts, plays, and films. 250 N.W. Broad, Southern Pines, NC 28387. (910) 692-3611; www.sunrisetheater.com

Knollwood House B&B

Star/Montgomery County

Piney Woods Pottery

Owned and operated by Georgia and Johnnie Maness, Piney Woods Pottery is well known for specialty angels, dogwoods, roses, magnolias, and sculpted whimsical figures such as snowmen, clowns, and angels. Commissions are accepted. 1430 Ether Rd., Star, NC 27356. Mon.–Sat., 9 A.M.–5 P.M. (910) 572-3554; www.visitseagrove.com

Troy/Montgomery County

The Acorn Collection

This quaint general store offers Seagrove pottery, Native American handmade jewelry, candles, handmade glass beads, and local arts and crafts. The shop is located in a historic hotel that was formerly a drugstore. 401 N. Main St., Troy, NC 27271. Mon.–Wed. and Fri., 10 A.M.–5 P.M.; Thurs., 10 A.M.–6 P.M.; Sat., 10 A.M.–3 P.M. (910) 572-3170; troyacorn@earthlink.net

The Blair House B&B

This historic home was built in 1893 by country lawyer Joseph Reese Blair. Completely renovated in 2001, the B&B offers four guest suites. The home has been family owned for more than 100 years. 105 Blair St., Troy, NC 27371. (910) 572-2100; www.blairhousebb.com

Fall Tour of Historic Homes

The Montgomery County Historical Society hosts the Fall Tour of Historic Homes. Stops include the Blair House, the Allen House, the Nance House, the Russell House, the Pope House, and the Clark House. Walking and driving tours can include these Victorian homes as well as country farm homes and estates. Troy, NC 27371. Held the first Sun. in Nov., 2–5 P.M. Admission fee. (910) 576-8781; rhuntley@connectnc.net

The Interiors Company

This retail shop in "the Yellow House" features handmade gift items, accessories, hand-painted furniture, and interior-design services. 429 N. Main St., Troy, NC 27371. Tues.–Fri., 10 A.M.–5 P.M. (910) 572-3030; interiorscompany@earthlink.net

Montgomery County Chamber of Commerce

The chamber offers a wealth of information on the area's attractions, businesses, and quality-of-life amenities. 444 N. Main St., Troy, NC 27371. Mon.–Fri., 8 A.M.–5 P.M. (910) 572-4300; www.montgomery-county.com

Troyfest

This celebration of American heritage and independence is held the Saturday before the Fourth of July. Street festivities include a parade, free games for children, food, and crafts. An evening performance features local bands and performing artists. Main St., Troy, NC 27371. Free. (910) 572-3661; adminasst@troy.nc.us

Wadesboro/Anson County

Anson County Arts Council

This gallery and shop features local artists' work, including woodcarvings, ceramics, and paintings. 110 S. Rutherford St., Wadesboro, NC 28170. (704) 694-4950; www.ansoncountyartscouncil.org

Anson County Tourism and Anson County Chamber of Commerce

This is a good source of visitor and tourist information. 107 E. Wade St., Wadesboro, NC 28170. (704) 694-4181; www.discoveranson.com

Ashe-Covington Medical Museum

Built in 1890, this historic house owned by Dr. Edmund Ashe and Dr. Jimmy Covington is now a museum showcasing artifacts of medical life and the history of Anson County. 206 E. Wade St., Wadesboro, NC 28170. Mon.–Fri., 9:30 A.M.–1 P.M. Call for group tours. Free. (704) 694-6694; www.ansonhistoric.org

Anson County Arts Council
Anson County Tourism

Boggan-Hammond House and Alexander Little Wing

The original house was built in 1783 by Captain Patrick Boggan, who donated the land for the town of Wadesboro. This colorful Irishman and 98 Regulators signed the Protest Paper of April 2, 1768. In 1839, Alexander Little made an addition to the original structure. Both houses feature period furnishings and artifacts, including items from the original structures. 206 E. Wade St., Wadesboro, NC 28170. Tues.–Fri., 9 A.M.–1 P.M.; call for an appointment. Free. (910) 694-6694; www.ansonhistoric.org

Anson Visitors Center *Anson County Tourism*

The Caudle House

This Spanish Colonial Revival house (circa 1926) sits atop a secluded wooded hill. The three guest rooms have private baths and cable TV. A full breakfast and light afternoon refreshments are included. Full kitchen and dining-room facilities are available on request. 614 Winoka Circle, Wadesboro, NC 28170. (704) 694-3990 or (704) 694-3542

Boggan-Hammond House *Anson County Tourism*

Fancy Crafts/Granny Hollow Pottery

This charming and unique gift and collectibles shop features North Carolina handicrafts, pottery, artwork, picture framing, candles, jewelry, handbags, flags and banners, birdhouses, goat-milk bath products, North Carolina wines, lamps, and much more. Among the pottery items created on-site are unique sculptures (a collaboration by Danny Beachum and Mike Jackson) and other beautiful hand-thrown pieces that are both functional and decorative. 217 S. Greene St., Wadesboro, NC 28170. Mon.–Fri., 9:30 A.M.–5:30 P.M.; Sat., 9:30 A.M.–4 P.M. (704) 694-2625; www.fancycrafts.net or www.grannyhollowpottery.net

The Caudle House *Anson County Tourism*

Forever Inn B&B

This beautiful 1910 Queen Anne B&B has many original architectural features, such as high ceilings, wood floors, leaded-glass windows, fireplace mantels, a wraparound porch, French doors, and more. The three spacious guest rooms have cable TV. Wireless Internet access is available. A full breakfast is served in the large mahogany dining room. 214 S. Greene St., Wadesboro, NC 28170. (704) 695-1304; www.theforeverinn.com

Ashe-Covington Medical Museum *Anson County Tourism* (p. 303)

GA's Beads and Designs

GA's offers antiques, collectibles, James Price pottery pieces, and beads galore, including ready-to-sell bead necklaces, earrings, and bracelets. You can also design your own, or learn how to make your own jewelry. The shop's jewelry includes abalone, turquoise, crystals, and sterling wire-wrapped pendants. 115 S. Greene St., Wadesboro, NC 28170. Mon.–Fri., 11 A.M.–6 P.M.; Sat., 9 A.M.–1 P.M. (704) 694-6550

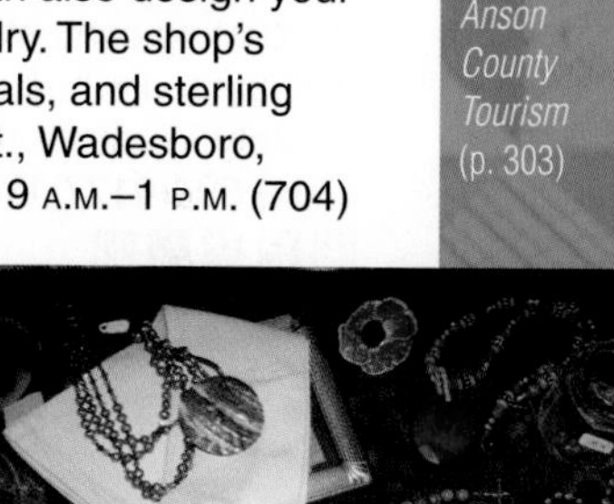

GA's Beads and Designs *Anson County Tourism*

H. W. Little and Co.

Anson County's oldest retail business (circa 1895) still offers hardware essentials, including paint, lumber, plywood, plumbing supplies, fertilizer, and assorted tools and equipment. Fishing rods and reels, hooks, sinkers, line, and bobbers are also available. 109 S. Greene St., Wadesboro, NC 28170. Mon.–Fri., 7:30 A.M.–5 P.M.; Sat., 8 A.M.–noon. (704) 694-2214

Lacy's

This shop sells collectibles, including a wide range of Tom Clark Gnomes and gifts. It is located in historic downtown Wadesboro's shopping district. 121 S. Greene St., Wadesboro, NC 28170. Mon.–Fri., 9:30 A.M.–5:30 P.M.; Sat., 9:30 A.M.–1 P.M. (704) 694-4646; gibson58@alltel.net

Lord George Anson Antiques

This shop sells antiques and collectibles, glassware, books, postcards, cabinets, and odds 'n' ends. 305 Camden Rd., Wadesboro, NC 28170. Mon.–Sat., 9 A.M.–5 P.M. (910) 572-3784 or (910) 694-5886

H. W. Little and Co. *Anson County Tourism*

Lacy's
Anson County Tourism
(p. 305)

People Fest

This celebration of family and friends brings together 10,000 to 15,000 visitors each year. Special events and activities are scheduled throughout the day, including a 5K run and family walk, a three-on-three basketball tournament, a classic car show, and an evening talent show. Also featured are local bands and entertainers on the main stage. Children's activities include the popular tractor pull, sidewalk art, and pumpkin-decorating contests. Cultural events include two historic walking tours hosted by the Anson County Historical Society. Wadesboro, NC 28170. Held one day in Oct. Free. (704) 694-0177; info@peoplefest.org

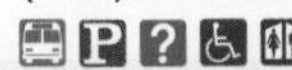

Lord George Anson Antiques
Anson County Tourism
(p. 305)

Rayfield Meat Center

This family-owned business sells handmade sausages with no preservatives. The meat comes from locally grown hogs and cattle. It also offers an in-house grill. 4450 Hwy 109 S., Wadesboro, NC 28170. Mon. and Sat., 6:30 A.M.–4 P.M.; Tues.–Fri., 6:30 A.M.–6 P.M. (704) 694-4384; www.sandhillsagriculture.com

Sooweet Treats

Sooweet Treats has a 1950s soda-shop ambiance, complete with checkerboard floor tiles. Snacks include cake squares, cupcakes, peanut butter balls, coconut balls, lemon squares, and cake by the slice. The selection varies day to day. Coffee and soft drinks are available. The shop also carries Ethan's Place antiques. 119 S. Greene St., Wadesboro, NC 28170. Tues.–Fri., 9 A.M.–5 P.M.; Sat., 9 A.M.–noon. (704) 994-9416; sooweettreats@alltel.net

Sullivan Place B&B

Originally part of the 1900s homestead and ginning village of Jesse William and Martha Flake Sullivan, Sullivan Place B&B is currently owned and operated by the Sullivans' granddaughter, Nancy Cornwell, and her husband, Milton.

The guest rooms blend harmoniously into the overall scheme, which features an eclectic blend of family antiques, original art, and a vaulted garden room with a panoramic view of the grounds and gardens. A full breakfast is served. 403 Park Rd., Wadesboro, NC 28170. (704) 694-2511

The Forever Inn B&B *Anson County Tourism* (p. 304)

Tom Little Museum

This small building houses artifacts representing historic Anson County. The Tom Little collection includes early farm implements, folk toys, trucks, and tractors. Visitors also enjoy the Fulton C. Allen Arrowhead Collection. 116 E. Wade St., Wadesboro, NC 28170. Tues.–Fri., 9 A.M.–1 P.M.; call for an appointment. Free. (704) 694-6694; www.ansonhistoric.org

Wade Street Originals

This mini-mall offers a wide variety of handmade crafts, original flower arrangements, figurines, collectibles, antiques, and seasonal items. 108 W. Wade St., Wadesboro, NC 28170. Wed.–Sat., 10 A.M.–6 P.M. (704) 694-2191 or (800) 440-2191; www.wsogifts.com

Wagram/Scotland County

Tom Little Museum *Anson County Tourism*

Cypress Bend Vineyard

This is the county's first muscadine vineyard and winery operation. Enjoy an afternoon or evening here and experience the tasting room, which features a full selection of the vineyard's wines. Stop by the gift shop as well. 21904 Riverton Rd., Wagram, NC 28396. Wed.–Sun., noon–6 P.M. (910) 369-0411; www.cypressbendvineyards.com

Newton Farms

Newton Farms grows and sells bulbs and cut flowers. Locally grown berries are also available in season. 25200 N. Turnpike Rd., Wagram, NC 28396. Open seasonally; call ahead. (910) 276-8570

Wade Street Originals *Anson County Tourism* (p. 307)

Odd Designs Pottery and Raku Jewelry

Odd Designs is owned and operated by artist Olivia Dowdy Brown, who works with mixed media including pottery, metal, paint, and fiber to create one-of-a-kind artworks and designs. Her work can be found in local galleries as well as regional shows. Annual shows include "Christmas in July" and various kiln openings. 26642 McNeill Lake Rd., Wagram, NC 28396. March–Oct., Tues.–Thurs., 9 A.M.–2 P.M., and by appointment. (910) 277-2620

West End/Moore County

Lighterwood Farm

This restored 1870 turpentine and tobacco farm features hiking trails and local and natural-history educational programs for the general public, schools, and civic groups. 535 Speight Rd., West End, NC 27376. Open by appointment. (910) 673-2828; www.sandhillsagriculture.com

Raft Swamp Farms (p. 295)

Burning Rubber and Riding the Rails

Cabarrus, Davidson, Davie, Iredell, Mecklenburg, Rowan, Stanly, and Union Counties

The economy and cultural traditions of counties along the lower I-85 corridor are often linked to engines, motors, and speed! During the heyday of the steam locomotive, the town of Spencer was home to one of Southern Railway's important service facilities. The Spencer Shops outfitted and repaired big steam engines that hauled Southern's passenger and freight trains. Today, the Spencer Shops are the site of the North Carolina Transportation Museum, where visitors can see a train depot, antique automobiles, and a fully restored roundhouse that includes 25 vintage steam engines.

A newer transportation tradition has made the region the heart of the largest spectator sport in America. Stock-car racing traces its roots to the era of Prohibition, when country boys used souped-up cars to deliver moonshine whiskey. Competition to prove who had the fastest car led to weekend races at tracks laid out in cow pastures and cornfields. In recent decades, the sport has expanded to venues like the Charlotte Motor Speedway, with fans embracing drivers like the late Dale Earnhardt of Cabarrus County. To understand this devotion, visitors can immerse themselves in stock-car culture by visiting sites along the Dale Trail in Kannapolis.

If you want a change of pace from traveling the interstates running through the region, consider taking side roads to experience rural and small-town life. Farms offer fun in the form of corn mazes and pumpkin patches, and vineyards and farmers' markets await the adventurous visitor. Those excited by steam engines and vintage stock cars can take in an antique tractor show and view the machines used to cultivate Piedmont fields in past generations.

Other arts and cultural opportunities abound on this trail. You'll find the first gold rush in America documented at Reed Gold Mine State Historic Site. Or you can sample nationally renowned Lexington barbecue or, better yet, attend the annual Barbecue Festival, which attracts visitors from around the Southeast. And Salisbury in Rowan County offers an African-American heritage trail and several Civil War sites.

Music lovers can hear bluegrass and country music performed in the intimate setting of Oakboro Music Hall. Also on the trail is Cannon Village, one of the largest and most intact mill villages in the world. The village now houses furniture showrooms, as well as the Fieldcrest Cannon Textile Museum.

Read on for a town-by-town description of attractions along the "Burning Rubber and Riding the Rails" trail.

Advance/Davie County

Hall's Berry Farm

At this family-owned organic blueberry farm, visitors can pick their own blueberries or purchase fruits already picked. Group tours are available. 130 Annie Ln., Advance, NC 27006. Open seasonally. Free. (336) 998-7246 or (336) 972-0909;hallsberryfarm@mail.com

Pick your own organic blueberries at Hall's Berry Farm.

Jones Nursery

This small, family-owned retail nursery offers 300 different varieties of hostas and many different shade perennials for gardeners. The 13 garden areas are designed around a collection of more than 700 varieties of hostas and shade plants, including registered hostas. 889 Underpass Rd., Advance, NC 27006. Open seasonally. Call for group tours. Free. (336) 998-4174; Jonesnsrv@yadtel.net

Albemarle/Stanly County

Dennis Vineyards, Inc.

This family-owned winery makes muscadine and fruit wines, growing nearly 100 percent of its muscadines and buying fruits from North Carolina farms. Festivals at the winery feature live music and food vendors. 24043 Endy Rd., Albemarle, NC 28001. Mon.–Sat., 10 A.M.–6 P.M. Tasting fees. (704) 982-6090; www.dennisvineyards.com

Uwharrie Vineyards

Uwharrie Vineyards

The vineyard features 35 acres of grapes. Wines include Chardonnay, Merlot, Cabernet Sauvignon, Noble (muscadine), Magnolia (scuppernong), White Syrah, Muscat (one of the oldest known wines), and peach. Special events include the Harvest Fest in October, Spring Fling at the end of April, and the vineyard wine club's four seasonal events. 28030 Austin Rd., Albemarle, NC 28001.

Tues.–Fri., 10 A.M.–6 P.M.; Sat., 9 A.M.–6 P.M.; Sun., noon–5 P.M. The tasting fee is $5; tours are free. (704) 982-9463; www.uwharrievineyards.com

Clemmons/Davidson County

Mrs. Hanes' Handmade Moravian Cookies

Mrs. Hanes' Handmade Moravian Cookies

One of the Moravian traditions of Old Salem is the wafer-thin cookie. This seventh-generation bakery produces six different flavors. 4643 Friedberg Church Rd., Clemmons, NC 27012. Mon.–Fri., 8 A.M.–5 P.M.; Sat., 9 A.M.–2 P.M. Arrive prior to 2:30 P.M. on weekdays to see cookies being made; the cost is $2 per person. (336) 764-1402 or (888) 764-1402; www.hanescookies.com

Concord/Cabarrus County

Sam Bass Gallery

NASCAR artist and motorsports designer Sam Bass paints great moments in motorsports history. The 10,000-square-foot building showcases the artist's collection of original paintings, fine art, limited-edition prints, and rare personal racing memorabilia. 6104 Performance Dr. S.W., Concord, NC 28027. Mon.–Fri., 10 A.M.–5 P.M., and by appointment; hours are extended during NASCAR events at Lowe's Motor Speedway and the holiday season. (704) 455-6915 or (800) 556-5464; www.sambass.com

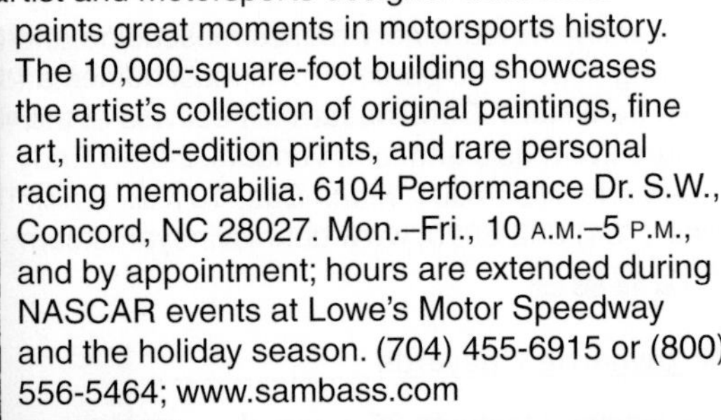

Sam Bass Gallery

Cooleemee/Davie County

Mill Village Museum

Surrounded by over 300 original mill houses, the historic Zachary-Holt House is home to a museum dedicated to the hardworking people who cleared land on the banks of the Yadkin River to build a cotton mill and homes for their families. 131 Church St., Cooleemee, NC 27014. Wed.–Sat., 10 A.M.–4 P.M. Large groups are scheduled by appointment. Free. (336) 284-6040; www.textileheritage.org

Denton/Davidson County

Denton Farm Park

The restored buildings include a general store, a church, a radio museum, a gristmill, a log cabin and barn, the Richmond Reid plantation house, a tramping barn, a blacksmith shop, a smokehouse, and a corncrib. The park is open to the public for the Doyle Lawson & Quicksilver Bluegrass Music Festival in May, the Southeast Old Threshers' Reunion in July, and Horse & Mule Days in October. Camping for RV clubs is available. 1072 Cranford Rd., Denton, NC 27239. Office, Mon.–Fri., 9 A.M.–5 P.M. Visit the Web site for schedule and fee information. (336) 859-2755 or (800) 458-2755; www.threshers.com

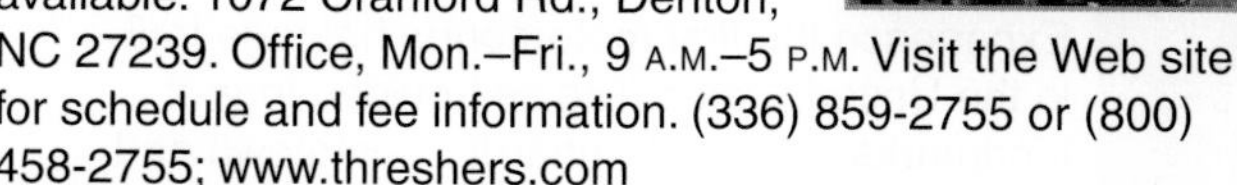

Southeast Old Threshers' Reunion at Denton Farm Park

Southern Spirit Gallery

The owners travel North Carolina for the best in hand-blown and stained glass, woodcarvings, wood turning, pottery, baskets, jewelry, woven goods, quilts, wall art, and more. 56 W. Salisbury St., Denton, NC 27239. Mon.–Fri., 10 A.M.–6 P.M.; Sat., 9:30 A.M.–4:30 P.M. (336) 859-9797; www.southernspiritgallery.com

Huntersville/Mecklenburg County

Carolina Raptor Center

Part of Latta Plantation Nature Preserve, the center is one of the country's premier rehabilitation and environmental education organizations for wounded birds of prey. 6000 Sample Rd., Huntersville, NC 28078. Mon.–Sat., 10 A.M.–5 P.M.; Sun., noon–5 P.M.; closed New Year's, Easter, Thanksgiving, and Christmas. The cost is \$6 for adults, \$5 for

American Kestrel *Carolina Raptor Center*

Sewing lesson at Historic Latta Plantation

seniors, and $4 for students; children under five are free. (704) 875-6521; www.carolinaraptorcenter.org

Historic Latta Plantation

This early-19th-century historic cotton plantation and living-history farm features a visitor center, the main plantation house, outbuildings, cotton crops, gardens, and period livestock. 5225 Sample Rd., Huntersville, NC 28078. Memorial Day–Labor Day, Mon.–Sat., 10 A.M.–5 P.M.; Sun., 1–5 P.M.; closed Mon. during the rest of the year. The cost is $6 for adults and $5 for seniors and students; children under five are free. (704) 875-2312; www.lattaplantation.org

Kannapolis/Cabarrus County

The Dale Trail

The Dale Trail

Experience the first motorsports heritage trail in the United States. The self-guided tour of landmarks in Dale Earnhardt's hometown and neighboring communities includes an exhibit of photos at the Cabarrus Visitor Center. Free copies of the collectible Dale Trail map and brochure are available. Exit 60 off I-85 along Dale Earnhardt Boulevard and beyond, Kannapolis, NC 28083. Most sites are open Mon.–Fri. during regular business hours; check the Web site for the various sites. Free. (704) 782-4340 or (800) 848-3740; www.daletrail.com

Lexington/Davidson County

The Barbecue Center

The Barbecue Festival

In business since 1956, this restaurant is known for its Lexington-style barbecue and its colossal banana splits. Residents often challenge unsuspecting guests to eat a whole banana split. The Barbecue Center has been featured on ABC's *Good Morning America* and Bobby Flay's show on the Food Network. 900 N. Main St.,

Lexington, NC 27292. Mon.–Wed., 6–9 P.M.; Thurs.–Sat., 6–10 P.M. (336) 248-4633; www.barbecuecenter.com

The Barbecue Festival

In addition to barbecue, this annual festival features local, regional, and national entertainers on five different stages, along with more than 300 artisans and craftsmen, special attractions, rides, and games. Uptown Lexington, NC 27293. Held on one of the last two Saturdays in Oct. (336) 956-1880; www.barbecuefestival.com

Bob Timberlake Furniture *The Bob Timberlake Gallery*

The Bob Timberlake Gallery

The gallery showcases famed North Carolina artist Bob Timberlake's popular line of furniture, home furnishings, gifts, and collectibles, as well as his original artwork. 1714 E. Center St. Ext., Lexington, NC 27292. Mon.–Sat., 10 A.M.–5 P.M. (336) 249-4428 or (800) 244-0095; www.bobtimberlake.com

Boone's Cave Park

This 110-acre park was designated a North Carolina Natural Heritage Area in 1987. The cave for which the park is named is an 80-foot-long crevice at the base of the Yadkin River. Boone's Cave Rd., Lexington, NC 27293. Open daily, sunrise–sunset. Free. (336) 242-4285; trip@visitdavidsoncounty.com

Barred Owl *Carolina Raptor Center*

The Candy Factory

This tempting store sells hundreds of candies, including locally produced pure sugar stick candy and puffs from the Piedmont Candy Company, a family-owned business. In addition to its confections, the store features antiques and toys. 15 N. Main St., Lexington, NC 27292. Mon.–Thurs., 10 A.M.–5:30 P.M.; Fri., 10 A.M.–7:30 P.M.; Sat., 10 A.M.–4 P.M. (336) 249-6770; www.sweettoothgifts.com

Childress Vineyards

Childress Vineyards

NASCAR team owner Richard Childress's signature winery is located in the Yadkin Valley. The Bistro, which features Italian cuisine infused with Southern flavor, is open for lunch. 1000 Childress Vineyards Rd., Lexington, NC 27293. Spring–fall, Mon.–Sat., 10 A.M.–6 P.M.; Sun., noon–6 P.M.; winter, Mon.–Thurs., 10 A.M.–5 P.M.; Fri.–Sat., 10 A.M.–6 P.M., Sun., noon–5 P.M. Tasting fees. (336) 236-9463; www.childressvineyards.com

Cook's BBQ

Cook's is known for old-style barbecue, smoked over an open pit of hickory embers. A fish fry is featured Friday and Saturday nights and all day Sunday. 366 Valiant Dr., Lexington, NC 27292. Wed.–Thurs., 11 A.M.–2 P.M. and 4:30–8 P.M.; Fri., 11 A.M.–2 P.M. and 4–8:30 P.M.; Sat., 11 A.M.–8:30 P.M.; Sun., 11 A.M.–8 P.M. (336) 798-1928; apayne1@triad.rr.com

David Fritts Outdoors

This major fishing tournament winner's gallery includes the "Walk through a Lifetime of Fishing." David Fritts Outdoors is also a boat dealer that offers service on many makes of outboards. 4343 Old US Hwy 52, Lexington, NC 27295. Mon.–Fri., 8:30 A.M.–5:30 P.M.; Sat., 8:30 A.M.–1 P.M. (336) 731-2232 or (877) 700-1976; www.davidfrittsoutdoors.com

2007 Z-20 Ranger at David Fritts Outdoors

Davidson County Historical Museum

Located in the historic Old Davidson County Courthouse on the square in Lexington, this museum features permanent exhibits about the building and the county's manufacturing history. Changing exhibits are presented in the restored 19th-century courtroom. 2 S. Main St., Lexington, NC 27292. Tues.–Fri., 10 A.M.–4 P.M.; also open the first Sun. of each month. Free. (336) 242-2035; www.co.davidson.nc.us/museum

Edward C. Smith Civic Center of Lexington

Formerly the Carolina Theatre, this facility meets the social, entertainment, arts, business, and educational needs of Lexington citizens. It features a large collection of black-and-white photos depicting life in Lexington between 1890 and 1950. 217 S. Main St., Lexington, NC 27292. Office, Mon.–Fri., 9:30 A.M.–5 P.M. Ticket prices vary. (336) 249-7875; mcburkhart@lexcominc.net

Full Moon Pottery

This studio features traditional hand-thrown, wheel-turned pottery. Products include utilitarian Seagrove-style dinnerware and face jugs made with rainbow and salt glazes. 510 Swicegood-Waitman Rd., Lexington, NC 27295. Mon.–Sat., 9 A.M.–3:30 P.M. (336) 956-2691; fullmoonpottery@yahoo.com

Potter Frank Ray creates a vase at Full Moon Pottery. *Willie Edwards*

Historic Uptown Lexington Walking Tour

The tour takes a little more than an hour and features one of the most beautiful old courthouses in America. Brochures are available at the chamber of commerce and in the Davidson County Historical Museum, located inside the old courthouse. 220 N. Main St., Lexington, NC 27293. Most shops are open Mon.–Sat. Free. (336) 249-0383; www.uptownlexington.com

Lexington Drug

Visit one of the few remaining true soda fountains in North Carolina and the only one in Davidson County. You can enjoy orangeade or lemonade, delicious locally made pimento cheese, homegrown tomato sandwiches, and real milk shakes and sundaes. 405 E. Center St., Lexington, NC 27293. Mon.–Fri., 8:30 A.M.–6 P.M.; Sat., 8:30 A.M.–4 P.M. (336) 248-5623

Lexington Multi-Cultural Festival City of *Lexington Recreation Department*

Lexington Multi-Cultural Festival

This annual daylong festival features five international villages devoted to dance, music, entertainment, displays, food, and children's activities. Finch Park, Paul Beck Rd., Lexington, NC 27292. Held the first Sat. in May, 10 A.M.–6 P.M. Free. (336) 248-3960 or (336) 248-3964; www.lexingtonnc.net/recreation/index.asp

Savor the flavor of Lexington-style BBQ at The Barbecue Center *Willie Edwards* (p. 314-15)

Taste of Lexington

This festival at the end of April offers the chance for visitors to discover Lexington—along with art, music, dance, and food. Edward C. Smith Civic Center, 217 S. Main St., Lexington, NC 27293. Ticket prices vary. (336) 225-5811 or (336) 249-7265; www.taste-of-lexington.com

Uptown Lexington Annual Christmas Open House

Lexington's holiday season starts the Sunday afternoon before Thanksgiving. Horse-drawn carriage rides from the square, live Christmas music performed on three stages, and a "North Pole Express" train for children are all part of the fun. 220 N. Main St., Lexington, NC 27293. Sun., 1–5 P.M. Free. (336) 249-0383; www.uptownlexington.com

Marshville/Union County

Ceramic horse at MAD Ceramics (p. 320)

Aw Shucks! Corn Maze and Pumpkin Patch

A trail through the woods connects two corn mazes. Visitors can use a map to search for trivia inside the mazes, or they can take a look from a 12-foot tower. Friday and Saturday nights in mid-October feature "the Field of Screams." 710 Forest Hills School Rd. S., Marshville, NC 28103. Sat., 11 A.M.–10 P.M.; Sun., 2–6 P.M.; weekdays are available upon request. The mazes operate Sept.–Nov.; other months are available for parties and gatherings. Call or visit the Web site for rates. (704) 517-5622; www.AwShucksCornMaze.com

Rusty Pistons Antique Tractor Show

The three-day show features old and new tractors, hayrides, bluegrass, homemade ice cream, a 2,000-gallon freshwater aquarium stocked with North Carolina fish, hit-and-miss engines, corn shellers, sky divers, helicopter rides, and experimental aircraft flybys. 7035 Olive Branch Rd., Marshville, NC 28103. Held the last weekend in Apr. before Mother's Day. Fri.–Sat., 8 A.M.–6 P.M.; Sun., 8 A.M.–4 P.M. Call for rates. (704) 624-6105

Panning for gold at Reed Gold Mine *N.C. Division of State Historic Sites*

Midland/Cabarrus County

Reed Gold Mine State Historic Site

In 1799, 12-year-old Conrad Reed brought a 17-pound shiny rock home. It was used as a doorstop for three years before it was determined to be gold. Soon, gold mining spread throughout the Piedmont and foothills and became an important contributor to the region's economy. North Carolina led the nation in gold production until 1848. 9621 Reed Mine Rd., Midland, NC 28107. Apr.–Oct., Tues.–Sat., 9 A.M.–5 P.M.; Nov.–March, Tues.–Sat., 10 A.M.–4 P.M.; closed on holidays; the panning area is closed Nov.–March. Admission and tours are free; the fee for gold panning is $2 (Apr.–Oct.). (704) 721-4653; www.reedmine.com or www.nchistoricsites.org/reed/reed

Mocksville/Davie County

Davie County Arts Council

This beautifully renovated building in historic downtown Mocksville includes the Brock Performing Arts Center. Visitors enjoy a variety of programs, among them a performing-arts season, visual-arts workshops, and exhibitions. 622 N. Main St., Mocksville, NC 27028. Mon.–Fri., 9 A.M.–5 P.M.; box office, noon–5 P.M. Rates vary. (336) 751-3000; www.daviearts.org

Horse bowl at MAD Ceramics (p. 320)

Davie County Chamber of Commerce

135 S. Salisbury St., Mocksville, NC 27028. Mon.–Fri., 9 A.M.–5 P.M. (336) 751-3304; www.daviecounty.com

MAD Ceramics

One of the largest studios in the state, this ceramic store serves wholesale and retail markets. Bisque is available for purchase and can be shipped. The shop manufactures its own "JR's Blue Ribbon Casting Slip," with delivery available. 118 Sayto St., Mocksville, NC 27028. Mon. and Fri., 10 A.M.–1 P.M. and 6–9 P.M.; Tues., 10 A.M.–1 P.M.; Wed., 6–9 P.M. Call or visit the Web site for rates. (336) 751-7655; www.Horseramics.com

RayLen Vineyards & Winery

Visit the tasting room to select from among the award-winning European varietal wines. RayLen's five to six festivals each year include music and wine tastings. 3577 Hwy 158, Mocksville, NC 27028. Mon.–Sat., 11 A.M.–6 P.M. Tasting fees. (336) 998-3100; www.raylenvineyards.com

Red Pig Bar-B-Q

Enjoy a 50-year legacy of pit-cooked barbecue and hot hush puppies at this down-home country café. You can order a vegetable plate that includes everything from home-style green beans to fried squash or okra. Sunday dinner includes barbecued chicken halves, meat loaf, country-style steak, and more. 7136 NC Hwy 801 S., Mocksville, NC 27028. Open daily, 6 A.M.–9 P.M. (336) 284-4650; destkay@yahoo.com

Monroe/Union County

Southern Piedmont Artists Guild Exhibition

The guild features an ongoing exhibition at Southern Piedmont Community College. The shows change about every two months. The exhibit area is open during school hours. Southern Piedmont Community College, Building A, 4209 Old Charlotte Hwy, Monroe, NC 28112. Mon.–Fri.,

RayLen Vineyards & Winery

8 A.M.–10 P.M. Free. (704) 225-8743; www.spartguild.com

Windcrest Farm & Greenhouse

Mushrooms at Windcrest Farm & Greenhouse

This family farm features a variety of organic herbs, vegetables, and fruits. Heirloom tomatoes, peppers, and salad greens are a specialty. 518 Greenfield Dr., Monroe, NC 28112. Open seasonally. (704) 764-7746; www.windcrestorganics.com

Mooresville/Iredell County

"Cotton" Ketchie's Landmark Galleries

This gallery in downtown Mooresville features the original watercolors and limited-edition prints of nationally recognized artist Cotton Ketchie. 212 N. Main St., Mooresville, NC 28115. Mon.–Sat., 9 A.M.–5 P.M. (704) 664-4122 or (800) 842-8604; www.landmark-galleries.com

David Miller, Leather Artist

Watch as artist David Miller intricately hand-tools leather goods such as belts, phone cases, billfolds, and mouse pads. 171 Market Rd., Mooresville, NC 28115. (704) 663-3472; whitmillers@aol.com

Lazy 5 Ranch

Gagliardo's Grill

Billed as "Where the Food Meets the Flame," the restaurant cooks over hickory and oak wood. The works of local artists hang on the walls, and there's often live music. 427 E. Statesville Ave., Suite 100, Mooresville, NC 28115. Mon.–Thurs., 11 A.M.–9 P.M.; Fri., 11 A.M.–10 P.M.; Sat., 5–10 P.M. (704) 662-0344; www.gagliardosgrill.com

Lazy 5 Ranch

This unique ranch features more than 750 animals from around the world. Visitors can observe animals—including giraffes, rhinos, buffalo, deer, antelopes, and ostriches—from six continents. 15100 Hwy 150, Mooresville, NC 28115. Mon.–Sat., 9 A.M.–one hour before sunset; Sun., 1 P.M.–one hour before sunset. The cost is $8.50 for adults and $5.50 for seniors and children two–11; children under two are free. (704) 663-5100; www.lazy5ranch.com

Blacksmith at President James K. Polk State Historic Site (p. 324)

Memory Lane Auto Museum

This museum features more than 150 unique racing and historical vehicles, including horseless carriages, classic cars, movie cars, racecars, motorcycles, tractors, and antique toys. 769 River Hwy, Mooresville, NC 28117. March–Nov., Mon.–Sat., 10 A.M.–5 P.M.; Dec.–Feb., Fri.–Sat., 10 A.M.–5 P.M. The cost is $8 for adults and $6 for children six–12; children under six are free. (704) 662-3673 or (877) 270-3509; www.memorylaneautomuseum.com

Mount Pleasant/Cabarrus County

Four Acres Farm

The farm helps children and their parents understand where food really comes from. Visitors can observe different types of animals and learn their names, their breeds, and other interesting facts. 3150 Mount Pleasant Rd., Mount Pleasant, NC 28124. Open by appointment. Call for rates. (704) 788-4396; fouracresfarm@hotmail.com

Oakboro/Stanly County

Big Lick Bluegrass Festival

Some of the hottest and most entertaining bluegrass groups thrill thousands at the annual Big Lick Bluegrass Festival. The event typically takes place the second weekend of June. 12743 NC Hwy 205, Oakboro, NC 28129. Noon–midnight. Admission fee. (704) 985-6987; www.hinsonauction.com

The Fountain Grill

Constructed in the 1920s, the grill has been home to various businesses. Framed photographs depicting Oakboro history are displayed, as are paintings by a local artist. 213 N. Main St., Oakboro, NC 28129. Mon. and Wed.–Thurs., 11 A.M.–2 P.M. and 4:30–9 P.M.; Fri., 11 A.M.–2 P.M. and 4:30–10 P.M.; Sat., 4–10 P.M.; Sun., 11 A.M.–3 P.M. (704) 485-3649; www.oakboromusichall.com/grill.htm

James K. Polk home (p. 324)

Oakboro Music Hall

The hall, located in a 1920s building, has gained a reputation as a showcase for bluegrass music. 215 N. Main St., Oakboro, NC 28129. Fees vary. (704) 485-3649; www.oakboromusichall.com

Oakboro Regional Museum of History

This museum features permanent exhibits exploring the town's origins, its people, and its institutions. Some artifacts on display date back 10,000 years. 231 N. Main St., Oakboro, NC 28129. Sun.–Mon., 2–4 P.M.; Thurs., 10 A.M.–noon. Free. (704) 485-3612; www.oakboro.com/museum2.htm

Ron Taylor Fine Arts

Here, you'll find original paintings and prints by North Carolina realist artist Ron Taylor, as well as pottery, photography, baskets, woodcarvings, and decoys by local and regional artists. This is also the home of the Bechtler Art Gallery, with works from the Bechtler family collection of modern contemporary art. 113 N. Main St., Oakboro, NC 28129. Tues.–Fri., 10 A.M.–5 P.M.; Sat., 9 A.M.–1 P.M. (704) 485-8080; www.rontaylorfinearts.com

Spinning at President James K. Polk State Historic Site (p. 324)

Pineville/Mecklenburg County

President James K. Polk State Historic Site

Located on land owned by the parents of Polk, the 11th United States president, the state historic site commemorates events in the Polk administration, including the Mexican-American War and the annexation of California. 12031 Lancaster Hwy, Pineville, NC 28134. Apr.–Oct., Tues.–Sat., 9 A.M.–5 P.M.; Nov.–March, Tues.–Sat., 10 A.M.–4 P.M. Free. (704) 889-7145; www.polk.nchistoricsites.org

Salisbury/Rowan County

Abstract stainless steel sculpture by Michael Baker Studios

African American Heritage Trail

This self-guided tour chronicles the historic moments and everyday lives of generations of African-Americans who contributed to the industrial, artistic, cultural, and spiritual life of Salisbury. 204 E. Innes St., Suite 120, Salisbury, NC 28144. Mon.–Fri., 9 A.M.–5 P.M.; Sat., 10 A.M.–4 P.M.; Sun., 1–4 P.M. Free. (704) 638-3100 or (800) 332-2343; www.visitsalisburync.com

Brent Smith Pottery

A former partner in the Green Goat Gallery in Spencer, Brent Smith now works and sells his excellent pottery from his home. 4885 Stokes Ferry Rd., Salisbury, NC 28146. (704) 633-1989; brents100@aol.com

Carolina Lily at the Farm

You can see century-old boxwoods and magnolias at this antique country farm place. Special events include the Queen for a Day Tea Party, Spring Art at the Farm, the Last Call for Fall Antique and Craft Show, and a Christmas open house. 1375 Kern Carlton Rd., Salisbury, NC 28146. Wed.–Sat., 10 A.M.–5 P.M.; closed in Jan. Free. (704) 639-0033; www.carolinalily.com

Dr. Josephus W. Hall House

This antebellum house is listed on the National Register of Historic Places. Docents dressed in period costumes host a journey through time, describing the history of Salisbury and the Hall family since 1859. 226 S. Jackson St., Salisbury, NC 28145. Sat.–Sun., 1–4 P.M. Admission fee. (704) 636-0103; www.historicsalisbury.org

Michael Baker Studios

This working artist's studio features the contemporary stainless-steel sculpture of Michael Baker. His sculpture ranges from tabletop and pedestal sizes to large, outdoor garden pieces and wall sculpture. 122 E. Innes St., Salisbury, NC 28144. Open by appointment. (704) 798-0047; www.michaelbaker.com

October Tour of Historic Houses

This annual two-day tour focuses on the architectural and historical features of structures in Salisbury. 215 Depot St., Salisbury, NC 28145. Usually held the second weekend in Oct.; call to confirm dates and times. Admission fee. (704) 636-0103; www.historicsalisbury.org

Rowan County Convention & Visitors Bureau

204 E. Innes St., Suite 120, Salisbury, NC 28144. Mon.–Fri., 9 A.M.–5 P.M.; Sat., 10 A.M.–4 P.M.; Sun., 1–4 P.M. Fees are charged for trolley tours. (704) 638-3100 or (800) 332-2343; www.visitsalisburync.com

Gaze at interesting works of art at Waterworks Visual Arts Center.

Salisbury Symphony Orchestra

The concert season runs from October through April. Catawba College, 2300 W. Innes St., Salisbury, NC 28145. Ticket prices vary. (704) 637-4314; www.salisburysymphony.org

Waterworks Visual Arts Center

Founded in 1959 as the Rowan Art Guild, this nonprofit group is located in Salisbury's first waterworks plant. The center provides art exhibitions, education, and outreach. 123 E. Liberty St., Salisbury, NC 28144. Tues.–Sat., 10 A.M.–5 P.M.; closed on major holidays. Free. (704) 636-1882; www.waterworks.org

Spencer/Rowan County

The Art Station

This gallery features original works and prints by local and regional artists. The works capture the beauty and charm of the South. The gallery is located in what was once Southern Railroad's company store. 514 S. Salisbury Ave., Spencer, NC 28159. Tues.–Fri., 10 A.M.–5:30 P.M.; Sat., 10 A.M.–1 P.M. (704) 633-6410 or (877) 273-2408; rgettys@vnet.net

Green Goat Gallery

Featuring fine, folk, and functional art and crafts from regional and national artists, this gallery is housed in an elegant turn-of-the-century commercial building with an original pressed-tin ceiling and exposed brick walls. In the rear of the building, classes are held at the Blue Ewe Yoga Studio. Upstairs are the art studios of portraitist Cara Reische and stained-glass artist Jon Palmer. 516 S. Salisbury Ave., Spencer, NC 28159. Tues.–Sat., 10:30 A.M.–5:30 P.M. (704) 639-0606; www.greengoatgallery.com

North Carolina Transportation Museum State Historic Site

The museum houses antique rail equipment, including steam and diesel locomotives, cabooses, and passenger and freight cars. It includes a 37-bay roundhouse and the Back Shop. Visitors will also find a plane, as well as automobiles from 1901 to the 1980s. 411 S. Salisbury Ave., Spencer, NC 28159. Apr.–Oct., Mon.–Sat., 9 A.M.–5 P.M.; Sun., 1–5 P.M.; Nov.–March, Tues.–Sat., 10 A.M.–4 P.M.; Sun., 1–4 P.M. The exhibits are free; fees are charged for train and turntable rides. (704) 636-2889 or (877) NCTM-FUN; www.nctrans.org

N.C. Transportation Museum
N.C. Historic Sites

Statesville/Iredell County

Laws Stained Glass Studios, Inc.

This unique business has provided stained-glass windows for churches and residences since 1946. Visitors will find all types of stained glass, craft supplies, and sketches of beautiful windows. 824 Turnersburg Rd., Statesville, NC 28625. Mon.–Fri., 9 A.M.–5 P.M.; Sat., 9 A.M.–noon. (704) 876-3463 or (800) 820-1292; www.lawsstainedglass.com

Locally grown tomatoes at Statesville Rotary Farmers' Market *N.C. Arts Council*

Statesville Rotary Farmers' Market

This multi-county farmers' market, run by the Rotary Club of Statesville, features fresh local produce and other homegrown products. Statesville Police Dept. parking lot, E. Sharpe St., Statesville, NC 27677. May–Oct., Mon., 4–7 P.M.; Wed. and Sat., 7 A.M.–noon. (704) 873-6457; ritadusty@roadrunner.com

Thomasville/Davidson County

Everybody's Day

Everybody's Day

North Carolina's oldest festival features 200 arts-and-crafts vendors, two food courts offering a host of culinary delights, rides and games for children, and national and regional entertainment. Downtown Thomasville, NC 27361. Held the last Sat. of Sept., 9 A.M.–5 P.M. Free. (336) 475-6134; www.everybodysday.com

Stephen Sebastian Gallery

This gallery and showroom features the paintings and etchings of nationally known artist Stephen Sebastian. The artist, who can often be found working in the upstairs studio, welcomes visitors. 8 Randolph St., Thomasville, NC 27360. Wed.–Fri., 10 A.M.–5 P.M.; Sat., 10 A.M.–3 P.M. Admission is charged for some shows. (336) 475-3363; etch77@northstate.net

Madelyn's In the Grove

Union Grove/Iredell County

Madelyn's in the Grove

This 1934 Tudor-style bed-and-breakfast is set on nine acres and features five rooms with private baths. A full three-course breakfast is served. Afternoon snacks and evening desserts are also available. 1836 W. Memorial Hwy, Union Grove, NC 28689. (704) 539-4151 or (800) 948-4473; www.madelyns.com

Waxhaw/Union County

Fox Farm

The farm offers 12 miles of trails around gorgeous pastures and barns. Horseback riding and numerous special events and clinics are on the schedule, including annual benefits held each spring. 7505 Sims Rd., Waxhaw, NC 28173. Fees vary; donations are requested to benefit events such as Farmpraise and Barnful of Quilts. (704) 243-0113; fox@alltel.net

The Museum of the Waxhaws and the Kudzu Festival

President Andrew Jackson was born in the Waxhaws in 1767. In addition to serving as the site of a Jackson memorial, the museum honors the Waxhaw Indians and the Scots-Irish. A highlight of the year is the Kudzu Festival, which showcases the vine's versatility. 8215 Waxhaw Hwy (Hwy 75 E.), Waxhaw, NC 28173. Fri.–Sat., 10 A.M.–5 P.M.;

Sun., 2–5 P.M. The Kudzu Festival is held the last Sat. of Aug., 10 A.M.–5 P.M. Admission fee. (704) 843-1832; www.visitmonroenc.org

Stewart's Village Gallery

This gallery includes the studio of potter Bill Stewart, along with the work of more than 250 American craft artists. Pottery, jewelry, iron and metal works, and wood, glass, and garden art are all on display. 116 McDonald St., Waxhaw, NC 28173. Mon.–Sat., 10 A.M.–5 P.M.; Sun., 1–5 P.M. (704) 843-5638; www.stewartsvillagegallery.com

Watercolor of Tharpes Mill by Cotton Ketchie at "Cotton" Ketchie's Landmark Galleries

Pictures from the Piedmont

Alexander, Catawba, Cleveland, Gaston, and Lincoln Counties

The blue highways of the western Piedmont often follow old roadbeds. Two of the oldest routes, Sherrill's Path and Island Ford Road, are offshoots of Pennsylvania's Great Wagon Road, which brought thousands of German and Scots-Irish settlers to this region of North Carolina. By the Civil War, their old fields were among the most productive in the state for wheat, fruit orchards, cotton, dairy products, and livestock.

Apple growers, some with a reputation for saving and popularizing heirloom varieties, still thrive today. North Carolina is one of the nation's top apple producers. Farmers in this region invite families to reinvent fun with you-pick orchard experiences. Sample a crisp apple fresh off the tree or take home homemade applesauce, apple butter, or cider.

The Piedmont's rich clay also solved a dilemma for early-19th-century residents in the Catawba River Valley who needed food storage containers and tableware. Local farmers-turned-potters found ways to finish their pots with an alkaline glaze in distinctive shades of brown and green. These days, old Catawba Valley pots are highly prized by collectors. Fortunately, artists in the region carry on the tradition and produce beautiful pottery available in their studios and through local galleries.

The area is an important hub for the state's historic textile industry as well. The Catawba River and other streams, creeks, and rivers were accessible and powerful sources of energy for 19th-century cotton mills. Industrialization in the next century spurred the construction of complexes like the Loray Mill in Gastonia, the largest mill under one roof when it was constructed in 1902. The building, along with a surrounding mill village, is now part of an architectural heritage driving tour of Gaston County.

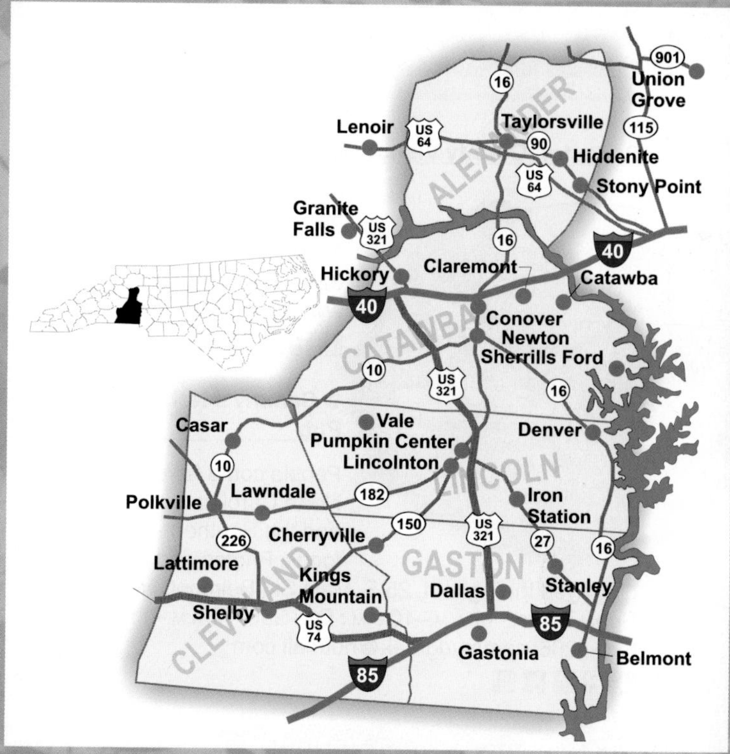

The rolling terrain and low mountain ranges of the region offer scenic and recreational experiences. Visit Crowders Mountain State Park for hiking, camping, and rock climbing. Rising 1,625 feet, Crowders provides spectacular vistas of the surrounding Piedmont plateau.

Nearby Kings Mountain, which sits astride the state line of North and South Carolina, was designated by Congress as a national military park to commemorate a victory by American patriots over American loyalists during the Revolutionary War.

One of the state's most popular gardens, the Daniel Stowe Botanical Garden, is located here on 450 acres near Lake Wylie. Nine major themed gardens with magnificent fountains and canals and plants from around the world are featured.

Festivals for all occasions, community theaters, and regional museums also celebrate the cultural fabric of the area. Read on for town-by-town descriptions of the attractions that make up the "Pictures from the Piedmont" trail.

Belmont/Gaston County

Gaston County Visitor Center

Sammy's Neighborhood Pub *Karen A. Blum*

620 N. Main St., Belmont, NC 28012. Mon.–Fri., 8:30 A.M.–5 P.M.; Sat., 10 A.M.–4 P.M. (704) 825-4044 or (800) 849-9994; www.gastontourism.com

Sammy's Neighborhood Pub

People come here for the North Carolina microbrews and the Southern-style comfort foods. Photos and artwork are displayed throughout. 25 S. Main St., Belmont, NC 28012. Sun.–Thurs., 11 A.M.–10 P.M.; Fri.–Sat., 11 A.M.–11 P.M. (704) 825-4266; sammydgreek@hotmail.com

Catawba/Catawba County

Historic Murray's Mill

Murray's Mill is listed on the National Register. Features include the intact 1913 mill; the 1890s Murray & Minges General Store; the 1880s wheat house, currently used as an exhibition gallery; and the 1913 John Murray House. 1489 Murray's Mill Rd., Catawba, NC 28609. Fri.–Sat., 9 A.M.–4 P.M.; Sun., 1:30–4:30 P.M.; closed Jan.–Feb. Free. (828) 241-4299; www.catawbahistory.org

Cherryville/Gaston County

Cherry Blossom Festival

Cherry pies, tarts, turnovers—oh, my! This fest offers two music stages, art, train rides, antique cars and trucks, and plenty of cherries. Main St., Cherryville, NC 28021. Held the last weekend in Apr. Fri., 5–10 P.M.; Sat., 10 A.M.–5 P.M. (704) 435-3451; www.cityofcherryville.com

Cherryville Historical Museum *Karen A. Blum*

Cherryville Historical Museum & Quilting Bee

The three floors at this museum include an authentic Bull Durham wall mural (one of only four existing) and a special "New Year's Shooters" exhibit. Try your hand at the Saturday quilting bee. 109 E. Main St., Cherryville, NC 28021. Sat., 10 A.M.–2 P.M., and by appointment. (704) 435-8011; www.cityofcherryville.com

Conover/Catawba County

Ira Cline Farm

Fruit lovers may pick their own strawberries and blueberries or let the farm staff do it for them. Make sure you have Grandma's pie recipes ready! 4444 Lee Cline Rd., Conover, NC 28613. Mon.–Sat., 8 A.M.–7 P.M. (828) 464-5942

Dallas/Gaston County

Maple Springs Farm

Kids' activities, strawberries, blackberries, veggies, and more are available here. Fall brings hayrides to the pumpkin patch, school tours, the Berry Land Maze, and a learning center. 906 Dallas-Stanley Hwy (Hwy 275), Dallas, NC 28034. Mon.–Sat., 9.A.M.–6:30 P.M.; Sun., 1–6 P.M.; closed in Aug. and in the winter. Call for prices. (704) 922-8688; http://maplespringsfarm.home.mindspring.com

Denver/Lincoln County

BH Black Pottery Spring and Fall Sales

Bobbie Black creates wheel-thrown and hand-built collectibles. Bobbie's face jugs honor the traditions of Catawba Valley potters, but her style includes a diversity of glazes and patterns. 8890 Graham Point Ln., Denver, NC 28037. Sales are held the last Sat. in Apr. and the first Sat. in Nov.; also open by appointment. (704) 483-3246; www.bhblackpottery.com

Pick your own blackberries at Maple Springs Farm. *Karen A. Blum*

Handmade teaset at BH Black Pottery (p. 333)

The Blue Heron B&B and Studio on Lake Norman

The only B&B in Lincoln County with access to Lake Norman, it's also home to Hartzog Pottery. Local fishing guides and a boat dock are available. 4339 Little Fork Cove Rd., Denver, NC 28037. (704) 483-4408; www.blueherononlakenorman.com

Denver Days Fall Festival

Held for four days each September, this festival features arts and crafts, amusement-park rides, and popular performers and bands. Food vendors serve up everything from Italian sausages to deep-fried Oreos, and brew aficionados can quench their thirst at the beer garden. Hwy 16, Denver, NC 28037. Held Wed.–Sun., afternoon–evening. Fees are charged for parking and rides. (704) 622-9901; www.denverdays.com

Grateful Growers Farm

Enjoy the view from the Blue Heron B&B and Studio on Lake Norman.

Grateful Growers offers catered meals using farm-fresh products. Bring a cooler so you can purchase delicious, wholesome chicken, free-range eggs, pork, shiitake mushrooms, and organic produce. 3006 Mack Ballard Rd., Denver, NC 28037. Sat., 10 A.M.–2 P.M., and by appointment. (828) 234-5182; www.ggfarm.com

Strawberry Festival

This May festival has an array of strawberry vendors, crafts, foods, a petting zoo, and games, plus the Miss Strawberry Pageant. It is sponsored by the East Lincoln High PTA. 6471 Hwy 73, Denver, NC 28037. 8 A.M.–2 P.M. (704) 736-1860; dlhsolutions@bellsouth.net

Gastonia/Gaston County

Arts at the Pavilion Fest

Bluegrass, Latin, beach, soul, rock-and-roll, Americana, and steel-drum music combine with a fine arts-and-crafts festival in this one-of-a-kind event. Rotary Centennial Pavilion, 121 E. Main St., Gastonia, NC 28052. Held on a Sat. in May, 10 A.M.–9 P.M. (704) 865-5044; www.GastoniaDowntown.org

Arts at the Pavilion Fest *Town of Gastonia*

Bluegill Pottery

This is the gallery and studio of well-known local artist Vicki Gill, who makes functional and decorative pottery. Vicki also schedules throwing and hand-building pottery classes. 4522 Wilkinson Blvd., Gastonia, NC 28056. Mon.–Fri., noon–5 P.M. Call ahead. (704) 824-9928; www.bluegillpottery.com

Gastonia's Downtown Alive!

People dance and sing and groove to the music of bands like the Embers, the Fantastic Shakers, the Spontanes, and the Chairmen of the Board. 162 S. South St., Gastonia, NC 28052. Held on summer evenings. (704) 865-5044; www.GastoniaDowntown.org

Bluegill Pottery

Katy-Did Antiques and Gifts

This store features rare antique finds and unique gifts that evoke big-city sophistication—without the big-city prices. 116 E. Main Ave., Gastonia, NC 28052. Mon.–Fri., 9 A.M.–5 P.M.; Sat., 10 A.M.–5 P.M. (704) 864-1090; katydidantiques@bellsouth.com

Hickory/Catawba County

Aquarius Stained Glass Studio

This studio features custom-made stained-glass pieces by artist John Falcone. 219 First Ave. N.W., Suite 104, Hickory,

NC 28601. Tours are available by appointment. (828) 322-4418

Artful Living

This is the area's largest resource for unique, original, and reproduction artworks by local and regional artists. 2220 Hwy 70 S.E., Suite 352, Hickory, NC 28602. Mon.–Sat., 9 A.M.–6 P.M.; Sun., 1–5 P.M. (828) 328-9500; www.ArtfulLivingGallery.com

Catawba Valley Pottery and Antiques Festival

More than 100 juried artists, including the Catawba Valley's most renowned potters, bring Southern traditional pottery to this fest every March. Antiques, furniture, and folk art are available, too. 1960 13th Ave. S.E., Hickory, NC 28603. Admission fee. (828) 324-7294; www.catawbahistory.org

Find handcrafted woodcarvings at Eddie Hamrick and the Twisted Tree Studio and Gallery. *Karen A. Blum*

Derfla

This artist's vibrant oil paintings with unusual color schemes include people, animals, landscapes, and abstracts. Works are also on display locally at the Twisted Tree Gallery. 543 Seventh St. N.W., Hickory, NC 28601. Open by appointment. (828) 781-5707; www.derfla.tv

Downtown Hickory Art Crawls

The crawls feature the works of approximately 50 artists, including musicians, poets, sculptors, and painters, at 18 galleries and studios. Wine tastings and restaurant stops round out the experience. Held in downtown Hickory on selected Thursdays in Apr., June, Sept., and Nov. (828) 322-1121; www.downtownhickory.com/1-ArtCrawl.html

Eddie Hamrick and the Twisted Tree Studio and Gallery

Eddie Hamrick is devoted to the arts of woodcarving and traditional 18th-century manufacturing. His Twisted Tree

Studio and Gallery offers visitors the opportunity to watch him work. 335 First Ave. S.E., Hickory, NC 28602. Studio, Mon.–Fri., 8 A.M.–5 P.M.; gallery, Wed.–Sat., 10 A.M.–6 P.M. (828) 244-4148; www.thetwistedtree.com

Full Circle Arts

Harper House *Karen A. Blum*

Full Circle is a not-for-profit artists' cooperative gallery near downtown in a historic home shared with Glory Bee Studios. It offers paintings, drawings, sculpture, jewelry, and fiber. Classes are available. 327 Second Ave. N.W., Hickory, NC 28603. Wed.–Sat., noon–6 P.M., and by appointment. (828) 322-7545; www.fullcirclearts.org

Ginger Creek Vineyards

Ginger Creek is a family-owned and -operated vineyard and winery set in the picturesque foothills. Handcrafted traditional Southern muscadine, scuppernong, and fruit wines are the specialties. 858 John Cline Rd., Hickory, NC 28681. Thurs.–Sat., noon–6 P.M.; Sun., by appointment. (828) 635-0327; www.ncagr.com/NCproducts/ShowSite.asp?ID=2595

Harper House/Hickory History Center

The 1887 Harper House is one of the finest examples of Queen Anne interior styling in the state. The Craftsman-style Lyerly-Hambrick House on the grounds is the home of the Betty Allen Education Center and the Margaret Huggins Exhibition Gallery. 310 N. Center St., Hickory, NC 28601. Fri.–Sat., 9 A.M.–4 P.M.; Sun., 1:30–4:30 P.M.; Tues.–Thurs., open for groups by appointment. (828) 324-7294; www.catawbahistory.org

Hickory Community Theatre

This performing-arts venue is in the 1921 historic Hickory City Hall Building. Theatrical offerings range from family fare such as Disney's *Beauty and the Beast* to avant-garde productions such as *Equus*. 30 Third St. N.W., Hickory, NC

Hickory Community Theatre *Karen A. Blum*

28601. Performances are held Sept.–May; box office, Tues.–Fri., noon–5 P.M. (828) 327-3855; www.hct.org

Hickory Farmers' Market

The market offers fresh locally grown produce, including organic potted plants and herbs, cut flowers, honey, preserves, fresh-baked goods, handmade soaps, and much more. Government Ave. and Second St. S.W., Hickory, NC 28603. Wed., 2–6 P.M.; Sat., 7 A.M.–1 P.M. (828) 308-6508; www.hickoryfarmersmarket.com

Julia Rush Fine Crafts *Karen A. Blum*

Hickory Hops

More than 30 brewers offering 100 different beers are on hand for Hickory Hops. In addition to quenching their thirst, beer lovers can enjoy the music of three live bands. Free water and soft drinks are available. Union Square, Hickory, NC 28601. Held the second Sat. in Apr., 1–7 P.M. Tickets are required. (828) 322-1121; www.hickoryhops.com

Hickory Metro Convention and Visitors Bureau

1960-A 13th Ave. S.E., Hickory, NC 28601. Mon.–Fri., 9 A.M.–5 P.M. (828) 322-1335 or (800) 509-2444; www.hickorymetro.com

Hickory Museum of Art

The collection at North Carolina's second-oldest art museum emphasizes American paintings, prints, studio art glass, American and North Carolina pottery, and Southern contemporary folk art. 243 Third Ave. N.E., Hickory, NC 28603. Tues.–Sat., 10 A.M.–4 P.M.; Sun., 1–4 P.M. Free. (828) 327-8576; www.HickoryMuseumofArt.org

Island Style Restaurant

Visit Island Style Restaurant for some great Jamaican food, plus walls decorated with work by local artists. Performances by local musicians are held monthly. 206 Union Square, Hickory, NC 28601. Mon.–Wed., 11 A.M.–

9 P.M.; Thurs.–Fri., 11 A.M.–10 P.M.; Sat., noon–10 P.M. (828) 327 9300; www.IslandStylehickory.com

Jacob Fork Gallery and Garden

Jacob Fork is a destination for discerning collectors searching for fine American handicrafts for home and garden. It boasts 2,000 square feet of gallery space and an acre of landscaped gardens. You'll find delightful clay, jewelry, and metalwork. 4912 Hwy 127 S., Hickory, NC 28602. Tues.–Sat., 9:30 A.M.–5:30 P.M.; Sun., 1–5 P.M. (704) 462-1877; www.jacobforkgallery.com

Julia Rush Fine Crafts

This stunning gallery of contemporary American crafts features jewelry, pottery, stained and blown glass, metal sculpture, wind chimes, wood works, candles, cards, incense, and more. 216 Union Square (Main Ave. N.W. and Second St. N.W.), Hickory, NC 28601. Mon.–Fri., 9:30 A.M.–6 P.M.; Sat., 10 A.M.–5:30 P.M. (828) 324-0409; www.juliarush.com

Oktoberfest

This fun three-day festival in mid-October is filled with music, food, crafts, and great activities for kids. Union Square (Main Ave. N.W.), Hickory, NC 28601. Fri., noon–11:30 P.M.; Sat., 10 A.M.–11:30 P.M.; Sun., noon–5 P.M. Admission fee. (828) 322-1121; www.hickoryoktoberfest.com

Rose Mary Cheek Photography

The artist works in digital and manipulative formats. Her specialties include fine-art portraiture, photography restoration, scenics, and landscapes. 322 Ninth Ave. N.W., Hickory, NC 28601. Open Mon.–Sat. by appointment. (828) 322-2862 or (800) 328-1598; www.rosemarycheek.com

The Sally Company

Artist Sally Fox has devoted her talents to creating functional art, such as her custom

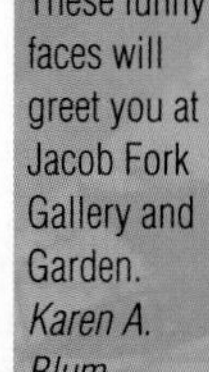

These funny faces will greet you at Jacob Fork Gallery and Garden. *Karen A. Blum*

The Sally Company *Karen A. Blum* (p. 339)

linens and her hand-painted canvas mats to welcome each season. Sally's "Homes for Small Birds" can be found in many gardens. 246 C Shoppes on the Square, Hickory, NC 28601. Tues.–Fri., 10 A.M.–5:30 P.M.; Sat., 10 A.M.–3 P.M. (828) 431-4400; williamfox@charter.net

Hiddenite/Alexander County

Hiddenite Center

The center promotes local history and culture and fosters self-expression in the arts and crafts. Classes, festivals, and theater are offered. 176 Hiddenite Church Rd., Hiddenite, NC 28636. Mon.–Fri., 9 A.M.–4:30 P.M.; open on weekends by appointment and during special events. A minimal fee is charged. (828) 632–6966; www.hiddenitecenter.com

Hiddenite Center *Karen A. Blum*

Iron Station/Lincoln County

Berry Hill Farm

If you love the sweet taste of fresh-picked, old-fashioned strawberries but don't like to get dirty, this is the place for you. 2400 Hudson Poultry Rd., Iron Station, NC 28080. Strawberries are available in May only, Mon.–Fri., 8 A.M.–6:30 P.M.; Sat., 8 A.M.–3 P.M.; Sun., 1–5 P.M.; call about other seasonal produce and off-season products. (704) 748-1488

Cedar Lake Christmas Tree Farm

In addition to Christmas trees, wreaths, roping, and swag, the farm features cute farm animals, haystacks, and hay tunnels for climbing. 5829 Hwy 27, Iron Station, NC 28080. Open from the day after Thanksgiving to Dec. 20, Mon.–Sat., 10 A.M.–8 P.M.; Sun., noon–8 P.M. (704) 201-8922; www.cedarlaketreefarm.com

Cedar Lake Christmas Tree Farm

Pick your own grapes for winemaking at Lockman Muscadine Vineyard. *Karen A. Blum*

Lockman Muscadine Vineyard

This small family vineyard grows only muscadine and scuppernong grapes. Families enjoy pick-your-own outings when the fruit is ripe. Delicious cider and homemade jellies are available all year! 4590 Orchard Rd., Iron Station, NC 28080. Hours are seasonal. Pick-your-own grapes are sold on the honor system. (704) 732-6637; www.lockmanvineyard.com

P ?

Kings Mountain/Cleveland County

Lineberger's Killdeer Farm

A variety of fruits and vegetables are available to the public at this retail farm market. The pick-your-own option is available for some vegetables and for all the farm's fruit crops except peaches. 300 Goforth Rd., Kings Mountain, NC 28086. Open daily in May; open Mon.–Sat., mid-Apr.–Apr. 30 and June–Halloween. (704) 739-6602; fruitgrower@netzero.net

P ?

Spoonin' It with Jerry

This unique shop showcases handmade hardwood spoons, some utilitarian and some artistic, crafted from Appalachian and other select hardwoods. Wood collages are also for sale. 404 Maner Rd., Kings Mountain, NC 28086. Open by appointment. (704) 734-0248; www.spooninitwithjerry.com

P

Lattimore/Cleveland County

Lattimore Farms

This field full of bright red berries is open April to June. Strawberries are sold prepicked or on a pick-your-own basis. 318 Peachtree Rd., Lattimore, NC 28089. Mon.–Sat., 8:30 A.M.–dark; Sun., 1:30–6 P.M. (704) 434-7190; alexlattimore14@hotmail.com

P ?

Berry Hill Farm *Karen A. Blum*

Lawndale/Cleveland County

Dedmond Pottery

Potters Corine Guseman and Hal Dedmond live and work in this restored tenant farmer's house built in the early 1900s. Both are featured artists at Redsky Gallery in Charlotte, Blue Moon Gallery in Cliffside, and Jacob Fork Gallery in Hickory. 537-1 Belwood Lawndale Rd., Lawndale, NC 28090. Mon., 10 A.M.–5 P.M. (704) 538-1057; www.dedmondpottery.com

Knob Creek Farms and Creamery *Karen A. Blum*

Knob Creek Farms and Creamery

Stop by for some homemade ice cream—strawberry, peach, apple, blackberry, pumpkin, and more. The farm grows strawberries, peaches, nectarines, cantaloupes, blackberries, muscadines, pumpkins, and apples. School groups are welcome. 6417 Fallston Rd., Lawndale, NC 28090. Apr.–Dec., Mon.–Fri., 8 A.M.–6 P.M. (704) 538-5573; jbcrotts@hotmail.com

Redbone Willy's Trading Company

This nostalgic general store has homemade ice cream, baked goods, candy, fudge, and other delights served on-site in the BoneHead Café. Redbone Willy's DeStarté Bed and Breakfast is next door. 6533 Fallston Rd., Lawndale, NC 28090. Mon.–Sat., 10 A.M.–6 P.M.; Sun., 1–6 P.M. (704) 538-3670 or (866) 538-3670; www.redbonewilly.com

Redbone Willy's Trading Company *Karen A. Blum*

Walker Farms and Art

This family-operated store sells homegrown and local produce, as well as art by Kenny Walker. Stop by for some vine-ripened fruits and vegetables fresh from the field, or try a cup of homemade ice cream. 3834 Polkville Rd. (Hwy 226 N.), Lawndale, NC 28090. May–Oct., Mon.–Fri., noon–6 P.M.; Sat., 8:30 A.M.–4 P.M. (704) 482-0588; kennywalker6@aol.com

Lenoir/Alexander County

Richard Wright Pottery

Richard Wright, whose pottery is located on a 150-year-old farm, uses only hand-dug clay, which he fires in an old-style groundhog kiln. All pots are hand-turned and come in various sizes, from coffee mugs to very large vessels. 1177 Emmanuel Barn Ln., Lenoir, NC 28645. Open on weekends and by appointment. Call ahead. (828) 759-0073; rwwnc@yahoo.com

Lincolnton/Lincoln County

Alive After Five

These outdoor concerts featuring regional music draw more than 2,000 people to downtown Lincolnton. 1 Court Square, Lincolnton, NC 28092. Apr.–Sept., 6–9 P.M. Free. (704) 736-8915; www.lovablelincolnton.org

Take some pottery home from Frazier Handmade Pottery and Gift Gallery. *Karen A. Blum*

Catawba River Trader Antiques

The shop specializes in Southern handmade furniture, pottery, and accessories. 110 E. Water St., Lincolnton, NC 28037. Tues. and Thurs.–Fri., 10 A.M.–4 P.M.; Wed., 10 A.M.–1 P.M.; Sat., 10 A.M.–2 P.M. (704) 735-1155

Frazier Handmade Pottery and Gift Gallery

This is the pottery studio of artist Kimbrell Frazier. The gallery is the retail outlet for Kim's unique handmade dinnerware and accessories. Stop by to see what she is creating today and to browse the gallery for that special piece. 2547 E. Main St., Lincolnton, NC 28092. Tues.–Fri., 10 A.M.–4 P.M.; Sat., 10 A.M.–2 P.M. (704) 477-8406; www.frazierpottery.com

Hog Happenin'

This annual event brings motorcycle owners and barbecue teams together in downtown Lincolnton. 1 Court Square, Lincolnton, NC 28092. Held the first weekend in June, Fri., 6–9 P.M.; Sat., 10 A.M.–6 P.M. Free. (704) 736-8915; www.hoghappenin.org

Lincoln County Apple Festival

Festival goers flock to Lincolnton for this premier festival of apples, art, and culture. With 150 booths and upwards of 40,000 visitors annually, the Apple Festival celebrates all things apple. Among the attractions are local crafters and artists, music, and activities for the kids. Downtown Lincolnton, NC 28092. Held the second Sat. in Sept., 9 A.M.–4 P.M. Free. (704) 736-8452; www.ces.ncsu.edu/copubs/community/tourism/001/

Furniture exhibit at Lincoln County Museum of History *Karen A. Blum*

Lincoln County Farmers' Market

Traditional growers and organic farmers sell their vegetables, sausage, eggs, and meats here. Local musicians and local artists make special appearances. 250 W. Water St., Lincolnton, NC 28092. Open in Apr., Sat., 7 A.M.–sellout; June–Sept., Tues. and Sat., 7 A.M.–sellout; Thurs., 4 P.M.–sellout. (704) 736-8461; www.lincolncountyfarmersmarket.com

Lincoln County Museum of History

The museum maintains a large collection of manuscripts, photographs, and original documents from 1770 to the present. 403 E. Main St., Lincolnton, NC 28092. Office, Mon.–Fri., 9 A.M.–5 P.M.; museum, Tues.–Thurs., 1–5 P.M.; Sun., 2–5 P.M. Free. (704) 748-9090; asso6377@bellsouth.net

Lincoln Theatre Guild

The guild offers live stage productions, the Footlights Drama Camp, and open-air Shakespeare performances in July. 403 E. Main St., Lincolnton, NC 28093. Office, Mon., Wed., and Fri., 9 A.M.–1 P.M. Fees are charged for performances. (704) 735-2281; www.lincolntheatreguild.org

Pleasant Retreat Academy/ Memorial Hall

Built between 1817 and 1820, the building is the oldest brick structure in Lincolnton. It is listed on the National Register of Historic Places. 129 E. Pine St., Lincolnton, NC 28092. Open by appointment. Free. (704) 735-8048

Pleasant Retreat Academy/ Memorial Hall *Karen A. Blum*

Ramsour-Reinhardt Cemetery

Christian Reinhardt and Jacob Ramsour, both associated with the Revolutionary War battle at Ramsour's Mill, are buried at the cemetery, along with other members of their families. Andrews Dr., Lincolnton, NC 28092. (704) 748-9090; asso6377@bellsouth.net

Rising Sun Pottery

Rising Sun Pottery offers pottery classes, retail gallery pottery sales, and a wholesale and retail dealership for clay, tools, and related pottery and clay equipment. 209 S. Academy St., Lincolnton, NC 28092. Tues.–Thurs., 10 A.M.–4 P.M. and 5:30–9:30 P.M.; Fri.–Sat., 10 A.M.–5 P.M. (704) 735-5820; www.RisingSunPottery.com

Take a class at Rising Sun Pottery. *Karen A. Blum*

St. Luke's Episcopal Church and Cemetery

Constructed in 1842, this is the earliest Episcopal church in town and one of the first in the county. The hand-carved altar and choir stall are ornate and decorative examples of the Gothic Revival style. 303 N. Cedar St., Lincolnton, NC 28092. Open by appointment except on Sun. (704) 732-9179; www.episcopallincolntonnc.org

Lowell/Gaston County

JS Pottery

The shop features a variety of handcrafted, functional pottery with lead-free glazes. Its wares may be used in the oven or the microwave and are dishwasher safe. Tour groups are welcome. 205 W. First St., Lowell, NC 28098.

St. Luke's Episcopal Church and Cemetery *Karen A. Blum*

Mon.–Sat., 9:30 A.M.–5:30 P.M., and by appointment. (704) 824-7767; www.jspottery.com

Newton/Catawba County

Annual Catawba Valley Storytelling Festival at Historic Murray's Mill

Learn about racing history at the Catawba County Museum of History. *Karen A. Blum*

Storytellers from across the state share their ancient art with more than 1,400 second- and third-graders from the western Piedmont, as well as the public. 1489 Murray's Mill Rd., Catawba, NC 28609. Held the first week of May. Admission fee. (828) 465-0383; www.catawbahistory.org

Catawba County Museum of History

Collections include agricultural tools, furniture, and implements forged from hand-dug iron ore. Two full-scale antebellum parlors have been reconstructed and preserved in the museum. 30 N. College Ave., Newton, NC 28658. Wed.–Sat., 9 A.M.–4 P.M.; Sun., 1:30–4:30 P.M. Free. (828) 465-0383; www.catawbahistory.org

Hart Square

Handcarved items at Buffalo Creek Gallery *Karen A. Blum*

Hart Square is the largest collection of historic log buildings in the United States. Each year on the fourth Saturday in October, demonstrations are offered to the public. Dating from 1782 to 1873, the 70 log structures—chapels, barns, houses, shops, and more—are all furnished. Newton, NC 28658. Admission is $25; directions are sent with the tickets. (828) 465-0383; www.catawbahistory.org

Murray's Mill Harvest Folk Festival

This celebration of Catawba County's agricultural heritage features bluegrass, country, and gospel bands, exhibits, demonstrations, crafts, and activities for the family. 1489 Murray's Mill Rd., Catawba, NC 28609. Held the last weekend in Sept., Sat., 9 A.M.–5 P.M.; Sun., 1–5 P.M. Admission fee. (828) 465-0383; www.catawbahistory.org

O My Soap!

The Trott House Inn *Karen A. Blum*

Soaps, scrubs, buckwheat pillows, eye pillows, cherry seed pillows, and many other bath products are created by artist Dorothy Samson. Small groups, including homeschool students, can watch the soap-making process. 2572 W. NC Hwy 10, Newton, NC 28658. Mon.–Fri., 10 A.M.–5 P.M. Call in advance. (828) 465-4455; www.omysoap.com

The Trott House Inn

Nestled amid beautiful pecan trees in the heart of the foothills, the Trott House Inn offers guests a brief respite from everyday life. Relax in the comfort of this Colonial Revival home. 802 N. Main Ave., Newton, NC 28658. (828) 465-0404 or (877) 435-7994; www.trotthouse.com

Pumpkin Center/Lincoln County

Madison/Derr Iron Furnace

The 12-acre site of an early iron furnace was purchased by the Lincoln County Historic Properties Commission in 1998. A historic house was moved to the site, with plans to continue development of a county historic park and museum. Madison Furnace Trail, Pumpkin Center, NC 28092. Open by appointment. Free. (704) 748-9090; asso6377@bellsouth.net

Shelby/Cleveland County

Buffalo Creek Gallery *Karen A. Blum*

Buffalo Creek Gallery

This nonprofit artists' cooperative gallery features the work of 24 artists in almost every medium. The gallery is staffed at all times by a member artist. 104 E.

Warren St., Shelby, NC 28150. Mon.–Sat., 10 A.M.–6 P.M. (704) 487-0256; www.buffalocreekgallery.com

Carolina Pottery Festival

This one-day event features more than 100 potters, as well as pottery demonstrations. Door prizes are given throughout the day. 1751 E. Marion St., Shelby, NC 28152. Held the second Sat. in Nov., 10 A.M.–4 P.M. Admission is charged for adults; children are free. (704) 824-9928; www.carolinapotteryfestival.org

Cleveland County Arts Council *Karen A. Blum*

Cleveland County Arts Council–Sponsored Festivals

The arts council is home to an art gallery featuring the works of local and regional artists. Events include a film festival in July, a music festival in October, and a holiday art sale. 111 S. Washington St., Shelby, NC 28150. Mon.–Fri., 9 A.M.–5 P.M. Admission to the gallery is free; fees are charged for some programs. (704) 484-2787; www.ccartscouncil.org

Hallelujah Acres Café

If you're hungry and want to eat healthy, try this café's all-you-can-eat salad bar. Many dishes are prepared using the fresh-picked vegetables and fruits grown in the organic garden and greenhouses located on-site. 900 S. Post Rd., Shelby, NC 28150. Café, Mon.–Sat., 11 A.M.–2 P.M.; store, Mon.–Fri., 9 A.M.–7 P.M.; Sat., 9 A.M.–3 P.M. (704) 481-1700 or (800) 915-9355; www.hacres.com

Ron Philbeck Pottery

Organic groceries at Hallelujah Acres Café *Karen A. Blum*

Ron produces beautiful handmade soda-glazed pottery. Displays in the showroom include pots for the home and kitchen. Pots are thrown on a manual treadle wheel. 757 Wallace Grove Rd., Shelby, NC 28150. Open daily, 10 A.M.–6 P.M. (704) 480-6046; www.philbeckstudios.com

Shelby Farmers' Market

The market, open year-round, features vendors who sell fruit, vegetables, flowers, baked items, and meat. 200 W. Warren St., Shelby, NC 28150. Tues.–Sat., 7 A.M.–6 P.M. (704) 484-3100; www.uptownshelby.org

Synergy Studios and Gallery

Synergy Studios and Gallery houses artists working in six different media—stained glass, basketry, fiber arts, painting, and both hand-built and thrown ceramics. 212-B W. Warren St., Shelby, NC 28150. Open most weekdays, 10 A.M.–5 P.M. Since the artists have varying schedules, call ahead. (704) 487-0144; synergystudios5@netscape.net

Make time to feed an ostrich at Birdbrain Ostrich Ranch, Inc.

Sherrills Ford/Catawba County

Birdbrain Ostrich Ranch, Inc.

Raising chemical-free livestock without steroids or growth hormones, Birdbrain Ostrich Ranch is a small farm with approximately 50 ostriches of various ages. 6691 Little Mountain Rd., Sherrills Ford, NC 28673. Open seasonally. Call to arrange a tour. (704) 483-1620 or (877) 733-7849; www.birdbrainranch.com

Stanley/Gaston County

Apple Orchard Farm

This family farm provides all-natural beef and pork and seasonal produce such as tomatoes, squash, okra, cucumbers, corn, apples, and figs. Stop by the roadside stand for fresh farm goods. 640 Mariposa Rd., Stanley, NC 28164. Garden season, Mon.–Sat., 8 A.M.–8 P.M.; open year-round for meat sales. Small group tours are available by appointment. (704) 263-2635; www.agr.state.nc.us/ncproducts/ShowSite.asp?ID=2366

Get a custom stained-glass window at Synergy Studios and Gallery. *Karen A. Blum*

Taylorsville /Alexander County

Alexander County Chamber of Commerce

16 W. Main Ave., Taylorsville, NC 28681. Mon.–Fri., 9 A.M.–5 P.M. (828) 632-1096; www.alexandercountychamber.com

Art in the Shop (Not Your Usual Art Show)

True to its name, this annual two-day festival is a delightful combination of music from area songwriters and visual arts from local and regional artists. 274 Bobby Godfrey Ln., Taylorsville, NC 28681. Held the first weekend in Oct., 10 A.M.–6 P.M. Free. (828) 632-0106; www.artintheshop.net

Alexander County Chamber of Commerce *Karen A. Blum*

Bearpaw Trading Co.

This place is two shops in one: the Bearpaw Gallery and the Blue Gems Rock Shop. The gallery features artwork by local and regional artists and craftspeople, gifts, used books, and candles. The rock shop features local gems and minerals; it also buys, sells, trades, and cuts gemstones. 546 W. Main Ave., Taylorsville, NC 28681. Tues.–Sat., 10 A.M.–6 P.M. (828) 632-2324 or (866) 242-5077; www.bearpawtrading.com

Bearpaw Trading Company *Karen A. Blum*

Burgin Art

The gallery specializes in portraits that reflect the subjects' personal interests, murals, pen-and-ink home renderings, and promotional materials. 942 Carrigan Rd., Taylorsville, NC 28681. Open by appointment. (828) 632-2256

Deal Orchards

Beautiful orchards of apples, peaches, nectarines, and Asian pears cover the hillsides at Deal Orchards. Tractor-pulled wagon rides, a picnic area, educational program, and a sunflower maze are available to groups of 20 or more in September and October. 7400 NC Hwy 16 N., Taylorsville, NC 28681. Open 8 A.M.–5 P.M. in season. Call for admission fees and tour details. (828) 632-2304; alanappledude@aol.com

H and H Arena

H and H offers a place to ride your horse or watch equine events, including team ropings, rodeos, barrel races, cuttings, team pennings, and other horse shows. Team-roping horses, roping steers, prospects, and brood mares are for sale. 311 Ned Herman Rd., Taylorsville, NC 28681. Admission is free for most events except rodeos. (828) 312-9891; www.hharena.com

Pick your own apples at J and A Orchard.

J and A Orchard

Owners Jimmy and Alice Land share their beautiful view with anyone who stops by to fill a bucket or bag with sun-warmed fruit. Old and new apple varieties, persimmons, Asian pears, plums, peaches, nectarines, and other fruits are available. 25 Reidland Rd., Taylorsville, NC 28681. Labor Day–mid-Oct., Mon.–Sat., 9 A.M.–6 P.M.; Sun., 1–6 P.M. (828) 632-6497

Leon Fagan Custom Chain Saw Carvings

Leon Fagan carves wood with a chain saw and white quartz rock with an air chisel, a chop saw, a hammer, and a chisel. You'll know you've found his workshop when you see the eight-foot Indian chief landmark at the driveway of his home. 7195 US Hwy 64/90 W., Taylorsville, NC 28681. Open by appointment. (828) 632-4928; rondafagan@aol.com

Richard Sinclair—The Shop

Using his welder like most people use a glue gun, metal artist Richard Sinclair creates fantastic, whimsical art sculptures using salvaged or recycled metal and stone. 274 Bobby Godfrey Ln., Taylorsville, NC 28681-8282. Open by appointment. (828) 632-0106; www.artintheshop.net

Relax with a cup of coffee at The Spilled Bean Coffee Shop. *Karen A. Blum*

The Spilled Bean Coffee Shop

This unique gathering place features original paintings and other artwork for sale, live music, poetry readings, and spaces to read, play board games, watch a free movie, and catch up with friends. The coffeehouse offers custom-blended beverages. 81 NC Hwy 16 N., Suite A, Taylorsville, NC 28681. Mon.–Sat., 7 A.M.–7 P.M. (828) 632-5007; thespilledbean@yahoo.com

Taylorsville Hometown Apple Festival

Two stages, 150-plus vendors, carriage rides, the Kid's Korner, food, arts and crafts, an apple-peeling contest, and an apple dessert contest are highlights of the festival. 239 E. Main St., Taylorsville, NC 28681. Held the third Sat. in Oct., 9 A.M.–5 P.M. Free. (828) 632-4451; Lenny_Rogers@ncsu.edu

Vale/Lincoln County

Arie's Gallery

Featuring Reinhardt family artwork depicting life in Catawba County in the early 1900s, the gallery is located off Hwy 10 behind Banoak School. 4427 White Rd., Vale, NC 28168. Open by appointment. (704) 462-1907; www.angelfire.com/ab/jagstudio/index.html

Get a fresh, North Carolina Christmas tree from Helms Christmas Tree Farm. *Karen A. Blum*

Helms Christmas Tree Farm

More than 5,000 Christmas trees are spread along the gently rolling hills of this farm. Wreaths, garlands, stands, refreshments, hayrides, and marshmallow roasts are offered. Blueberries are sold in the summer. 6345 Christmas Tree Ln., Vale, NC 28168. Nov. 19–Dec. 20, daily, 9 A.M.–6 P.M.; July 15–Aug. 15, Thurs.–Sat., 7 A.M.–2 P.M. Tours, hayrides, and a picnic area are available by appointment. (704) 276-1835; henryhelms@bellsouth.net

Studio Ross

Lynne Ross loves light, be it natural or manufactured, and its revelation of forms and colors. She works in oils, acrylics, and pastels. 8430 Reeps Grove Church Rd., Vale, NC 28168. Open for studio visits by appointment. Classes are offered in summer and early fall; costs vary; bartering is also an option. (704) 276-1915; rosstown@bellsouth.net

Vernon Boyles Vegetable Farm

The farm grows corn, cucumbers, tomatoes, squash, hot and sweet peppers, green beans, okra, onions, October beans, pumpkins, greens, peas, cantaloupes, and watermelons. You can buy produce at its roadside stand. 5443 Hwy 27 W., Vale, NC 28168. Open daily during harvest time, 8:30 A.M.–7 P.M. (704) 276-1496

WoodMill Winery offers a large selection of wine. *Karen A. Blum*

WoodMill Winery

WoodMill Winery grows the sweet Southern grape known as the muscadine. Recognized for its extraordinary flavor, the grape is renowned for producing exceptional jellies, desserts, and the popular muscadine wine. 1350 Woodmill Winery Ln., Vale, NC 28168. Thurs.–Fri. and Sun., 1–6 P.M.; Sat., 10 A.M.–6 P.M.; open Mon.–Wed. by appointment. (704) 736-7733; www.woodmillwinery.com

Apples so fresh they are still on the tree at Deal Orchards. *Karen A. Blum* (p. 350)

Foothills, Vineyards, and Old-Time Music

Forsyth, Rockingham, Stokes, Surry, and Yadkin Counties

Visitors can view some of the state's most scenic landscapes, hear some of our nation's most acclaimed music traditions, and taste one of the South's newest cash crops in North Carolina's northwestern Piedmont.

Here, land rises into the escarpment that forms the eastern slope of the Blue Ridge Mountains. Streams from the region's highlands merge into the rivers that, over the millennia, have eroded valleys into the rolling hills. For generations, corn and tobacco were cultivated in fields near these waterways and in the shadows of the mountains. While barns and farmhouses still dot the landscape, farmers these days are more likely to grow garlic, strawberries, and apples. And more and more farmers raise grapes and process the delicate fruit into fine wines.

In fact, the counties featured on this trail are considered by many to be the heart of North Carolina's wine industry. Visitors will discover Chardonnay, Cabernet, Syrah, and Sangiovese at these regional wineries—ready to be tasted, purchased, and served at home dinner parties. Winemakers are eager to show off the vines and explain the methods they use to create their own varieties.

This area also lays claim to some of the richest music-making traditions in the South. Rural farm communities with names like Round Peak, Pine Ridge, Skull Camp, Low Gap, and Beulah are home to generations of fiddlers, banjo players, and guitarists. Their powerful brand of string-band music is now emulated by younger players throughout the nation and in countries around the world.

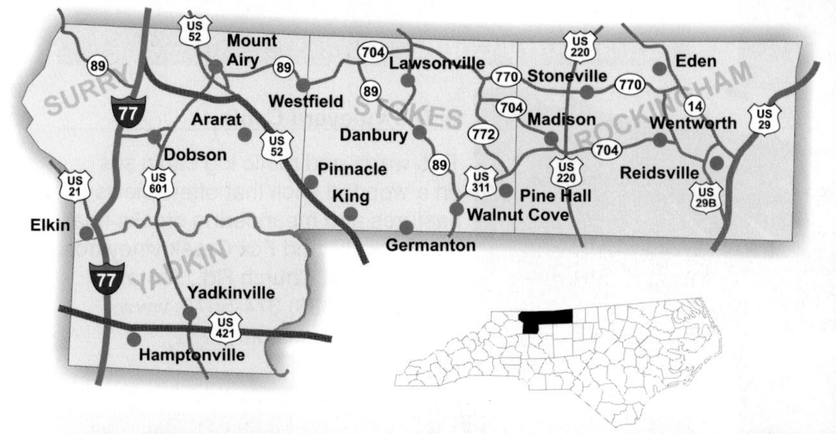

Traditional music continues to be performed live at dances, fiddlers' conventions, and hometown oprys held throughout the region.

In the town of Eden, the community pays homage to the accomplishments of a former textile-mill worker named Charlie Poole, whose singing and banjo playing are acknowledged as building blocks for modern country music. Although Poole died in 1931, his early recordings recently garnered a Grammy nomination. A music festival bearing his name is presented every June.

If recreation and natural resources are among your main interests, visit Hanging Rock State Park or Pilot Mountain State Park. You can hike trails or test your rock-climbing skills to reach the pinnacles for views of the Piedmont plateau stretching to the horizon. And while you are in the area, take in Horne Creek Farm, an educational center dedicated to preserving North Carolina's rural heritage. This state historic site adjacent to the Yadkin River is restored to its appearance at the turn of the 20th century.

So, let the fiddles ring, the banjos sing, and the wines take wing at the "Foothills, Vineyards, and Old-Time Music" trail.

Ararat/Surry County

The cozy Vineyard Cabin

The Vineyard Cabin

This warm and rustic log cabin sits on a wooded knoll that offers views of pastures and meandering creeks near the Rock Hill and Fox Creek vineyards. 510 Rock Hill Church Rd., Ararat, NC 27007. (336) 374-5078; www.rockhillvineyards.com

P ?

Bethania/Forsyth County

Bethania Historic District

Learn about the first planned Moravian settlement in North Carolina as you discover historic Bethania. Its National Historic Landmark District includes Bethania Moravian Church (circa 1809), the Wolff-Moser House (1780), and the Alpha Chapel (circa 1894). Free. (336) 922-0434; www.townofbethania.org

P ?

Clemmons/Forsyth County

Tanglewood Festival of Lights

This is one of the largest and most spectacular light shows in the Southeast. From storybook scenes to holiday themes, over 100 displays with nearly a million lights fill Tanglewood Park with the joy of the holiday season. 4061 Clemmons Rd., Clemmons, NC 27012. Early Nov.–Jan. 1, nightly, 6–11 P.M. (336) 778-6300; www.co.forsyth.nc.us/Tanglewood

P ?

Danbury/Stokes County

Dan River Art Market

Dan River Art Market

The Dan River Art Market in historic Danbury, started by the Stokes and Rockingham county arts councils, features the finest in local handcrafted artwork by 75 area artists and crafters. Original paintings and prints, pottery, stained and blown glass, masks, ironwork, pewter, baskets, quilts, woodcarvings, wooden toys, natural soaps, jewelry, Indian flutes, lamps, and contemporary and traditional art are available. 108 N. Main St., Danbury, NC 27016. Mon.–Fri., 8:30 A.M.–5 P.M.; Sat.–Sun., 1-5 P.M. (336) 593-2808; www.stokesarts.org

The Dan River Company Kayak & Canoe Rental

Take a break from driving by renting a kayak or canoe. This riverside company arranges trips from two hours to two days, covering 40 miles of the Dan River. There are areas appropriate for novice paddlers, too. It is located adjacent to Hanging Rock State Park's Dan River Access. 1110 Flinchum Rd., Danbury, NC 27016. Rental and guide fees are charged. (336) 593-2628; www.danrivercompany.com

Priddy General Store and "Pickin' at Priddy's"

This two-story frame country store (circa 1888) was an all-in-one post office, voting station, and bank. Enjoy live bluegrass music during "Pickin' at Priddy's" every October. The store is well known for antiques, "newtiques," old-fashioned candy favorites, overalls, groceries, and hardware. 2121 Sheppard Mill Rd., Danbury, NC 27016. Mon.–Sat, 8 A.M.–6 P.M. (336) 593-8786; www.visitstokesnc.com

Stokes County Arts Council Gallery

Monthly exhibitions of paintings, pottery, and stained glass by local artists are on display. 500 N. Main St., Danbury, NC 27016. Mon.–Fri., 8:30 A.M.–5 P.M. Free. (336) 593-8159; www.stokesarts.org

Whippoorwill Inn Guest House

You'll find family-style suites with kitchenettes and fireplaces and a country-style welcome in this quiet inn that sits on a beautiful overlook. Old Church Rd., Danbury, NC 27016. (336) 420-9122; www.whippoorwillinn.com

Delicious dinner at The Wolf's Lair Restaurant *Black Wolf Vineyards* (p. 358)

Dobson/Surry County

Stone cabin solitude at Black Wolf Vineyards

Black Wolf Vineyards & Wolf's Lair Restaurant

This enterprise is located at the north end of the Yadkin Valley, North Carolina's first designated viticulture area. The vineyard tasting room has sweeping panoramas stretching from the foothills to the Blue Ridge Mountains. Visitors can take a walk to a spring-fed wellhouse and a "secret garden." 283 Vineyard Lane (off US Hwy 601 north of Dobson), Dobson, NC 27017. Wine tastings, Mon.–Sat., 11 A.M.–2:30 P.M.; Sun., noon–4 P.M. Tasting fees. (336) 374-2532; www.blackwolfvineyards.com

The Rockford Inn

Rockford Inn

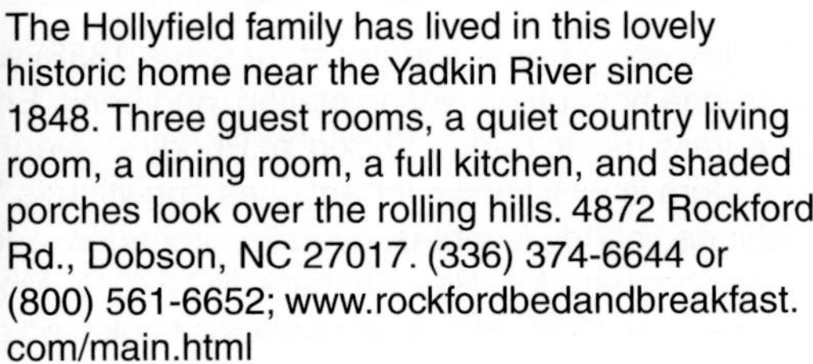

The Hollyfield family has lived in this lovely historic home near the Yadkin River since 1848. Three guest rooms, a quiet country living room, a dining room, a full kitchen, and shaded porches look over the rolling hills. 4872 Rockford Rd., Dobson, NC 27017. (336) 374-6644 or (800) 561-6652; www.rockfordbedandbreakfast.com/main.html

Shelton Vineyards

Come picnic or catch a summer concert at the largest family-owned estate winery in North Carolina. Beautifully landscaped grounds, a spacious visitor center, and a shop with award-winning wines and picnic supplies are located here. This vineyard is an inspiration to many in the viticulture region. 286 Cabernet Ln., Dobson, NC 27017. Mon.–Sat., 10 A.M.–6 P.M.; Sun., 1-6 P.M.; call for Jan.–Feb. hours. Tour and tasting fees are charged. (336) 366-4724; www.sheltonvineyards.com

These grapes at Shelton Vineyards will make a fine wine.

Stony Knoll Vineyards

Van and Cathy Coe are the latest in the family to inhabit Stony Knoll (circa 1896), a North Carolina Centennial Farm. Today, a mixture of grape varieties has replaced tobacco and corn on these rolling hills. 1143 Stony Knoll Rd., Dobson, NC 27017. Sat., noon–6 P.M.; Sun., 2–4 P.M.; and by appointment. Tasting fees. (336) 374-5752; www.stonyknollvineyards.com

Stony Knoll Vineyards

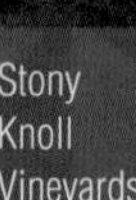

Eden/Rockingham County

Charlie Poole Music Festival

Musical legend Charlie Poole—Eden resident, mill worker, 1920s singer and banjo player—was a pioneer of modern country music. The festival features the best in old-time and bluegrass music and a prestigious competition focusing on Poole-style instrumentation. Camping is available. Fairgrounds, Eden, NC 27289. Held the second weekend in June. Admission fee. (336) 623-1043; www.charlie-poole.com

Elkin Farmers' Market

Elkin/Surry County

Elkin Farmers' Market

Area farmers and gardeners, many with organic vegetables and fruits, offer a range from baby lettuce and French green beans to good, all-American fresh corn on the cob! Downtown Elkin, NC 28621. Sat., 8 A.M.–noon. (336) 835-9800; www.localharvest.org/farmers-markets/M13050

Foothills Arts Council/Yadkin Valley Craft Guild Gallery & Shop

You will find handpainted shutters and so much more at Foothills Arts Council.

The arts council hosts a permanent craft shop run by the new Yadkin Valley Craft Guild. More than 100 craft professionals display works of clay, wood, fabric, photography, paper, glass, metals, and original jewelry. 129 Church St., Elkin, NC 28621. Mon.–Thurs., 10 A.M.–4 P.M.; Sat., 11 A.M.–2 P.M. (336) 835-2025; www.foothillsartscouncil.org or www.yadkinvalleycraftguild.org

Germanton/Stokes County

Germanton Vineyard Winery & Art Gallery

In addition to producing excellent wines, Germanton offers works by 80 local artists in its gallery. 3530 Hwy 8/65, Germanton, NC 27019. Tues.–Fri., 10 A.M.–6 P.M.; Sat., 9 A.M.–5 P.M. (336) 969-6121 or (800) 322-2894; www.germantongallery.com

Hamptonville/Yadkin County

Buck Shoals Vineyard & Winery

Buck Shoals features wines from grapes grown on-site. The vineyard has a log-cabin tasting room; wine tastings include samples of six wines. Free tours are offered on weekends. 6121 Vintner Way, Hamptonville, NC 27020. Wed.–Thurs., 11 A.M.–5 P.M.; Fri.–Sat., 11 A.M.–6 P.M.; Sun., 1–5 P.M. Tasting fees. (336) 468-9274; www.buckshoalsvineyard.com

Buck Shoals Vineyard & Winery

Kernersville/Forsyth County

Körner's Folly

In the late 1800s, Jule Körner set out to create a combination bachelor's quarters, artist's studio, office, billiard room, ballroom, carriage house, and stables. The design reportedly caused a cousin to comment, "That will surely be Jule Körner's folly." And thus it has been known to this day. 413 S. Main St., Kernersville, NC 27284. Thurs.–Sat., 10 A.M.–3 P.M.; Sun., 1–5 P.M. Admission is $6 for adults and $3 for children five–16; children four and under are free. (336) 996-7922; www.kornersfolly.org

Laurel Gray Vineyards

This family-owned and -operated vineyard features estate-grown French varietal wines. You can stroll the beautiful rose gardens and take an educational vineyard tour. The tasting room is a restored 1930s milking parlor. 5726 Old Hwy 421, Hamptonville, NC 27020. Wed.–Fri., 10 A.M.–6 P.M.; Sat.,

10 A.M.–5 P.M.; Sun., 1–5 P.M. Tasting fees. (336) 468-9463; www.laurelgray.com

King/Stokes County

Geraniums in bloom at Mitchell's Nursery & Greenhouse

Mitchell's Nursery & Greenhouse

Geraniums, lilies, mums, pansies, trees, and shrubs are available. 1088 W. Dalton Rd., King, NC 27021. Nov.–Feb., Mon.–Fri., 7:30 A.M.–5 P.M.; Sat., 7:30 A.M.–4 P.M.; March–Oct., Mon.–Fri., 7:30 A.M.–6 P.M.; Sat., 7:30 A.M.–4 P.M. (336) 983-4107; www.mitchellsnurseryandgreenhouse.com

One Way Architectural Antiques

One Way Architectural Antiques & Show

Architectural garden art, wrought iron, statues, doors, and gates—the architectural remnants in abundance here seem to inspire creativity. On the first weekend in May, a show with 30 artists, food, and entertainment is held in the gardens. 127 Bob Rierson St., King, NC 27021. Sat., 9 A.M.–4 P.M.; Tues.–Fri., by appointment. (336) 983-6790; www.onewayantiques.com

Tim Bruce Art Studio

A native of North Carolina, Tim creates stunning originals and giclée limited editions of wildlife, pastoral, and maritime scenes. 367 E. King St., King, NC 27021. Daily, 8 A.M.–6 P.M. (336) 985-0648; www.timbruce.com

Tim Bruce Art Studio

Lawsonville/Stokes County

Southwyck Farm B&B

Furnished with 18th-century American, Oriental, and English antiques, captains' memorabilia, waterfowl art, and handcrafted afghans, Southwyck Farm has six guest rooms and 38 acres with trails, animals, and fishing.

1070 Southwyck Farm Rd., Lawsonville, NC 27022. (336) 593-8006 or (866) 593-8006; www.southwyckfarm.com

Madison/Rockingham County

Blackmon Amphitheatre *Hobart Jones*

Riverside Farms

You can stop by the farm stand or pick your own produce at this family farm. Bountiful fresh strawberries, melons, apples, plums, corn, juicy tomatoes, and even hanging baskets are available. 241 Rierson Rd., Madison, NC 27025. Daily, 8 A.M.–6 P.M. in season. (336) 427-5937

Mount Airy/Surry County

Andy Griffith Playhouse

The original stage floor where native son Andy Griffith first performed still serves actors, musicians, and dancers for festivals, classes, workshops, jam sessions, and concerts. The playhouse is also home to the Surry Arts Council. 218 Rockford St., Mount Airy, NC 27030. Mon.–Fri., 8 A.M.–5 P.M. (336) 786-7998 or (800) 286-6193; www.surryarts.org

Blackmon Amphitheatre

Summer-series events like the “Living Storybook” series, an outdoor drama, and great Carolina beach bands are scheduled weekly. 218 Rockford St., Mount Airy, NC 27030. (336) 786-7998 or (800) 286-6193; www.surryarts.org

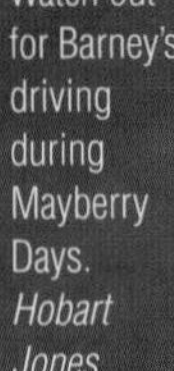

Watch out for Barney's driving during Mayberry Days. *Hobart Jones*

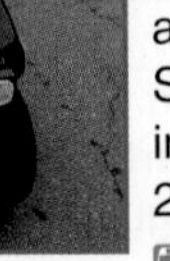

Mayberry Days

This family festival celebrates the magic of *The Andy Griffith Show*, when life was simpler. Stars from the show, tribute artists, and thousands of fans come for bluegrass music, trivia contests, and the Mayberry Days Pig Cookoff. 218 Rockford St., Mount Airy, NC 27030. Held the last weekend in Sept., Thurs.–Sun. (336) 786-7998 or (800) 286-6193; www.surryarts.org

Mount Airy Farmers' Market

Homemade goodies at the Mount Airy Farmers' Market *Hobart Jones*

At the Andy Griffith Playhouse parking lot, homemade jellies, breads, and cakes nestle with delicious fruits and vegetables, flowers, and herbs. 218 Rockford St., Mount Airy, NC 27030. May–Oct., Tues., 4–6 P.M. (336) 786-7998 or (800) 286-6193; www.surryarts.org

Mount Airy Fiddlers Convention

This convention attracts old-time music enthusiasts and performers for a week of jams, competitions, camping, and just plain old-time fun! If you enjoy old-time music, you'll love the small-town flavor of this exciting, foot-tapping musical event. 691 W. Lebanon St., Mount Airy, NC 27030. Held the first full weekend in June. (336) 786-7998 or (800) 286-6193; www.surryarts.org

Grab your fiddle and join in at the Mount Airy Fiddlers Convention. *Hobart Jones*

Round Peak Winery

Delicious Chardonnay, Merlot, Sangiovese, Cabernet Franc, Cabernet Sauvignon, Nebbiolo, Rosé, and Sweet Rosé wines blend with sweet old-time Round Peak–style fiddle performances. Quilts and crafts are for sale. 765 Round Peak Church Rd., Mount Airy, NC 27030. Mon. and Thurs.–Fri., 10 A.M.–5 P.M.; Sun., noon–5 P.M.; or by appointment. Tasting fees. (336) 352-5595; www.roundpeak.com

Saturday *Merry-Go-Round* at the Downtown Cinema Theatre

This Art Deco theater is home to one of America's longest-running live bluegrass radio programs: WPAQ-AM 740's *Merry-Go-Round*. The free bluegrass and old-time music jam session is on Saturday from 9 to 11 A.M., prior to the free live radio show, which airs from 11 A.M. to 1:30 P.M. 142 N. Main St., Mount Airy, NC 27030. (336) 786-2222 or (800) 286-6193; www.surryarts.org

Foothills and vineyards at Round Peak Winery

Enjoy a tasty pork chop sandwich at Snappy Lunch. *Hobart Jones*

Snappy Lunch

This 1923 restaurant is the place where Andy Griffith (and later on TV, Andy Taylor and Barney Fife) dined in style. It features the famous "Pork Chop Sandwich," which you can have your way with chili, slaw, mustard, onion, and tomato. 125 N. Main St., Mount Airy, NC 27030. Mon.–Wed. and Fri., 5:45 A.M.–1:45 P.M.; Thurs. and Sat., 5:45 A.M.–1:15 P.M. (336) 786-4931; www.thesnappylunch.com

Tommy Jarrell Festival

This festival celebrates the life and music of the late old-time music icon Thomas Jefferson Jarrell with jams, a Friday-night dance, and a Saturday birthday concert with old-time musicians, some of them North Carolina Folk Heritage awardees. 218 Rockford St., Mount Airy, NC 27030. Held the last weekend in Feb., Thurs.–Sat. Admission fee. (336) 786-7998 or (800) 286-6193; www.surryarts.org

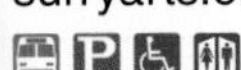

Tommy Jarrell Festival *Hobart Jones*

Pine Hall/Stokes County

Rose Cabin Retreat

This quaint 1930s log cabin is the perfect setting for a getaway. Rose Cabin Retreat is within earshot of the Dan River, famous for canoeing, kayaking, and tubing. 1871 Pine Hall Rd., Pine Hall, NC 27042. (336) 591-4861

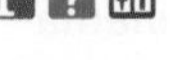

Pinnacle/Surry County

Horne Creek Living Historical Farm State Historic Site

Costumed guides interpret everyday life during the early 20th century. The site features traditional music on "Toe-Tappin' Saturdays," wood chopping, corn shucking, holiday carols, and an apple orchard. 308 Horne Creek Farm Rd., Pinnacle, NC 27043. Tues.–Sat., 10 A.M.–4 P.M.; closed on major holidays. (336) 325-2298; www.nchistoricsites.org

Learn about North Carolina's agricultural history. *N.C. Historic Sites*

Reidsville/Rockingham County

Cornerstone Garlic Farm

Turban, Asiatic, Porcelain, Rocambole, and Shantung Purple are just a few of the 15 garlics at this small family farm, which also has shiitake mushrooms. The farm's organic practices yield delicious results. Fresh vegetables, blackberries, and herbs are available, too. 1249 Tate Rd., Reidsville, NC 27320. Open by appointment. (336) 349-5106; www.home.bellsouth.net/p/s/community.dll?ep=16&ext=1&groupid=140532&ck

Learn to garlic braid at Cornerstone Garlic Farm.

Mural & Artwork Home Studio

You won't want to miss Elizabeth Boles's 60-foot scenic mural in downtown Eden. The artist teaches and works at her home studio. 335 Richardson Rd., Reidsville, NC 27320. Call for an appointment. (336) 342-0991 or (336) 932-0122; www.HelloGreensboro.com/Art/elizabethartist.cfm

Mural & Artwork Home Studio

Rockingham County Farmers' Market

Seasonal berries, apples, melons, and veggies are available, as are baked goods, honey, goat cheese, organic meats, jams, and jellies. Photography, pottery, and art treasures by local artists can be found inside the log buildings. 1944 Wentworth St., Reidsville, NC 27320. May–Oct., Sat., 8 A.M.–1 P.M.; Wed., 3–6 P.M. (336) 634-5652; www.co.rockingham.nc.us/farmark.htm

Stoneville/Rockingham County

Tuttle's Berry & Vegetable Farm

From beets to turnips, from pumpkins to perennials and cut flowers, this farm is a joy. You'll find Christmas trees and holiday wreaths on Sundays in November and December. Hwy 135, Stoneville, NC 27048. Open for produce Apr.–Nov., Mon.–Sat., 9 A.M.–6 P.M.; the greenhouse is open year-round. (336) 623-2024

Rockingham County Farmers' Market

Walnut Cove/Stokes County

Hillbilly Hideaway Restaurant

Fine Southern hospitality awaits at Hillbilly Hideaway. Start with homemade hoecakes and save room for delicious made-from-scratch desserts. Fresh veggies from the area are also featured. 4335 Pine Hall Rd., Walnut Cove, NC 27052. Fri.–Sat., 4–9 P.M.; Sun., 8 A.M.–8:30 P.M. (336) 591-4861

JL Artistry

This working studio and gallery of stained-glass artist and lifelike bird and animal woodcarver Jan Lukens is in an 1830s Moravian-style home. She does glass fusing and slumping processes, heating glass in a kiln. 2348 NC Hwy 65 E., Walnut Cove, NC 27052. Open by appointment. (336) 591-7504; JLartistry@msn.com

Old Farmhouse Inn

The log portion of the Old Farmhouse Inn is pre–Civil War. The antiques, the farm memorabilia, and the lovely lawns all add to the sense of peace. Two suites provide modern comfort in a delightful rustic setting. 3117 Hwy 89 E., Walnut Cove, NC 27052. (336) 591-7635; www.visitstokesnc.com

Squires Inn

Squires Inn

Originally part of a 1,700-acre tobacco plantation, this historic 1850s home was a frequent retreat for tobacco baron R. J. Reynolds. Built with valley timber, the house has been authentically restored. Much of the original hand-hewn log structure still exists, such as the 12-foot-tall tiger oak and stained-glass front door. 1117 Watts Rd., Walnut Cove, NC 27052. (336) 591-5653; www.squiresinn.com

Hanging Rock State Park *N.C. Division of State Parks and Recreation*

Wentworth/Rockingham County

Dan River Art Market Gift Shop

Over 200 artists bring their angels, birdhouses, folk art, chairs, quilts, and sundry handcrafted treasures to the gift shop in the historic 1850s Martin-Irving House. 1122 NC Hwy 65, Wentworth, NC 27375. Sept.–Dec. and March–June, Mon.–Fri., 10 A.M.–4 P.M.; also open on Sat. from the second Sat. in Nov. to the third Sat. in Dec. (336) 349-4039; www.members.aol.com/oldbeeg/ArtWork.html

Westfield/Stokes County

Hanging Rock Outdoor Center

Stokes County's oldest and only full-service outfitter offers private canoe and kayak instruction. It also organizes lazy family canoe trips, overnighters, and even whitewater trips. 3466 Moores Spring Rd., Westfield, NC 27053. Early March–late Nov. (336) 593-8283; www.hroconline.com

Hanging Rock Outdoor Center

Yadkinville/Yadkin County

Moonshine Heritage Farm

Ever tasted a pawpaw? A persimmon? Want to learn about heritage farm animals and gardens? This farm's goats, sheep, and hens can help, as can JoJo the llama. You can gather eggs, stroll to the Shacktown Farmers' Market, walk the back 40, or just sit in the swing and dream. 2721 Shacktown Rd., Yadkinville, NC 27055-5703. (336) 961-3035; mutter@triad.rr.com

Yadkin Valley Grape Festival

The popular festival, held the third Saturday in October, gathers music, food, fun, and many vintage grapes. It also has a chili cookoff, children's activities, and specialty crafts. A benefit motorcycle ride through the vineyards begins in the morning. 205 S. Jackson St., Yadkinville, NC 27055. (336) 679-2200; www.yadkinchamber.org

Yadkin Valley Grape Festival *Yadkin County Chamber of Commerce and Visitor Center*

Index